J. D. TANT -- TEXAS PREACHER

A BIOGRAPHY

FANNING YATER TANT

FAITH and FACTS PRESS

Indianapolis, Indiana 46268

Printed in the United States of America

INTERNATIONAL STANDARD BOOK NUMBER
0-88407-029-8

J. D. TANT

(At age sixty)

NANNIE YATER TANT

(At age fifty)

JEFFERSON DAVID TANT

INDEX

FOREWORD

I started this work with the expectation of writing a biography. The reader will quickly discover, however, that the book is more autobiographical than biographical. It is composed in large part of quotations from the writings of J. D. Tant and Nannie Yater Tant. Over a period of fifteen years (1932-1947) my mother prepared a manuscript of nearly two hundred typewritten pages which she entitled, "Reminiscences Of A Pioneer Preacher's Wife". The manuscript has never been published, and the reader of this volume will find many quotations from it in these pages cited simply as "Reminiscences".

Over a period of fifty years J. D. Tant wrote hundreds of articles to the religious journals, and in many of them he would make reference to the same events and experiences. Quotations from him appearing in this volume are credited to the principal article giving the information, but in a few instances (perhaps a dozen) that main article or story has been filled in with details appearing in other accounts of the same experience.

The battle for the truth waged by Jefferson Davis Tant is an age-lasting one. It shall never be completely won, nor completely lost, until the last trump shall sound. It is a battle which every gospel preacher, in every age, must fight in one way or another. This book is the story of the heroic life of one gospel preacher and the fight he made for the truth. It is dedicated to young gospel preachers in general, and to Jefferson David Tant, grandson and namesake of J. D. Tant, in particular; and is sent forth with the fervent prayer that it may serve to strengthen and encourage these valiant young men to stand firmly for the Truth, "holding fast the faithful word" and contending earnestly

"for the faith which was once delivered unto the saints."
In doing so they will prove themselves worthy fellow-workers with that great host of godly men who have preceded them, and who shall follow them, in the greatest calling among men.

—Fanning Yater Tant

CHAPTER I

SON OF THE CONFEDERACY

Tuesday, May 20, 1864, was a beautiful spring day in north Georgia. The red clay hills were now covered with a lush green carpet of grass, and the singing birds gave an air of peaceful serenity to all who cared to listen.

But there were few that day who listened. For Georgia was in the grip of a paralyzing terror. The Yankees were coming. General Braxton Bragg had withdrawn his battered Confederate troops from the bloody battle at Missionary Ridge the preceding fall, and had wintered at Dalton, in Northwest Georgia. There he had been replaced in command by General Joseph E. Johnston. The two leading generals of the Union, Ulysses S. Grant and William Tecumseh Sherman, had met in Nashville, Tennessee, on March 17, and had arranged for a great concerted double movement to crush the Confederacy. Grant was to move against the Army of Northern Virginia under Lee, and at the same time Sherman was to try to crush the Army of Tennessee under Johnston. Sherman's campaign in Georgia got quickly under way, and the furious fighting at Resaca had left several thousand dead on both sides.

Johnston kept retreating before Sherman, cautiously seeking some way to catch a part of Sherman's army separated from the rest, or to force a battle in positions advantageous to his smaller numbers. But Sherman was a master tactician. He was caught at disadvantage once or twice, but quickly recovered himself, and kept applying the relentless pressure. It began to seem to the weary men in gray that every time one blue-coated warrior fell beneath their sharp-shooting accuracy, two others sprang from the blood-soaked soil to take his place. There was no relief, no rest for the bone-tired, grim faced, and gaunt-eyed men who daily retreated before that swelling tide of blue.

The spring of 1864 found the Confederacy gradually coming to a realization that the war was lost. Bitter fighting would drag on for a full year yet, and thousands more on both sides would fall; but the tide had turned at Gettysburg, Antietam, and Vicksburg. These were mortal wounds from which there could be no recovery. Nothing remained now but the slow, horrible, and inevitable death throes of what four years ago had seemed a nation, mighty and invincible. Not only was the Confederacy doomed, but she would carry with her into oblivion a whole civilization, a way of life.

General Sherman ("Old Cump") had given his soldiers a very simple code by which to fight. "We must," he had said, "make old and young, rich and poor, feel the hard hand of war." The will of the people to resist must be broken. It was not enough to defeat the armies in the field; the people themselves must be subdued. To do that job Sherman had inaugurated a scorched earth policy that was destined to make his name live in infamy in the South. He was a paradox — the most cruel and ruthless force in destroying the South, yet one of the most thoughtful and considerate in her Reconstruction. He made a holocaust of Atlanta, then told its mayor: "When peace does come, I will share with you my last cracker. But now. . . . go. . . and take with you the old and feeble. Feed and nurse them until the mad passions of men cool down, and allow the Union and peace to settle over your old homes." After having smashed the city with artillery, flame, and unspeakable suffering, Sherman staged theatrical benefits for 17 nights in the ruined metropolis to raise $8,000.00 for Confederate needy.

Henry Grady, southern journalist, who was one of the

leaders in the Reconstruction, once made the wry comment
that Sherman was "careless with fire." He was mistaken.
Sherman was not careless; he deliberately and methodically
applied the torch to Atlanta. He ordered the destruction
of every Confederate military installation in the city, and
then looked on with indifference as 5,000 private homes
went skyward in the roaring flames along with warehouses
and ammunition dumps. This was Sherman — vicious,
cruel beyond measure, yet having purpose and method in
every move he made. "War is hell," he had said, and he
was eager to get the terrible ordeal over as quickly as
possible. Perhaps he felt there was compassion and mercy
in bringing destruction swiftly and completely rather than
in stretching out the agony over longer months with mild-
ness and moderation.

The destruction of Atlanta was but the climax to a campaign that had extended all the way across northern Georgia, a campaign that had left that state prostrate and
bleeding. As Sherman's legions pressed ever harder on
the retreating Confederates there had been almost daily
skirmishes and patrol engagements. In some of these brief
but bloody encounters there had been as many as three or
four hundred men on each side; in others, only four or
five, or perhaps a dozen, might have clashed. But the
movement southward continued, certain, inevitable, irre-
sistible. Looming ahead before Atlanta could ever be
taken would be the great battle of Kenesaw Mountain. But
between Resaca and Kenesaw there were three or four
sharp battles to be fought, the heaviest of these being the
engagement at New Hope Church in Paulding County.

This Battle of New Hope Church was fought May 25-28,
1864. Several thousand men were engaged on each side.
Official casualty lists tell that 3,500 Federal soldiers were
killed here; the Confederates reported their losses at about
one half that number. Old timers in Georgia, however, who

were present after the war when the bodies of the Union dead were removed to a Federal Cemetery, swore that no less than "ten thousand dead Yanks" were dug out of the trenches and makeshift graves where they had been hastily buried. They reported the Confederate dead, who were also removed to a new resting place, at only a fraction of that number. Naturally! By all counts, however, it was a major engagement.

II

It was Tuesday, May 20. A patrol of Union soldiers, some fifteen or twenty in number, were scouting the area, foraging for food and provisions. They were on the very spot where five days hence the massed roar of cannons and the screaming wail of flying lead and steel would write another bloody page in American history and name it the "Battle of New Hope Church." The young sergeant in command turned in his saddle, waved to his men and motioned with his arm off to the right. The horsemen turned off the dusty road and came galloping down a tree-shaded lane to a large two-storied frame house. The house was set well back from the road in a beautiful grove of majestic oak trees.

There were no slave-quarters to be seen near this place, for this was the home of one of those prosperous, non-slave-holding farmers of Georgia, a class of thrifty and industrious men, growing rather rapidly in the South in the years immediately preceding the Civil War. Many of these farmers had never been slave-holders; others had owned slaves, but for either moral convictions or economic reasons had freed them. They worked their own lands, hiring either negro or white labor as they needed it. Some of them had regularly employed "hired hands" who lived on the place.

The particular farm home toward which the Union patrol was riding this late spring day belonged to a man who was at that very hour encamped with General Robert E. Lee in Virginia. He had not been home since he left the first week in July, 1861, nearly three years ago. Throughout the war he had served with Company K, 14th Georgia Infantry, and was with them on this fateful day in May. He was not a slave-holder, and had never been one; he was a well-to-do independent farmer, the owner of eleven farms, all situated in Paulding County, or just across the line in Crawford County. When he left home that July day, he had left his wife and four small sons (the youngest only eight days old) in the beautiful home, assuring them he would be gone only a very short time. He had several men as overseers of the various farms, and had given careful instructions to each of them as to what was to be done during the three or four months he expected to be gone. Like most Southerners, he was confident the war would end in a matter of a few weeks, and that he would be home in plenty of time to oversee the picking of the cotton, which was already knee-high when he left.

Several times during the long years of his absence his wife had written him, asking permission to abandon the farm and flee with the children into southern Georgia or Florida. As the weary months dragged by, more and more of her neighbors and friends were doing this. She wanted to take her brood and go with them. But her husband was hard to convince. "One Reb can whip ten Yanks any day," he wrote her. "You stay right there where you are. They'll never get that far." So she stayed.

The patrol stopped outside the yard.

"Halloo in there!" called out the leader, cupping his hand to his mouth.

A young woman came to the door, with a three year old boy holding to her dress and peeking around the voluminous skirts at the strange men beyond the fence.

"Ma'am," said the soldier courteously, doffing his hat, "I'll have to ask you to get your children and leave the house. I have orders to search your place for contraband."

Without a word the woman reached down and picked up the little boy, called out to two other small boys to come with her, and walked out into the yard. The oldest boy in the family, now fourteen years of age, was not at home and his mother was grateful for that. He had joined in with a wandering band of guerillas, who were waging a sharp hit and run fight against the invaders. Had he been home, he would undoubtedly have been shot or else imprisoned, as he had managed to get together a tattered and much-too-big uniform of gray, which he proudly wore. The mother and her three small sons stood disconsolately and fearfully in the corner of the yard while their house was systematically searched for food or contraband. Nothing was found.

The smallest boy was holding a large pet dog between his legs, playing with him, not realizing what was happening. The dog, however, sensed the danger and tension in the air. The hair on the back of his neck began to bristle, and a low growl rumbled from his throat as a blue-clad soldier came near. With a quick jump the dog broke loose from his young master and made a lunge at the soldier, the growl breaking into a full-throated angry snarl. The startled soldier jumped backward, aiming a swift kick at the charging dog. Almost in the same movement he brought his rifle to his shoulder, took quick aim, and sent a bullet crashing through the dog's head just as the frightened little boy jumped forward to retrieve his pet. The dying dog fell at his master's feet.

The work of the patrol was finished. They had found no contraband in the house. But this place belonged to a Confederate soldier. Their orders were explicit; they were to do what had to be done to break the spirit of the people. Calling off his men to one side, the leader of the patrol himself went back into the house and applied a torch to some of the inflammable furnishings and drapes. The young mother darted toward the house, bent on rescuing some precious heirlooms; but a sharply barked order by the sergeant brought two soldiers quickly to her side who grabbed her and held her despite her furious struggling. As the flames began to lick through the windows and the soft crackle of burning wood turned gradually into a roaring inferno, the sobbing woman was dragged to the corner of the yard and released by the two soldiers. Her three small sons stood helplessly by, comprehending only vaguely the enormity of the catastrophe that had befallen them. Meanwhile, fire was also applied to the barns, the smokehouse, and to every building on the place. Rampaging flames from nearly a dozen barns, sheds, and farm buildings quickly combined with the blaze of the burning house to send a pall of smoke high into the heavens in the still summer air.

Young Jefferson Davis Tant, son of the Confederacy, not yet three years old by one full month, watched with terror stricken eyes as he received his first real taste of the kind of world into which he had been born.

III

All wars are alike. There is the horrible carnage of the battlefield, and there is the dumb terror and suffering of the civilian population. As the hungry flames swept through her home and through every building on the place, Mattie Lloyd Tant hugged her little sons to her bosom in the corner of the big yard and wept.

Sixteen years prior to this day she had married William Tant. She was born in Marion, South Carolina, on February 7, 1827, only a few years after her parents had come to America from their native Ireland. When Mattie (who

had been christened Martha) was three or four years old,
the family had moved to Cass County (now Crawford County), Georgia, where she had grown to womanhood as a
close neighbor of the large Tant family, also lately come
from Ireland. There were some six or eight Tant boys,
but Mattie had yielded her heart to William, who was
younger than she by some four months. William had been
born in Jackson County, Georgia, on June 15, 1827, and
was a true son of Ireland, with his sky blue eyes, his flam-
ing red hair (and temper to match), and a tongue that
dripped blarney. Mattie was the "black Irish" strain, with
dark skin, and eyes that were a deep shade of brown, deep-
set and piercing.

William Tant and Mattie Lloyd were married in Cass
County, Georgia, on Sunday, December 18, 1848. Neither
the Tants nor the Lloyds had been slave-holders, but both
families had prospered after coming to America, and both
were moderately well to do. William and Mattie were given
a rather respectable marriage dowry by both families, and
decided to move south a few miles, to Paulding County, to
buy a small farm.

By good management and a considerable talent for trading (which was to show itself years later in his youngest
son), William Tant had been able rapidly to expand his
holdings. Within ten years from the day he settled in
Paulding County, he was considered wealthy, and was well
on his way toward becoming one of the biggest land-owners
in that part of the State. He had acquired no less than
eleven farms in the general area south of Cartersville, and
had built a beautiful two-storied mansion, set well back
in a big grove of oak trees, to house his growing family.
He was constantly expanding his real estate holdings. All
his farms were either leased out, or else were under man-
agers who were directly responsible to Tant. Although
some of the farms were leased out to slave-holders, Tant

himself had no slaves, and would never use them when he could get other labor to work his crops. Occasionally he would hire or lease a group of slaves from some neighboring plantation, but only when he was unable to find any others to do the work. He took little or no interest in politics, regarding the hot-headed arguments of his slaveholding neighbors as being rather silly. To him, hard work and thrift and careful management were the things that counted. He had little time to argue the merits of the Missouri Compromise or the Gadsden Purchase.

The passing years saw the family of William and Mattie Tant increasing in number, as well as their farms. First-born was John, who made his appearance on September 6, 1850; three years later, a second son, Franklin Daniel, joined the family on December 15, 1853. James Monroe, third in line, was born on October 15, 1857; and Jefferson Davis, named in honor of the newly chosen President of the Confederacy, was born on June 28, 1861. When those ill-fated shots at Fort Sumter had heralded the opening of the bloody fratracidal conflict, like thousands of other non-slave-holding Southerners, Tant laid aside his tools and took up his rifle to defend his homeland. He felt as did many others (and didn't hesitate to say so) that it was "a rich man's war, and a poor man's fight." And although he could hardly be classed as a "poor man", he had had little association with the politicians, the "states'right" advocates, and the wealthy slave-holders and landed aristocracy. He was a relative new-comer to Paulding County, and no doubt the object of a certain amount of envy and jealousy since he had so rapidly advanced his fortunes; he was also in all probability subject to a degree of suspicion since he refused to own slaves even when he was obviously more than able to buy them. But, regardless of how it started, once the conflict was joined, there was no turning back. It was simply elementary that a man would

defend his home. And if, as they were constantly being
told, the Yankees were bent on invading them and enslav-
ing the people of the South, then a man's duty was plain.

The four years that William Tant fought under the Confederate flag were years of incredible suffering, hardship,
and loneliness. Fighting at first under General P. G. T.
Beauregarde, he was transferred later to Lee's army in
Virginia. It was his sad lot to be among the battle-scarred,
weary, and ragged heroes who witnessed the final curtain
ring down at Appomatox, almost four years to the day
after that first tragic cannon blast at Fort Sumter. Not
once during those four years had Tant had a furlough;
not once had he seen the family whom he had left. Letters
were exchanged, but mail was slow and uncertain. It would
sometimes take a letter as much as three months to go
from Georgia to Virginia. And many never reached their
destination at all. It is likely that William, as a soldier,
had very little understanding of how dire was the threat
to his home and family. Propaganda, then as now, was
necessary to keep up the morale of the men in battle. It
was hardly likely that they would be told their own states
were being invaded and their own homes destroyed by the
enemy.

IV

As the flames began to subside, and the roaring furnace
of what an hour earlier had been a beautiful house died
down, Mattie Tant gathered her weeping children together
and started walking through the fields to the east. Long
columns of black smoke, ascending lazily into the sky from
every direction, told her that her neighbors were reaping
the same cruel treatment she had received. No point in
trying to turn to them for help. Their homes had been
burned as hers had been. This was war. General Sherman had decreed that the will of the people to resist must

be broken; and the way to break it was by a scorched earth policy of total devastation. For that decision Sherman will be remembered and hated as long as the story of the "Lost Cause" shall live in the memories of men.

Nearly seventy years after those frightful days, Jefferson Davis Tant wrote of them:

"I was born in Paulding County, Georgia, 1861. I was only eight days old when my father started for the war, and was four years old when he returned. I was taught that he was my father, and I must respect him. When father started to the war, we owned eleven farms in North Georgia, and we were considered 'well-to-do'. Our home was on the New Hope Church battleground. After the battle nothing was left on the farm but some oak trees. My dear mother and my oldest brother walked twenty-two miles to where they heard of a wheat field outside of the army's march, and pulled up two bushels of wheat, beat it out on a rail the next day, and brought it home. For three months we lived under an oak tree, with nothing to eat except boiled wheat with salted water put in it. The salt was obtained by my mother's digging up the ground where the smokehouse had stood and boiling the dirt to get the salt from it. While we lived under that oak tree we were often visited by roving groups of Yankee soldiers. They offered us no physical hurt, but seemed to take a great delight in teasing me, and teaching me to swear most prodigiously. They would tell me a long list of curse words to call various men in the group, and then would laugh uproariously and slap their legs when I repeated the oaths after them. I was a pretty good size boy before I ever learned that "damnyankee" was two words.

We were in the line of Sherman's march through Georgia, sixty miles wide and three hundred miles long. Not a cow, horse, hog, nor house was left. All were burned or taken. Germany in her bloodiest days was never any meaner than the Yankee soldiers under Sherman. They not only outraged every girl in our

country, but stood guard with their guns and made
the negro men commit the same crime on white girls.
When my father came home from the war, all deeds
and records of our farms had been burned. He got
Babe Forsythe, a lawyer, to get up other deeds. The
lawyer had all the deeds made to himself, sold all the
farms, made deeds to them, and left the country. This
left us at the bottom. Father moved south four hundred miles, with a wagon of his own make and a pair
of broken-down oxen he had found wandering around
after the war. For nine long years we struggled
against the hardships of life." (Gospel X-Ray, p 283.)

Those years following the war were very difficult. This
was the era of the "carpet-bagger." Society was disor-
ganized; violence was common, and the cruel aftermath
of war brought disease, poverty, malnutrition, and squalor.
William Tant worked valiantly for his family, but he was
a broken man. Four years of warfare, living in the open,
sleeping on wet ground, forced marches, days without food,
had ruined his health. He had walked all the way home
from Appomatox, doing the last fifty miles of it without
even stopping for rest. He was weak from hunger when
he arrived home — to find his house burned to the ground,
his stock all stolen or destroyed, his wife and children
gaunt-eyed and half-starved. His baby, Jefferson Davis,
now a big-eyed child of four, with the shrivelled arms and
legs and the distended stomach that spoke all too eloquently
of malnutrition, had never seen the red-bearded stranger
who tried to pick him up and hold him in his lap. He ran
screaming in fright to his mother.

Less than a year after returning to his desolated home,
William Tant received the further crushing blow of having
all his lands stolen from him by the unscrupulous Babe
Forsythe. This was the end. There was no point in try-
ing to get a new start in this part of the country. So
Tant gathered his pitiably meager belongings together,

piled stuff and family into the makeshift wagon he had devised, and moved to the south, to Brooks County.

Life in south Georgia showed little improvement over Paulding County. Tant tried to rent a small farm for a few years, tried his hand at trading again (at which he had been so phenomenally successful before the war), tried carpentery, tried anything and everything he could find to feed his family. Nothing ever turned out right.

V

In 1873 the Tant family had reached the point of desperation. And this was the year young Jefferson Davis got snake bitten. He was now twelve years old, and had never been to school a day in his life. He had spent the day on the creek bank, trying to catch a catfish for the supper table. No luck. As he was threading his way back through the well-beaten path, brushing against the ferns and weeds that overlapped the trail, he felt a sudden sharp sting in his left leg just below the knee. He had heard no sound, but as he jumped back involuntarily, he caught a glimpse of the slithering shiny back of a moccasin, rapidly losing himself in the grass. Jeff picked up a stone and hurled it with all his strength at the wriggling snake, then seized a short stick and chased after his attacker. The snake soon lost itself in the underbrush, and young Jeff picked up his fishing pole and started on toward the house. It was nearly a mile away, and before he had covered half the distance, he began to feel dizzy and nauseated. He decided he had better hurry and get home before the poison killed him. He began to run.

By the time he reached the clearing where the crude little patched-up shack stood, he was staggering wildly. He would start toward the house but before he had taken three steps it would seem to disappear in a whirling, crazily tilting landscape, only to bob up again on the opposite side of the clearing. Every time he tried to move toward it, the house disappeared and came up somewhere else. The boy felt a great throbbing roar in his ears, and the sight began to fail in his eyes. Terror took hold of him.

"Mammy!", he screamed. "Jim, Mollie, come and get me!" Jeff stumbled on, whimpering with fright.

Little Mollie, newest member of the family, having been born in Brooks County on February 4, 1868, was the first to hear his cries. She quickly called her mother, and Mattie Tant ran to her semi-conscious boy, picked him up in her arms, and carried him into the cabin. This was a crude two-room shack, used by a negro family before the war, but abandoned by them when the "carpet-baggers" had come and moved them into town. William Tant had patched up the miserable hut with scraps of board from a nearby saw-mill.

For nearly a week the issue as to whether Jeff would live or die was in doubt. There were no doctors in that section, but there were many well known "home remedies" for snake bite, all of which were tried. The child was given several stiff shots of corn whiskey. The place where the snake had struck was cut open with a razor and a cud of chewing tobacco (well chewed by William for that very purpose) was placed in the wound and bound tightly there. The fever did not break for four days, and Jeff's delirium lasted for two days after that. But a remarkably strong constitution (which was to stand him in good stead in the hard and rugged years ahead which destiny had mapped out for him) finally brought him through, enabling him to recover from the snake bite as well as from the treatment. During his sickness, as he was burning with high fever, he used to watch the sun come up each morning, shining through the huge cracks in the cabin, and tell himself that he would be dead before it sank in the west. And as the last rays of sunlight faded from the cabin walls in the evening, he felt sure he would die before it rose again. But he lived. And gradually, as the days went by in slow progression, he began to mend.

As he convalesced, the young patient began to grow increasingly restless and fretful. He began to worry his mother with daily pleadings that she let him go back into the woods, back to the small stream for more fishing. But Mattie was fearful of other snakes and unwilling to let him venture out so soon again. This irked the boy, and he took out his irritation on his five year old sister. At last the bickering between the two became so bad that Mattie Tant told her husband he would have to take a hand in the matter.

He did. And sent young Jeff to the neighborhood school, some three miles away. This was a new experience to the lad. But he took to it with an insatiable appetite. Those few days in school (he went six weeks) opened up a whole new world to him. He learned to read, learned the elementary rules of simple arithmetic, and had some practice in spelling. There were no free schools in Georgia at that time; all students paid tuition. After six weeks William Tant had exhausted his meager funds, and Jeff had to drop out of school. But this brief encounter with "learning" kindled a fire in the breast of the country lad which was never to be extinguished. He began to discover the wonderful world of books; he read everything he could lay his hands on — newspapers, magazines, the Bible, school books, anything that had printing on it. His choice of reading matter in post-Civil War Georgia was limited indeed; but such as it was he devoured voraciously.

By 1876 William Tant had come to believe that his only hope and the only hope for his family lay in the west — in Texas. Fabulous stories had seeped back to Georgia about the opportunities in this new frontier. Vast tracts of rich prairie land could be had for less than a dollar an

acre; fortunes were being made in cattle. Georgia was
under the rule of the carpet-baggers; there was no chance
ever to get ahead, or even to make a decent living in this
part of the world. Many of his old wartime comrades had
already gone west, some of them going all the way to California, some stopping in Colorado, and a great number
of them stopping with their families in Texas. Andrew
Tant, William's older brother had moved to Texas shortly
after the war closed, settling on a farm a few miles south
of Austin, and was doing well.

In the fall of 1876, after his few acres of cotton had
been picked, William Tant packed all his worldly goods into
four or five wooden boxes, gathered his wife and three
sons and one daughter together, and left for Texas. John,
the oldest son, was now married, and remained in Georgia.
But Dan, Jim, Jeff, and Mollie, with their parents, set their
faces to the West. They came by train to Memphis, Tennessee, then managed to get a wagon train going on into
the land of promise. After a long and tiring journey they
reached their destination, a lonely farm about fifteen miles
south of Austin.

Andrew Tant gave them a hearty welcome.

CHAPTER II

THE BRONC BUSTER

Texas in the 1870's was an untamed country. The huge cattle drives up the Chisholm Trail to the Kansas railroads were at their height. A six-shooter was standard equipment for cowboys and all travelers. Indian raids were still a thing to be reckoned with, particularly the depredations of the savage Comanches. Wild game was plentiful, including buffalo, deer, and antelope.

When William Tant brought his family to his brother's home in the waning months of 1876, it was with high hopes of making a new life for himself and his loved ones in this virgin wilderness. He had no money, no tools, no education; but he did have a willingness to work, and an indomitable courage.

Unfortunately, also, he had something else, a weakness not uncommon to the Irish — a love for red whiskey. Through the thirteen years of life that were left to him he waged a noble but losing fight against the bottle. Somehow, the fortunes that were being made in Texas always eluded him. The rich strike was always just beyond his reach. After only a few days at his brother's place, William heard of a rich farming area in Collin County, Texas; he bought an old worn out wagon and a team to take his family back three hundred miles to that section. Camping one night near Dallas, he happened to be talking with a passing traveler who told him of a fine farm near Forest Grove, not far from McKinney, which he might rent. Tant came on to this community, rented the farm, and for two years tried to raise a crop. But the Texas weather, and Texas methods of farming were too much for him. After two years he was badly in debt, and saw little chance of ever getting out. About that time he managed to get a job with a construction crew, building a railroad in southwest Texas.

For the next two years William worked as a "powder monkey," setting the charges of powder and blasting huge chunks of earth and stone into the air. It was a dangerous job, but the ex-Confederate soldier was not unhappy with it, and it did give him a regular monthly income, however small, to send home to his family. His Irish temper was usually (but not always) well under control, and his wit was quick and penetrating. He was not a large man physically, perhaps five feet seven inches in height, and never weighing more than 160 pounds. His health improved somewhat in the dry, invigorating air of the southwest, and he was unusually strong and agile. He managed to hold his own with the tough crew with which he worked, both as to work, repartee — and the bottle.

Meanwhile, his family was growing up. Young Jeff's memory of those early years remained vivid to the end of his life. He wrote:

"At the age of fourteen. (while still in Georgia), I joined the Methodist Church, and began preaching for them when I was nineteen. At fifteen years of age, with my parents, I moved from Georgia to Texas. About this time I became interested in an education, and fortunately was located near a high school; but unfortunately I had only one dollar to supply all my earthly needs. I invested that dollar in three yards of cloth, from which my mother made me a pair of pants. I started to school. There were no free schools in Texas then. I did not have a single school book, and began my education with only one pair of pants. At school I would dodge around the children and study my lessons on their books with them, until one day a school-mate cursed me and told me that if my old daddy could not get me any books, I had better quit.

This discouraged me, and I stated my troubles to my teacher, who agreed that he would leave one window unfastened each night, and for me to come and get all the books containing my lessons for the next day, learn my lessons, and put the books back next morning before school. This I did for two years, and many times would three o'clock in the morning find me after my lessons with a little brass lamp to study by.

"Days came and went. I was in the school room all day and never looked at a book — yet at the recitation time I seldom missed answering all questions. The children begged me to tell them how I knew my lessons without studying. This I kept as a profound secret, and the news soon spread that I was an idiot. As this seemed to be so near my nature, I acted my part well. People often visited the school, anxious to see 'old man Tant's idiot boy that learned his lessons without studying'. This I kept up for two years, at the end of which time an old lady heard of my desire for an education, sent for me, and loaned me twenty dollars to buy my school books. The last two years I was in school I was in a class alone. I had passed all the other students — not because I had more ability, but because I used what I had.

"In that day and time about four years was the limit of an education. Now it takes from ten to twenty-five years to get through school. After school was out I worked at home, and each fall helped to gather the crop. I then would hire out to pick cotton until I had enough money to pay my tuition and enough to buy a common suit of clothes to wear the next school year. In the community where I lived we started a Sunday School when I was seventeen years old. One hundred and fifty students and teachers were enrolled; and because I did not have sense enough to see my mistakes and be disheartened by them, I was elected Superintendent of the Sunday School, and for the first time in my life I stood before a large congregation and read the word of God and tried to pray.

"About this time I thought I was up on vocal music and began to teach in different communities. Metho-

dist preachers were easily made, as the demand was
more for lung power and the ability to get up excitement than for brain power to teach the people. Because of this I stood high with them, and passed my
examination for a preacher at nineteen." (Gospel X-
Ray, p. 284.)

II

The Reverend Jefferson Davis Tant, duly ordained in
the Methodist ministry, became a circuit-rider in North
Texas in the year 1880. There was just one problem: he
had no "circuit" to ride, nothing to ride it on, and no salary
to live on while riding. About all he did have was a limit-
less zeal, an unbounded faith in God, and a certainty that
God would make a way for him somehow. His mother
was a devout and God-fearing woman, reared a Methodist,
and her heart overflowed with gratitude when God saw
fit to give her youngest son "the call." She knew that
according to family tradition young Jeff's great grand-
father had once been a Catholic priest in Ireland, but had
fallen into disfavor with his superiors over a sacred relic
which he had accidentally dropped and broken. He had
fled from Ireland to America, abandoning his Catholic religion while doing so — and also changing his name from
"O'Fell" to "Tant". This latter name had been an inven-
tion, made up by taking the first letter from the given
name of each of his four brothers - Theodore, Andrew,
Nathan, and Thomas. In America the erstwhile priest had
married, reared a large family, and three of his grandsons
had fought under the flag of the Confederacy. He had
not been particularly religiously inclined in the new world.

But now the hand of God was again laid on the family,
Mattie felt, and her son was to wear the cloth! Her heart
was happy within her at the thought, and she thanked
God for having given her this comfort and great joy in
her declining years. She was only fifty-three years old

when Jeff was ordained, but her life had been filled with hardship and suffering, and her health was failing. From his boyhood she had sensed the deep spiritual powers of this child of war. Through the weary years of privation and poverty she had seen him grow intellectually and spiritually. And now, by God's grace, she would see him stand in the pulpit and speak the blessed gospel!

Tant's life in the Methodist ministry, however, was destined to be a short one. He was ordained in the fall of 1880, and spent the rest of that year and the early months of 1881 in a diligent proclamation of Methodist doctrine. He knew practically nothing of it, but he had "lung-power" and was unusually successful in raising an audience to a high pitch of excitement and frenzy by the very intensity of his own feelings. He preached in school-houses, in private homes, and often in the open air as the summer months of 1881 came on.

It was midnight in early July, 1881. A bright moon overhead shone intermittently through the pale fleecy clouds drifting slowly across her face. A camp meeting is in progress. The young Methodist preacher who has been making such a sensation in North Texas these past few months is standing on a crude wooden platform, sweating and shouting. His words have little meaning, and at times are almost incoherent as he momentarily chokes up from his own overwhelming emotional fervor. A sobbing scream pierces the night air, followed by sympathetic groans and cries from all over the audience. There is no roof over these people, and the hot summer breezes are heavy with an oppressive humidity. In the pulpit Jeff Tant, standing just a fraction under six feet tall, slender as a reed, and with eyes deep-sunk and intense, so brown they almost seem black, continues to pour forth pleas and exhortations. He has an hypnotic spell upon his audience;

they are responding to him as the waving grass yields to the passing wind.

Tant was no orator. The rolling periods, the fine alliterative phraseology and the great swelling crescendos of the professional speaker of his day were as foreign to his nature as they were unknown to his intellect. He had a great power to move people, but it lay in his own total and unalloyed sincerity, his complete belief in what he was doing, his unquestioning acceptance of the absolute and final truth of his message. These people were unlettered, and many of them illiterate. Their lives were filled with hardship and danger and toil. Tant was one of them. He spoke their language. He knew what had meaning to them and what did not. The rough jest, often crude or even bordering on obscenity if judged by the standards of a more cultured and effete society, was taken in stride by these farmers of the frontier. They roared with unrestrained laughter as the young preacher gave utterance to some witticism, or put a hilarious turn or twist to some common saying of the day. The laughter relaxed them, and made them sympathetic and eager listeners as the tone of the sermon turned from humor to solemnity, and from witticisms to worshipful awe and gravity. This was not the studied play of a trained speaker; it was the natural and unconscious action and reaction between a speaker and an audience entirely en rapport. Tant was not aware that he was using any psychology at all. He simply spoke as he felt — and he felt with an intensity and a sensitivity far deeper than most men of his day, or of any day.

During the spring of 1881, Tant had had occasion to hear two "Campbellite" preachers in North Texas whose simple explanations of Bible teaching had a profoundly disturbing effect on him. A part of his duties as a Methodist preacher was to sprinkle babies. He had faithfully followed this custom (although he himself had been immersed in the

Methodist Church while still in Georgia), and had not ques-
tioned its scripturalness. But John M. McKinney of Mc-
Kinney, Texas, and Ben Falkner of near Forest Grove were
holding meetings over much of the same area where Tant
was preaching, and he had occasion to hear each of them
several times. Like most frontier preachers of their day
their lessons were simple and elementary, and highly emotional. But even their poor exposition of the Scriptures
disturbed Tant. They were reading verses from the Bible
and explaining them in a way he had never even dreamed
of before. Nearly thirty years later he wrote:

> "Old Brother John M. McKinney of McKinney, Tex-
> as, and Ben Falkner, now of Wylie, were the first
> Christian preachers I ever heard preach; yet when I
> look back and compare their preaching to that of the
> religious world, I am surprised at their success. Their
> preaching was but little above the sectarian world;
> and to associate with the sects, to often call upon sec-
> tarian preachers to lead prayer in their meetings, was
> so common that all the sects thought they were re-
> garded as Christians and saw little use to change. Long
> since, Ben Falkner took an aggressive stand among the
> innovators; and Brother McKinney was not aggressive
> on either side. They never benefited the cause of apos-
> tolic Christianity much in Texas." (Firm Foundation,
> January 26, 1909.)

Perhaps not. But after hearing their sermons it is true
that Tant himself began to be considerably disturbed about
the subject of baptism, particularly about infant sprinkling. These men had challenged any in their audience to
find one verse in the Bible (just one!) that even hinted that
any infant was ever sprinkled for any cause. Tant was in-
dignant at such preaching. He began a careful search of
the Scripture to find the verse. He read the entire New
Testament through; then began to read the Old Testament. He could not find a verse that fully satisfied him.

He was familiar with the argument made on the "household" baptisms of Cornelius and the Philippian jailor, but these stories left him still with a nagging sort of uncertainty. He wanted something more definite with which to confront the "Campbellites." It was unthinkable to him that the great Methodist scholars, who could read Greek and Hebrew with as much ease as English, could be mistaken in this matter.

So the search went on, with a growing feeling of desperation as day passed after day without the looked for verse turning up.

Spring turned into summer, and Tant decided to try his luck in a different part of the state. Jim Tant, his older brother who was now married, wanted to move down near their relatives in the Austin area, hoping that the dry climate there might improve his health a bit. He had found the humidity of east Texas rather hard for him to take. The family of Andrew Tant was a large one, and Jim kept getting letters from his cousins south of Austin telling him of the fine land, the wonderful climate, and the "fortunes to be made" in that area of Texas. The decision to move was made. Jeff decided to go along. Although the young Methodist preacher had been phenomenally successful in North Texas, the lure of a new country was strong upon him. He had the not uncommon feeling that "a prophet is not without honor save in his own country and among his own people." Perhaps among strangers he could do even greater things for Christ than he could here in Collin County where he had lived for five years and had gone to school.

There was one deciding factor, however, in bringing matters to a head. The family of Andrew Tant had written that there was a great desire on the part of the community to have a singing school. Was young Jeff up on music enough to teach a singing school? That settled the matter. Tant had attended a few singing schools in North Texas, and with unbounded confidence in himself felt sure that he was well qualified to teach. He decided to go south with Jim and his wife, and teach singing schools as well as preach Methodist doctrine. Maybe singing schools would support better than preaching! As yet he had received no money for his preaching, just food and shelter and a few cast off pieces of clothing that were no longer serviceable to their owners.

III

The Tant caravan (they went in two covered wagons) reached Buda, between Austin and San Marcos, about the middle of July, 1881. The final week at Forest Grove had been one of the most exciting in the young minister's life. On the very night before the wagons left the next morning he had closed out the biggest "revival" he had yet conducted. Shouting, crying, and wild hallelujahs! had rent the night air until almost day break. There had been many who "got through," and Tant felt that the hand of God was indeed with him.

The journey to Buda took nearly ten days. Almost immediately upon their arriving there a singing school was organized. Tant was the teacher. The school quickly turned into a singing school and a revival combined. The excitement here began to mount as it had in Collin County. The young preacher undoubtedly lacked many things, but nobody could deny his tremendous earnestness and his ability to inspire his audience with enthusiasm.

Only a few days after reaching San Marcos, and while engaged in the singing school and the revival, Tant had gotten a job on a nearby ranch as a "bronc buster." He was now twenty years of age, and although slender, weighing about 150 pounds, his long hours of hard work had made his muscles like whip-cord. He stood straight and erect, disdaining the slouching gait and lazy posture af-

fected by most cowboys of the day. He knew little of
horses, but was certain he could do whatever was necessary to break them to the saddle. Breaking wild horses is
a job that is soon learned or soon abandoned. Tant learned.
He was thrown as many as nine times in one day from the
same horse; but had an uncanny knack for learning the
tricks of the trade, and rapidly developed into an expert
rider. Successful ranchers were reluctant to have their
regular cowboys break the wild horses, as it not infrequent-
ly laid a man up for a week, or might even cause him to be
off the job for a month or two recuperating from a broken
arm or a leg or some cracked ribs. This was expensive.
The job was a dangerous one. For this cause professional
"bronc busters" were in demand, and usually went from
ranch to ranch, breaking the horses and training them to
the saddle and the bit. Tant got $5.00 per head for each
horse he broke and trained. This would require sometimes as much as three or four weeks, but he usually had
five or six in the process of being broken at the same time.
Each horse had to be ridden the first time, which was the
"breaking", then he had to be ridden every day for a couple
of weeks to make sure he was not too dangerous or untamed
to turn over to the cowboys for further training. Even
when the professional "buster" was through with a horse
and turned him over to one of the cowboys, the training
and taming were still far from complete. It usually took
two or three months of daily riding before a horse could be
gradually worked into the regular string.

Tant describes his life in those years:

"As to myself, I followed music teaching and farming and breaking wild horses for a living, getting $5.00
a horse for each one I would break to ride. I preached
all summer in protracted meetings, besides each Lord's
day near my home in crop time. I have held many a
protracted meeting and picked 300 pounds of cotton

each day, then preached each night for two weeks at a time. Also I became a reckless rider and many times have I been condemned for riding wild horses and driving so fast, as many thought "bronc busting" belonged to the cowboy and not to the preacher. A few times in life I have been challenged to run horse races during my meetings, some of the boys thinking that any man who could ride a broncho should be able to run a race." (Firm Foundation, January 26, 1909.)

It was early in August, 1881, less than a month after he had come to Buda, that Tant first came in contact with W. H. D. Carrington, a man who was to influence his life profoundly. Carrington was in a gospel meeting at the little town of Buda. This was only a few miles from the ranch where Tant was making his home, and he decided to ride over one night to hear what the "Campbellite" preacher had to say. Any kind of meeting was a social event, furnishing the occasion for visiting and meeting old friends as well as for making new ones. Tant was deeply shaken by Carrington's preaching from the very first night he went. All the doubts that had plagued him earlier in the year when he had heard John McKinney and Ben Falkner preach now returned with multiplied force. Carrington was an able historian, having an excellent knowledge of both secular and church history, particularly as it concerned the origin and development of the various denominational bodies. All this was an entirely new world to young Tant. If he had ever stopped to think about the origin of the Methodist Church, he had brushed the question aside as being unimportant. The important thing was to have "the Spirit," and he knew he had that! His feelings constituted all the evidence he needed or wanted.

But night after night Carrington's preaching was penetrating that conviction, increasing doubts and uncertainty and confusion in the young preacher's mind. Was it possible, he began to ask himself, that the Methodist Church was wrong? Had he been preaching something foreign to God's word in preaching Methodist doctrine? Could his godly mother be mistaken? A thousand questions arose to torment him. Returning from the meeting, he would sometimes spend all the rest of the night checking the passages of Scripture which Carrington had used. The first rays of the morning sun would find him sitting on the side of his bed, the little brass lamp flickering on the table beside him, and with an open Bible spread out on his knees, reading, reading, reading . . . and beginning to be filled with a dread and a terror that almost paralyzed him.

At last the situation became intolerable. Tant realized with an unutterable sense of apprehension that he had been preaching error; and that if he had died in that condition, he would have stood in the final judgment of God condemned and damned forever! It was a frightening and dreadful experience. He had stood, he felt, on the very brink of hell, blindly, calmly, and with never a thought or a fear as to his condition. Cold sweat began to break out on his brow, and a great trembling came over him. Physical weakness overwhelmed him so that he was robbed even of the power to stand on his feet. It was an experience he never forgot, a shock to his soul that was to give a sense of urgency and tremendous appeal to all his preaching for sixty years to come. But for the grace of God (and W. H. D. Carrington!) he might have gone right on his way through life — and into hell!

On August 14, 1881, Tant came forward in Carrington's meeting and gave the aged preacher his hand. He was openly weeping as he did so, weeping from fear, from gratitude, and from the awful realization that his mother, his father, his brothers, and his sister, were all still in the error which he was leaving. Since he had been immersed, he was received into fellowship by the Buda church on his statement that he was "satisfied" with his baptism.

It was only one week later (and after many lengthy conversations with Carrington) that young Jefferson Davis Tant was given his "license" to preach in the church of Christ. He was so much a stranger to all at Buda that the penman who wrote out the letter of commendation did not even know his given name or initials, and left a long blank space before the name "Tant". He wrote:

To the Brethren of the Church of Christ in Texas:

This will commend to your kind consideration our beloved brother ——————— Tant, who is authorized to preach the word, organize and take the oversight of Sunday Schools, and baptize any converts he may be instrumental in converting to Christ.

August 21st, 1881   Signed:

J. D. Cady   W. H. D. Carrington
          Elders   Evangelist of Church of Christ
W. M. Bills   W. E. Nelson
                    Evangelist of Church of Christ

CHAPTER III

PREACHING IN EAST TEXAS

Tant's "joining the Campbellites" immediately shut him off from association with his Methodist friends. This represented no great financial sacrifice, however, as his ministerial stipend from the Methodists had been exactly nothing. He had made his living by teaching singing schools, breaking horses, and picking cotton. This he continued to do.

Immediately after being "shaken in" by the Church of Christ in Buda, Tant started to preach "the faith of which he once made havoc." He felt awkward and ill at ease in his new relations, hardly knowing how to preach a sermon except in the fashion of high excitement, shouting, and intense emotionalism of the Methodists. But he knew that God's word was true, and set himself to study it with a passion that would not be daunted. He read everything pertaining to the Bible on which he could lay his hands. He formed the habit of underlining Bible verses that were of particular importance or interest to him. Some of his old Bibles show scarcely a chapter from Genesis to Revelation without one or more verses underlined, and some of them have whole chapters underlined.

All through the fall of 1881 Tant preached as he had opportunity or could make appointments. He held several meetings in the little country communities out from Buda, meanwhile continuing his work as a horse trainer, and picking cotton or working out as a hired man when he could get no horses to break. He was a willing worker, possessed of unusual physical stamina in a land where strong men were the rule rather than the exception, and he worked with a haste and a concentration that at times almost seemed frenzied. He was forever in a hurry. And when the day's work was done, and the last weary cowboy or cotton-picker would drop off into a heavy and dreamless sleep, worn to exhaustion by the gruelling pace that had been set, Tant would either be on his horse riding off to some preaching appointment, or straining his eyes by the flickering light of a coal oil brass lamp, reading the Bible or perhaps some book of history, philosophy, science, or metaphysics. Rarely did he get to bed before midnight, a trait he kept all through life. Usually he was the first one up in the morning. Five hours a night seemed to be all the sleep he needed or desired. He had great ability to relax almost instantaneously and completely, and could catch a "cat-nap" even while riding a horse, or plow, or wagon. When the men knocked off work at noon, Tant would eat his simple meal, stretch out on the ground, and be fast asleep in three minutes. He would sleep for fifteen or twenty minutes, then be ready to go back to work, fully rested and refreshed.

Realizing that he could never be anything but a hired hand unless he began to farm for himself, in the spring of 1882 Tant rented a small farm some ten or twelve miles east and north of San Marcos. The rental agreement was the customary "share-cropping" arrangement of the day, in which the landlord received one-fourth of the cotton and one-third of the corn grown on his place, the renter furnishing all the tools, teams, and work of planting, cultivating and harvesting. The young farmer-preacher threw himself into this new venture with great energy. This was one of the most successful and financially rewarding years of his life — although he still received nothing at all for his preaching.

"The third year of my ministerial work (1882) I made a fine crop, picked fifteen bales of cotton myself, made $1,700.00 on the farm. I then bought a small farm, improved it, located my parents on it, and sought larger fields of usefulness." (Christian Leader, 1932.)

II

The year 1883 found Tant working hard on his small farm, his family sharing in his toil. Living with him at this time were his father and mother, and his only sister, Mollie, a beautiful girl of fifteen, just turning into womanhood. William Tant had returned from his railroad construction work, his health having begun to fail somewhat. He was not able to do any of the heavy work on the farm, but did help in every way he could with the chores and the lighter work.

This year was a milestone in Tant's life. For it was in 1883 that he received his very first compensation as a preacher of God's word. He held several meetings through the year, and preached nearly every Sunday in some schoolhouse or rural community. He would work all week on the farm, then ride his horse to these preaching appointments, preach on Saturday night, Sunday morning, Sunday afternoon, and again on Sunday night, then ride half the night to get home in time to catch a little sleep before going to the field on Monday morning. No day ended which did not find him either in some place preaching, or poring over some book by the light of that coal oil lamp.

When the year ended, Tant checked back through his records and found he had received a total compensation for this year of preaching in the amount of $9.75. Of this, $5.00 had come as a wedding fee. This was his fourth year as a preacher. Fortunately, the cotton crop was good this year, and the little farm produced enough to meet all payments due on the mortgage, buy groceries and clothes, and still leave a slight surplus. Tant felt that his star of destiny was on the rise. For the first time in his life, he was able to look forward to some sort of financial security and stability. The whole family was happy, and the outlook was brighter than it had ever been since that fateful day when the gods of war had devastated their home and their hopes in Georgia.

Late in the fall of 1883, Tant wrote to C. M. Wilmeth, who at that time was perhaps the leading preacher in Texas, and who was the "state evangelist," asking his help in furthering his usefulness as a gospel preacher. This was at a period in the history of Texas congregations when the churches were practicing a type of "sponsored cooperation" which enabled them to combine their resources under a single eldership (called by Carroll Kendrick a "receiving, managing, and disbursing evangelistic committee") for the support of one or more evangelists to work in the state. The Missionary Society had not yet invaded Texas, and the disciples of the state, numbering perhaps 30,000 all told, had for a number of years been conducting annual "lectureships," or "consultation meetings," usually referred to by them simply as the "State Meeting." Wilmeth's support was supplied out of the funds raised through these meetings.

A report of these days is given by Tant:

"At that time we had no Missionary Society in Texas. We were not divided at any place except Pearl and Bryan Streets, Dallas, and San Marcos. The organ had been introduced in both of these places, and had divided the congregations. There was a cooperation among all the churches, and a meeting of messengers each year. A strong man was selected and sent out to strengthen the weak and build up new congregations. The noted C. M. Wilmeth was selected to do this work. I wrote Wilmeth of my escape from sectarianism, of my ability as a gospel preacher, and asked his help to locate me in a larger field. Wilmeth wrote me a kind letter, telling me that for two years he had been look-

ing for a Timothy to travel with him to do the odds
and ends, to lead songs, to help answer his mail, to
often go before him and start his meeting while he
remained behind to close the meeting he was in. He
also added that the churches paid him $1,200.00 a year,
and at each place he would put my work before the
church in connection with his, and he was sure I could
get my railroad fare and $200.00 to $300.00 a year.

"I knew I could hire a hand to work on the farm and
see after my parents for $150.00 a year, and if I could
only get $200.00, this would leave me $50.00 a year to
clothe myself; and since the salary was so far above
the $9.75 I had received I accepted his offer gladly.
I sold what surplus things we could spare from the
farm, and arranged to meet Brother Wilmeth in San
Antonio in November of '83. There was to be a meeting at that place of the preachers of southwest Texas
to look after the mission at San Antonio where Brother
D. Pennington was located on a salary of $50.00 per
month, with forty-eight members meeting in a rented
hall. At that meeting the noted G. L. Surber, just
back from Australia, A. L. Bush, and D. Pennington
were all grand loyal preachers; but all went to the digressives when division came. But Pennington repented and came back home before he died. After one
week's wrangling among the preachers without any
good, the mission was left with Brother Pennington.

"During that week Wilmeth was too busy wrangling
with the preachers to tell the Lord about my work, so
he and I started to Hempstead, Texas, for a mission
meeting. I had $13.00 which I had brought from home
with me, and hoped the Lord would hear of my work
at Hempstead and send me a collection before that
amount gave out. At Hempstead it was my work to
lead songs, ring the bell, build the fires, go for Wilmeth's mail, and write letters for him.

"I had neglected writing in school and could not
write any better than Joe Warlick or F. B. Srygley,
and some times when I would write letters of our coming, some of them would be put aside until we could
get there to explain what was meant. Others were returned with a letter stating that they had no one in

the church who could read Greek or Hebrew, or who
was familiar with Egyptian hieroglyphics. We would
have to get some one else to write. Wilmeth soon saw
that I could do him no good. We had a fine meeting
at Hempstead, but Wilmeth forgot to tell the Lord
about my work. About this time he was called home,
and left me there to go to Groesbeck to start his next
meeting when he should write me. My $13.00 had run
down to $2.65. I waited in Hempstead six weeks be-
fore I heard from Wilmeth. He wrote me that he
could not use me. I could look out for something else.

"I was then one hundred and fifty miles from home,
had spent two months' time and my work without one
cent. The thought then came to me to go back home
by rail (being careful to get off the rails each time the
train passed), get me another team and go to work.

"About that time old Brother George W. Harvey,
one of the grandest men God ever made, came by, going
to Montgomery County for a meeting, and took me
with him. Brother Harvey put new life into me and
declared that I would succeed if I would stay by my
gun. We went to Willis, Texas, and had a grand meeting. Brother Harvey told them of my condition, and
got them to hire me to teach their school. But they
told me that the pupils had run off two teachers before
that time, and they had some fears about my being
able to control them. I told them I could teach the
school, but they might have to employ two doctors to
wait on their children, as I proposed to be manager of
the school.

"At the close of the first month I had whipped thir-
ty-two children and proved to them that I was equal
to the occasion. During the two years I taught there,
I seldom did any more whipping. I remember the last
outbreak; I whipped five grown young ladies one day
and a married woman. The trustees came to me and
wanted me to sign a contract to teach the school five
years and build up a first class school. But I learned
that if I did, quite a number of men intended sending
their wives to school, and for fear I might get into deep
water I quit the school forever after the second term.
In addition to my school salary I was paid $92.00 for

my preaching that year, which was a considerable advance over my first four years." (Christian Leader, 1932.)

III

Very shortly after closing out the school in Willis, Tant had a letter from John McKinney, inviting him to come back to Collin County and hold a meeting in the Forest Grove Church. He had been gone from that section for four years now, having left there as a Methodist preacher. But word of his conversion had come to his old friends there, and the brethren had decided that it would be a good thing to have him back for a meeting. His sensational success as a Methodist evangelist was still remembered here, and it was felt that he might have some considerable influence among his Methodist friends and relatives. Tant was delighted at the opportunity:

"To go back among my old school mates a Christian preacher made me very happy. The meeting was held in the Forest Grove church house, where I had preached when a Methodist preacher. Perhaps fifty of my old school mates attended. The meeting was great. Twenty-two were baptized. A special call was made the last day to support me well. John McKinney and Ben Falkner helped in all the meetings, yet they were treated as all home preachers are when a church sends off for a big preacher — they were not counted in the support. They gave me $18.00 for that meeting, the two home preachers putting in $4.00 of that amount. At that time Forest Grove only numbered one hundred and fifty members, were not worth over $200,000.00, and not expected to pay much. It cost me $15.00 to go and come to that meeting, which left me $3.00". (Christian Leader, 1932.)

The meager support for this meeting brought discouragement and disappointment to Tant. He knew that Forest Grove was (for that day) an extremely wealthy congregation; they had held a truly fine meeting; everybody had been lavish in praise for his preaching. And they had paid him $18.00. He could see nothing left for clothes or the support of his family (father, mother, and sister) after the railroad fare was paid. He sincerely began to wonder if God had "called" him to preach or not. If so, why was he not given a living support? Maybe it was all a mistake. He knew he had found the true church. But was he ever going to be a preacher in that church? Did he not have a duty to his aged parents and to his young sister which demanded that he engage in some sort of work that would provide a decent living for them? He wanted to preach, but did God want him to? He had been trying it for five years now, and had received a total income of $119.75 for the five years' work. It certainly was not because he was not successful in his work; the big crowds, the high interest, the many baptisms all disproved that. Where lay the fault?

It was while this mood was upon him that he decided once again to go into the school-room. Perhaps this, rather than the pulpit, was his calling. He had been eminently successful in his two terms at Willis. The pay was not large ($40.00 a month in the Willis school), but it was certain and could be depended upon. It was at this juncture that the trustees of a nearby school approached him, and asked him to become the teacher of their school. The salary would be $60.00 per month — and for a ten month school! This was quite unusual in Texas at that time, but apparently the arrangement was for two school terms of five months each. Most of the children had to work on the farms, and many fathers felt they could not spare the whole family from the fields; so each child must go to school for five months and then work on the farm for the other seven months. Half the children in the community would go to one term of school, then they would go back to the fields and their brothers and sisters would come to the next term. Tant was told that if he would take the school, he could preach every Sunday he desired to, could hold as many singing schools at night as he might wish, and would have the entire months of July and August for meetings.

This was a fabulous offer. With singing schools, meetings, and other remuneration it would mean an income of not less than $1,000.00 per pear, with almost unlimited opportunity for church work. Tant had decided after Willis to leave the school-room forever, but this offer was too attractive to turn down. The fact that he had received only $18.00 for the greatest meeting of his preaching career up to this date, plus the additional fact of mortgage payments coming due on his farm, and a family looking to him for support had more than a little influence on his decision. He agreed to teach the school.

From Forest Grove, after having agreed to return to start the school in September, Tant returned to Willis in Montgomery County to attend a "co-operative meeting" of some fourteen churches, scattered over seven counties in southeast Texas. Purpose of the meeting was to discuss plans for supporting an evangelist to give full time to preaching the gospel in these seven counties. Perhaps some explanation of these "cooperative meetings" is in order:

"Before the war, it was common for brethren to meet together in what was often referred to as "Co-operation Meetings," "Consultation Meetings," and sometimes "District Meetings," or "State Meetings," depending upon their extent. These comparatively innocent meetings were nothing more than mass gatherings to discuss problems relative to the advancement of the church. Everybody was invited so there was no tendency of a segregation into "clergy" or "laity," named or unnamed. No influence toward coercion was put toward any of the churches.

"Carroll Kendrick left his home in Kentucky in 1851 to move to Texas. In the west Kendrick became a most influential preacher. It was he who introduced "State Meetings" to Texas churches. These meetings were mass gatherings of brethren at specific locations to discuss the work of the church. It was not a missionary society, although in these earlier years Kendrick was not averse to societies. Before the war, Kendrick and Tolbert Fanning discussed these societies at great length through the Gospel Advocate, Kendrick affirming their right to exist. After the war when Lipscomb came prominently to the front in the Advocate, Kendrick and Lipscomb had a great misunderstanding. When Lipscomb visited Texas in 1872, he attended the State Meeting held at Bryan, but was ignored and discourteously treated by Kendrick. Afterwards, rumors of Kendrick's disapproval of Lipscomb reached the Advocate editor, and Lipscomb blazed forth with a sizzling chastening for Carroll Kendrick. Although afterward, Lipscomb regretted what he had done, the harm was done, and the personal feelings between Carroll Kendrick and David Lipscomb were never the most fraternal.

"Although in the last fifteen years of his life, Kendrick opposed the missionary society, for several years earlier he had spoken favorably of them. At the State Meeting held in Dallas in July, 1876, Kendrick spoke, favoring adopting a plan to do missionary work in Texas. T. W. Caskey openly objected on the ground that the plan was just another Louisville plan, whitewashed over. So the suggestion was killed. (West: Search For The Ancient Order, Vol. II, p. 421.)

For two years Brother George W. Harvey had been supported by these fourteen churches in Montgomery, Walker, Harris, Grimes, San Jacinto, Waller, and Brazos counties. He was a great hulking man, who had come out of the Civil War unable to read or write. He had married a fine Christian woman who taught him his ABC's, and turned his interest toward spiritual things. Brother Ed Dabney con-

verted him to Christ, and for several years now this unlettered, but noble man had been preaching the gospel. He
was a wonderfully poor speaker, but was so completely
consecrated to the Lord that his atrocious grammar and
halting delivery were soon forgotten by those who heard
him. His work in visiting and in private conversation was
far more effective than the more eloquent pulpit efforts of
many others. But now his health was failing, and he
wanted to leave east Texas and travel farther west, hoping
the dry air and invigorating climate of the west might restore him.

IV

When Brother Harvey made known to the brethren who
were supporting him that he desired to leave that field for
work farther west, they asked him whom they might secure to follow in his work in these seven east Texas counties. Harvey reminded them of young J. D. Tant, who had
been so very successful in his two school terms at Willis,
and who showed great promise as a gospel preacher. They
asked him to get in touch with Tant, and invite him to attend the next "cooperation meeting," which was scheduled
to be held at Willis in about three or four weeks.

Harvey immediately dispatched a letter to Tant, who
was just about that time closing his fine meeting at Forest Grove, asking him to come to Willis to talk to the brethren about preaching for them in east Texas. Although
Tant had already agreed to teach school in Collin County,
he had about a month before school was to start, so thought
he might as well go down to Willis and attend the meeting.
A "committee" waited on him and told him they would like
for him to take Brother Harvey's place in that field. They
told him the support would be $600.00 a year. Tant de-
murred. He told them he had already agreed to teach
school in Collin County, and that, besides, he was unable to

come for the $600.00 they planned to pay since he had his father, mother, and sister to support, and was trying to pay off the mortgage on his small farm near San Marcos. Tant was also fearful (having lived in Willis for two school terms and knowing something of the weakness of the brethren so far as their contributions were concerned) that these fourteen churches might not be able to raise the $600.00 they were promising. However, at the insistence of the "committee", he agreed to think over their proposition for two days before giving them a definite refusal.

Within those two days great pressure was brought on Tant to persuade him to accept the work. Brother Harvey came to him and told him that all eyes were looking to him, and that it surely must be God's will that he give up all thought of teaching and set his mind once and forever to the proclamation of the gospel. Judge McCaleb and M. C. Leslie added their words to Harvey's, telling Tant that he must abandon all thought of any career except a full time proclamation of God's word. Tant told Harvey that he was fearful the fourteen churches might not be able to raise the $600.00 they were promising. Harvey responded by saying that they already had $269.00 in the treasury to start with, and that he felt confident the additional $331.00 could be raised without any trouble. It was Harvey who had rescued Tant once before from defeat and discouragement, and had persuaded the brethren at Willis to hire him for their school teacher. He was such a good man in his own life, so utterly dedicated to the Lord, that he had a wonderfully persuasive way with the twenty-four-year-old Tant.

At last Tant capitulated. The fact that Judge McCaleb's beautiful daughter, in whom Tant was more than a little interested, had added her persuasive voice to the chorus to get him to stay, may, or may not, have helped him to decide. He told the "committee" he would accept the work, that he would rather preach the gospel for $600.00 a year than to teach school for $1,000.00 a year, and that he was ready to start to work immediately. He wrote a long letter back to the Collin County people, telling them exactly why he was asking to be released from his promise to teach their school. Since most of them were members of the church, or else very religiously inclined men, they understood Tant's reasons for requesting a release, and did not feel badly toward him for it. He had feared they might.

The interesting work of preaching in southeast Texas began in August, 1885. Tant describes the following months in these words:

"There were fewer than half a dozen church houses in the seven counties. During the entire year of 1885 I preached in three houses only. I was expected to go and live among the people and preach from house to house. Brethren knew nothing of monthly appointments then. In that country most all were hunters and each community had a code of signals to talk with their hunting horns. I was welcome at any farm home.

"I would go up to any home, tell them I wanted to preach that night. The man would get out his hunting horn and blow till all his neighbors would hear and answer. Then he could tell them where to meet that night. A different signal was given to tell whether the meeting was for a party, preaching, or to go hunting. By nine o'clock at night the house would be filled with men, women, and children, and from ten to thirty dogs out in the yard frequently making things lively by pulling off a free fight. I have often preached at one of these houses with two or three to baptize the next morning. I would usually spend five nights each week preaching around in the community, each man insisting that I must preach at his home the next night. Then on Saturday night, Sunday, and Sunday night, all would go to the school-house and I would close my meeting. On Monday morning I would start out to find another place. I only had about five sermons when I started, and no book but the Bible, and no preacher in Texas who would have recommended me for anything other than an honest ignoramus.

"In after years, when I had held successful meetings in more than a dozen states, and had met most of the strong debaters among the denominations, I met old Brother Harvey at Abilene, Texas, and he thought I was a wonder! He told me there might have been bigger fools than I was, but he had never met them. He stated that many times when he and I were out preaching together, brethren would come to him and tell him that I was a disgrace to the church on account of my ignorance and poor teaching, and beg him to talk to me and get me to quit preaching and go back to the farm. But with my bull dog disposition he would tell them to 'let the boy alone; he is doing no harm, and he will come to the front some day'.

"The agreement between my brethren and me was that I must spend all my time in those seven counties, making my own appointments. I was to ride to those appointments when any one would lend me a horse, otherwise I must walk. Not only was I expected to be a good walker, but a good swimmer as well. I have had to swim as often as seven times to reach my appointment. Several times when on a borrowed horse I have ridden forty miles in the night, laid down on the saddle blanket to sleep two or three hours, and then gone on the next day.

"On one occasion I got off the train in the morning at Navasota, Texas, was to commence a protracted meeting forty-two miles east that night. It would cost me $3.00 to go round by Houston and up to Willis, within four miles of my meeting. I had the $3.00, but felt like if I could save it by walking to my appointment, I would be doing the right thing. The train ran my way twenty-eight miles to Montgomery, but as they had no connection to make, and made one trip a day on their own time, I could not wait for them. Taking my grip in my hand, I left the train and walked down the track to Montgomery, twenty-eight miles; made it by 4:00 p. m., borrowed a horse and went on twelve miles, and got there on time to fill my appointment. The train came into Montgomery at 9:00

o'clock that night, and when the editor of the local paper wrote them up for letting passengers get off and walk and beat them in by five hours the people seemed to enjoy the incident

"Next morning I borrowed another horse and rode back twelve miles to carry my first borrowed horse home. That was the last meeting Brother Harvey helped in. There were forty-five additions.

"After this big meeting near Willis, I pulled up to Grimes County to resurrect a dead church. I found this church had been composed of kinfolks, who are the meanest people on earth to settle church troubles among. The church had been meeting for worship until the past Christmas, at which time many of the members had got drunk, including one elder. I would rather try to make a whistle out of pig's tail than try to rule some churches by some so-called elders.

"I went to this community, and told a brother my mission. He informed me that some of the members were still bitter enemies. It would never in life do to bring them together, as some would be killed. But I set the next day to discuss the matter. Only two brethren met me. I argued with them that the church was bound to go to hell in their present condition. I thought the best thing to do was to bring all together and settle all trouble. If they wanted to fight, I thought the best thing was to pull it off, and let two or three members kill each other and go to the devil. Such would bring about a state of sorrow and humiliation among the rest of the members and perhaps convert them to the Lord, and they could be saved.

"This suggestion was accepted, and the next day the whole community came out, as they usually do to a church fuss. I brought the matter out from every angle. Each had to tell how good he was, and how all the meanness was in the other fellow. During the trial I had to get up three times and set one of the elders down, who got up to use the direct operation of the Devil's spirit on another member. But finally I struck the right key. They all tuned in and all confessed their wrongs to each other and came back to Christ.

"They then said we must have a meeting. But I

told them we were not ready for a meeting yet. I got five wagons to go with me the next day to the post mill, bought lumber, all went back and commenced to work. In two weeks we had completed the first church house my brethren ever owned in Grimes County. I then held the meeting in their new church house, which resulted in thirty-five additions. I heard of that church many years later, and they were still on the main track.

"Later I made a date to go there for a meeting. It was forty-five miles from where I was. I tried for two days to borrow a horse, but all were at work, so I knew I would have to walk. I bought a pair of new shoes, and started out afoot. In four miles my new shoes had skinned my feet. I pulled them off, put them over my shoulder with my old time saddle bags, and continued the other ten miles afoot and bare-footed. I put up that night with the county judge. He and his family were all members of the church. All were glad to see me, but no one knew I had come afoot. Next morning I got out of town, pulled off my shoes, and started off afoot and bare-footed again. I walked about eight miles, and stopped for dinner with one of the elders — a wealthy man who had 5,000 acres in one body, and was running thirty-seven plows. I told him my terrible condition, and begged him for a horse to ride. He said he was sorry, but none of his horses were broken to ride. I told him I could ride anything that had hair on it. He then claimed he was far behind in his plowing, was looking for rain, had negroes hired to plow, and could not possibly spare a horse.

"I then asked this brother if he had a bull he could loan me. He said he had two fine bulls, and would be glad to loan me either of them, but they were out on the range.

("But at this juncture I must stop to apologize. Years ago I was relating this incident in Kentucky and two of my preaching brethren became shocked because I said 'bull' in the presence of a man's wife and two daughters. They wrote the Gospel Advocate that I was too vulgar to have my reports in the Advocate, and for ten years I was barred from the Advocate.

But Brother J. C. McQuiddy, a godly man, saw his mis-- take, and came out in the **Advocate** with an apology before he died.

"Having been reared in Texas, I did not know it was any more vulgar to say 'bull' than to say 'man'. But N. B. Hardeman, good authority on such matters, wrote me that I should be refined east of the Missis- sippi River, and should not say 'bull' but 'Mr. Cow' or 'Mrs. Cow's husband'. So all my brethren east of the Mississippi know I mean Mrs. Cow's husband if I use the word over there.)

"But the old brother started me off afoot. His wife stopped me at the gate, sent a negro boy to the barn to get her saddle mare, and informed me before her hus- band that she was not a 'Christian' but a Baptist, and that she thought it an outrage the way my brethren treated me. She told me to take her mare, and to bring her back when the meeting was over.

"Before reaching my appointment, we had a heavy rain. I came to a swimming creek, and thought I could get in the saddle and swim across without get- ting wet, but found the mare would not swim with me on her. When she had waded until we were both four feet under water, I came to the top as I could not get my breath under the water. I swam over, pulled the mare after me, pulled off all my clothes and wrung the water out. By all work I could not get one of my new shoes on, so I rode on eight more miles. I got in late, and the house was crowded. I walked down the aisle with one shoe on and the other in my hand, set it on the pulpit, preached a fine sermon, and went home with Brother Gown.

"Brother Gown and his wife were good people, but like many others failed to do their duty. He asked me how much he and his wife should give in mission work each year, stating they had given nothing that year. I told him it did not take much to support a preacher, and I thought God would be pleased if he paid as much to missions as he and his wife paid for tobacco and snuff. He and I ran up his books and saw that he and his wife had paid $37.50 that year for tobacco. Noth-

ing for mission work.   I am sure many of my brethren
could tell the same tale.

"I continued my work all the year, and went to Willis
to make final report.   I reported one church house
built, one church house repaired, three new congregations started, one hundred and sixty-six baptized during the year in my territory.   The $269.00 that was in
the treasury when I started had dwindled down to
$235.50 before it got to me.   All the churches felt like
they had done their duty.   The new converts thought
the Lord was supporting me, and the $600.00 I was
trusting the Lord for did not come — for I was trusting five or six hundred ungodly brethren.   From that
day until now I trust the Lord and myself, knowing
that many of the brethren fall far short of duty.

"I then decided the Lord had not called me to preach;
that I would quit the whole outfit and seek some honorable vocation.   I went home (to San Marcos), paid
out all the money I had on debts, borrowed $20.00, and
went to Rockdale, Texas, to become a real book agent.

"But misfortune met me there.   Before I had sold
a single book, I met Brother John Lincoln, a great
gospel preacher.   He rebuked me for turning Jonah-
like, and assured me there was success at the front if
I would but push ahead and stick to my work.   He told
me the churches of Christ in Bell County had offered
him a thousand dollars a year to evangelize for them,
and by his influence he was sure he could get them to
put me to work for $600.00 a year.   He loaned me a
horse; wrote me a letter of recommendation, and sent
me off to Bell County to look for work."   (Firm Foundation, Feb. 23, 1909.)

CHAPTER IV

THE AUSTIN STATE MEETING

The year 1886 was a memorable one in the history of the church of Christ in Texas, as well as in the life of J. D. Tant. This year marked the beginning of the Texas Christian Missionary Society, an event which took place at Austin in the month of July, and in which event Tant was a participant — on the opposition.

For many years the brethren in Texas had been in the habit of holding their "Cooperation Meetings," "Consultation Meetings," sometimes called "District Meetings," or "State Meetings." The State Meetings had gradually become an annual affair, moving from year to year to whatever city or church might invite them. These meetings were simply mass meetings of any and all who cared to attend. They were not organized at all to begin with, no minutes were kept, no secretaries were appointed, and no official action of any kind was taken. They usually lasted from three to five days, during which time brethren visited with one another, talked about their mutual problems, listened to a number of good sermons, sang, ate, — and mostly just visited. In the sparsely settled frontier, with perhaps only about 30,000 Christians in all the state, these State Meetings provided a wonderful opportunity for visiting and social intercourse. Carroll Kendrick of Kentucky had first introduced such meetings to Texas before the Civil War.

"For all practical intents there were missionary societies on a state-wide basis, but Kendrick's had a more conservative flavoring to them. State Meetings were held annually at which every phase of the work in Texas was discussed. Whatever missionary work was

agreed upon, was then put under the eldership of a
local church, usually the church at Sherman.   The
more conservative element among the brethren eased
their consciences by imagining that since the work
was under the elders at Sherman, it was not a missionary society of the human variety.   By 1886, the
more 'progressive' element in Texas succeeded in ditch-
ing the Old State Meeting idea, and establishing the
Texas Christian Missionary Society.   For two years in
advance of this, every informed brother in Texas knew
the attempt would be made to establish the Society.
Many were certain that if the effort succeeded, it
would mean an open division in Texas.   So, during
these anxious months preceding 1886, the question of
church cooperation with particular emphasis upon the
affairs in Texas, gained wide publicity in every period-
ical in the brotherhood . . .

"David Lipscomb followed the opposite track in logic
to that once pursued by Alexander Campbell, and maintained that the church universal had no organic existence.   All thinking about the work of the church must
begin and end with the local congregation.   The local
congregation was the largest unit of God's people
known to the Bible . . . "   (West: **Life And Times of
David Lipscomb**, p. 191.)

At the State Meeting in Sherman in 1885, W. K. Homan
had put forth a resolution to form a State Missionary Society. C. M. Wilmeth, R. C. Horn, Thomas Moore, W. H.
Wright, and others had managed to defeat the move.   Another effort was made at a meeting in Thorp's Spring in
January, 1886. This too was defeated. But the "progressive" brethren were determined to get the society going,
one way or another; so they came to the Austin State
Meeting in July, 1886, with a great number of girls and
women who were pledged in advance to vote the Society into existence. They were instructed to watch Chalmers
McPherson, and on his signal, to vote in whatever way he
might indicate. McPherson, the acknowledged leader in

the move, even had the effrontery to send out word that
all who were opposed to the Society should stay away from
Austin.

II

Tant had been "shaken in" by the church in Buda, Texas, on his Methodist immersion. This was in August, 1881.
He had not given any serious thought to this matter until
Austin McGary began to emphasize the necessity of the
sinner's knowing that he was a sinner at the time of baptism, and understanding that his baptism put him into
Christ. This matter of "sect baptism" became one of the
bitterest fights within the church in the 1880's and 1890's.
Generally speaking, David Lipscomb and the brethren who
were associated with the Gospel Advocate took the position
it was not necessary that a man understand that his baptism was "for the remission of sins," but that any man who
was immersed with a sincere desire to obey God was in
truth and in reality baptized into Christ — even though he
had thought he was already in Christ and had had his sins
forgiven before the act of baptism. If such a man after
being baptized affiliated himself with some denomination,
all he had to do to become a faithful Christian was to re-
nounce his denominational affiliation and take his stand
among the people of God.

Brotherhood periodicals of these years are filled with reports of gospel meetings in which so many persons were
baptized, and so many others "came from the denominations." Tant was one who had "come from a denomination." He had given very little thought to the matter until 1885. Then he came in contact with J. F. Grubbs.
Here is what happened:

"While in Bell County in 1885 I met J. F. Grubbs,
who was attending the Wilmeth-Little debate. Grubbs
had recently taken a stand for the one baptism and

condemned sect baptism in all its forms. Just before this time, at Austin, Texas, there came upon the stage of action one of the most remarkable men who ever took a stand with the people of God. This man was A. McGary, who was the founder of the Firm Foundation, the paper for which I am writing today. McGary was unknown and unheard of until the Firm Foundation broke forth like a great meteor across the religious world, making war on all innovations and condemning the practices of many of the oldest fathers in the church.

"When the first issue of the Firm Foundation came out only 500 copies were published, and many of them were shoved under the bed, for McGary did not know whom to send them to. But in a short time men and women came to his support by the thousands, and before the first year was out, the paper was read all over the state of Texas, and in many other states.

"I met almost the first issue with hatred because it condemned me for trying to palm off on God my sectarian immersion for scriptural baptism when it taught that God would not accept the same. With bitter denunciations did I condemn it, and when it had run a year and rested a month for McGary to visit in east Texas, I truly hoped and prayed it would never start again. In the meantime, I looked the matter over, discussed baptism with McGary, Jack McCarty, Goodwin, Allen, and others, and by that time I was up on all the sophistry Campbell and others who favor sect baptism ever used. When I met Grubbs the first time I found him gone off after McGary; I waded into him with all the arguments and sophistry at hand, and felt good when I left him because the brethren told me I had downed him in the matter. When Grubbs came back to Holland, John Durst and Dr. Mahon had scattered the so-called 'McGary doctrine' in that part and I was more than anxious to turn Grubbs down the second time. But no man ever caught Grubbs twice by the same trick, and every point I made, he met on my own ground, turned each argument against me, and thoroughly proved to my satisfaction as well as to all who heard that I was wrong. And to make me feel

more humiliated than ever, he turned to me and said:
" 'Now, Brother Tant, you know that I know you know
you are wrong; but you have hugged this sophistry so
long that you are too stubborn to surrender now, but
just as soon as your better judgment gives you courage enough to lay it aside and seek scriptural baptism,
it makes no difference where I am or what I am doing, I'll quit all and come and baptize you.'

"And there I secretly resolved that I would give it up
and obey the Lord, but that Grubbs should never baptize me. After three months of seeking rest and finding none, I got on my borrowed horse and rode one
hundred and twenty-seven miles to Austin to get John
S. Durst, one of God's grandest men, to baptize me.

"As to poor Brother Grubbs, he it was who in argument led me to see the truth, and proved to be one of
my truest friends. Grubbs was one of the ablest
preachers and debaters in the church of Christ. Many
times have I sat under his preaching and wept like a
child, and if I had been worth a hundred thousand dollars, I would gladly have given it all to have been able
to preach as he did. But Grubbs, poor soul, was only
a man, short-sighted and weak in the flesh. He was
side-tracked in the great prohibition fight in Texas in
188?, espoused the anti-prohibition side, was turned
down by the church, held up by the saloon element, became discouraged, was lost to the church, lost to his
family, and I fear in eternity will be lost to God and to
heaven. He deserted home and a fine family, and the
last I heard of him he was arguing infidelity. It
makes me weep today when I think how I loved him,
how grand he was, and how low he fell. Would to
God the doctrine of once in grace, always in grace,
which was first proclaimed by the Devil, were true.
I could then think of Grubbs with the hope of meeting
him in glory where all his evil works will be burned up.
Notwithstanding his great mistakes, I believe in eternity there will be many people in heaven who would
not have been there had it not been for J. F. Grubbs.
I still love him for the good he did." (Firm foundation, March 2, 1909.)

III

It was John Lincoln of Davilla, Texas, who saved Tant
from being a "sure enough book agent." Accusing him of
being like Jonah, and running from responsibility, Lincoln
had persuaded the young preacher to try once more to
make a go of his preaching. He had pictured in glowing
terms the great opportunities in Bell County, the eagerness of the brethren there to support a man in evangelistic
work, and how much good Tant could do in turning souls
from darkness to light by the truth of the gospel.

As a final clincher to his persuasive argument he had
offered to loan a horse, and to write a letter of introduction and recommendation to the church in Holland, in Bell
County, which was taking the lead in trying to get a man
in the field. Tant continues the story:

"So he loaned me his horse, wrote the papers, and
started me to Bell County. I went in full hope, stated
my mission, and found all anxious to help in the work,
save a few. One sister, at that time worth two hundred and forty thousand dollars, was anxious to see
the work go on, but as she had just bought eleven
thousand acres of land, and needed all the money to
pay for it, she could not help. Another brother, who
had a fine home and eighty thousand dollars loaned
out on interest, promised ten dollars; but was unable
to pay that much when it came due. The church at
Holland was then worth one hundred and fifty thousand dollars, and declared the work ought to be done,
and they would gladly help if I would spend one month
at my own charges, working over the county to get
the churches all to send messengers to this town a
month later to see if all the members would help support a man; and then to see if I was the man they
wanted.

"I spent one month, for which I received not one
cent, stirring up the churches to support a preacher
in that county. At the end of said month, I found we
had twenty-two congregations in the county, six

church buildings, and a thousand members, worth at least two million dollars, but not able to support a man all his time.

"After one month's work among the churches of Bell County, we all met at Holland to see about sending out an evangelist. Only two churches outside of Holland were represented by messengers. It was agreed that I should go out as an evangelist at $50.00 a month. I was to raise whatever money I could on the field, both by preaching and by work, and the church at Holland would fill out what was lacking." (Firm Foundation, February 16, 1909.)

"I boarded with Captain A. J. Dallas, who had sixteen young horses to break to ride, and as he let me break a new one each trip I took to preach, I did not have to walk any that year. I preached under the direction of the Holland Church at $50.00 per month for four and one-half months." (Firm Foundation, March 2, 1909).

"During the spring of 1886 I held some fine meetings in Bell and Williamson counties. One was a camp-meeting at Bartlett, on the old time order. Hundreds came and camped. I sent to California and got the help of the noted Carroll Kendrick for this meeting. Kendrick had spent twenty years preaching in Texas, and had brought about twenty thousand into the church, ten thousand of that number being in Texas. He had started out fifty young men to preaching, and had a wonderful influence for good.

"Many brethren came from a distance to attend that meeting. Many had not met Kendrick for twenty years, and much rejoicing and shouting continued from day to day. From fifteen hundred to four thousand were in regular attendance. Forty-five were added. Kendrick was paid $150.00 for his work, and I received $76.00 for what I did in the meeting. Kendrick was the most incessant worker and most thorough Bible teacher I ever worked with. Seven hours a day was his limit to work in a protracted meeting, and no day fell below that. His order was to rise with the sun, walk around and ring the bell until all awoke. Those who could leave the camp went to the stand. Here we spent one hour in short talks by men and women, in prayer, and in songs. This was called our 'social' meeting, held for the purpose of edifying one another. Then all went to breakfast, and were called together again at ten o'clock. All must carry their Bibles, and we spent one hour in Bible reading. Each person was called upon to read a passage of scripture upon the subject we had. Then Brother Kendrick spent one hour commenting upon what we had read, after which all went to dinner.

"At three o'clock we came together and spent two hours as we had in the morning. After this service, I went to the water and did the baptizing, Brother Kendrick seldom going to the baptizing. We came together again at seven, and spent thirty minutes in song, thirty minutes in reading and prayer, one hour in Brother Kendrick's preaching to us. Thus ended one day's work. Would to God those spiritual feasts and days of Bible study would be renewed in the church of God. But brethren have grown so busy of late years, and have so much to care about that none have time to camp at a meeting, and at few places do they have time to have a service in the day time. So the preacher, instead of getting in seven hours a day in his meeting, is compelled to waste his time and put in only thirty minutes each night, as few can stand to hear a preacher longer than that." (Firm Foundation, March 23, 1909.)

Tant continued his preaching all through the spring and early summer. By this time he had developed considerably in his preaching ability, having put in endless hours of study and reading. He had tremendous powers of concentration, and once he became immersed in any task, whether writing, reading, or plowing, he was oblivious to all that took place around him. He would habitually take a book in his hands when he mounted his horse to ride to a preaching appointment; and as the horse paced the dusty road (or, more likely, kept a steady trot, for Tant was constitutionally in a hurry, and never wanted to go at any

gait slower than the fastest possible), his rider would likely be digesting the pages of some book on church history,
or trying to make rough pencil marks under a verse in
the Bible, or perhaps staring steadily and unseeingly into
space as he committed some passage to memory.

So the days and weeks passed swiftly in that spring of
1886.

"Then it turned dry, the brethren feared a drouth,
and that the other churches would not come to their
assistance. I made a report and showed that I had
baptized fifty-three during that time, and had received
from the field a total of $129.00 (most of it paid me
by Capt. Dallas for breaking his young horses for
him). This left the church at Holland owing me
$96.00, according to our agreement. They told me they
all liked my work, but for fear they could not pay me,
they would turn me loose to do the best I could. So
I did not hold them responsible for the $50.00 per
month. They did me like nearly all churches do nearly all preachers — turned me out owing me money
they never did pay. I guess they will pay me at the
judgment day." (Firm Foundation, March 2, 1909.)

It was June 28, 1886, Tant's twenty-fifth birthday, when
Holland let him go.

IV

The tension in Texas mounted steadily toward the "State
Meeting," scheduled to open the first session of a four day
gathering in Austin on Wednesday, July 7, 1886, at ten
o'clock in the morning. For nearly twenty years (since
1867) it had been the custom of the Texas brethren to
meet in these annual meetings for reports, discussions,
and agreement as to which church would be the host for
the next meeting, and which eldership would act as the
"receiving, managing, and disbursing evangelistic committee" for the year. Carroll Kendrick described their practice:

". . . . The churches sent messengers, pledges, etc.,
and the meetings chose evangelists and a committee
from among themselves to act for them from one meeting to the next. Each meeting determined the time
and place for the next, and each meeting chose its own
chairman, secretary, treasurer, and evangelizing committee. We have very little machinery about these
meetings. We had out some years from twelve to
eighteen evangelists, and never any trouble with them
or their salaries . . . . . .

"I think we should never have had any serious difficulty among Texas preachers or churches; but preachers came from the East, and human organizations were
urged to great disadvantage. To guard against these
evils, and seeing we had the example for it (Acts 11:
27-30), we requested first the elders of the church at
Austin to act as a receiving, managing and disbursing
evangelizing committee. Afterward and for several
years, the elders of the church at Sherman did this,
and the work went on increasingly well. It was hindered some, and finally, two years ago, greatly interrupted by a human organization, in opposition to all
our efforts . . . . ." (Christian Leader, September 25,
1888.)

Prior to the advent of the Firm Foundation the Texas
periodicals of greatest influence among the brethren were
The Christian Preacher, which had begun publication in
1875 under the name of The Texas Christian Monthly, and
The Christian Messenger, which also started about 1875,
and was edited by T. R. Burnett of Bonham. Of course,
the Gospel Advocate was well circulated also, particularly
among the families who had migrated from Tennessee.
The Christian Standard, chief journal of the "progressive"
brethren, being a northern paper, had almost no circulation among the Texas disciples.

C. M. Wilmeth was editing The Christian Preacher, and
was taking a positive stand against the innovations which
were wreaking such havoc among churches east of the

Mississippi River. The "progressive" element in Texas were chafing under this sustained attack, and there was much talk among them as to what could be done to remove Wilmeth from his job as editor. J. D. Tant writes:

"Up till this time Wilmeth still held his position as state evangelist, sent out by the church at Waco. There could be no charge against Wilmeth's preaching, nor his work, but his work was growing in favor among the people, and as he was then editor of a religious paper, published in Texas, known as The Christian Preacher, all knew that they could never build up a human society as long as said paper was circulated among the people. So there was a scheme to be put before the next state convention to not allow any man to be state evangelist who was editor of a paper. The next state meeting was called at Austin in July, 1886, and for the first and last time I attended a state meeting. I remembered that God had said, "Thou shalt not follow a multitude to do evil." (Ex. 23:2.) Knowing the restlessness of man to depart from God in all big conventions, I have kept from them ever since.

"There were many noted characters in that convention who plead hard not to depart from the old land marks, but continue to work in the old ways. Among the number I remember E. Hansborough, W. H. D. Carrington, C. Kendrick, W. E. Hawkins, R. O. Charles, Charles Carlton, J. A. Clark, T. W. Caskey, C. M. Wilmeth, and Cam Hill, who are now sleeping with the dead. While these aged soldiers earnestly pleaded for a respect for God's word, there was also a younger element of preachers who cared not for the gospel as held by their fathers, but they led a great congregation of frivolous girls and worldly-minded boys who wanted to have a human society to be like the denominations around them. Of the older brethren who were there and fought the society, Caskey, Carlton, Hawkins, and Hill finally went with them and died as rebels against God, working in the human society; but the rest died believing the church is the only society ordained of

God, through which the gospel should be preached to
all the world.

"Cross firing was done in this convention, each side
maintaining bravely its position until the third day.
Then a test vote came as to whether next year we
should send up to this convention 'messengers' or 'delegates.' Old Brother Charles Carlton, who was president of Carlton College at Bonham, got up and made
a talk showing that the word 'delegate' is a legislative
word, carrying with it authority to act for others, and
that if we sent delegates, we must delegate to them
authority to act for the churches they should respectively represent, and that such acts would be human,
without divine authority. On the other hand, if we
sent 'messengers," such could only bear messages from
the churches, and have no authority, and such would
be according to the Bible.

"But the younger element of preachers, led by Chalmers McPherson, R. D. Smith, W. K. Homan, A. J.
Bush, and Dick Kendrick, was working hard to come
out from under church rule, and organize a human
society. They came to the convention, bringing with
them many girls to vote on all subjects they wanted
voted upon; and when the test vote came, these aged
brethren were turned down by a majority vote of these
silly girls, and the convention voted to send 'delegates'
to the next state meeting.

"All then realized that the delegates must go to
some place as well as from some place; so the next
step was to vote as to whether or not we would have a
human society like the sects around us. This vote was
put before the house, and when C. McPherson held up
his finger as a signal to all the girls carried there to
vote, all voted and the society element triumphed. At
this moment I witnessed a scene almost equal to the
crucifixion of the Son of God; a scene great enough to
cause angels to weep, whereas the demons of hell would
shout for joy. As soon as the society vote carried,
one woman shouted out, 'Thank God! We have a
society at last!' Another yelled, 'All is peace on the
Potomac tonight!'

"McPherson started up the old song which was written. to honor God, but there used to please the devil, 'All Hail The Power of Jesus' Name.' Amidst the cheering, stamping of feet, and clap of hands, this song was sung — while such godly men as C. Kendrick, W. H. D. Carrington, J. A. Clark, C. M. Wilmeth, and R. M. Gano, and others sat weeping like children at the burial of their mother. I hope never to witness another such scene." (Firm Foundation, March 23, 1909.)

"I was bitterly condemned by R. D. Smith, a leader among them at that time, because I told him I would live to see the digressives practicing the mourners' bench system of getting religion, and accepting sprinkling for baptism." (Christian Leader, 1932.)

"This was the beginning of the human society in Texas. It was their general claim that if we can only get a society with business principles, we will soon take the world for Christ. The society work has been carried on in Texas for twenty-two years now, and there has never been more fraud, deception, false swearing, and robbery than has been committed by these brethren during the past twenty-two years to introduce instrumental music, to gain church houses built by society opposers, and setting traps to catch preachers and put them to work for the society." (Firm Foundation, March 23, 1909.)

When it became evident that the cheering, shouting girls who had come with the young "progressive" preachers would be able to out-vote the older brethren, and that they would vote in a body in whatever way McPherson indicated by the raising of his finger, amid a scene of general confusion and extremely high tension, the venerable W. H. D. Carrington finally got the floor for an announcement. His speech was brief but eloquent. He asked that all in this assembly who were interested in doing God's will, and wanted the churches to continue to work on a Scriptural basis, without a man-made society, should arise immediately, leave this meeting and retire to the basement for a meeting of their own. A goodly number, particularly the aged brethren, got up and left. There were some boos, hisses, and cat-calls as they marched out. They went to the basement for a brief session. Carrington was asked to serve as Chairman of the meeting, which he did. His young convert and protege, J. D. Tant, was elected as secretary. A short discussion followed, but all were so overwhelmed and wrought up emotionally over the scene that had taken place upstairs that the meeting soon adjourned. Another short session of this group was held the next morning (Saturday), at which time it was decided that the elders of the Pearl and Bryan Streets Church in Dallas would be the "receiving, managing, and disbursing" eldership for the next year, and that the next State Meeting would be held with the Pearl and Bryan Church. Meanwhile, the other group, upstairs, had decided to have their next meeting in Dallas with the church on Commerce Street.

These two separate "State Meetings" were held the next year, 1887, in Dallas at the same time. Committees from each group met trying to seek some ground of reconciliation. But all in vain. The die was now cast. Division, meaning total separation, was to be the order in Texas henceforth.

CHAPTER V

LAURA WARREN

The Austin State Meeting, sad as it was, was not a total loss for J. D. Tant. For he had come to the meeting with interests matrimonial as well as ecclesiastical. He was now twenty-five years of age, fully matured into manhood, wearing the rather over-size mustache which was the style of the day, but disdaining both sideburns and beard. The sideburns he looked upon as foppish; the beard was a nuisance and hard to keep clean. His hair was straight and of a rather light brown color; he wore it parted on the left. His clothes were cheap and plain, often unpressed, but never dirty. He had been reared in abject poverty, and in circumstances that bordered on squalor, but in his own being he had developed habits of personal cleanliness that were far removed from the slovenly character of many of his generation. He could tolerate and seem oblivious to any kind of dirt and filth, or even rancid stench, so long as his own person was clean.

Tant came to the Austin meeting with the hope of finding a suitable wife. While he had had ample opportunity to know many marriageable girls, and had had casual friendships, he had never seriously courted any of them. He was too busy trying to establish himself as a preacher of the gospel, trying to provide a home for his father, mother, and sister, and trying to meet the ever present burden of debt to give any real thought to matrimony. His books, which he bought when he could get a few cents together, and borrowed if he found himself totally without funds (which was as often the case as not) were fascinating. He spent hour after hour poring over them, reading, marking, studying, making notations on the margin. Into such utter dedication of life, the pleasure to be derived from feminine company had not yet registered. Tant was not anti-social, but rather just absorbed, pre-occupied. He simply had not yet found time for girls.

But now it was time for a change. He writes:

"At that time I was twenty-five years old, and had carefully trained myself against the love of women until I should become of marriageable age. I decided a man was too young to marry under twenty-eight years of age. I had set my time to marry at that age, and was patiently awaiting the time.

"In this connection I wish to add that many brilliant young minds are dormant today, and many young men who would have been leading preachers today have lost their influence in the Master's cause by marrying too young. Being unable to pull to the top with a wife and a continually increasing family, they soon became discouraged in the studies and efforts to preach, and drift out into some more profitable employment that they may be able to support their families.

"Early marriage is seldom, if ever best, and no young man trying to make a preacher of himself should bind himself to a woman until he is twenty-eight or thirty years of age. This will give him age and sense enough to seek out an intelligent companion who can be much help to him as a minister of the gospel. A man can hardly realize the fatal mistake hundreds of our young preachers have made in marrying, unless he could travel and be in their homes as I have been for the past twenty-five years. On an average, all women are good enough for all men, yet few women have the love of Christ at heart enough and are willing to inform themselves enough to be preachers' wives. Many times do I hear of some preacher: 'His wife is a great drawback to his usefulness and work.' Whereas, if said preacher had waited longer, and used more judgment in his selection, it would be just as easy to say: 'That preacher's wife has been the making of him.' There are a number of fine Christian women in this world who would make congenial and helpful companions to our preachers if the preachers would only take time to look around and not be in too great a hurry to marry.

"So I went to the Austin State Meeting with one leading thought, to get a wife. By the close of the first day, I had selected three girls whom I thought would be suitable for the work, and then watched them closely for two days longer to let the future determine which one I wanted. Being a stranger to all, I could give neither the preference, only hoping the Lord might direct me in this as in all other matters. But finally the test came. At the close of the last day of my observation, a vote was taken in the house as to whether to send delegates or messengers to the state convention. After some arguments by able brethren about the meaning of the two words, showing that 'delegate' is a legislative word, carrying authority, but 'messenger', a Bible word, bearing only a message, I watched the three girls vote. Two of them voted for delegates, the third for messengers. This one item, a test of loyalty to God's word, also decided me at once as to the one I preferred to stand by me and help me in the great battle of life, as I tried to fight for God and his cause.

"I had the same idea then that I have now, that when you want anything done you must do it; so I went to the girl at once, told her who I was, and sought a private conversation with her. I told her why I had come to Austin, and that I had selected her to be my future companion, provided our natures blended and we could realize the hand of God would be with us in our work after knowing each other as we were. I told her my intention was to marry in five years, and if she could see nothing across her pathway that would prevent her from being the wife of a Christian minister, we would commence a correspondence, looking forward to an engagement and marriage at the proper time.

"We commenced a correspondence at that time which continued four years, meeting only four times during those four years, and on the 26th of March, 1890, Laura Warren of Austin, Texas, a teacher, and

I were made one by the law of God and man. We were married at Georgetown, Texas, by the grand and lamented E. Hansborough. A more devoted wife and a more godly woman could not have been found. She was a preacher's wife from every standpoint, a helper in all things, and one who lived at home and helped run the farm while I was out preaching the gospel of the Son of God." (Firm Foundation, March 30, 1909.)

II

Tant went directly from the State Meeting at Austin to his gospel meeting at Georgetown, thirty miles north of Austin. He was still riding his borrowed horse, probably borrowed from Capt. Dallas, although he does not say. Following the Georgetown meeting, he went to Bee House in Coryell County for a meeting in September. Twenty-one were baptized, among the number being J. M. Tuttle, whom Tant in after years described as "a grand, godly man," and who preached the gospel in New Mexico for a number of years.

It was during the Bee House meeting that Tant worked up his first debate. Interest and excitement were high in the community, and among the number baptized were several prominent members of the Baptist Church. The Baptists challenged Tant for a debate. He replied that he would get C. M. Wilmeth to meet any man they wanted to put up. The Baptists retorted by saying that Tant was the one who had "torn up the community," and it must be Tant who would "either fight or run;" they would accept nobody else. Tant then accepted the challenge.

Once it was agreed that Tant would do the debating, the next question for settlement was the matter of propositions. Tant told them he would mail them the propositions the next week. He felt too inexperienced and uninformed to draw up sensible propositions. Debating was a matter of most serious consequence, and great care was given to the exact wording of a proposition. As quickly as he could get away from the meeting, Tant mounted his horse (borrowed) and rode to Austin to get the help of McGary and Hansborough in wording the proposition. He writes:

"Notwithstanding I had been preaching for years, I was not smart enough to get up propositions, and waited until I got to Austin to get help to formulate a sensible proposition. Since then I have held more than one hundred debates, and have long since learned a proposition stated has but little to do with the debate, for no sectarian can stick to a stated proposition.

"So now I debate issues and not propositions, and I will affirm anything the sects deny, or deny anything they will affirm, and in more than half the debates I now hold, I don't know what the propositions are until I reach the debate." (Firm Foundation April 6, 1909.)

The debate at Bee House was a great success. The Baptists had secured their greatest debater of the day, W. A. Jarrell to meet the unknown young "Campbellite," and had come in great numbers to enjoy the slaughter. The debate was set for the first week in November. At the appointed hour an audience of perhaps six hundred had gathered, and were waiting for the opening gun to be fired.

But there was no opening gun. A Baptist preacher came to the platform and read a telegram from Jarrell, saying that he was ill and could not come. He said his brethren had known for several days that Jarrell was sick, but had hoped right up to the last minute that he would recover sufficiently to go on with the discussion. No one else was willing to go into the debate on such short notice; so the Baptists asked for a delay of one month so that they could either give Jarrell time to recover, or else could get another man. This extension was agreeable to all — and nobody was happier than Tant.

Finally, the month was up, and the opposing sides were drawn up for the encounter. It was now the first week in

December, 1886. It developed that Jarrell still felt unable to undertake the job, and a Baptist preacher by the name of W. N. Leak was put forward in his place. Leak came to the discussion with great preparation. He brought a trunk filled with books, so many, in fact, that it took two of his strong brethren straining under the load to carry the trunk into the building. It was the common feeling of many of the Baptists that Leak was even better than Jarrell, although younger and lacking Jarrell's reputation, and that he would make an utter fool of the uneducated Campbellite.

Tant had as his moderator J. F. Grubbs, the man who had taught him the truth on "sect" baptism, a debater of considerable ability. In his first speech Leak mispronounced a Greek word he was trying to write on the board, and also mis-spelled it. Grubbs rose to his feet and asked Leak what he was trying to say and what word he was trying to spell. When Leak told him, Grubbs gave him the proper pronunciation, and then slowly spelled the word out for him. This so disconcerted and confused the Baptist debater that he appeared crest-fallen and uncertain for the rest of the discussion.

The final night of the discussion found the two men debating the direct operation of the Holy Spirit. Leak frankly said that this was Baptist doctrine, but that he felt it was in error and did not believe it. Tant then asked him to sign an agreement to the effect that the Holy Spirit operates through "means," and not directly on the sinner's heart. Leak said this represented his conviction, and he would gladly sign a statement to that effect. The statement was quickly put into writing, and both Tant and Leak signed it.

As a result of this debate, nine people were baptized from the Baptist church and five from the Methodists. Tant says that this first debate "really put me on the warpath." His great success here convinced him once and forever of the value of public discussions. He was having a first taste of the kind of teaching for which he was going to develop and never lose the keenest kind of appetite. He discovered he had a gift for repartee which delighted his audiences; under pressure he could turn the most serious and weighty argument of his opponent into a witticism or bit of drollery that could be devastating. Whether the argument was answered or not, Tant took the crowd. For months afterward they would be repeating and re-telling his sallies, and recounting the discomfiture and embarrassment of his opponent under the barbs. The debate at Bee House was the first of nearly 350 such discussions which Tant was destined to hold before his life should close.

III

Immediately following the Bee House debate the brethren there propositioned Tant that he should move to Coryell County and do the work of an evangelist. Enthusiasm was high following the victory over Leak and the Baptists. But Tant was hesitant. He had his small farm south of Austin, and felt heavily the responsibility of caring for his aged parents and his young sister. It was difficult to manage the farm while he was constantly away from it; and mortgage payments had to be met. But still the opportunity in Coryell County seemed to be a great and challenging one. Tant finally decided to lay the whole matter frankly before the brethren at Bee House. He says:

"I told them my trouble. I had a small farm with almost $1,000.00 against it, a father and mother and sister to support. But a negro had come to me just before I started from home and had offered me $1,-800.00 cash for my farm. I had thought it was worth more, and had refused the offer; but I was willing to return home, take the $1,800.00 for the farm, pay all my debts, if I could do no better, and return and preach for them. I told them, however, if they were willing to raise $1,000.00 and pay me out of debt, I would bind myself to go and preach for them all the time for two years. This would enable me to lift the mortgage on my farm, provide a suitable home for my father and mother and sister, and leave me free then to come and preach for them. Nothing suited them better. Ten of them quickly got up a note for the $1,000.00. One brother knew a man who had the money and wanted to loan it. They told me to go home and get all my things ready, and they would send me the check the last of December. I could pay all my debts and come back and be their evangelist for two years. I felt happy to think my debts would be paid, and I could continue preaching the word.

"I went home and assured all my creditors that I would be able to meet all obligations when due, for I thought all brethren were true to their word. Just before my debt was due, I wrote for the check — and got a letter stating that they did not go to see the man about the money until they got my letter, and the man in the meantime had let the money out; and it would be best for me to make other arrangements, as they did not know where they could get the money. Just two days before my notes were due, I sold my place for $1,200.00 and paid all debts." (Gospel X-Ray, p. 289.)

Shortly after the first of the year, 1887, Tant moved his family to Hamilton, county seat of Hamilton County, Texas. He had sold his farm south of Austin, paid all his debts, and had come out with a few household possessions and a total cash capital of $47.00. He borrowed a horse, made the 150 miles ride to Hamilton, there found a farm of 160 acres with an old two-story house on it, which he could buy for $2,000.00. He had borrowed $100.00 for a down payment, purchased the place, and had gone back to Austin to get his family and move to the new home.

Hamilton was to be the home of J. D. Tant now for nearly fifteen years, his longest residence in any one place during the eighty years of his life. More than any other place in life he referred to this as "home," and often expressed regret that he had ever moved from it. For the first three years of his residence there, 1887, 1888, 1889, he was supported by six small congregations in the section, and gave his full time to preaching in Hamilton, Coryell, and Lampassas counties. The agreement was that for eight months in the year he was to go where these little churches wanted him to, and for four months (sixteen weeks) he was to pick his own place for meetings, but each meeting was to be within one of the three counties. The church at Hamilton took the lead in commending this work to other churches, and encouraging them to participate in it.

Tant often looked back upon those three years as some of the finest work of his life. He writes:

"During these three years the little congregation (at Hamilton) paid me, first year, $504.00; second year, $454.00; third year, $602.00. Within the three years I baptized seven hundred people, set to work twenty-one congregations; and fourteen debates were held within the three counties." (Gospel X-Ray, p. 291.)

Tant made many friends in Hamilton, and on his leaving there was presented with a handsomely engraved "Letter of Recommendation," a fairly common practice in those days. It is an interesting commentary on the times to note the businesses of the men who signed the letter:

To Whom It May Concern

"We, the business men of Hamilton, Texas, who have known and dealt with J. D. Tant for the many years he has been among us, have found him an honorable gentleman, prompt in all his dealings, and one whose credit is first class: F. H. Baker; W. F. Taylor & Sons; John L. Spurlin; A. H. Watson; W. A. Martin & Brother; E. F. Catterton; A. M. Edmiston; J. Y. Durham; B. F. Scruggs (merchants); A. J. Collier (shoemaker); W. M. Sparkman (photographer); Joe T. Williams; J.

T. James & Sons (druggists); M. Cox (restaurant);
Walter Cook (jeweler); R. O. Misner (postmaster);
G. H. Boynton (editor, 'The Hamilton Herald'); E. A.
Perry (cashier, Hamilton National Bank); W. P. Fer-
guson (barber); B. West; J. T. Taylor; Hawkins &
Rogers (blacksmiths); N. M. Phelps; E. R. Williams;
L. V. Manning; B. F. Watson (saloons and restaur-
ants); Buck & Carter (editors, 'The Rustler'); J. T.
May (confectionery); T. J. Johnson (grain dealer); J.
Stass (editor, 'The Journal-News'); J. H. Taylor (har-
ness and saddlery).

Tant's only sister, Mollie, seven years younger than he,
was a fine alto singer, and often went with him to his meetings. She was the first convert Tant had ever baptized,
and he had a deep affection for her. She was an excellent
rider (side-saddle; no lady of that day could ever have
agreed to riding astride), and did not hesitate to spur her
mount to full gallop, taking ditches and fences with reckless abandon. Among the things she left with her brother
when death quenched her gay spirit at the early age of
twenty-two was this brief message, written in the first
year of the residence at Hamilton, and when she was only
nineteen.

Hamilton, Texas
November 14, 1887

Mr. Eddie Connell,
Esteemed Friend:

Your highly appreciated little missive received a few
days since. It was the first letter I have received from
L. H. in a long time. I suppose all my friends there
have forgotten me; and I think you came very near to
forgetting me. I wrote to your sister, Annie, five or
six weeks ago, and have not received an answer yet.
Also I wrote to Missouri and Madie three or four weeks
ago, and they have not answered me either. I suppose
they have also found new friends and have forsaken
me.

The debate is over. I attended all the time. Had a

real nice time. Brother Randolph Clark was in a
meeting at Hamilton last week. Only one addition.
Brother is at home now, but will leave Wednesday or
Thursday, and oh! I will be so lonesome when he
leaves.

Mr. Eddie, you said if I were there, you thought I
would liven things up a bit, as you think I am of a
"lively nature." But I have been here in this lonely
place so long that I am almost lifeless myself, I think.
I wish I could hear you play on the fiddle. I like music
so much, and play the accordion sometimes myself; but
hurt one of my fingers the other day and can't play
much now.

I notice you never sent the picture, nor even mentioned it. Have you forgotten all about it? Write
soon to your

True Friend,
Mollie Tant

Tant, meanwhile, was continuing his correspondence with
Laura Warren, the Austin school teacher, to whom he had
made such a frank proposal at the Austin State Meeting.
The course of their courtship can only be surmised, for records of it are non-existent. She was about one hundred
twenty-five miles from Hamilton, and it would seem that
the average young man in love might have been able to
visit her more than four times in four years; but Tant was
not an average young man. He had no occasion to be
traveling in the direction of Austin on any preaching mission, all his work being confined to Hamilton, Coryell, and
Lampassas counties; and a trip strictly for courting was
out of character for him.

He had a job to do for his Master first. His own love
life must be fitted, one way or another, into that. If his
sweetheart felt aggrieved or neglected that she did not
come first in his life, and should become resentful that he
placed his work above her, then obviously she would not be
a suitable wife! Tant knew that once they were married

he would be gone from home for weeks, sometimes months, at a time. It would not do then to discover that he had a wife who would feel neglected or mistreated at the absence of her lover, or who would be demanding of his time. Marriage was important; but preaching the gospel was more important. Any woman who married J. D. Tant must realize from the very first that she occupied a secondary place in his heart; his work as a gospel preacher came first. Making a woman happy by time and attention and the elaborate entertainment commonly expected and given was not a part of his courtship. One does not find it difficult to surmise that the long absences, the brief visits, and the general tenor of this four year courtship were deliberately contrived as a test.

Laura Warren met the test. If she ever complained or chided at all, there is no indication of it. She served the same Master as her lover; the work he was doing was the work that was closest to her heart too. If fidelity to that Master kept her sweetheart from her side when she longed to be near him, she was comforted by the thought that he was busily engaged in doing the greatest job on earth — preaching the gospel of salvation to lost men. Her own pleasure and her own desires could be sacrificed for the kingdom of heaven's sake.

IV

Two children were born to Laura in the four short years of her marriage to J. D. Tant. First born was a boy, Ira, who came in May, 1891. Fair of skin, and with eyes as blue as the skies of Texas on a summer day, he was a sweet and docile child, mild and gentle for all the ten years of his brief life. Two years after Ira was born came a girl, Davis, who was dark where her brother was fair; and volatile and restless where he was gentle. Davis was only one year old when her mother was taken by death.

In a later age Laura Tant's illness would have been only an inconvenience. But she lived before the advent of the wonder drugs by which pneumonia has been conquered. Tant was away from home nearly all the time now, and on Laura fell the responsibility of managing the farm. She was a city girl, knowing little of farm life. But with willingness and intelligence, she set about to inform herself and to become as proficient here as she had been in the school-room. She learned how to feed the stock, how to tend the hogs, chickens, milk the cow, and was even beginning to gain some elementary understanding of the problems of plowing, planting, and harvesting.

A cow got sick during a frigid "norther" about the middle of December. Laura went to the barn to try to determine what to do for the creature, and spent some time there trying to bed the cow down, and see that she was protected from the freezing blast of cold air. Laura herself was chilled to the bone, and was shaking with fatigue and the cold when she came back to the house. But instead of going to bed and trying to regain the circulation in her numbed hands and feet and limbs, she got to work on some household cleaning, trying to get the place in order for the return of her husband. Tant was engaged in a gospel meeting with the Little Elm congregation, a few miles from Temple, Texas, and was scheduled to return home the next week. He was staying in the home of Brother John Keeney, a friend of many years.

The next morning after her work with the sick cow, Laura awakened with a high fever, and a deep congestion in her chest. She stayed in bed most of the day, trying to overcome the cold with the usual home remedies of the time. But the cold got worse. A doctor was called. After his examination, he immediately sent a telegram to Tant, advising him to return to Hamilton at one. Tant closed his meeting without further ceremony and drove his team and buggy straight through to Hamilton without stopping. It took him a day and a night to get there. Upon his arrival he found his wife in a losing battle with pneumonia. Another doctor was called in for consultation, and finally, two more. But hour by hour Laura seemed to grow worse. No remedy could stay the agonizing congestion which kept her gasping for oxygen.

When Tant finally abandoned hope for the life of his beloved, he set about as best he could to help her prepare for the long journey. He told her in her quieter moments that the fight looked hopeless, and that she must prepare her heart and mind to meet God. Laura was shocked and terrified at first. But with the calm acceptance of the inevitable by her companion, her fright was soon allayed. "Do not be frightened, Dearest," Tant soothed her as her strength ebbed, "Our God is with us, and will see us through this hour. You will soon see Mollie. I will be lonely without you; but God has other work for me to do. I wish it were otherwise, and that we could go together. But the separation will not be for long."

"Jeff," she whispered, "will you marry again? I want you to. Wait a decent time, and then find some good Christian woman to be mother to my babies and a helper to you. God has laid his hand upon you, and he expects much from you. Do not disappoint Him; and do not disappoint me."

Tant was unable to speak, but could only try to choke back the sobs that were tearing his throat, and squeeze tightly the hand that lay still and warm between his own. There was no answering pressure. At the early age of twenty-eight, Laura Tant had tiredly resigned her spirit into the hands of God and closed her eyes in the final sleep.

Fifteen years later, Tant wrote of that sorrowful hour:

"We made our home at Hamilton, Texas, and fought life's battles together for almost four years. Then on the 4th day of January, 1894, after a hard fight, with four doctors to help me, we lost the battle to pneumonia. The messenger of death hovered around our home, exercised his authority, and called our loved one to the home of the blest, and no one had the power to say, 'No'. So the heavy cloud of sorrow and gloom hung over our home, and where once joy, sunshine, and happiness had been, mourning and sorrow came. I was left alone with a little boy and girl, and Laura was laid to rest in the old Hamilton graveyard, where she still awaits the coming forth of all the dead at the last day. Since that time, our oldest child, Ira, has been laid to rest by her side.

"While many changes and also many cares have come and gone since these great troubles crossed our home, I often find myself wondering over these sad scenes and trying to reconcile myself as to what death is anyway. I know I have tried to be faithful to God and do my duty, yet in the hardest battle of life, I have been called home five times in seven years to weep at the burial of father, mother, sister, wife, and son. All are now sleeping side by side in the old cemetery at Hamilton. I am different from some men. Brother Jack McCarty says death softens him and makes him a better man. But it produces a different effect on me. It makes me harder and more defiant all the time. If I could get the old sectarian idea into my head that God kills our kin to make us love Him, I would have neither love nor respect for such a god. But Jesus recognized the devil, and not God, as being the author of death, and claimed that he came to destroy him who had the power of death, even the devil. I look upon death as forced upon me by my enemies. Jesus comes at death, not as a death angel, but as a guide to lead me through the valley of the shadow of death that I shall fear no evil." (Firm Foundation, March 30, 1909.)

CHAPTER VI

NANNIE GREEN YATER

The year that followed the death of his wife was one of the busiest, and certainly one of the hardest, of Tant's life. He secured the services of a man named George Applewhite and his wife to move into his home, work the farm, and take care of his two motherless children. His own heart was so overwhelmed with grief that he could barely stand to come home to Hamilton from his meetings. He moved his own personal things out of the house on the hill, and got a room down in the town. When he was in Hamilton between meetings, he went out and worked all day in the fields with Applewhite, scarcely going near the house. Had it not been for his love for little Ira and Davis, he would have preferred to stay away from Hamilton all the time.

Often at night, after a hard day's work in visiting, and perhaps preaching to an audience of a thousand people, Tant would go to his room utterly exhausted, and weep out of sheer loneliness. It ate at his heart like a disease. He was naturally gregarious and loved to be among people. But he missed Laura so dreadfully much. He felt he could never marry again; and was much too busy at first to give even a passing thought to the subject.

But as spring turned into summer, and summer into fall, he began to recover from the first numbing grief of Laura's death. And he began to think more and more of his motherless children. He remembered Laura's dying request of him that he find some good Christian woman to be a mother to her babies. Maggie Applewhite was a poor substitute, he knew. No doubt she was doing her best with Ira and Davis, but she was a poor house-keeper, and Tant felt certain his children were being neglected. George Applewhite was a rather helpless, inefficient sort of worker on the farm, and the whole place was growing more forlorn and desolate looking by the week.

In the winter of 1894-95, a year after Laura's death, Tant began to give some serious thought to the question of marrying again. He went to Kentucky for some meetings, and there met Miss Lyle Booker of Eminence. She was a brilliant and talented woman, and Tant was much impressed by her intelligence — and by her obvious interest in him. But she was in delicate health, and Tant knew she could never stand the rough life of the frontier. He did not permit his genuine respect and affection for her to blind him to the more practical aspects of life and his situation.

In the autumn of 1894, back in Texas, Tant had decided he would begin seriously to look for a wife. Laura had been dead for nearly a year now, and his children ought to have a mother. He did not want to marry for at least another year, perhaps two more years, but he could at least begin to look around now. Before he married again he wanted to be certain of the one whom he chose. He felt that since he was so constantly on the road in his preaching (and would under no circumstance consider stopping) it might be well for him to pick out some girl who seemed worthy, go to her as he had to Laura Warren at Austin, and ask her to commence a correspondence with him, looking forward to marriage one year or perhaps two years hence. This had worked well with Laura; perhaps it would work again.

After carefully "analyzing" all the girls he knew, and trying to consider from every standpoint both their virtures and their faults, Tant finally made up his mind he would try to marry Earle Parker, a beautiful young widow from Wills Point, Texas, who was then a student in Carr-

Burdette College at Sherman. She was intelligent, well-bred, strong and healthy. Tant felt she would make an excellent mother for his children, and a companion for him. Abruptly, as was his nature, he sought a meeting with Earle, told her frankly what was in his mind, and asked if she would consider becoming his wife provided they found out after a suitable time and correspondence that their natures "blended."

This sort of proposal did not suit the young widow Parker. She was of a more romantic disposition, and rather wanted a man to sweep her off her feet. Tant's proposal was altogether too cold-blooded and objective. Then, too, she wanted a degree of security and wealth which she felt she could never have with a preacher — any preacher —, and especially Tant. She told him so, explaining that she was deeply touched and flattered by his request, but that she did not love him and would not marry him. W-e-l-l she did not think she would marry him!

This had an effect that might have been predicted. Tant immediately became certain that he did love Earle Parker, and that she must become his wife. That one or two year period he had contemplated for becoming "acquainted" was, after all, not necessary. He urged her to agree to an immediate wedding. But Earle was still uncertain. She wavered a bit. This ardent wooing was more to her liking, and more in the nature of what she desired from a sweetheart, but still she could not be certain. Tant had seemed so cool at first, so matter-of-fact. To him love and marriage were a sort of — well, a business agreement.

For several weeks Earle kept Tant dangling. She finally agreed to marry him; changed her mind the next day and told him she would not. Then she relented and told him maybe she would. Only to tell him bluntly the next week that she was certain he could never provide her the kind of home she wanted, and the romance was off. Permanently.

Tant was piqued and hurt. He was perhaps the most eligible "catch" in Texas for Christian girls desiring to marry a gospel preacher. He was already well established, being in great demand by congregations all over the nation for gospel meetings; his home was set up; and he was quite handsome by the standards of the day. That his marriage proposal should be turned down wounded his sense of self-respect far more deeply than anything that had ever happened to him. Or ever would.

Still smarting over his rebuff, Tant went again to Kentucky for a series of meetings that would last for some six weeks. He went again to the Booker home in Eminence. Lyle Booker was in many respects the very opposite of Earle Parker. Earle was strong, healthy, and high spirited. Lyle was serious, studious, and extremely pious. She spent her days in reading and study; was poised, highly intelligent, and profoundly interested in the work of the Lord. Her delicate health was the one big factor in causing Tant to feel that he could never marry her.

Tant stayed in the Booker home for about a month. He was putting the finishing work on his book of sermons, "The True Way," and Lyle helped him greatly. She was always sympathetic, understanding, and deeply devoted to him. Had her health been more robust, there is little doubt that Tant would have married her on his "re-bound" from his sad experience with Earle Parker. He told Lyle of his love for Earle, but could not quite bring himself to tell her of the final rejection. This was the ultimate humiliation, and even his dearest friends were not permitted to guess the depth of the wound he had suffered.

II

On his way home to Texas from Kentucky, sometime between Christmas, 1894, and the New Year, 1895, Tant stopped by the Gospel Advocate office in Nashville, Tennessee, for a long visit with David Lipscomb. This was the first time they had ever met in person, although they had naturally known of each other for a number of years. Tant had occasionally submitted an article to the Gospel Advocate, and his meetings were quite often reported. Following his visit with Lipscomb, the editor of the Gospel Advocate inserted this brief statement in his journal:

"Elsewhere in this issue will be found the salutatory of Brother J. D. Tant of Hamilton, Texas. He begins work as field editor. He will spend his time in the field preaching and representing our publications. It is not understood by his taking a position with us that he agrees with all the positions of the Advocate. Neither do we ask this. It is not to be expected that men who think for themselves will agree upon matters of opinion. But it is different as to matters of faith. In this we see eye to eye and speak the same things. We all teach faith, repentance, and baptism in order to the remission of sins. We cannot see how a man who is loyal to the truth can do otherwise . . .

"Above all things we realize our duty is to preach the gospel as it is in Christ Jesus without addition or subtraction. We want men to work with us who are determined to do this, and not to know anything save Jesus Christ and him crucified. We are anxious for those to help us in this glorious work whose speech and preaching are not with enticing words of men's wisdom 'but in demonstration of the Spirit and of power', that our faith should not stand in the wisdom of men, but in the power of God. We wish we could unite the North, East, West, and South on this broad, catholic, and scriptural basis. Who will help us?

"We believe that Brother Tant's work with us will be conducive of good, and that those who are faithful to the word of God will be brought to a better understanding of each other, and into a closer union. 'But if we walk in the light, as he is in the light, we have fellowship one with another, and the blood of Jesus Christ his Son, cleanseth us from all sin."

To this Tant responded immediately following Lipscomb's article:

"I hail with gladness the opportunity of coming before the brethren as a co-laborer on the Advocate, earnestly praying God's blessings will be upon me in trying to preach the gospel through this channel.

"It has been my desire during the past five years to become connected with some gospel paper, believing it would enable me to do more good; yet I had no idea when I went to Nashville of entering on the work so soon; but, after prayerfully considering the matter, and realizing that Brother Burnett could not reach the tenth part of the field, we all thought best I should become Field Editor of the Advocate, and travel not only in Texas, but elsewhere, as the Master's cause might demand. If this is the Lord's work, and I am doing his will, certainly it will succeed. My only desire in the whole matter is to be found faithfully preaching the word. And while Brother Lipscomb and I differ on some questions, especially the baptism question, still we do not deem the difference of such magnitude as to keep us from working together on the Advocate for the salvation of men. And while it is generally known my friendship has been with the Firm Foundation in past years, still I hope it will also be known that my connection with the Advocate will not weaken my love for the Firm Foundation, or any other paper that is earnestly contending for the faith." (Gospel Advocate, January 17, 1895.)

III

During one of his visits to Earle Parker in Carr-Burdette College, Tant had become re-acquainted with Nannie Green Yater, whom he had met first at her home in Grandview, Texas, when he had held a meeting there in July, 1894.

Nannie Green Yater was the great-great granddaughter of Henry Yater, a German subject, who had emigrated from his native land to America in 1765. On his way over, while in mid-ocean, his wife had given birth to a son, who was given the name, Henry, after the father. This birth took place on August 15, 1765. When the Revolutionary War broke out in 1776, Henry Yater, Sr. enlisted with the British army as a loyal subject of King George III. After three years of fighting with the British, Yater was captured by the Colonial Army, made to understand that the Colonials were fighting to break the very kind of tyranny he had fled Germany to escape, and promptly thereupon joined the Colonial army. He fought on the rest of the war under General George Washington.

Peter Yater, son of Henry Yater, Jr. was born June 9, 1800. He married Nancy McManus, and they became the parents of nine children, the second among them being named William Madison Yater. This boy was born on June 9, 1826, his father's twenty-sixth birthday. Peter Yater was killed by lightning on June 13, 1838, and is buried in the old family graveyard at Lancaster, Kentucky.

William Madison Yater was married on June 10, 1855, to Fannie Buckner Mills of Kentucky. The Mills family were wealthy slave-owners, (as were also the Buckners.) One of the latter, General Simon Bolivar Buckner, became a Confederate officer of considerable distinction in the Civil War. At first the Mills family had been strongly opposed to the marriage of their daughter, Fannie, to William Yater. They had even tried to break up the match by sending Fannie to Columbia, Missouri, to visit with an uncle and an aunt. It was while Fannie Mills was in Missouri that she heard the ancient gospel from the lips of John T. Johnson, who was holding a meeting in Columbia at the time. Before the meeting was over, she had abandoned her Baptist faith and had been baptized by Johnson into the body of Christ. Her family, staunch Baptists all, were horrified at Fannie's having "joined the Campbellites." But being more than a little strong-willed, Fannie had argued the question with them with considerable spirit, and had defended her views so strongly from the Scriptures that her parents floundered helplessly in their attempts to confute her. They were finally reconciled to her being a "Campbellite" however, and forgave her, but never themselves left the Baptist Church.

When Fannie Buckner Mills had married William Yater, her father had made her a wedding gift of a beautiful coach, with six perfectly matched white horses, and two slave girls as her personal servants. The Yaters had lived at Hartsville, Tennessee, for the first years of their marriage, but had moved in 1878 to Johnson County, Texas. They were a close knit family, somewhat more prosperous than most of their neighbors, and were given some local distinction because one of the Democratic powers in the United States Senate during the 1880's and 1890's was Roger Quarles Mills, senator from Texas, a brother to Mrs. William Yater.

Nannie Green Yater, daughter of William and Fannie Mills Yater, was born February 13, 1874. She was the seventh of thirteen children and even from babyhood was the "pet" of the family. She had an unusually gentle and amiable disposition, was deeply spiritual, and was baptized when thirteen years of age. Later in life, shortly before her marriage, she became fearful that she had not properly understood what she was doing when baptized at thirteen, and had asked C. R. Nichol, then but a "boy preacher" to immerse her again.

Nannie grew to young womanhood amid the usual farm surroundings of Texas in the 1880's. She learned to work in the field, particularly at cotton picking time, but spent most of her time helping in the work of the house. When the Civil War had freed the slaves, the two young negro girls given as a wedding present to Fannie Mills Yater, had insisted on staying with their mistress. She had kept them in Tennessee, taught both of them the truth of the gospel, and had seen them baptized into Christ. She had then arranged marriage for both girls with two good negro men in the community, and the girls and their husbands had continued to live and work on the Yater farm. The Yater babies had all been nursed and cared for by one or the other of these "black mammies", and had loved them, and been loved by them, in a way difficult for a later age to understand. When the Yaters moved to Texas in 1878, the two negro families wanted to go with them; but Fannie Yater thought it better to leave them in Tennessee, and not let them take the uncertain venture into what was then regarded as the "wild frontier" of Texas. So the Yaters in Texas had no servants, and the girls learned to do the house-work, as well as to help in the fields when the need was pressing.

Nannie Green Yater, graduating from high school, had taught school for two years, then had entered Carr-Burdette College, a school for girls operated by Brother and Sister A. O. Carr at Sherman, Texas. Her father had died on March 19, 1891, and she was now largely self dependent. She had borrowed money from W. P. "Uncle Billy" Richardson to pay for her schooling, and was working hard, intending to make school teaching her work in life. By the spring of 1895 she had almost completed the work for her degree, and was due to graduate within a few weeks. It was at this period that she came in contact again with J. D. Tant, whom she had first met at Grandview, her home, the previous summer when he had come there for a gospel meeting.

IV

About this time the bitter fight over "re-baptism" was being waged through the periodicals of the brotherhood. It was the teaching of the **Gospel Advocate** under David

J. D. TANT AND LAURA WARREN
(At the time of their marriage, 1890)

Lipscomb that any sincere persons who was immersed "to obey God" was scripturally baptized, whether he realized at the time that his baptism was "for remission of sins or not." He held the remission of sins to be simply a promised blessing (one among a multitude) coming from such obedience, and that it was not necessary for a sinner to understand all, or for that part, any, of the blessings that came as a result of his obedience.

In Texas, the Firm Foundation was begun in 1884 by Austin McGary for the expressed purpose of combatting Lipscomb's teaching on this subject.

"A McGary, to his enemies, became known as a 'hobbyist' on the 're-baptism' issue. McGary admittedly established his journal to preach against false baptism. He did not think of it as baptism. The issue was this: Churches over the country had been in the habit of accepting persons from the Baptist Church and other denominations into the church of Christ on their sectarian baptism. McGary believed that denominational baptism did not require the knowledge on the part of the recipient that he was being baptized 'for the remission of sins' — as the New Testament authorized. He felt that a person who had been baptized only 'to obey God' had not obeyed with proper understanding and had not in actuality been baptized in the first place. McGary also fought 'Our Plea', an idea connected to the baptism questions. Years before, Alexander Campbell had uttered 'Our Plea', a call for the union of all of those who had been immersed. In McGary's day most of the brotherhood were still following the 'Our Plea' idea of accepting all immersed persons into the church. The Firm Foundation was the only paper against this practice, the Gospel Advocate itself fighting on the other side. McGary and others, however, continued their articles against the 'shakers', the brethren who merely 'shook the hand' of the person desiring membership in the church. J. A. Harding and McGary conducted a written debate on the subject. In this debate, printed in tract form, McGary set the issue as:

'Does the Lord authorize immersion of such persons as do not know for what he commanded them to 'go down into the water'?" (Cubstead: The Firm Foundation, 1884-1957, an unpublished manuscript.)

In Grandview, Texas, Mrs. Fannie Yater had followed the controversy with keen interest. A very intelligent woman, and one of strong convictions, she had been a reader of the Gospel Advocate from its very first issue. She was a personal friend to both David Lipscomb and Tolbert Fanning, and had even named one of her sons, Tolbert Fanning Yater. (And, incidentally, in turn, the author of this book was named after this uncle of his, omitting the Tolbert, and being simply Fanning Yater Tant.)

The progress of the discussion was such as to convince Mrs. Yater that McGary and his associates had the better of the argument from a scriptural point of view. All her natural inclinations and personal preferences were on the side of Lipscomb and the Advocate. But she could not withstand the simple and obvious truth of McGary's reasoning. She became an ardent advocate of the Firm Foundation's position. It was largely through her influence that the little church at Grandview invited J. D. Tant, who was known to share McGary's convictions on baptism, to come to Grandview for a meeting. This took place in July 1894. It was at this meeting that Tant first made the acquaintance of Nannie Green Yater.

Neither of them was much interested in the other at first. While Nannie was much impressed with Tant as a preacher, she was critical of him as a man. She had been reared in a cultured home, and sharing a rather family trait of the Yaters, had never suffered unduly from any feelings of inferiority. The Yaters were intelligent, articulate, and for the Texas of that day, a family well above the average in wealth and social standing. Tant as a preacher she liked; but Tant as a man, or as a possible candidate for her

hand in marriage, was not in the Yater's social class. She
had no thoughts of him at all in that direction. As for
Tant, his grief over Laura, now in her grave only six
months, was far too poignant as yet for him to be even re-
motely interested in any woman. So the meeting at Grandview continued for two weeks, Nannie becoming more and
more impressed with Tant's intelligence and Bible knowledge; but neither of them having any thoughts at all beyond good friendship.

But six months later it was a different story. By this
time Tant had made his disastrous play for Earl Parker
and had been turned down. He had visited her at Carr-
Burdette College several times, and had become very well
acquainted with a number of the girls there, among them
being his friend of the previous summer, Nannie Yater.
He wrote some of the girls a letter:

Ladonia, Texas
Jan. 6, 1895

Dearest Nannie, Effie, Zanona, and Mattie (But not
Earle Parker):

I know you girls think I have treated you mean;
which I have; and ask forgiveness. But you know not
the work I have done since we met. I stayed at the
Booker home (in Eminence, Kentucky) and wrote continually for 12 days, Lyle also helping. But that work
is off of hand, and my book of 40 sermons and 25 diagrams is now in the hands of the printer, and will be
out in 40 days.

I am now field editor of the Gospel Advocate for
Texas. And if it is taken at the College, you can keep
up with me through it. I'll be in Sherman this week on
that business, as we have near 50 subscribers there.
Will be there next Sunday, and guess I'll preach while
there. Hope you all can go out. What has gone with
Earle Parker? I heard as I passed through Wills
Point Thursday that she was there, but I did not stop,
as I was anxious to reach Dallas.

In fact, I don't guess we (Earle and I) will ever pull in double harness, nor even in parallel lines, but crosswise. I wrote her roughly in my last letter. I thought she needed tending to, and I sure tended to her! Perhaps I shocked her modesty in my last when I said 'Perhaps one year from now your name will be Mrs. (?), and another year from that you will be rocking a cradle.' That was all I said. But, after all, I guess I loved Earle too much. Some men are fools over some women. But if I ever love again, I'll know first the girl loves me.

Lyle Booker and I parted as good friends. She is the most intelligent girl I ever met. If her health had been good, and some other things I may tell you about when we meet, no telling what might have come next.

Hope you girls are all getting along well, and are well pleased. Shall come to see you when I get to Sherman, perhaps Saturday. Give my love to Brother and Sister Carr, and that old maid Mattie Webb.

Yours in love for you all,
J. D. Tant

Just learned all are well at home. I shall go home from Sherman after I work over my buggy.

While this letter was addressed to four girls in Carr-Burdette College, it seems pretty obvious that it was intended mainly for Nannie Yater, the first named. At any rate, she was the one who finally got the letter and kept it — for more than sixty years. This apparently marked the real beginning of Tant's courtship of Nannie Yater, a courtship which was to end at the marriage altar some two years later.

The forthcoming visit to Sherman, which he mentions in the letter, was a momentous one.

V

The church at Sherman, Texas, had been divided over the introduction of instrumental music into the worship. Shortly after T. B. Larimore had held his great meeting there, the digressives had come in and captured almost the entire congregation. The controversy dragged on for many weary months, with charges and counter charges growing more bitter by the day. At last the matter came to the civil courts for settlement over property rights. While the lawsuit was still on the docket, and before it came to trial, both sides agreed, as a last desperate resort, to call in J. D. Tant to work on the problem to see if the matter could be resolved or compromised in any way to avoid the open disgrace of a court trial. Tant had held meetings in Sherman in the past, and was highly respected by both groups. There was some desire to have T. B. Larimore come back and try to work out the problem, but he made it clear that he was reluctant to have anything at all to do with these church splits, preferring to hold himself aloof from them. Tant came to Sherman and worked very hard for some two weeks, making upward of 500 calls and interviews, pleading with angry brethren to come to some agreement. He was finally successful, and wrote:

"I know all will rejoice with me to learn the noted church trouble and lawsuit over church property at Sherman, Texas, is now settled satisfactorily to all. For twelve days I have let my work on the paper go, and Brother J. P. Loving for the organ party and I for the other side have worked faithfully to restore peace and end the disgrace.

"At times we found much opposition on both sides, but finally struck a stand to which all agreed. The organ and society brethren who call themselves the First Christian Church of Sherman, and number nearly two hundred members, offered to sell their interest in the house and lot to the anti-organ and anti-society brethren, who are known as the Church of Christ worshipping on East Houston Street, and number about two hundred and seventy-five members, for the sum of $2,250.00, being about one half the value of the house and lot.

"Both parties are now going to meet, confess their wrongs and hard sayings about each other, and part in peace. The Church of Christ will continue to meet in the old house, and the organ brethren will either go to Central or build.

"All recognize the settlement as being best, and getting the matter out of court, as both sides are satisfied with this, and could not be if settled by law. I alone seem to be the loser in the settlement of this trouble, as it had been stated by myself, that if I settled the trouble, the organ would be mine; but two or three old maids, declaring that where the organ went they would be bound to go, caused me in order to avoid future trouble to let the organ go.

"In the settlement of this trouble, J. P. Loving, one of the elders of the organ party, worked with me, and manifested the spirit of a Christian gentleman from every standpoint . . . . . .

"Ever since these disturbers started in their disorganizing work at Austin, eight years ago, I feared there would be danger ahead, but never thought it would be so great. Certainly it is well to look after the instructions of Paul, who said, 'Mark them which cause divisions and offenses contrary to the doctrine which we have learned, and avoid them.'

¶'I call to mind the churches at Burnet, Wolfe City, Corsicana, Gatesville, Comanche, Manor, Hillsboro, Granbury, Weatherford, and last, but not least, Sherman — all have been disturbed, and most of them divided by those disorganizers introducing instrumental music, women societies, and other unscriptural things that divide . . ." (Gospel Advocate, February 7, 1895.)

Tant may have "let his work go" so far as promoting the interests of the Gospel Advocate was concerned, but evidence is not lacking that even in the midst of his campaign at Sherman he found time for several brief dates with Nannie Yater at Carr-Burdette College. This was not easy to arrange ordinarily, but apparently Brother and

Sister Carr were willing to relax their strict rules a bit in this particular case, and permit dates which usually would have been forbidden. Nannie was now a mature woman of twenty-two years, and a great favorite of the Carrs, holding the highest scholastic record of any girl in the school. Tant was, from their point of view, a highly eligible widower, and a man of whom both the Carrs were very fond. At any rate, the association with Nannie progressed rapidly enough that by late spring of 1895 Tant's wounded pride at Earle Parker's rejection was becoming but a dim and distant memory. Thoughts, pleasant thoughts, of Nannie Yater were increasingly filling his heart.

The next several weeks following the Sherman visit were spent in an intensive drive to get subscriptions for the Gospel Advocate. Tant was widely known throughout Texas, was in great demand as a gospel preacher, and had a ready welcome wherever he went. His record number of invitations for gospel meetings received in one year was 269, but for thirty years or more he never received less than a hundred invitations a year. In his old age the invitations declined rapidly. When it is recalled that in the entire nation there were less than three thousand churches left who were loyal to the truth when the digression had run its course (about eight thousand congregations had gone with the digression), Tant's record becomes even more impressive. To enjoy the same degree of popularity fifty years later, when the number of congregations had increased by five fold or more, an evangelist would have had to receive twelve hundred to fifteen hundred calls a year for meetings. But Tant's strong fight against the digression had endeared him to a great host of little congregations, small groups of brethren who had been put out of their church buildings, and who were struggling valiantly in the face of bitter opposition to build up a loyal church.

To these people, J. D. Tant was a fearless champion of
truth, a strong and mighty warrior who would not quail
before any opponent. When he came into their meetings
and sought subscriptions to a gospel paper, the response
was immediate and generous. The subscription list of the
Gospel Advocate began to show a great increase, particularly in Texas.

The last week in March, 1895, Tant held a meeting in
Quinlan, Texas, which he reports as follows:

"Quinlan is a railroad town fifty miles northeast of
Dallas, where I went last week to hold a mission meeting. Brother Stout secured the Methodist house for
me, and the attendance was large from the beginning.
One Methodist, one Presbyterian, and two Baptist
preachers were in attendance all the time, and many
claimed they had never heard our brethren preach before. All things went well for a few nights, but in
answering some questions propounded, I stated the
sprinkled went down to the judgment bar of God without a promise of salvation, and that most Arminians
taught infant damnation. This seemed to be too much
for the Methodist preacher's theological organs to di-
gest.

"He claimed my statement was an unmitigated falsehood and came from the spirit of the devil, and that
a man who would make such a statement would do
anything. I promised to prove my statement the next
night or take it back. Next night came. I showed
that John Wesley, in his Doctrinal Tracts, page 251,
taught infant damnation, and that Dr. Wall and Jacob
Ditzler did the same, and that even the Methodist
Discipline prayed in baptizing a child for God to wash
and sanctify him, and that the old Adam might be
buried in him, all of which showed they thought the
child a sinner. Many seemed to be surprised that the
Methodists taught such.

"A universal desire took hold of the Methodists at
once and the community for a discussion. I promised
to arrange propositions and time, but the preacher,

thinking the effects of our work must be killed then,
required a discussion of their nine articles of faith,
and that we arrange for the general discussion when
we got through with that. We selected the Presbyterian preacher as Moderator, and went to work. The
last night of the investigation the Methodists decided
to have no more debating. The preacher's wife told
me it was her first, and she prayed to God it would
be her last, debate. I am sure much good was accomplished in the investigation. F. L. Young, one of our
able gospel preachers, was with me one day." (Gospel
Advocate, April 11, 1895.)

CHAPTER VII

MARRIAGE, MEXICO, OR SUICIDE?

In May, 1895, Tant held a meeting in Georgetown, Texas. The congregation there had divided the year before over the introduction of the organ. The non-instrument brethren, numbering about eighty members, were in the majority. There was no property to fight over, since the church up to this time had never owned a building in Georgetown, but had been meeting in a lodge hall. When the split came, however, the non-instrument brethren left this place of worship, went into North Georgetown, and through the good influence of Brother House of Fort Worth, built a very neat and comfortable frame house. Whereupon the instrument brethren, not to be outdone, went into South Georgetown and built them a bigger and finer house than North Georgetown. Tant was called for a meeting with the North Georgetown congregation. He had preached quite a bit in the town and the surrounding country in other years, and it was in Georgetown that he had married Laura Warren five years previously. He writes:

"I have many friends belonging to the organ congregation at Georgetown who love to hear the story of the cross, and who attended my meeting. Seeing our large congregation of earnest listeners, they gave me an invitation to move to South Georgetown and preach the gospel to them. I then met with the elders and deacons of South Georgetown and submitted two propositions:

(1) I would preach for them a week, and they could conduct the song service, and use the organ, BUT I must preach one sermon telling why I objected to the organ.

(107)

> (2) If they preferred, they could move the organ
> out; then Brother Horton (the song leader)
> would go with me and all the North George-
> town church, and all would work together and
> sing together without those things that di-
> vide, and we would try to teach sinners the
> way of life.

"The latter proposition was readily accepted by the
elders and deacons, and all seemed to rejoice to think
we could work together as we did in bygone years
before the things were agitated that have caused so
much division in Texas.

"I announced the meeting in North Georgetown;
and the elders at South Georgetown did the same on
Sunday morning. All looked forward to Monday night
to open one of the grandest meetings we thought would
ever be held in Georgetown. But, alas! the ruling
woman power had not been consulted by the elders of
South Georgetown; and as most all organ and society
congregations of Texas have long since ceased to recognize any power save the pastor and woman power that
has brought about this evil, and has fulfilled the prophecy of Isaiah, who said, 'As for my people, children
are their oppressors, and women rule over them.'
(Isa. 3:12), so it was in Georgetown.

"Three women in the church, who seemed to think
more of the organ than the rule of the elders and
deacons, just said the meeting could not be and leave
out their idol, the organ. This caused the elders to
submit to the humiliating act of calling in the meeting
and requesting me please not to come." (Gospel Advocate, 1895, page 396.)

II

Other things were on Tant's mind at Georgetown besides the meeting and the trouble with the digressives.
He objected strenuously to women ruling over the church,
but he had no objection to women as such, and certainly
not to one woman in particular, Nannie Yater. In a letter

to this one, marked "Private, Personal, and Confidential" on the envelope, he wrote:

Georgetown, Texas
May 17, 1895

Dearest Nannie:

Thinking you have treated me somewhat shabbily since leaving Carr-Burdette College, I thought of writing you a few lines this morning.

Since Earle Parker and I made a decision to go our separate ways, I have been considering seriously, is it best for me to (1) commit suicide, (2) go to Old Mexico, (3) get married. And as it is hard for me to decide, I write you for some advice along that line.

Which would you advise me to do? And in order for you to be able to give advice, I want you to understand plainly that should marriage be my lot, you will be called upon to play a part on the other side. Perhaps, Nannie, no one knows me better than you. I am getting too old for foolishness. Neither can I love again and make the foolish mistake I did in loving Earle Parker without knowing such will be reciprocated. I have made the mathematical calculation, and think you come nearer filling the demand than any other. Having that thought in view, I now desire some time in the near future to meet you and have a private conversation on all these things. Let us thoroughly understand each other; and then if we decide we can be an advantage to each other, and that our lives will be happy together, why should we not learn to love each other better than all others, and finally marry?

Dearest One, consider this matter seriously. Much depends on it. I go to north of Dallas next month and can stop over a night. Speak out plainly, and let me hear from you. Are you willing for me to have the conversation with you? Are you willing we should court as special friends? Are you willing to look forward to a consummation of our love in marriage if all things prove favorable? If you know anything that could prevent such, we had better not start down the road to which there is no ending . . . . .

Would like to write you much this morning, but do not have time. Am in a good meeting here. Davis was down with the measles and a broken arm when I left home, but guess she is well now as they have not written.

Write me at Hamilton. Speak as you desire on the subject of which I write.

Truly your brother,
J. D. Tant

How the cultured and gentle Nannie Yater took this strange letter can be only surmised. But the surmise is not too difficult to make in view of the tone of aggrieved and injured innocence with which Tant responded to her one week later from Killeen, Texas:

Killeen, Bell County, Texas
May 23, 1895

Dearest Nannie:

Your letter to hand, and glad to hear from you. But, to some extent, like yourself, I am surprised at the letter. If it be true that (1) I sent you a proposition looking forward to courtship and marriage, and (2) claimed at the same time I had not one bit of love for you, then I was indeed crazy, as you say. (Mrs. May Powell, the first girl I ever courted, and who now lives at Georgetown, told me I had gone "crazy" about Earle Parker. Now I can see such was true.) You certainly know to the contrary, however, for you will know how I have often expressed myself to you.

In my letter to you I only expected to convey the thought I could not bear to think of loving you with all my heart, and then find out, when it was too late, that such had not been reciprocated. Sad has been my experience along that line, and before I shall ever try to give another girl all my heart, I must count the cost, and try this time not to love in vain. Am I right or wrong on this point?

In your reply you state: (1) you do not love me well enough to marry me; and (2) you said I do not love you at all! Now, why did you not qualify the second statement as you did the first?

Then you ask, Can there be happiness in a married life without love? I answer you: There can be no scriptural marriage without love. And even in this matter I shall trust that the hand of 'Him who guides me aright' in all things shall direct me here also. But can true love exist long upon an object unworthy of the name? I can never claim to be the husband of any woman until I can answer these questions with an unwavering firmness: Among them all, can I love her best? Can I love her as my own life? Can I treat her always as myself?

But before this love comes about, I had rather sit down and ask myself, Does she suit me? Is she the one I need? Will she help me in the work to which my life is given? Can I prove true to her in every way? Is it best to love at this time? And after these, and many other questions, are propounded, and answered, THEN, I think, is the time to tell her of love. Let these things be settled in my mind first, and after they are answered, I ask, why should we not learn to love each other?

If a love is based upon this kind of foundation, I see no reason for it to give way. Love is so deceptive, and so blinded to all faults, that I think it best to calmly consider all the ground before love comes — when it is possible to do so.

Having these thoughts in mind in writing you, I think your remark just a little unkind to call my love for you "platonic," and to accuse me of wanting to marry you without loving you with all my heart. There have been few times in our acquaintance that I have not known it would be but little effort on my part to love you with all my heart. But knowing myself and my circumstances, I dared not let myself entertain such thoughts lest it prevent me from proving true along other lines. There is One who has first claim on my life; I must be true to Him regardless of the cost.

Now to your second paragraph: You seem not to know what I meant by a "mathematical calculation",

and do not think you "could ever marry by the double
rule of three." Well, I thought you heard me joke
Earle Parker enough on my way to Kentucky that you
would remember how I told her I expected to compare
all her good points and all her weak points with all
Lyle Booker's good points and weak points, and then
take the one who stood highest. I only used this term
that you might understand my idea. But, to be more
serious in this matter, I do want you to understand
plainly that my thought of love to you is based on a
"mathematical calculation." And the same process
shall continue to exist I trust in all our married life
should such ever be. In this affair I have tried to do
as the wise man did (Luke 14:28-29); I tried to count
the cost. And in my examination I tried to consider
myself as I am, and you as you are. I then thought
of the position each must occupy, and what would be
counted on from both. Knowing so well I was seeking
a companion, not a boss, nor a servant, I tried to ask
myself: am I willing to add the better qualities where
I may be deficient? am I willing to subtract the things
from my life that may be wrong, etc.? But from the
tone of your letter, it looks like you don't think you
can be deficient in anything! Perhaps Sister Carr
did not miss it so far when she told me you were the
most obstinate girl she ever met!

Yes, I deliberately made a "mathematical calculation" on your case, and decided that of all the 1,000
girls who would jump at the chance to marry me, you
suit me best. And I can learn to love you for life.
Now, if you think such wrong, state your objections.

I thought McGarvey's letter grand. Yes, I'll kiss
Ira for you — and bring the same to you when I come.
Don't let me forget to deliver it in person.

So far I have been answering your letter. Now, of
myself: will say I am in a meeting here, and will continue through Sunday. Then off home for one day
and night, then to Orangeville, east of McKinney.
Looking over my work, I see I'll be at Grandview on
Wednesday night, and should the congregation there
decide a talk might benefit them any, I will be willing

to talk to them. But you can let them be the judges in this matter.

Shall I come to the old lady Yater's late Wednesday afternoon for dinner? I think it will be afternoon before I reach there. Have never travelled the country from Kimball, and don't know how far it is, nor which way I'll go. Should it be raining when I reach home, as it is now, of course I'll not go through in my buggy. If not raining, however, I'll be there if the Lord wills.

Finally, dear girl, remember this: you and I today are standing at the gateway leading down the path in which the most serious thoughts of life should engage our time. Should it be true that love and marriage should ever be considered by us, then every step should be taken with caution, and every thought considered with care. Remember that nothing but darkness lies out before you in thinking of becoming a companion of mine. Most of the time you will be by yourself; have to milk your own cow; cut your own wood; run the pigs; feed the chickens; throw things at the cats; squall at the dogs. And you will even have to direct the little wandering feet of my motherless children in the way the Master would have them go. Sometimes there will not be enough to wear; you will be deprived of the pleasures of this life, and will be considered in this world nothing but a "preacher's wife." And should it be true that our home will be blessed with other children, then your troubles and cares will increase. And in all these things I can only promise I'll love you with all my heart, and strive and pray that I will ever be true to you and never disappoint you. Such is poor recompense, indeed, for so great a sacrifice on your part. Perhaps you could find a hundred men who could promise you all that I can offer — and wealth and security in addition. Then be very sure it is the will of the Lord that you fill this position before you ever say "yes."

And should we both ever decide best to pledge our love to each other, I trust in all these things we may not act in haste, but may count the cost from every

angle, and once our decision is made, we may ever
remain true to it. I want no foolishness in this matter; no more uncertainty in love affairs. It makes me
so CONFOUNDED MAD every time I think of my
recent love affair that I can sometimes scarcely control myself. To think I would be fool enough to deeply
love one who did not appreciate nor reciprocate makes
me think I have compromised all my pride, and acted
like a fool of the first degree. I hope such may never
be repeated in this life. If it be true that our hearts
shall learn to beat as one, then may we well decide
there is an Unseen Hand ever ready to guide us, to
bear us up when we fall, controlling and over-ruling
all our affairs to his glory and to our good. May the
God of love, mercy, and peace protect you in all things.
Write me at Killeen, and write by Wednesday for me
to get it before I leave.

J. D. Tant

III

Tant closed his meeting at Killeen, went on home to
Hamilton as he had planned, went to Grandview for his
Wednesday night visit there. He ate dinner, as planned,
at "the old lady Yater's" — a most unfortunate designa-
tion, about which he was to hear much in years to come,
and which came very near to wrecking all his hopes of
marriage to the "old lady Yater's" daughter, Nannie. Then
he went on to Orangeville:

"I spent a week at Orangeville, and found about
sixty members living in that part, who, I fear, are not
(with a few exceptions) contending for the faith as
earnestly as they should. I then spent two days with
the faithful brethren at Bonham, who had been driven
out of their house by the introduction of innovations;
but they had built them a beautiful house, where they
could meet and worship God according to the New
Testament plan . . . .

"From Bonham I went to Cooper and pitched my
tent for the first tent meeting of the year. We commenced this meeting under the most unfavorable cir-

cumstances, as it was rain, mud, and water almost every day. But for seventeen days I ceased not to preach the gospel two and three times a day. The brethren all had a mind to work, and the Lord heard our prayers and gave the increase — fifty-eight confessions and six reclaimed, bringing a total of sixty-four as the final result.

To some extent this meeting came out ahead of Paul's. At Cooper the jailor, the county judge, and also the devil out of the third party printing office were among the number who went to work in the Lord's vineyard." (Gospel Advocate, July 25, 1895.)

Tant was now getting more calls for debates than he could possibly manage. In his report of the Cooper meeting he mentions five calls for debates that fall. But as he had planned to spend the months of November and December working in behalf of the Advocate, he recommended that the brethren either get Joe S. Warlick or H. F. Oliver to take over some of these discussions. Warlick was five years younger than Tant, but was already making a considerable reputation for himself as a debater. Oliver, three years Tant's senior, had not begun to preach until past thirty years of age, but was showing great ability. Tant had been his "sponsor" and backer in leaving secular work and devoting all his time to preaching.

But neither rain, mud, five debates, nor fifty-eight baptisms could take Tant's mind completely away from the one he sought. So from Cooper, right in the beginning of his three-sermons-a-day meeting, he wrote:

Cooper, Texas
June 20, 1895

Dearest Loved One:

After preaching at Bonham Monday and Tuesday nights (and met one of my old girl friends, whom I baptized some years ago. She still loves me.) I came here yesterday by driving 40 miles through the black

mud. Last night I got eleven letters, but knew none
would be from you. Today I went by the postoffice
and got twelve more. After looking over them I felt
sad to note that your letter was not there; but later,
passing by the office again, I got the letter I wanted.
It had been overlooked.

Have worked hard all day getting up my tent. All
things are now ready for my meeting to commence
tomorrow night — and I with twenty-four letters to
answer now commence the work by writing you first.
Then I'll write Lyle Booker. One of the letters I have
is from her. I'd not heard from her in a long, long
time, and wrote her last week, as I feared evil had
befallen her. But a letter today tells me the thing
I had suspected, she had over-worked herself and had
been ill. I regret I cannot send you Lyle's letter and
also the best compliment of my book yet from the
Eminence paper; but she asked that I send the clip-
ping and her letter on to a lady friend of hers in Gar-
land.

Now to the things of your letter: No, dear I did
not intend to convey the idea that I was charging you
with being unwise from a financial standpoint in your
love of me. I did not charge that you were unwise —
but I do now! What have I to offer you for the life
you would have to live? Staying by yourself, cutting
the wood, milking the cow (if any to milk), whipping
Davis for fighting Ira, bringing your own water from
the well, 150 yards away, building your own fires, and
cooking what little bread and meat you might have —
and with me at home occasionally. And for all these
things I can only promise to love you with all my
heart. Many who are able to take care of you in the
way you have been accustomed to could likewise promise to love you with all their heart. So, Nannie dear,
remember that should you ever marry me, yours will
be a hard lot. I would not deceive you in this. There
is Another who has first claim on my life, my time,
my thoughts — you must come second.

You wrote me once you did not love me enough to
think of marrying me; later, you wrote you had closed

up the channel of your affections so completely you did not know whether you could ever love me or not, and advised me to withhold my love from you till you could decide whether you loved me or not. And now, in your last letter, you seem to be confirmed in your conviction that I had only written you in a passion, and you felt sorry for me, and would do anything you could to help me — even to trying to mend the forever broken ties between Earle and myself. You even emphasized that if Earle and I got married you would NOT commit suicide. I'm sure you wouldn't!

But I am astonished at this late date by your reasoning on the matter. Take a look: (1) you ask me not to love you until you can decide whether or not you love me, then (2) you turn right around and say you cannot decide whether you love me or not until I decide whether or not I love you enough to marry. Oh, the logic of the feminine mind! But if I were called upon this very hour to make my choice among the 1,999 (or more) girls who would marry me at a moment's notice, my Nannie Yater is the one I would choose. And I wish that you had as large an acquaintance to choose from But after all, what use is there in working a year to get money to buy a horse, and then learn that the horse is not for sale. (Excuse the comparison, but it does hold in business affairs.)

❧ Now to a few things in general: At the present I see no hope of my being able to be with you much for the next few months. Perhaps the greatest necessity of life demands our being together now, but my work is such that I simply cannot abandon it. I cannot come to you, therefore I ask, can you and will you attend the Thornton meeting, commencing Monday night after the fourth Sunday in July and continuing through the second Sunday in August? If I do not get to go home before then, Ira and Davis will come to see me there if Applewhite can get off to bring them. Can you come to this meeting? You have many friends there with whom you can stay.

Just got a letter from Brother Wells stating the church at Sherman is counting on me holding them a meeting there this fall. I also have a letter from

home telling me (which I rejoice to hear) that the
infamous **Christian Courier** of Dallas has suspended
for a while. But I must close now. I am very tired,
been working hard all day. I shall hope and work and
pray for a good meeting here. Write me here, and
answer this letter as you think best.

> "Now I'll lay me down to sleep
> Thinking of one so far away;
> Committing all to Him who'll keep
> And guide us both along our way.
> And should our hearts soon beat as one
> And purest love to us be given,
> I'll recognize the will of Him,
> And pray He'll guide us both to heaven.
> And in the Paradise of God
> When all shall meet in heavenly rest,
> I'll still observe His precious word,
> And say, 'He knoweth all things best'.
>
> —J. D. Tant

IV

Not all of Tant's letters to his sweetheart were as long
as that one. But what he lacked in length, he made up
in frequency. All through that summer of 1895 he wrote
constantly, chiding Nannie for her indecision, telling her
how many hundreds of girls (sometimes it was thousands)
would have been delighted at the chance to marry him,
reminding her that her lot would be one of loneliness, hardship, and unending sacrifice if she decided to share his
life. The letters alternated passages of intense feeling and
devotion with paragraphs of joking banter and badinage.
But he did not joke about his preaching. This was a subject too sacred to permit of any kind of levity. He was
back home in Hamilton on July 10, when he wrote:

"I wish so much you were here this evening. I have
been writing all day. And everything on the place
looks quite torn up this evening. However, I think
Maggie Applewhite will get up after awhile to try to

get the place straightened out before I leave. The peach trees (about 100 of them) are loaded down. It makes me sad to realize the fruit will all be gone ere I return home again.

"I send you the questions I received at Cooper in one night. Some nights there were more, some less; but I got quite a number all the time. Are you coming to the Thornton meeting? I am so tired of dealing in uncertainties. But enough of this for this time. I've got to finish four or five letters and get them ready for the Hamilton mail hack which leaves tomorrow at 6:30 a.m. Ira and Davis both look well, but you cannot imagine how it tears my heart to leave them again in the morning."

A few weeks later a letter dated, "Bremond, Texas, Monday morning, July 22, 1895," gives an interesting sidelight on Tant's work and correspondence through the summer. He writes:

"Just got a very nice letter from a Baptist preacher in West, Texas, yesterday, charging I was afraid to meet him, and that I must take back a charge of calling him a liar; else he would do me as Sam Jones did the Tyler mayor. I wrote him at once that I looked upon him as the most consummate liar in Texas, void of truth and principle, a living demonstration of total depravity, and that I was here in Bremond and would pay half his fare if he wanted to come over here to whip me. Or, if he would come and get the Baptists to endorse him, we would have a debate. So I will be looking for him, but don't know which he is coming for, the fight or the debate. Think I'll enjoy it either way . . . .

"Am glad you got a school in West, and are going there to teach. My bitterest enemies live there. And I hope you may learn from them some of the dark as well as the bright side of my life."

V

One of the most popular features of the Gospel Advocate

in the 1890's was a column entitled "Burnett's Budget," written by Brother T. R. Burnett, at that time of Dallas, Texas. Burnett had a pen that was sometimes dripping with wormwood and gall, but he was invariably "readable," and his biting sarcasm caused many a reader to chuckle, even as he winced under the lash. Burnett once gave the description of the Advocate bill of fare as it was stated to him by a friend in Texas: "Lipscomb furnishes the bacon and greens; Sewell, the peach pie; Howard, the chicken dumpling; Srygley, the spice; Burnett, the pepper; McQuiddy, the sugar; and Tant, the gravy." (Gospel Advocate, April 11, 1895.)

A sample of Tant's "gravy" can be had from his report of the debate he had with G. A. Strain, Universalist, at Grapeland, Houston County, Texas, the last four days in August, 1895. He reported:

"The debate is now over, was largely attended, and much interest was manifested all the way through.

Dr. G. A. Strain is the noted Universalist debater of East Texas. He is above ordinary as a speaker, one among the most unscrupulous men I have ever met, and works for victory all the time instead of truth. He knows but little about the Bible, and has no idea as to a proper division of the same — still thinks we are under the law of Moses, that Christ came at the fall of Jerusalem, and that the judgment is past already. He ridicules faith in Christ, repentance, and baptism; claims that we go to heaven for doing good, and that infidels, on an average, are more benevolent than preachers. He says they will get to heaven first. He teaches that punishment is confined to this life, and that a man is punished for the sin he may commit on the day he commits it; God, he says will not run a credit system.

I was more forcibly impressed than ever that Universalism is the most deceptive form of infidelity we ave among us. Strain's main power is crying and appealing to sympathy for success. He had recently met Wilmeth and Bearden in debate, and at the close of each debate had gathered all the scattered Universalists and organized a church, claiming the congregation came as a result of the debate. I learned that Strain had fifteen or twenty believers in Universalism around Grapeland, and at the close of the discussion he planned to open the door of his church and have them all join and organize a Universalist Church. But four days of Bible teaching wrought considerable change, and he could get only two to come forward and take their stand with him on Universalism. I preached on Sunday after the debate closed, and had five additions to the church of God." (Gospel Advocate, October 3, 1895.)

The Tant-Strain debate was one of the most exciting ever held in East Texas, and attracted huge throngs. Universalism was something apart from the usual denominationalism of the day, and was predicated on the idea that God is so good, tender, merciful, and compassionate that he could never conceivably condemn any soul to eternal punishment. During the Grapeland discussion, Dr. Strain was put under considerable pressure to meet Tant in a series of debates on the subject all over East Texas. At first he readily agreed to do so, but as the debate progressed he had less and less to say about future discussions. Finally, the last day of the debate, the matter came to a show down. Strain was asked to sign an agreement to meet Tant the very next week in a second debate at any one of five or six towns where the Churches of Christ wanted it to come. He firmly refused.

Throughout the entire debate Tant had been very sick, but had made no reference to his illness, and apparently Strain had never detected it. Coming back to Hamilton for a day or two after the Grapeland affair, Tant wrote to Nannie:

J. D. TANT
(Picture made at Lexington,Oklahoma, 1895)

Hamilton Tex
Sept. 5 - 95.

Dearest Nannie. I am home
again as Strain refused to meet
me in our 2nd debate this week it
left me out so I am here and
will preach rest of this week.
I have been sick had
the hottest fever in Austin
last Monday week ago I ever had
in my life. fever did not
cool on me for 5 days.
I took 2d closses of Quinine
5 grs and closed every time
I burnt mwhich the fever at its
higher. I broke the fever but
could not bear it thunder when
I quit.
I wrote you a long letter
from Liberty Hill. stated things
plain as I could & predict you
reply there and at Grapeland
but they came to winters place.
I was surprised to get your
letter here yesterday. So I
ask you to repeat your
letter and questions again.
Yes dear I am booked for
Blooming & 4 & 5 Sunday

Hamilton, Texas
Sept. 5, 1895

Dearest Nannie:

I am home again as Strain refused to meet me in our second debate this week. It let me out, so I am home and will preach here the rest of this week.

I have been sick. Had the hottest fever in Austin last Monday a week ago I have ever had in my life. Fever did not cool down for five days. I took 20 doses of quinine, five grains each dose every two hours, with the fever at its highest. I broke the fever, but could not hear it thunder when I quit. This was during the debate with Strain.

Yes, dear, I am booked for Blooming Grove the fourth and fifth Sundays in September. And I would rather meet you there than any living person. I have to go back to Thornton soon to meet Jarrell in debate. Wrote Cannon today telling him I would stay with him. Would write you more at this time, but 24 letters is the number I have directed before me to answer. So I write this short note to let you know I have not forgotten you. If you can do so, write me this week, and I will get it by Monday night here. After this, to Cooper, Delta County, Texas.

J. D. Tant

V

It was on the last day of the Blooming Grove meeting, September 29, 1895, that Nannie Yater finally gave her promise to become Tant's wife. The decision had not been a difficult one for her, in spite of the disapproval of her family. The Yaters did not disapprove of J. D. Tant the gospel preacher; they were all greatly impressed with his ability and his knowledge of the scriptures. They had a profound respect for his willingness to stand fast for the truth as he found it set forth in the Bible. But it was their almost unanimous judgment that the life of a preacher's wife (especially if that preacher happened to be J. D. Tant) would be far, far too strenuous and difficult for one of

Nannie's gentle nature and background in life. They let their thoughts be conveyed to her in a hundred subtle ways, but were at first far too wise to be outspoken and direct in their opposition. They knew that the cultured and soft-spoken Nannie had an iron will, and once she had made up her mind it would be difficult indeed to change. So day after day they cautiously talked around the subject of her infatuation for Tant, offering mild observations and thinly veiled hints as to what the demands would be on any woman so unfortunate as to marry him.

But the favorite child of the Yaters had ideas of her own. From the very beginning she had been fascinated by this strange man. He was so different from any one she had ever known in her life. She had not lacked for suitors; indeed, had had more than her share. But none of them interested her as did Tant. His blunt, direct approach to life was a challenge that intrigued her. And beneath his brashness, his bluff outward crudity, she thought she detected a sensitiveness, a rare and intense capacity for tremendous feeling, for emotions both of joy or of pain. Others might see only the man who laughed and joked and poked fun at their most cherished idols; Nannie saw beneath that protective shell a man capable of great love, great sacrifices, and great and noble life. The warnings of her family, subtle at first and later not so subtle, fell on deaf ears.

Once she had made up her mind that Tant loved her, and that all his bluster and bragging about the "one thousand girls" who would have jumped at the chance to marry him was simply an effort to cover up his real feelings, she gave herself wholly and without reserve to planning for her future life with him. Her betrothal day was a sacred and treasured anniversary during the nearly half-century she lived with this man who had won her heart.

Coming back to Hamilton briefly after the Blooming Grove meeting, Tant wrote:

Hamilton, Texas
October 4, 1895

Dearest Loved One:

After a hard day's work, a few parting words, a night's sleep, and then off to Putnam if the Lord wills. I am staying at home one day longer than I had planned, but hope to make the railroad connection and be at Putnam on time. Am up with my writing, and have straightened out my books, which had begun to look like a pig-pen. I now have all things in order for my next trip, but am not feeling very well.

Just got a letter from Jack McCarty. He is a grand man, and I love him. Wish he could see and fall in love with you. He and I then might have a tilt for you. You could not keep from loving him. He is not rough like I am. Also had a letter from J. W. Strode apologizing for his write-up of me.

May the angel of peace guard and protect the little girl I love dearer than all others till we meet again. And may the strong arm of Him who doeth all things well be beneath us in all our earthly wanderings. Write me at Putnam.

Sacredly yours,
J. D. Tant

Nannie Yater had secured her school at West, Texas, some twenty miles from Waco. All through the fall and winter of 1895-1896 Tant made every effort possible to go by West, either going to his meetings or coming from them, to visit her. He was not very successful in this. Leaving Hamilton on October 5, he had gone to Putnam, about thirty miles east of Abilene, but had been hurriedly called from there to Ladonia, in Fannin County, where they were having trouble in the church. From Putnam he wrote:

"I know much depends on my going to Ladonia, so, by the help of God, I commence there tomorrow night.

Will run till Sunday night before my debate starts at 2:00 o'clock Monday afternoon. Such will knock me out of going home, going to West, or seeing you before the debate. But I think it best for me to go. But can almost be certain that I'll spend Monday after the debate at West."

Then for the first time in one of his letters Tant mentioned a thing that was to be a major item in Nannie's life. He wrote:

"As for you writing for me, I don't see how I can get along without it, yet I am afraid to send you my book to copy, for fear it might be lost in the mail."

Tant's penmanship was vigorous, bold, and consistently illegible. It became a standing joke with him and with others. All the years of his life he was to have letter after letter returned with the request that it be typed, or else copied by someone who could write a legible hand. After he married Nannie (and apparently for some months before) he never sent an article to the papers, or a book or pamphlet to the publishers that she did not copy. She wrote a beautifully clear and simple hand, smooth, even, and of copy-book clarity, and the years did not cause her to lose this fine art. Even now, as this book is being prepared, although she is in her mid-eighties, her handwriting is as even and smooth as it was sixty years ago. Tant was a prolific writer and gave her much practice in copying articles for him. Quite often she would make three copies of the same article, one for the Gospel Advocate, one for the Firm Foundation, and one for the Christian Leader.

His letter from Putnam continues:

"I only got to preach three nights at Cottonwood, and never started a meeting with more interest. But felt duty bound to leave.

"Am glad you are improving physically, and hope you can soon tip the scales at 130. But enough of this for now, as I have a few more things to do here before

train time. I have to come back here in one month to
moderate in a debate. Just got a letter from Joe Warlick. I'll be with him in his debate at Killeen."

VI

One of the most interesting debates of this period in
Tant's life was the one held for six nights in late October
at Thornton, Texas, with W. A. Jarrell, a Baptist. Tant
writes:

"Jarrel acted gentlemanly, and was much kinder
than I ever heard him in former debates. He also
made the ablest defense of Baptist doctrine I ever
heard him make. His greatest power is on total depravity. As for the debate, it will speak for itself. It
was taken down by a stenographer, and will be published in the Thornton Topics, and will continue for one
year, or near that time. Write John Fuller, Thornton,
Texas, if you wish to subscribe to the paper. No doubt
you will learn much about Baptist doctrine in that
time. As for myself, I am sure I made the ablest defense for the Bible and the church of Christ that I
ever made in my life. Notwithstanding all this, I only
represented one side. Dr. W. A. Jarrel, the most noted debater in the South among the Baptists, represented the other. So far as mopping up the earth with Jarrel, or crushing out the Baptist doctrine like breaking
dry eggshells with a sledge hammer, and that our side
was the only one in the fight, this I claim is not true.
I represented one side; Jarrel the other. I have held
about fifty debates during the past ten years, and
while I am sure much good has resulted from them,
yet it has never been mine to hold a one-sided debate,
nor to attend one in which our side did it all and the
other fellow did nothing. I have only read about those
debates in some of our papers!" (Gospel Advocate,
November 21, 1895.)

The debate was duly published in the Thornton Topics,
and attracted a great number of new subscribers to that
county paper.

CHAPTER VIII

PREACHING AND DEBATING

The fall of 1895 was a busy one. Now that the question of his marriage to Nannie Yater was settled, Tant plunged into one of the hardest seasons of his life — preaching, debating, traveling. He and Nannie planned a fifteen-month engagement. This was her idea, not his. Refusing to let her family put up the money for her education, Nannie had borrowed funds from a long time friend of the family, W. P. (Uncle Billy) Richardson to pay her way through Carr-Burdette College. She refused to marry Tant until her debt was paid, and refused to let him help pay it. She was determined to enter her marriage with him as a part-. ner, not as a burden. This fifteen months would give her time to teach for a full year, and half another year. It would also give Tant time to try to work through a part of the great back-log of meetings he had promised and which were pressing him for fulfilment. In December, 1895, Tant held a meeting at Sherman, Texas, with eight baptisms.

It was during this meeting that an incident occurred which was to start one of those famous "Tant stories" circulating. Staying in the home of one of the brethren who had a small farm on the outskirts of town, Tant was told to "just make yourself at home."

The good farmer and his wife went out to the barn and chicken-house late in the evening to attend to some of the chores, leaving Tant and three or four small children in the house. About fifteen minutes after leaving the house the farmer and his wife heard unearthly screams coming from the house — screams of outraged protest and childish anger. Rushing back from the barn as quickly as they could cover the distance, they found Tant firmly holding their seven-year-old son between his knees, vigorously scrubbing his neck and ears with soap and water, calmly ignoring the blood-curdling protests of his small victim.

"Why, Brother Tant," said the startled housewife, "what on earth has happened?"

"Sister," replied her guest in deadly seriousness, "you told me to make myself at home; and, before God, if I had anything in my home as filthy as this child here, I couldn't rest till I'd cleaned it up!"

From the Sherman meeting Tant went directly to his home and children at Hamilton. This was the second Christmas he had spent at home in twelve years. From there on Christmas Eve he wrote to Nannie:

> Hamilton, Texas
> December 24, 1895

Dearest Loved One:

I closed out at Sherman last Sunday night with eight additions. Came to Dallas Sunday night after the service, then on to Cleburne Monday morning. I had to wait there till noon; and hoped you might be home for the holidays; but several inquiries revealed you were still at West. So I went on to McGregor, caught a freight train out of there to Hico, which I reached at 5:45 P.M. I then hired a team and driver, and got here to Hamilton at 10:00 P.M. Rain, rain, rain, — but all things look pretty today. I have everything so torn up around here I can hardly tell what I am doing; but am trying to catch up with the absolutely necessary things so I can leave Thursday night for Cleburne. I hope to see you for a few minutes there at that time; then have to go on to Dallas Thursday night, then to Paris the next day for the Denton-Weaver debate. Immediately following that debate I go to Cooper for the Tant-Ballard debate, which starts Monday night, January 13. This means I'll be in debates for twelve straight days.

I am mailing you three copies of a sectarian paper

which I have been taking for nine years.   Don't suppose you ever saw it, but I think it good.

From Cooper, Texas, on January 9, came a letter telling of the debate with Ballard:

"Only a few moments before debating time this morning, but I must write you.   Your letter came yesterday, and I was so glad to hear, as I was beginning to feel like you were unduly prolonging your time in writing me.

The Tant-Ballard debate is now at its highest pitch; and I must say Ballard is one of the most dishonest and unscrupulous men I ever met.   DuPont and Jarrel have both so recommended him to me.   They are Baptists and so is Ballard; but the half they never told me!   The Methodists are hot.   Some have talked about stopping the debate in their house.   Ballard told Brother Grimble last night that from no standpoint would he ever again be induced to meet me in debate. He says I am too rough and ungentlemanly.   Which shows how the thing is going.   We are speaking three sessions each day.   Which means I have to speak six times a day, thirty minutes each time.   I am a little tired but think I will hold up O.K.

A letter from Sherman informs me that W. A. Jarrel will be my man there instead of Williams.   We meet Monday night.   Twelve days debating without interruption is too much for me!"

The local newspaper at Paris carried a blow-by-blow account of the Tant-Ballard discussion, along with some editorial comment as to the value of such debates.   The paper reports:

"The debate came off pursuant to announcement, and was marked with much acrimonious feeling between the two ministers, and there were some very exciting passage between them.

"Two moderators were selected at the beginning of the debate, a representative of each of the two churches, and after agreeing to use the King James version of the Bible as authority in the discussion, the forensic pugilists shook hands and proceeded. Frequently while Elder Tant had the floor, Rev. Mr. Ballard called out, interrupting him, and insisting that Tant was not using the King James Version. Finally, Ballard remarked that this was the twenty-sixth time he had had to interrupt and correct Tant on his use of some version other than the King James. Tant called Ballard a liar. Ballard replied that he was too much of a gentleman to resent the insult by having a fight right there in the pulpit. At this point the moderators took over and told the pugilists to quit their foolishness and get back to the subject. The debate proceeded without actually coming to the point of pulling wool, but a marked coolness existed between them during the balance of the controversy and scant courtesy was shown.

"After the series of debates were over, Tant was very anxious to hold another debate. He said he was willing to let two infidels act as umpires, and decide which man had the best of the argument and was telling the truth. But Mr. Ballard refused to debate with Tant any more under any kind of circumstances, saying he was no gentleman."

Immediately following the Tant-Ballard at Cooper, the Tant-Jarrel debate at Sherman took place. Tant had debated Jarrel in October at Thornton, Texas, and had been highly impressed by his opponent's fairness and courtesy. The men had a mutual respect for each other, and excellent order prevailed throughout, in sharp contrast to the encounter just closed with Ballard. The discussion was held in the old Houston Street Christian Church building, and was bitterly opposed by both the First Baptist Church in Sherman and the Central Christian Church (digressive). In spite of this opposition, however, an average attendance of 1,000 people each night gathered to listen to the two speakers. Tant reported:

"Never in life did I hold a debate in which universal good feeling seemed to pervade the entire community more than at Sherman. Elder Jarrel was kind and courteous all the way through, and I am sure lasting good was accomplished . . . . . .

"The debate was held for six days. The brethren paid me $10.00 in money, and boarded me while I was there. As I was out only $12.00 traveling expenses for the debate, I contributed $2.00 above what I was paid for the privilege of preaching the gospel to so many in Sherman.

"Had the Sherman brethren appointed two or three members at the beginning of the debate to look after the financial condition of affairs, I could have been supported, my children cared for, and the Church of Christ not brought under reproach.

"But frequently we forget the preacher has loved ones depending on him at home. In justice to the Sherman brethren, they promised to send me $40.00 later. As soon as they do, and the church at Grapeland sends me the $25.00 they promised for my debate with Strain there last August, I'll mention both in the Advocate." (Gospel Advocate, February 27, 1896).

Incidentally, the Sherman story had a rather interesting sequel. The brethren had promised Tant they would send him the additional money "when they picked the cotton in the fall." They did not send it, however, and nothing was said of it for many, many years. But in 1934, Tant, then well past seventy, and in rather difficult circumstances financially, wrote the church in Sherman, telling them he did not wish to push them or to appear impatient about the additional $40.00 they owed him, but that thirty-eight years had gone by, and he was just wondering if they had picked their cotton yet! If so, he would be deeply grateful to receive the rest of the support he had been promised.

The church secretary replied that none of the elders at Sherman had any memory of either the debate or the promise to pay for it, the record books had been searched and no mention had been found of any such debate or promise, and so far as the church at Sherman was concerned the matter was closed. The secretary made the additional statement that the elders felt they were not able to respond to his request because if they did, they might be swamped with letters from broken-down old preachers all over the nation presenting similar claims. The church sent nothing; but a few of the older members, hearing of the matter, sent a few dollars privately.

Not all of Tant's tilts, however, were with sectarian and denominational antagonists. He was as uncompromising with his own brethren when he thought them in error as with the Baptists or Methodists. In fact, because he felt some of them were deliberately betraying the cause of Christ for worldly popularity, he was, if anything, harder in his condemnation of them than of the sectarians. Perhaps the very atmosphere of the day made him more touchy and suspicious of his brethren than he would have been in calmer and more settled times. Here is a brief exchange with T. R. Burnett:

"Brother Burnett: It is reported that you attended the big convention and had a badge pinned on your lapel."

—J. D. Tant

To which Burnett responded:

"Yes, I attended the convention as a spectator to see how far the digressives had digressed from Jerusalem. But I wore no badge. One of the 'delegates' pulled off his badge and pinned it to my coat for amusement, but I removed it instantly, with the remark that 'I would not have that thing pinned to my horse's tail!' I told them I had not had the 'mark of the beast' on me in twenty years (since I left the Methodist Church) and did not propose to be marked and branded any more." (Gospel Advocate, January 9, 1896.)

On March 10, Tant wrote to Nannie from his home in
Hamilton:

"I write you a few lines tonight. I am at myself
again. Am working on the farm this week, helping
Applewhite. Planted grape-vines and potatoes yesterday. Also dug several post holes. Have been breaking land today until rained out. And when the ground
got too wet to plow, I came in and spent a couple of
hours breaking a wild pony, training him to the saddle and bit.

"I am also holding a meeting at Hamilton this week.
So far we have had a much better turn out than was
expected. I go to Cherokee next week. This has been
a lonesome week for me. For some reason I feel more
'lost' here at home without you than elsewhere."

Five days later another letter tells that Tant has now
been at home for ten days, the longest unbroken period
he has had there since the death of Laura twenty-seven
months before. He writes much of a proposed trip to
California in the spring of 1897, suggesting that they may
be gone as much as two years. He asks Nannie to think
it over, and then decide whether she would like it or not.
But apparently thoughts of California were only fleeting
ones, for in a later letter he seems to discount the trip,
and says he had rather stay at Hamilton.

II

Cherokee, San Saba County, Texas
March 22, 1896

Dearest Nannie:

Your letter to hand, and I'll take a few minutes to
answer this evening to be ready for the morning's
mail.

1st. Do you have a map of Texas? If not, I'll try
to furnish you one. Cherokee is 100 miles southwest
from Hamilton, through the country, 18 miles north
of Llano. It is not on the railroad, so I am here in

my buggy. I did not have to come by Cleburne to
reach Cherokee. Ira and Mrs. Bledsoe and her 13
year old girl from Hamilton came with me. She is a
"widder."

2nd. I think you are far off on Daniel 2:44. (a)
The image was one consisting of four parts, so it was
right to say 'these kings' in referring to the image,
or the four empires. (b) The kingdom God was to
set up was to break in pieces the iron the brass the
clay the silver and gold. (c) If the word 'these' does
not refer to the four kingdoms, why state God's kingdom would break the silver gold and brass, or the
three kingdoms that had preceded the Roman kingdom? See ch. 2:45. (d) It was in the year 483 A.D.
that the Roman Empire began to be divided into ten
toes, or kings. Then was the kingdom not set up till
that time? But if you claim it will be set up at the
second coming, all the Roman Empire went under in
1453. Was Daniel a failure as a prophet? Try again,
my girl! Your grammar won't stand the test.

3rd. I think you place too much stress on my letter
about Nona. I did not mean to say she was a heathen.
I think well enough of her, considering her faults.
But she has no use for me, nor for many of my friends.
I want you to be on your guard. Also, as I said, if
I get any time to spend from my work, I want to spend
it with you, and without too much interference from
either your friends or mine. Though I fear perhaps
I was selfish in my statement; and if you really want
her to go with us, write her, and I'll not say a word.

4th. Monday morning. As I did not get to finish
yesterday, I continue today. I preached three times
yesterday, and had the large school building packed.
Cherokee is an educational center, and they are building a college here now to cost $21,000.00. There are
not over 300 inhabitants, which should give you some
idea of their zeal and industry. I have held one nine
days' debate here, seven years ago, and have held five
protracted meetings here. I have some of my bitterest enemies in all of Texas right here. But I am growing just as fat and living just as long as if everybody

loved me. I denounced one man publicly here two years ago, naming him out. He hunted for me the next day (after I was gone), saying he was going to whip me on sight. Being told I had already left, he swore he would whip me soundly if I ever set foot in the town again. He repeated his threat a few days before I got here this time. But I've not seen him anywhere around. That reminds me, Brother Cochran, who was knocked in the head here last fall for preaching the gospel, died from the effects of the blow a short time ago.

I preach here tomorrow night, then to Star for a debate, and then home. If I could possibly get off Monday, I would come by and see you — but don't count on it."

One month later, Tant writes again from the Indian Territory of Oklahoma:

Quartz, Oklahoma
April 17, 1896

Dearest Loved One:

I am away up here in far away Oklahoma, 300 miles from you. And while all things are ordinarily well with me today, yet my heart is wandering far, far away from this place, lingering around the one I have learned to love with all my heart, often wondering will the time ever come when we shall walk life's road together.

I think I wrote you last from Haskell, Texas. I had a good meeting at Haskell. Preached in the digressive house; they have an organ there, and the church is divided. Our singing was very poor. They had a grand congregation there when I held them a meeting seven years ago. Next day I went by mail hack to Seymour, about 50 miles. Saw not more than a dozen houses in the entire distance, and not ten acres of waste land along the route. The land looks as fine as the land around Grandview, and sells from $2.00 to $5.00 per acre.

The church house at Seymour where they refused

to let me preach last year when Eddie Boyington was the preacher was opened to me this time, and the two elders who had said I could not preach there last year were on the front seat. Guess they have repented. A large crowd greeted me, and I preached a grand sermon (of course!) on "How To Study The Bible." Sold four of my sermon books, and spent the night with Senator Gass, an old friend of mine.

Next day I started for Quanah, perhaps 60 miles away. Got there at 7:00 o'clock, stopped at the hotel, and had my bill paid by a digressive elder. I preached that night in the digressive church building on "The Three Salvations," and had a very large congregation. Most of the people in this town are Methodists, or else belong to no church. Quanah is the town where I met J. F. Elder in debate last year.

Yesterday morning Dr. Smith and I started north to Mangum, some 60 miles away, in a hack. We reached that place at 6:00 o'clock in the evening, then came on four miles north of Mangum to spend the night. This morning we came on over here to Quartz, which is 15 miles east of where we spent the night. I am to preach here over two Sundays. Have four or five calls for meetings up here, and then two calls for debates. I simply can not stay for all the meetings; but will try to hold the two debates in connection with my preaching while here.

I plan to cut my stay in Indian Territory one week short and return to Seymour for a week's meeting south of here. I am staying in the home of Brother J. M. Tuttle. I baptized him in the fall of 1886 — together with his wife and daughter, who was then 12 years old. He was a Universalist at the time. Now he is the ablest preacher in this country, and his daughter is a fine teacher. But he is very poor, as most preachers are. He lives on the prairie. I can look from my window north a few hundred yards and see Headquarters Mountain, half a mile high, almost solid granite. I can look south for five or ten miles (but it doesn't appear to be over two miles) and see the noted Quartz Mountains, almost twice as high.

If I can get over to the Quartz Mountains and go up in them, I can look eastward some fifty or sixty miles and see the famous Navajo Mountains. Anywhere you look in this country you can see from five to twenty miles over beautiful rolling prairies without a single tree to obstruct your view. Wish you were with me. I am about one mile from the line of the Indian Reservation. They have one of their chief towns some ten miles from here, and Brother Tuttle and I plan to go over there one day. We will see a town full of people dressed like Adam and Eve were before God made them clothes. Some of the Indians wear blankets, hence are called 'blanket Indians,' but many of them wear not a stitch.

Quartz is the largest community in this county of Greer, which is 90 miles long and 40 miles wide. The county contains about 5,000 people at this time. A few years ago it had over 12,000, but the drouth of '93 and '94 drove many off. I am booked to preach at Quartz, Mangum (the county seat), Cottonwood, and Hess. If nothing prevents, I will debate at Mangum and Hess.

I notice that Brother Rice Daniels of Sherman is dead.

I don't know yet when I'll get to go to Lexington; it will be either the last of July or the last of August, or maybe September. Nothing would please me more than for you to go with me to Lexington, and also to Roby, Texas, the last of June; but as you seem to fear what 'they might say,' I suppose there is no point in suggesting it.

As to what I meant about preaching at Sherman on a 'stipulated salary," I meant exactly what I said. For the three years I spent half my time at West and Whiterock, I worked on a 'stipulated salary;' and I would not preach regularly for any church which would not pay it!

About your teaching all the year, if you can't make ends meet without it, go ahead and teach; but I may have to get a receipe somewhere for drying hide on the bones by the time I take you as my wife next December or January.

It is a still, clear, beautiful day. Yet I feel lonely without you. How much I would give if we could only spend one day somewhere together, aside from all the busy demands that so many people are constantly making on us. But, alas, the life we must live seems to make it impossible for us to have much time to ourselves. Write me at Mangum, Greer County, Oklahoma.

III

Nearly every report or article from Tant at this period, as well as his personal letters, reflects his sorrow and distress at the division caused in the ranks of the brethren by the introduction of the Society and instrumental music. He often preached in churches where he had held big meetings in years past, but which were now divided, torn, and discouraged by the trouble. A number of times he went to communities where the digressives had captured the whole congregation. Because of their regard for him, and no doubt remembering the great meetings of the past, many of these places invited him to preach for them. He often did so, even when they used the organ. But he always made it perfectly clear to them that he considered the organ an innovation contrary to God's will, and pleaded with them to discontinue its use, to break away from their societies, and to return to the "old paths" in which they had once worshipped God as a happy united people. Out of deference to his known convictions, a number of digressive churches would refrain from using the organ when Tant preached for them. In such cases, he usually chided the church for loving him more than they loved the Lord!

Why did the Society make such great head-way in Texas, and take over so many congregations and preachers? Probably Tant's own experience can furnish part of the answer. The churches were penurious and indifferent in their sup-

port of the preachers. Unless a man had some other
source of income than preaching, it was almost a certainty
that he would suffer untold hardships in trying to live on
the salary he got from preaching. Tant, for example, was
from 1890 to about 1910 one of the most sought after
preachers in the church. He had hundreds of calls for
meetings that he could never answer; the best churches
in Texas and many of the biggest in the nation were pleading with him to give them time for a meeting. Yet in all
his life he never got more than $1,500.00 in a single year
from preaching the gospel. And only once or twice did
he even come close to that figure. Usually he received
less than $1,000.00 a year, which would be the equivalent,
perhaps, of four or five times that amount now. But scores
of faithful preachers saw their families deprived of the
very necessities of life, their credit in the town no good,
and were constantly hounded and embarrassed by debts
they could not pay. Such men, unless fortified by powerful convictions, were highly susceptible to the attractive
prospects held out by the Society of adequate and certain
support. There can be little doubt that the "economic
argument" was in that day one of the most powerful of
all. And the churches themselves, even the loyal churches
which did not go with the digression, were shamefully
to blame for their own laxity and weakness in making
it possible for this argument to have such an appeal.

But while Tant along with most other gospel preachers
was sadly underpaid, he still had occasions when he felt
the brethren had done all they were able to do. Returning from a two-month tour of northwest Texas and Oklahoma in the early summer of 1896, he wrote:

"The brethren supported me more than they were
able, and with many sad partings and farewells, I bade
them goodbye, with a promise to return this fall or
next spring to preach the gospel again. I suppose that

there will be no debates on my return as Elder refuses to meet me again unless I will affirm the 'Campbellite' church; and as for Banks, I think he doesn't care for any more debating.

"To my brethren in Greer County I would say that our future coming and success will depend greatly upon how you live while I am gone. So don't be negligent in doing the things commanded you of God.

"After an absence of two months from home, in which I travelled about 1,200 miles and spoke 101 times, I am home again to see my dear children for two days. Then I will be off to Fort Worth for a three weeks' hard fight there. I am almost broken down, and badly in need of rest; but more than fifty calls for meetings that I could not answer the last two months tell me that the harvest is great, and the laborers are few. Only a few more years, and the fight will be over, the day's work ended; then how sweet that rest will be! I don't know what 'plan' I am working by, if reports be true. I have tried it now for twelve years, and am still living, and have not been out of meetings or debates two weeks at any one time in all those years. I know also that I am not working by the 'board' plan of sanctified common sense. The Lord says, 'Go.' I have gone, and have tried to be faithful. God has given the increase. I have been better supported, and have never seen near the hardships that the apostles saw while here. Why should I not be satisfied? To Him that doeth all things well be all the praise, not in the Society, but in the church of the living God." (Gospel Advocate, June 11, 1896.)

Nothing is more apparent in Tant's life than the awful sense of urgency under which he constantly lived. There was so much to do, so little time to do it in. He could barely take time even for courting; many of his letters to Nannie Yater urge her to come to the depot in Cleburne, or Waco, or wherever she might have been, and wave to him as the train goes through. Occasionally, as in the following instance, they could spend a few hours together.

This letter was written as he was preparing to go to Fort Worth for the three weeks' meeting there:

Hamilton, Texas
May 27, 1896

Dearest Loved One:

Your letter of yesterday came in on the same train I did from Morgan. Am glad to hear from you. I have been down town today paying off my debts, and getting things straightened out to start again. I look worse than an old mare on winter range suckling two colts, but hope I'll live over it. Hope I'll never spend two months like the past two. I will get to stay at home three days and four nights, and hope by Sunday to be O.K. again. Brother Marshall is preaching here now.

It may be possible I can stop off Saturday night, my only fear being that I'll get to talking to you and miss the train Sunday morning. But I could talk to you at your place until midnight, then come back to the depot and sleep four hours before train time. But in case there is any change of plans, and I do not get to spend the lay-over as I hope, you be sure to come down to the depot. It will not yet be dark when I get there. You can get Emma Taylor to come with you if you are afraid, and we can then go to your home and talk for a while. Perhaps you can even come to Fort Worth for the last week-end of my meeting there. When I came through there Monday night I went all through the depot looking for you. I thought you might have come down to spend a few minutes with me while the train was stopped. I saw a number of girls and boys who had come to the train, but not my Nannie.

Only a little over seven months' waiting, and then it shall be that you and I will walk the road of life together. I am constantly thinking of this, looking forward to our future. I can truly say I love you with all my heart. But I have seen so many troubles in life till I sometimes almost shudder when I think the hand of fate may yet cross our pathway before the seven months have gone . . . . .

That ominous sense of foreboding was not without some foundation, as became evident within a very few weeks.

But Tant went on to his Fort Worth meeting. The attendance was small, and nobody was baptized. But six did come from the Central Christian Church, a congregation which did not as yet have an organ, but which was definitely headed in that direction. Tant reported the meeting:

"I recognize South Fort Worth as one of the grandest fields in Texas to build up a strong, scriptural congregation. Almost ten thousand people in that part of town, and not a gospel church in all the field, save the little congregation in the central part of town, where Homer T. Wilson is preaching. They number eight hundred members, and support Brother Wilson.

"The brethren at South Fort Worth had hoped and prayed for the cooperation of this congregation during the meeting; but many of the members were so carried away over the Christian Endeavor Convention that was to meet at San Antonio that all, save half a dozen, forgot to come over to help in the meeting by their songs and prayers. Had the Central Church turned out and put in part of the money they spent in going to the Endeavor and Christian Conventions at Austin and San Antonio in supporting a gospel preacher in South Fort Worth for a year and establishing a congregation in North Fort Worth, in just a few years we could have from four to six congregations in Fort Worth. In so doing they would accord more with that life the Son of God and the apostles lived while here. Brethren, why not think seriously along this line? We still have many of the old brethren in Fort Worth who have been tried on a hundred battle-fields and have been true. They are becoming tired of the Society craze and innovations being introduced at Central Church. And if the brethren continue to be gov-

erned by the word of God in South Fort Worth, as
they have been doing, it will only be a question of
time until many others will come over from the Central Church and help them so soon as the organ and
other innovations are introduced there — which now
seems sure to come.

"Brethren, it is with sadness I have to call attention
to these things, recognizing the fact that many of
you will become my enemies by my telling you the
truth. But God commands that I reprove and rebuke
with all longsuffering and doctrine; and if my calling
attention to these things will cause a single member
to come back to the old landmarks before going too
far, I am willing to become your enemy in order to
save one soul, and, doing so, do my Master's will."
(Gospel Advocate, July 9, 1896.)

It could hardly be expected that Brother Homer T. Wil-
son could let this thrust pass without notice. He did not.
He responded one month later; in the Gospel Advocate,
August 6, 1896, he wrote:

"I very much regret that Brother J. D. Tant could
not hold a meeting for the 'South Side" church in this
city, and report the great success of that meeting,
without firing a parting salute at the Central Church.

"I dislike to engage in newspaper controversy, especially of a personal kind, and have always tried to
avoid it; but as 'Brother Tant has made some unkind
insinuations against the church of which I am pastor,
it is only just that an explanation should be made . . ."

Wilson then takes up Tant's statements, one by one,
and comments on them. He defends the Central Church
vigorously, telling how many have been baptized there the
past year, how much money they have contributed to mission work, and how little the South Side is doing by comparison. He declares:

"Well, I am free to say that if the South Side doesn't
soon get a preacher to lead them on to grander work,

their present manner of continuance will play out entirely. Our congregation with all its 'societies' and 'innovations' recently proposed raising two hundred dollars for the South Side Church. One of the elders wrote to a distinguished Tennessee preacher concerning a certain young man for the work, and the reply came back: 'He is too much tinctured with Firm Foundationism'.

"Our church, unscriptural as it is, gave over a thousand dollars for home and foreign missions last year. We have made no report of the work done, nor fired a single shot at others who differ from us as to the methods of doing the work. I held a meeting for the Central Church in May, resulting in fifty-four additions, the most of whom were by obedience. Very few of the members 'forgot to come'. If I had made a report of the meeting, it would have been a report of work done, not a fling at some imaginary monster.

"We are grateful for the information that the 'organ and a few other innovations are soon to be introduced'. This information, I am afraid, will cause those 'old veterans of a hundred battle-fields' to put on the warpaint again, and then there may be a 'waterloo' for somebody. The only people in our congregation who agitate the organ question are those who are opposed to it, and who, in their visions and dreams, like Brother Tant, see nothing but innovations accompanied by the sweet music of the organ.

"I am exceedingly tired of these unkind and unjust flings from either side of this unpleasant controversy. Let me kindly admonish Brother Tant that when he comes to South Side again to hold a meeting to 'preach the word', unmixed with bitterness and insinuations toward others, and perhaps his meeting will be more largely attended."

The organ was put into the Central Church within the year.

IV

On July 19 Tant closed a ten days' meeting at Cooper,

Texas, in which he had a bit of fun from the denominations.
He reports:

"We held a ten days' meeting at this place, with
sixteen baptisms, and there are five to take membership.   Cooper is where I held a meeting last year, and
sixty-five became obedient to the truth.   Last January
I met C. L. Ballard in debate there.   The Methodists
(Ballard is a Baptist, but the debate was held in the
Methodist building) claimed a great victory.   Ballard
stated publicly that he would never meet me again in
debate, as I did not treat him gentlemanly.   The
Methodists tried to freeze our meeting out by starting
one of their own a week before I got there.   However,
theirs went into the hands of a receiver for want of
attendance two days after ours began.   The Methodists then formed an agreement that they would not
ask any questions, would not attend the meeting, and
would not call my name any more than possible while
I was there.   Also some boys tried to help them out by
tying a sackful of tin cans to a horse's tail, and running
him through the many horses and vehicles there the
last night; but out of all these things the Lord delivered me, for almost all their young members broke
over and came.   Our meeting was largely attended all
the time and the tent would not begin to hold the
people the last night.   Some who had been Methodists
and Baptists were baptized during the meeting, which
shows that our defeat of Methodism in the debate
there with Ballard was productive of good."   (Gospel
Advocate, August 6, 1896.)

From Cooper, Tant went immediately to McGregor,
Texas, for a meeting, his third in that town.   He reports
a fine meeting with fifteen baptized.   While in this meeting he wrote Nannie Yater, expressing his regret that she
was planning to start another school term in September.
He wrote:

"While I want you to teach, yet I am planning on
stopping the same in January — or else defer our

marriage for a full year. You say something about a marriage date in June of next year. No. It doesn't suit me to marry in June for many reasons — the main one being I simply can not fit a summer wedding date into my meeting schedule. Do you think the hand of Fate may yet say 'No' to all our plans and dreams? Applewhite tells me that Sister Applewhite is practically bedfast most of the time. I do not think they will keep my children any longer than January. Davis and Ira both looked well, but Oh! how sad. I could only be with them three days, and then part again for three long months."

In late August and early September Tant held a meeting at Swan's Chapel, eight miles out from Anson, Texas; and finishing it, moved into Anson for ten days. Four were baptized at Swan's Chapel, and one at Anson. Concerning the latter meeting he wrote:

"Our meeting was not the success it should have been, on account of a Baptist meeting running at the same time with an imported preacher and an imported singer, with one piano, two organs, and a mourner's bench to draw. I think our meeting did good, as the Missionary and Primitive Baptists both seem anxious for an investigation. Propositions to that end were left, and if they don't back out, two debates at Anson in the near future will be the result of our meeting. To God be all the praise." (Gospel Advocate, October 1, 1896.)

From Anson Tant went to a school-house about ten miles west of Seymour, Texas, for his next meeting; then, closing there, moved five miles closer in toward town for another meeting. Here he ran into a bit of excitement:

"I have just closed a meeting of two weeks near Seymour under exciting circumstances all through. I held a meeting at the same point in May, and circulated many copies of my book, and baptized some members of the Baptist Church, which gave the Baptists no little trouble. The third night of the meeting Elder Jones, a Baptist preacher and former president of the Baptist College at Whitesboro, with some members, came out and claimed they had the right to the house for prayer meeting. Jones got up and for an hour and ten minutes I never had such an abuse. He claimed that I did not have enough sense to write a proposition, nor brains enough to understand Baptist doctrine; that what I was preaching would damn every soul who believed the same. Then all the Baptists got down and prayed that I might not have a single convert. But the meeting demonstrated a fulfillment of the Scripture which says, 'We know that God heareth not sinners' (Jno. 9:31); for all the prayers of the Baptist Church did no good, as we had three confessions, two of them from one of the leading Baptist families." (Gospel Advocate, October 15, 1896.)

When the Baptists had all finished praying, and Tant could get the floor, he told Jones that he was a moral coward and a slanderous liar in addition; he also added the information that Moody, his deacon, was likewise a slanderous liar, and that he would indict both of them for slander, but he knew they had no money and he could not collect from them when the court gave him the verdict, as most assuredly it would. Moody had a grown son in the house, and he and Conklin, another deacon stood up together and told Tant if they had the money to pay their fines they knew one "Campbellite" preacher that would get a thorough whipping that night. Tant then offered to pay their fines, and said he would tie one hand behind him while he whipped them both at the same time. They decided not to put him to the test.

Two of the Baptist girls who made the confession were daughters of a man named Jones (not the Baptist preacher), a leading member in the Baptist Church. He sent Tant word that if he baptized his daughters, he would do so over his dead body. Tant sent word back by the same messenger that he intended to baptize the girls, and would whip Jones too, if necessary, but would not kill him if he could keep from it, and would let him off with a good sound thrashing.   One of the girls was baptized, but the other was caught and forcibly restrained by her family. She vowed she would run away from home and be baptized just as soon as she could manage it.   Whether she ever did or not, the records do not reveal.

Meanwhile, the division within the church continued to grow more and more pronounced, and more and more bitter. Relative to his difficulty with the Baptists at Seymour, Tant wrote:

"In all these spats I learned from the Baptists that Brother T. G. Nance, the digressive preacher at Seymour (who was so busy arranging to hold a union meeting with the Methodists that he could not attend the meeting), stood in with the Baptists, telling Jones that I was not connected with the true church of Christ, only a stirrer of strife, and begging them not to pay any attention to me at all.   Brother Nance used to be a sound gospel preacher, but has departed from the ancient order of things.   May God forgive him at the last day."   (Gospel Advocate, October 15, 1896.)

The Baptists challenged Tant to defend his book, "The True Way," and the debate was scheduled for the first week in December.

While in this latter meeting near Seymour, Tant wrote to Nannie, thanking her for having copied some manuscripts for him, and saying, "you are the sweetest, cutest, and dearest thing imaginable.   I love you more and more all the time, and regret that I did not hug and kiss you the time we went to borrow the money.   We never see the things we lose till it is too late; but I hope I may never be guilty of letting such an opportunity slip again."   In the

same letter (dated Seymour, Texas, September 18, 1896)
he speaks of the work at Cleburne, Texas:

"Am glad Brother Kidwell is coming. Who is preaching for Cleburne now? If they get any encouragement
to build up a new congregation there, insist on their doing it. I'll preach for them if I can persuade Brother
———————— to help. You may have to court him to
get him interested in the work. If you have to marry
him to get him interested in the Cleburne work, do
so! Then I can marry his beautiful daughter, and you
can be my Ma, and be Ira's and Davis' grandma!"

J. D. TANT

NANNIE GREEN YATER

(At the time of their marriage, 1896)

CHAPTER IX

"THE OLD LADY YATER"

The rate of division among Texas churches was accelerating. At first there had been only a few, with confusion, uncertainty, and hesitation marking the actions of those who opposed the societies and the instruments. The society came first. This was the opening move in every church. We have not learned of any church which introduced the organ, but rejected the society. There were a great number, however, which worked through the society, but which at first rejected the organ. Some of them (Central Church in Fort Worth, for one) had worked with the society for a number of years before accepting the instrument. Tant was in the thick of this fight, and was one of the Texas preachers who tried valiantly, and so futilely, to stem the tide of digression. These faithful men saved a few scores of congregations, but approximately four times as many went with the digressives as remained loyal to the truth. When the final division came, and all had accepted the society and instruments who were going to do so, the battle-scarred veterans who had opposed the digression could survey the scene and estimate that only about one church in five had been saved. Eighty to ninety percent of Texas congregations had gone with the new movement.

Tant wrote in the fall of 1896:

"All brethren of Texas remember that at the last State meeting Brother W. H. Wright made a speech, urging those who are not satisfied with the Bible order of things (i.e. the digressives) to 'invade the churches', and introduce the organ and the society in all the congregations where such are not to be found, and to crush out, if possible, ignorant preachers who oppose the same. Also, you may remember my reply to him through the Advocate.

"Many young preachers took his advice, Brothers J. W. Marshall and Eddie Boyington among the number. These brethren came to Hamilton without an invitation from the church, and worked up an element to bring the society into the church there. This they did, and divided the church of God, and did more harm than both could do good there in five years.

"I now think the time has come for the 'invasion' to start from the other side. For ten years my brethren who have opposed these innovations have only stood on the defensive side, pleading with those brethren to respect the law of God, and not sow the seed of discord among brethren; but all our prayers and pleadings have been in vain. We have stood still. They have invaded, and the work of division has gone on till more than a hundred otherwise peaceful congregations are divided over untaught and unscriptural innovations. But of late I note encouraging surroundings, which demand that we rise in the power of Israel's God and carry the war into the midst of the troublers. The recent decision of the Supreme Court, which has been commented on in the **Firm Foundation, Christian Leader,** and other papers, shows that we are entitled to half of the property, at least, where this trouble comes. As many loyal brethren of Texas have been beaten out of their houses of worship, besides many thousands of dollars they have put into those church houses, without any love or respect shown them when they oppose those innovations, I now call through the **Advocate,** the **Firm Foundation,** the **Word of Truth,** and the **Christian Reporter** to see how many gospel preachers are willing to hold a three weeks' meeting in some town next year, and try to re-establish the ancient order of things in those places where the loyal brethren have been driven from their houses of worship." (**Gospel Advocate,** October 20, 1896.)

Tant then gives his plan as to how this ought to be done:

1. We write to some brother at each of these places and get the names of all who oppose these innovations.

2. The preacher with all who oppose the innovations, then send a request to the elders of the congregation, asking for the house to hold a meeting in, to preach the gospel independently of these outside 'helps'.

3. If the house be granted, use it; if not granted, get some other place.

4. Preach the gospel in kindness and love, without any rough language. Set forth the plain gospel facts, and show how all got along and worked together in peace before these innovations were introduced.

5. Show how we have been divided by them, and plead for a return to the ancient order of things.

6. Then all who oppose these innovations state plainly and in a kind petition to the other side that they cannot work with them; and plead with them to give up those things, and come back where we all can work as we did before they were introduced.

7. If they refuse, then ask them kindly for a half interest in the house. Let one side set a value on the property, and the other side have the say as to whether they will buy or sell.

8. If they refuse to do such, they then cut off all Bible right to be regarded as brethren. Then, as American citizens, demand our part of the property by law."
(Ibid, October 20, 1896.)

This was a new and drastic proposal generally for the brethren in Texas, but it met with a hearty response. Brother W. W. Sewell wrote in full support:

"I am pleased to see an article from Brother J. D. Tant on the subject, 'Invading the Churches'. I am glad to see Brother Tant coming to the front on this."
(Gospel Advocate, November 26, 1896.)

Sewell then relates that he has begun to urge this course on others, and has been following it himself for some time. He mentions several places in which this has been done, with varying results. He warns that the course will require great courage: "You have never met opposition until you undertake this work; at least that has been my experience."

II

Tant's courtship, meanwhile, was making progress. He and Nannie had agreed on the time for the wedding, either late December or January. He kept writing her teasing letters, telling her she had better be sure of herself, and that if she did not want him, there were five others who had told him they would be ready for him on the wedding date, just in case she backed out at the last moment. She wrote him late in August:

Grandview, Texas
August 27, 1896

My dear Brother Tant:

Yours of 24th received today, and I must say after one has been ironing all morning it is quite restful to read a nice long letter from one's best friend.

I would have been glad had you come by Tuesday. I spent the day at Sister Sowell's, sewing, but am sure I would have been much happier had you been there. Am glad, however, you spent the day so pleasantly.

If you think you can get Maggie, it might be the best thing for you to take her, as I come nearer looking like a "sack of bones" now than ever before in life. Am much thinner in flesh than when I got up from the fever last summer; but, notwithstanding this, I feel better and do more work than for many years. Maggie is plump all the time, and you like that. I think maybe I could live over it if you want her.

Yes, I think, too, Laura doesn't want to marry Williams if she could do any better. In fact, she told me she would not marry him if she could do any better, and did not have to sew for a living. I'm sorry she looks at marriage from that standpoint. She is a good girl and deserves to be happy in her marriage. I think she would like to have my sweetheart for hers, but I think I can't spare him now. The days and weeks seem too long when I am away from him for me to give him up to another for always. I'll be truly glad when I begin teaching, for I don't get so lonely without you then.

And then there is Lena Higgins making love to you, too. Well, it does seem they are determined to take you from me. I guess I'll have to make fair weather with Mr. Crank so as not to be left at the altar in the event you should skip with one or more of my rivals. Why not just go to Salt Lake City and take them all? So many are wanting you! Pray tell me what the attraction is!

I think Sister Sowell has named her twins Emily and Janie, for their grand-mothers. You ought to be ashamed of yourself to write me all that foolishness about preachers' wives. The next syllogism that comes, I think I'll have one to match it. Then you'll be willing to quit 'logic' for a while. Yours won't stand the test anyway. You don't draw the proper conclusions from your premises. No, I'm not at all uneasy. I think I've got a few ideas myself!

I think more of Brother Sowell than I did this time last year. I wrote to Callie Nichols last week. I think she is very sensible woman for wearing mother hubbards this hot weather. I wear them nearly all the time. I wish you would write Brother Sowell a letter congratulating him on his twins, and try to encourage him some. He is so down in the mouth since they came; thinks he can't get off any more to preach. But that is all a notion of his. Of course he can go. Five children are no more than one woman can care for.

I had a letter from my sister at Rio Vista yesterday. Old man Abney is to preach for them one Lord's day in September. Sister is much bothered. Says if they don't have some sound preaching there very soon, the place will go into the hands of the progressives. She urged me to insist that you come in September, and hold a week's meeting, or more. Brother Carnes' meeting there in July seems to have done no good at all. I am sure you could not find a field anywhere to work in to more profit for our Master. Brother Sowell wants to preach for them, but does not see how he can leave home soon. If you can't go, maybe you could

get some one else who is nearly as good a preacher as
you are to hold a meeting there. Maybe Brother Joe
Warlick, or Brother Oliver, or Brother Jack McCarty,
or somebody that can go. Don't send any 'soft-shell'
or weak material to that place . . .

I rather think I don't want to marry at church on
Sunday. I go to that place to worship, and I don't want
to have my mind disturbed by anything else. Then
wouldn't I feel like a goose, sitting up there and everybody in the house gazing at me while you are up in the
pulpit preaching and telling what Paul says about
wives obeying their husbands, etc. while I turn crim-
son, and everybody laughs! A pretty scene for the
hour of worship! No, thank you. Really, dear, I think
it best for us not to marry on Sunday. Don't you
think so, too? I think about the 23rd or 24th of December would be all right; or, if you are in a debate
then, we can wait until you get through. However, I
want you to be suited in the matter. The exact time
makes but little difference to me. But if we do marry
on Sunday, I would rather it would be at home.

Lovingly yours,
Nannie

III

Sometime in the fall of 1896 Tant pulled one of the biggest mistakes of his life, and one that was to bring untold
grief to Nannie, and to have an adverse effect on his relationship with the Yater family for the rest of his life. It
came very near to being that "hand of Fate" concerning
which he wrote with such forebodings, and which he feared
might say "No" to the Tant-Yater wedding plans. But it
was his own fault.

Nannie had told Tant that before she married him it
would be necessary for him to write her mother, Mrs. William M. Yater (who, incidentally, always signed herself by
her given name as "Mrs. Fannie Buckner Yater", or simply
as "F. B. Yater") and receive her blessings on the impend-

ing marriage. Nannie's father had been dead for five years now, and her mother was the recognized head of the Yater family — nine boys (including two dead) and four girls. All the children now living were grown, several of them married, and with children and in-laws, the Yater clan comprised a sizeable group of people. Grandview, Texas, was the little town in which the matriarch lived, as did also two of her married sons with their wives and families.

Tant wrote the letter, as Nannie requested, and it was a very nice letter — for him. But he wanted to make certain that the right "Mrs. Yater" received it. There were three women in the little town of Grandview under that name, and Tant persuaded himself that he did not know or did not remember the correct initials of Nannie's mother, so addressed his letter to:

"The Old Lady Yater
Grandview, Texas"

Repercussions to that missive were so painful that even after the lapse of more than sixty years, Nannie Yater Tant finds it embarrassing to recall the matter. Mrs. Yater herself was not so deeply insulted by it as were her children. She apparently ordered Tant from the house the next time he called on Nannie; and Nannie took the side of her betrothed, deeply hurt at his crude address to her mother, yet fiercely loyal to him in the face of her family's hostility.

Several weeks went by, and there was considerable uncertainty as to whether the wedding would take place in Grandview as planned or not. Nannie insisted that Tant come to Grandview and have the wedding in her home. Tant demurred. He told her that he felt sure her brothers would try to start a ruckus, and that while he did not mind whipping all seven of them, he did not want to do it on his wedding day. Nannie was adamant — the wedding would be at Grandview, and she would take care of her family. She did. The cultured and high-spirited Mrs. Yater (obviously out of deep love for her Nannie) wrote to her prospective son-in-law:

Grandview, Texas
November 18, 1896

Elder J. D. Tant
Dear Brother:

Notwithstanding you 'excused' me from the 'labor' of answering your last letter, the respect due you as a Christian brother demands that I should write to you and try to disabuse your mind somewhat as to the supposed animosity my children bear you. While I know you are fully impressed with the idea that their objection to your marrying their sister is of a personal nature, I think your better judgment will after you understand them, convince you to the contrary. It is quite natural that brothers should take an interest in the welfare of their sisters, especially when they have no father to advise. And it is proper the sisters should heed the cool advice of the brothers. But it seems sometimes 'tis the case they do not. In Nannie's case, for instance.

Nannie had arrived at an age she thought herself capable of making her own selection, and such was, and is, the case; but they looked at the union from a different standpoint to hers. They know Nannie's fastidiousness as regards the bearing of a man, and seeing you, as they thought, so different from the 'model' she ever held up, they were of the opinion the union of two natures so utterly uncongenial and inconsistent would result in a life, to her, most wretched, and therefore sought to convince her of that fact.

And now, since she seems to thoroughly understand your customs and ways, they have long since ceased to say anything in the matter, and feel that, as she thinks her future happiness depends upon the marriage, they will not interfere further. It is the desire of all of them and myself that all 'hostilities' be laid down, and the marriage take place in her Mother's house.

As to fearing any undue treatment from any one of them, you will rest assured that for their mother's sake, if for nothing else, they will treat you with utmost respect. They did all they could to prevent the marriage; you did all you could to bring it on. You were successful, and they, like the true and honorable men that they are, have lain down all objections, and will try to meet the issue as best they can. They all have ever loved the gentle sister, Nannie, above the rest. She was ever mild and amiable, and so considerate of the feelings of those with whom she had dealings. I beg of you, in the reconstruction of feelings, to accept my offerings of peace, and give us time to bridge over the unpleasantness, time to heal all wounds; and while I try to conciliate matters, I trust you will do the same.

My children are too sensitive about me. I cared not so much for the improper address, thinking 'twas just as you said, you did not know my name, but felt that you might have gotten my name from Nannie. However, I still tried to think 'twas one of your freaks of idiosyncrasy, and therefore was willing to let it go, trying to subdue my feelings. And had you deferred your visit a few days longer, I could have met you in a better frame of mind. I beg you to forget and forgive the unChristian reception I gave you. I do not desire to give dear Nannie one other pang. She has had enough in the contest to deserve nothing but smiles and caresses hereafter.

Submission has been my attribute when defeated in anything undertaken. And if you cannot act the way we desire without acting the hypocrite, why, it would be out of reason to demand it of you; therefore, will pass by all your inconsistencies and cover the same with the mantle of charity. If you are but kind to Nannie, 'tis all I ask. And I have no fears on that score. She will do her best for the good of your children. It would be against her nature and teaching to be unkind to anyone. As to my visiting you next spring, I cannot say that I shall. My indisposition to travel, and the change of habit necessary to the same, is ever attended with unpleasantness to me.

All I ask of you and Nannie is that you marry in my house, and let the wedding be a quiet one, only the relatives on each side to be in attendance. I am too feeble for much noise or bustle.

With best wishes for your happiness and prayer for God's blessing to be upon you, I claim to be still your friend,

F. B. Yater

In reading over my letter, I fear its expressions may seem harsh, but I pray you will not so construe it, for I entertain only good wishes for you.

IV

Readers of the modern Methodist Discipline may not be aware of the fact that a fundamental change in Methodist doctrine was brought about in the year 1910. Prior to that time the Discipline had clearly taught the doctrine of inherited depravity, and that infants were conceived and born in sin. The Discipline contained many expressions setting this forth such, for instance, as the "Order for the Administration of Baptism to Infants." This gave the formula for the Minister as follows: "Dearly Beloved, forasmuch as all men are conceived and born in sin, and that our Saviour Christ said, Except a man be born of water and of the Spirit he cannot enter into the kingdom of God; . . ."

It was to debate this question J. D. Tant, Christian, and J. C. Weaver, Methodist, met in a two-days' discussion at Moore's Spring the last of November, 1896. Tant reports:

"After lasting two days, this debate at Moore's Spring closed. Perhaps no debate like this was ever before held in Texas. Only one proposition was debated. I was to affirm, and Mr. Weaver was to say how long the debate should last. I expected to continue five days, but at the end of the second day, Mr. Weaver said he was through; so we quit.

"I affirmed: 'The Methodist Discipline teaches the doctrine of infant damnation to unbaptized children'.

I proved the following points from the Methodist Discipline, Wesley, and Watson's Institutes. They all teach:

1. The child is not washed.
2. The child is not sanctified.
3. The child is under God's wrath.
4. The old Adam is in the child.
5. The child has a carnal mind.
6. The child is corrupt.
7. The child is under the guilt of original sin.
8. Children deserve eternal misery.
9. They are dead in sin.
10. They have committed original sin.
11. The child is not a member of Christ.
12. Children are out of covenant relationship with God.
13. The child is not a child of God till baptized.
14. Children are obnoxious in God's sight.
15. Children cannot be saved without baptism.
16. Children are liable to eternal damnation.
17. God has tied us to infant baptism.
18. Outward baptism is necessary to salvation.
19. Baptism washes away original sin.
20. Baptism engrafts us into Christ.
21. Children are not born justified.
22. Children are not in the covenant of grace.
23. Baptism is a pledge to the parents of the child; for if it dies, God has pledged that he will save it if baptized.
24. The child is born sinful and unclean.

"I wrote these twenty-four items on the blackboard, and kept them before the people. Mr. Weaver denied that Methodists teach them. This I readily admitted, but showed that it was their doctrine, and pleaded with them to give up the same." (Gospel Advocate, December 10, 1896.)

Following the Tant-Weaver debate, it was necessary for Tant to return to Seymour to defend in a debate with the Baptists his book, "The True Way." From Seymour he

writes his last letter to Nannie Yater before their marriage,
now scheduled for December 30:

Seymour, Texas
December 19, 1896

Dearest Nannie:

I write a few lines tonight, which I suppose will be
the last letter for '96, . . . perhaps for life; who can
tell?

The Tant-Elder debate is now four days old. Perhaps it will close tomorrow night. It has been quite
strong at times, but I feel very happy tonight, for it is
a conceded fact that I am far ahead. I closed up the
defense of my book today, and will look after the Baptist Church tomorrow. Hair, wool, and feathers are
expected to fly.

Don't know where I'll go from here, perhaps to
Bowie or Fort Worth, or perhaps to Weatherford to see
my mother. I am quite tired tonight. Have not been
well since I left you. Hope you got the letter I sent
you from Fort Worth, with the notes in it for Schultz
and Lawson. I'll go down to Cleburne Tuesday, and
to Grandview on Wednesday if the Lord wills.

It will be impossible for me to go to Clifton on the
31st, as all things are ready for me to go home that
day. If I were to go to Clifton, could not get home till
Monday. The first is Friday, and bad luck to go home
then! I hope, dear, you will not think me unkind in not
going. If you desire, you can go down from McGregor,
but I cannot go and meet my engagements at home.
Just got a letter from Sowell. J. M. Tant may come
over with me. I am tired down tonight. Will have to
meet Cayce in January and Hall in July.

J. D. Tant

V

Fannie Mills Yater was four years younger than her sister, Nannie. But for two years she had been much in love
with a young medical student named Albert Gebhart. As
the time for Nannie's wedding drew closer day by day, and

the Yater household was astir with wedding plans, it was decided to make the affair a double wedding, with Nannie marrying Tant and Fannie Mills (who was never known by anything but her nickname of "Kanna") marrying her young medical student. Both the Yater girls were pleased with this arrangement, and feverish preparations were made accordingly.

The day for the wedding, Wednesday, December 30, 1896, was clear and warm and still — one of those beautiful mid-winter days such as only Texas can provide. The wedding was set for 2:00 o'clock in the afternoon, and by ceremony time the house was filled with guests, mostly relatives. Brother Felix C. Sowell, he of the five children and the discouraged feeling that he had too big a family ever to be worth much as a preacher, was to perform the rites. Although a Tennessean, he was the local preacher at Grandview, having come out about a year before this time to try his fortunes in the West.

Young Albert Gebhart, twenty-two years old, was scared to death. Timid and shy to start with, he had barely screwed up courage enough to propose to Kanna (and probably never would have without considerable encouragement from that source). He had an "all-gone" feeling that got worse and worse as the day progressed. It was not that he did not want to marry, but he was scared — just plain frightened. He loved Kanna well enough, but was over-awed by her family, and by the occasion. He was a country boy, from a poor family, and was desperately trying to work his way through medical school to become a doctor. The Yaters were a big family, rather well to do by the standards of that day, and Nannie was marrying the noted Christian preacher, J. D. Tant, in comparison with whom Gebhart felt like an awkward, illiterate country bumpkin. He had lain awake most of the night worrying

about the forthcoming event. Could he go through with it?
What if he said the wrong thing?

But finally he hit upon a wonderful solution! He would
go to Brother Sowell, and ask him to put the questions first
to Brother Tant and Nannie; he would listen, oh! so carefully to what Brother Tant said in response to the questions, and then he, Albert, would say exactly what Brother
Tant had said. This seemed like a perfect arrangement.
Brother Tant was a man of the world, a famous preacher
and debater, who never got rattled at anything, but was always completely composed and master of any situation.
Gebhart was so relieved at this bit of planning that he could
almost half-way enter into the festive spirit of the hour and
enjoy himself. Well, not exactly enjoy, but at least he
could endure it.

Gebhart made his arrangements with Sowell, as planned,
and received this friendly preacher's assurance that the
questions would go first to Brother Tant. When 2:00
o'clock came the ceremony got under way; all the guests
were quietly in their place. After a very lovely short address as to the meaning and sacredness of marriage, Brother Sowell asked both couples to join hands. He was going
to say one ceremony for both couples, asking them, in
turn, to give their responses. He propounded the first
question to the men:

"Do you, J. D. Tant and Albert Gebhart, each take the
one whose hand you hold to be your lawfully wedded wife,
to live together after God's ordinances in the holy estate
of matrimony? Do you promise and covenant, each of you,
before God and these witnesses, to be her loyal and faithful
husband, to love, honor, and cherish her in sickness and in
health, for better or for worse, and forsaking all others
keep yourself to her only so long as you both shall live? Do
you, J. D. Tant, so promise?"

In the still and solemn silence that followed this question, Tant's voice, charged with deep emotion, came forth strong and clear, and in measured accents:

"By the help of God, I do."

Then Sowell turned to Gebhart, and asked:

"And do you, Albert Gebhart, so promise?"

Sweat was glistening on Gebhart's forehead; and his pale and frightened face was quivering. His eyes were dilated enormously, and his breath was short and jerky. But he had listened, as best he could, to what Tant had said; so came forth bravely with a high-pitched and shaky, but clearly audible:

"B-b-b-by God, I do!"

In a stunned and breathless silence the ceremony went on.

But when the last "Amen" was said, and Tant took his bride in his arms to kiss her, there was a wild rush of the Yater boys to the kitchen, and from that area of the house for many minutes there could be heard strange choking sounds as though someone was being strangled to death, with an occasional explosive "whoop", and the loud smacking of open hands on leg or back.

CHAPTER X

AT HOME IN HAMILTON

Following the wedding, J. D. Tant and Nannie Yater Tant went immediately to their home at Hamilton, Texas. George Applewhite and his wife had been living in the house, keeping Tant's two children, Ira, a blue-eyed boy of five, and Davis, his three-year-old sister, who was as dark as her brother was fair. When Tant came with his new wife, the Applewhites vacated the place, and Nannie set herself to cleaning up the entire house, and trying also to win the love and affection of her two step-children. She was so successful in this latter task that these two children came to love her with an intensity that surpassed the love that natural children often have for their mothers. Perhaps the loneliness of their early years as orphans had something to do with it. That, and the fact that their father was almost constantly away from home, leaving Nannie to fill largely the place of both father and mother in their young hearts.

At first they were shy and shrinking. Nannie coaxed and begged them, and finally began to bribe them with candy and other goodies to let her get near them. They referred to her as "she" and "her" in talking to one another, and rarely addressed her directly. When Tant left on his first preaching tour some three weeks after the marriage, his bride could not restrain her tears. Several times during the first days of his absence the children would over-hear her sobbing softly. One day she heard Davis slip up close to Ira and ask,

"Wonder what she's crying about?"

"I dunno," responded Ira rather forlornly, "she's been crying like that ever since Papa left."

Nannie tells of those first days of her marriage:

"I believe it was the sixth day after we reached
Hamilton that my husband went to the far pasture to
build fence, and failed to leave all the water I needed
to do the house cleaning I had planned for that day.
Our water was furnished by a wind-mill which pumped
into an elevated tank about one hundred yards from
the house. We had no pipes from the tank to the house
then, but carried the water by hand in huge wooden
buckets.

"I took two buckets and proceeded to the well. I had
watched my husband the day before — how he pulled
a wire that hung over the top of the tank, which I
think, must have connected with a valve in the bottom.
An open pipe extended almost to the ground, a very
odd arrangement. I put my bucket under the pipe and
pulled the wire. The water gushed out, filling the
bucket instantly. I hastily removed bucket number
one, and put bucket number two in its place. It filled
as rapidly as the first. I gave the wire a jerk to shut
off the flow, as I had seen my husband do.

"The water kept coming.

"I pulled frantically on the wire, jerking it, jiggling
it, twisting it. All to no avail. I screamed for my husband. He was too far away. I ran to the house and
sent little Ira for his Papa as fast as his short legs
could carry him; then rushed back to the tank to take
one more despairing jerk at that wire to try to stop
the flow of water. It wouldn't stop. So I returned
to the house, excited and almost ready to cry because
I had wasted so much water. Water in Texas in the
1890's was precious, and of course living in town, I
had been accustomed to paying for every gallon used.

"I saw my husband come to the well, adjust the
valve to stop the flow of water, pick up the two buckets
I had left there in my excitement, and come on to the
house. My heart was filled with apprehension as he
approached. What would he say? It wasn't my fault,
I told myself defiantly. I didn't know how to work
that contraption. I stood in the door and waited as he
brought the two buckets and set them down on a shelf

on the back porch. Not a word did he say. I could stand it no longer, so I broke into tears and began to tell him what had happened, and how everything on the place was dilapidated and worn out. Not a gate had hinges, not a door had locks, several windows had the glass broken out. And that arrangement at the well was something a child ought to be ashamed of!

"I could say no more for his arms were around me and his lips planted a kiss on my cheek, and in words so tender and kind he told me that no harm had been done; the windmill would soon refill the tank, there was nothing to be concerned about. He said he knew the place had gone to wreck in the three years since Laura had died, but that it would soon be back in shape again, and everything would be all right.

"But my troubles with that windmill were not over by any means. My husband showed me how to work the cut-off valve, and explained other things about the system, cautioning me to be sure always to drain the pump at the well any time he was away and I thought it might freeze. I was quite vigilant on the job, taking no chances, and cut off the water every night. But in the month of February, my husband being away on a preaching tour, I met disaster. It was an unusually warm day, and I had worked hard all day in the yard. I was digging some flower beds, and carrying off trash that had accumulated on the place for years. In fact, the wood-pile had been put in the front yard, and Ira and I spent a good part of the day cleaning it up, raking up the chips and trash and hauling them off in his little express wagon. The day was Saturday.

"The day was so very warm that I felt spring had come, and was certain there could be no danger to the pump that night. By this time my husband had piped the water into the house, and I did not have to carry water from the well each day. So after our usual chores of milking the cows, feeding the chickens and pigs and ponies, and bringing in wood and kindling, I got Ira and Davis inside, shut the doors, pulling a heavy trunk in front of one and a bed in front of the other. There were no locks on the place, and in those early years I was terribly afraid in the dark.

"The wind suddenly ceased blowing from the south, and the stillness was like death; the darkness was as black as the tomb. But we, Ira, Davis, and I had our usual bed-time story; I read the children a chapter from the Bible, and we kneeled down and prayed together, then went to bed, tired but happy and at peace. We slept soundly until a Texas "norther" struck the house with a suddenness and a fury that shook the old place to its foundations. It was three o'clock Sunday morning.

"My first thought was for the pipes and the pump. I looked at the time. Three o'clock. Well, it would be daylight by five, and of course those pipes could not freeze in two hours. So I turned over and tried to go back to sleep. But I couldn't. It grew colder and colder. I thought I never knew it to turn so cold so fast. I looked at the clock again. Four o'clock. I began to grow uneasy about the pump. Finally casting all my fears aside, I got out of bed, bundled myself up in nearly everything I could get on, for by this time the wind must have been blowing at fifty miles an hour, and the blast was so frigid as to take my breath the moment I stepped outside, and went to the well.

"Too late! The rod would not turn. I was certain, however that it was not frozen solidly, so hurried back to the house, got an old bucket and put live coals of fire in it from the fire-place, put chips on the coals, and hurried back to the well. I put the bucket with the smouldering chips under the pipe where it was frozen, climbed the ladder (seventeen feet) to the top of the tank, and cut off the water. I thought the howling gale would surely blow me off the ladder a time or two, but it didn't. I saved the pipes from freezing, but not the pump. It froze and burst, and cost us $13.75 to have it repaired.

"In my husband's absence, several ladies in the Hamilton church seemed to vie with one another in doing every kindness for me in their power. Especially do I recall one occasion when a number of ladies brought food to our home, and gave me a 'surprise' dinner. Among them was Sister B————, a lady of strong convictions, her strongest being a holy antagonism to all second marriages. She had one child, a sweet little girl named Lucille. All through dinner she expounded her views on second marriages. Of course, I pretended not to notice. The other ladies in the room tried to turn the conversation, but without too much success. Thinking to divert her a bit, I caressed her little girl and remarked, 'Lucille. What a pretty name. You must have named her from the character in the book, 'Lucille'. Promptly she replied, 'Yes, I did. I think 'Lucille' is the finest thing Longfellow ever wrote.'

"I said nothing, but could see from the glances exchanged between the other women that they had caught her mistake the same as I.

"While my husband was a widower, an elderly spinster who was a fine artist, and who had been a close friend to Laura, his first wife, had painted a life size portrait of Laura, and had given it to Husband as a present. It was a beautiful piece of art, and I treasured it for Laura's children in coming years. I did not want them to forget their dead mother, but to always remember her with true and faithful love.

"Since the picture was too heavy to hang on a wall, I kept it on an easel in the front room, which we called the 'parlor.' After dinner was over, I arose and asked the ladies to come into the front room. Sister B.———— was one of the first in, and the first thing that caught her eye was the large portrait of Laura. As if shot from a cannon she dashed across the room, clasped her hands together, and fell to her knees before the picture, tremulously crying out as she swayed back and forth with eyes closed:

" 'Oh, Laura, sweetest, and purest, and best! An angel from God sent to this earth to show mortals what heaven is like. Too good, too beautiful, too lovely to be tarnished by the corruptible things of this earth, so God took you back to heaven'. Then turning to me, she said, 'No mortal on this earth can ever take her place'.

"I replied, 'I have been told she was a most excellent lady, and I'm sure all who knew her loved her. Although I did not know her, I will always love her because my husband loved her so truly." (**Reminiscences.**)

II

While Nannie at Hamilton was having her problems with windmills and Texas northers and "the sisters," Tant was continuing his relentless battle against digression and the devil. Early in March he wrote:

"More than once during the past year has the writer been condemned for his unceasing denunciation of Brother Homan's recognition of the pious unimmersed as Christians, and of Brother Bush's calling for mourners at Archer City, Brother Boen at Dublin, and Brother Saunders at Denton . . .

"The recent account of Brother Boen's meeting at Luling, as reported by Brother G. S. Kimberley in The Christian Courier of February 18, forever settles the matter that Brother Boen is not preaching the gospel, for no gospel preacher has ever left such a record.

"Brother Kimberley says, 'The meeting was run under the direction of the Christian Church, but on the cooperative principle. The results were twenty-five professions, distributed as follows: Christians, seven; Baptists, ten; Presbyterians, five; Methodists, two; Episcopalians, one. The interest was deep, and we are satisfied that it will result in lasting good to all the churches. Brother Boen was faithful in presenting the Bible plan of salvation, and its all-sufficiency as a rule of faith and practice. I think that we are better understood and more respected here than ever before.'

"Also I note in Courier of February 4 that Brother G. W. Lee preached an able sermon in the Central Christian Church in Dallas, giving his reasons for leaving the Methodist Church and uniting with the Disciples of Christ . . .

"What is gained by a Methodist becoming a Christian, when a so-called Christian preacher will preach in such a way to make seventeen Baptists, Methodists, and Presbyterians, while making seven Christians?

"Twenty-five years ago such a report would have been scorned out of any Christian paper. But how sad to note the departure of these brethren from the truth! An apostasy never reforms. I predict that twenty-five years hence sprinkling and infant baptism will be added to the already long list of errors practiced by these brethren who have gone out from us. May God help all lovers of truth to guard their work, and to put on the brake at the top of the hill." (Gospel Advocate, March 11, 1897.)

Tant had a debate scheduled with S. F. Cayce, editor of the Primitive Baptist, Martin, Tennessee, set for Anson, Texas, on March 1. Tant came; but Cayce did not. So Tant wrote:

"I left home February 26 for Anson, Jones County, where Elder Cayce and I were to have met in debate on March 1; but as it had been 'fore sot' from the foundation of the world that Elder Cayce would not be there, myself and many others were disappointed. I hope, though, it may not be contrary to God's decree that Cayce and I may yet meet some day at Anson.

"I preached twice at Anson, and learned that the brethren are still struggling hard to maintain their work for the truth, notwithstanding the financial embarrassment that has almost ruined the west. Brothers Ribble and Bishop, two boy preachers, are preaching regularly for the church at Anson. To those boy preachers I would say: 'Much experience and observation have taught me that it will be hard for you to succeed by preaching only once or twice a week at some stated places. Go out and preach all the time; stay at a place as long as you can do good; preach at least six times a week for the first four or five years; preach in the highways and school houses and among private families; do not wait till Sunday for a big crowd. If you can get as many as Philip had, preach the word, and rest assured God will give the increase'.

"From Anson I went to Abilene, and spent one day with Brother W. L. Gibbs, editor of the **Word and Work**, a religious paper of two years' standing. Brother Gibbs has crossed swords on some points with Brothers Jackson and Nall; but on the fundamental principles of Christianity — such as the establishment of the church, what a sinner must do to be saved, and how to live a Christian life — I found him in perfect agreement with the word of God, and see no necessity for the differences that sometimes exist among brethren on things of minor importance. Brother Gibbs is laboring to overthrow the fatal mistake of Campbell to unite all Christians on the Bible. He claims it has resulted in a human union of many sectarians, unscripturally taught, unscripturally converted, and unscripturally baptized, until the mixture has become so corrupt within itself that it cannot stand. Our aim should be to persuade men and women to become Christians by the Bible, and then the union will stand.

"On my way home from Abilene, I stopped one night in Fort Worth, and met with the faithful few on South Side. I learned that Brother Dunn is taking well with the brethren there. I also met Brother Perry Johnson, one of our able young preachers, who lives at Fort Worth and does the work of an evangelist in the neighboring towns." (**Gospel Advocate**, April 15, 1897.)

Always conscious of his responsibilities as a "field editor" of the **Gospel Advocate**, Tant constantly felt that he was falling short of his duties along that line. He confessed his shortcomings, and offered a partial explanation:

"To the Readers of the Advocate: I am almost ashamed to tell you I am still field editor of the **Advocate**, for I have done so little for its circulation during 1896; but five months of that time were spent in West Texas, where the brethren have been troubled by a four years' drouth, and were not able to buy their bread, clothes, and tobacco, and of course could not think of taking a religious paper, which comes after all these things; but I shall write more and work harder for the paper this year than ever before. Let us work, watch, and pray, and God will give the increase." (Gospel Advocate, April 22, 1897.)

True to his promise, Tant wrote more and worked harder for the paper in 1897 than he had the previous year. He had a series of ten articles in the journal that year under the title, "Advice To Young Preachers." He was now only thirty-six years of age himself, but already was regarded by others, and by himself, as a veteran. His debates had won him wide recognition among the churches, and he was in constant demand for meetings from all over the nation. His debate with S. F. Cayce, originally set for the first of March, was now re-scheduled to begin on July 7 at Anson, Texas. Brother S. A. Ribble, the boy preacher whom Tant had commended, had been able to work out the details of the new schedule after Cayce had failed to show at the first appointment.

Home briefly for a few days toward the end of March, Tant had time only to straighten out a few books before going to Bloomington in Greer County, Oklahoma, for a meeting. From that place he reported:

"I have just closed a grand meeting at this place with thirteen additions. Bloomington is where I preached two days last year, and baptized nine. These brethren, with the faithful few already there, went to work and have lived right since. They have built a small church, where the meeting was held. This is the only church building in Greer County, and shows the faith and zeal of the members of the church of Christ in that county . . . Our brethren have eight congregations in the county. Brothers Scruggs, Tuttle, Dial, McIntyre, Millwee and Sweet are the preachers. Brother W. M. McIntyre has done more preaching and baptizing than any other preacher in the county, and is hated by all the denominations, and is never called upon to help in their union meetings. This causes me to think he is a man of God, sound in the faith. A young man, to identify himself with the people of Greer County, and spend his entire time preaching, could be supported and do much good." (Gospel Advocate, April 29, 1897.)

In April, A. J. McCarty held a meeting at Hamilton. Tant was home for a part of the meeting and had a fine visit with McCarty, of whom he was especially fond. McCarty had lost his wife the same year Laura had died, some six months later, and he and Tant had suffered the loneliness of widowerhood together. Joe S. Warlick, a close friend of the Yater family, as well as of Tant and McCarty, had several times told Nannie Yater that Jack McCarty, and not J. D. Tant, was the man she ought to marry. McCarty, said Warlick, wasn't nearly so "rough" as Tant; and the sheltered and cherished favorite of the Yater family would find a far more congenial union with McCarty than with Tant.

But it had not worked that way. Nannie had given her heart to Tant before she ever got a chance to meet McCarty, and that was the end of the matter. But McCarty was a dear friend of the Tants for the balance of his life, and was a frequent visitor in the home. He had remained a widower only a little more than a year, having married his second wife, Eula B. Robinson, on December 21, 1895, a full year before Tant and Nannie were to be married.

Following the Hamilton meeting, Tant immediately began his travels again:

"After the McCarty meeting at Hamilton, I went to Franklin, Robertson County, where I preached in the opera house thirteen days. Brother McDaniel led the song service.

"We once had a church of Christ at Franklin, till

Brothers Saunders, Barber, and others worked the society and the organ in; then discord began and continued till finally the division took place. The Bible department went to the opera house, and the digressive part kept the church house.

"So far as I could learn, only two of the digressive members attended our meeting; the majority worked against us all they could. They even had a Presbyterian preacher to preach in the church house while I was preaching in the opera house. They drummed the town to get people to hear him. Some of them went out of the church house and tried to stop the country brethren who were on their way to hear me, and get them to hear the Presbyterian instead.

"It is thought by some that the digressives at Franklin will soon join the Presbyterians, as the Bible class is taught by a Presbyterian, and both the elders of the church are in his class. They had trouble some time ago, I was told, about his teaching that sprinkling was baptism. One of the leading sisters told them that if they submitted to such, she could no longer meet with them. She quit; they retained their Presbyterian teacher, but he agreed to say nothing more about baptism.

"From Franklin I went to Thornton, where in bygone years I have held four meetings, also a debate with W. A. Jarrel. I preached three days to large congregations, and baptized one young man.

"My next stop was at Hot Springs, Arkansas. I learned from a sister there that the cause of Christ is almost lost there.

"From Hot Springs I went to Little Rock, but failed to find any of the faithful. I met at prayer meeting with the digressives, where I met the only living daughter of old Brother 'Raccoon' John Smith. I also met Brother Browning, Arkansas State Evangelist, and Brother J. L. Darsie, 'pastor' at Little Rock. Both were working hard for the State Convention. (Gospel Advocate, July 8, 1897.)

II

The Tant family was rejoicing in the summer of 1897, for it was now apparent that the home was to be blessed with an addition. Tant had planned his work all through the year so as to permit a visit home about every month or six weeks, and sometimes he was able to stay for as much as five or six days, although two or three days was more often the case. After careful consultation with their doctor, and estimating the expected time of arrival for the baby as accurately as they could, November seemed to be the date to plan for. Tant wrote all the places where he had promised meetings for November and early December, telling them he would have to defer their meetings. This was Nannie's first baby, and he was going to take off a whole month to stay home with her until she recovered her strength. He would propably be preaching at Hamilton or some nearby school house during that month, but would be with his family through the day time, and could get some neighbor woman to stay with Nannie while he filled his preaching appointment each night, if needed.

But the best laid plans of mice and men . . .

On Wednesday night, September 22, Tant had preached his first sermon at Childress, Texas, three hundred miles from home. After the service that night he got a telegram from the doctor in Hamilton, telling him that his wife had delivered a premature baby that day, that she was dangerously sick, and that he should come home at once. The baby, a girl, weighed less than four pounds, and was expected to die at any moment.

Five people had made the "good confession" at Childress in that first service. Leaving word with the brethren to call the meeting off, or else try to get someone else to come in and continue it, Tant left on the very first train for Hamilton. Nannie reports the story:

"Railroad connections were extremely bad, and he was three days getting home. My mother, who lived at Grandview, Texas, one hundred miles away, beat him to me. I was glad to have her there, but those hours were dark ones for me. Until my mother came, I was alone except for a sweet neighbor girl who was ever faithful and true to me. She took the two children and went to a neighbor's house, and sent the woman back to stay with me while she kept the children. We sent for the doctor, and the baby came at five o'clock. No nurse, no hospital. Only a country doctor, and a good-hearted, but ignorant, country woman as helper.

"The night after my baby came, and before my mother got there, some of the neighbor women came in to 'sit up' with me. I had a fairly comfortable night, and next morning some of them cooked breakfast. One of the ladies finally came to my room and told the two or three ladies there that they could now go to the kitchen and eat, and that she would stay with me. They seemed to think I must not be left alone. Each lady began to volunteer to stay with me while the others ate. Sweet little Davis, then four years old, who ordinarily had a ravenous appetite, coolly climbed up into the bed beside me and stated firmly: 'I will stay with Mama and 'tend the baby. You can all go'. And there she sat." (Reminiscences.)

The third day after the baby was born, Tant arrived home. By this time his relationship with his mother-in-law was much improved, and the two of them worked side by side in doing the things necessary for Nannie and in trying to save the life of their tiny daughter and granddaughter. The baby, a full two months premature, was weak and delicate. Her survival seemed highly unlikely, but she was given every care that the medical skill of a country doctor and the wise and practical experience of a thirteen-times mother (for Fannie Mills Yater had given birth to an even 'baker's dozen') could provide.

The treatment was effective. It rapidly became evident that both mother and daughter were gaining strength, and, barring complications, both of them would live. By Sunday afternoon each had passed the crisis, and Nannie was insisting that she would very soon be up and on her feet again. She had good neighbors to help her, and her mother was planning to stay for another two or three weeks, since this was her first visit with the family since Nannie's marriage the previous December.

IV

These plans helped Tant make his decision to go on to Troupe, Texas, where he had a six days' debate scheduled with D. T. Brown, a Methodist. Nannie took the decision to leave her so soon somewhat philosophically:

"I believe nothing but death could have stopped him when he had a debate on hand. Some might say hell or high water could have done so; but I am sure the devil tried many times unsuccessfully to do the job, and I have known him to swim a creek as many as seven times to get to an appointment.

"So he stayed with me two days, saw that I was doing all right, and left me in my mother's care. Who on earth can love like a mother? Someone has truly said, 'For unwearying patience and unchanging tenderness, the love of a true mother stands next to the love of our Father in heaven'." (Reminiscences.)

The debate plans, however, were going slightly awry. Brown did not show up for the discussion. Tant tells the story of what happened:

"On September 28 I left wife in bed, with a baby six days old, and started for Troupe, where D. T. Brown (Methodist) and I were booked for a six days' debate.

"After reaching the ground, I learned that Brown would not be there; and, as Troupe is the place where R. M. Gano broke down with Weaver two years ago,

and the Methodists had blown so much, and Weaver
had claimed it was nothing uncommon for our preachers to get hoarse, or for their families to get sick, I
began to remind the Methodists about Weaver leaving
a few times himself. They soon learned we meant
business, and after telegraphing Weaver, Smith, and
Alderson of Sherman, they finally got Alderson, and
we began the debate six days after the appointed time.

"Alderson affirmed: 'Infant baptism', and 'sprinkling is baptism'. I affirmed: 'Baptism is for the remission of sins'. Alderson has some experience as a debater, having met T. W. Caskey, R. C. Horn, J. W.
Denton, J. A. Harding, B. A. Carr, and perhaps others
among the brethren.

"Alderson claimed that J. A. Harding is the nicest
man he ever met in debate, and J. N. Hall and J. D.
Tant are the greatest dodgers. He behaved himself in
all his speeches except one. In that one he got irri-
tated and called us 'Campbellites', but a genteel spank-
ing prevented his doing so again.

"After all, the debate passed off pleasantly. I look
upon Alderson as the most gentlemanly and ablest debater I ever met in the Methodist Church. While myself and the brethren at Troupe were well pleased with
the results of the debate, yet it was like all other
debates I ever held or attended in that it was a two-
sided affair. Alderson had studied his lesson well,
and made the ablest defense of Methodism I ever
heard." (Gospel Advocate, November 4, 1897.)

After the debate with Alderson, Tant returned to Hamilton for a three day visit with his family, then went back to
Childress, Texas, to resume the meeting which had been
interrupted there in September by the telegram calling him
home. He had a good meeting at Childress this time, baptizing several more, and was very happy to find the little
group of disciples there working hard to build up a strong
congregation. From Childress he came to Seymour, where
he had debated John F. Elder in December of the previous
year. Here he preached seven sermons and baptized seven

people. The Baptists were angry and bitter. He reports:

"The Baptists were bitter throughout. The whole Baptist Church, and Jones, their preacher, bolted that night while I was there. All of them got up and left just as I began to preach. Notwithstanding the hard work of the Baptists there to break up the church of Christ since the debate, the Baptists have baptized two little girls and the church of Christ has baptized fourteen in that part — four Baptists among the number." (Gospel Advocate, January 13, 1898.)

From Seymour Tant went to the little town of Howe, some ten miles south of Sherman. Here he found the digressives completely in control, but they respected him, and wanted him to preach:

"My next stop was at Howe, where we have a strong congregation holding to all the innovations that have divided the church in Texas. Notwithstanding these things, the elders selected me to preach a week on nothing but doctrinal themes. This I did with all my power. I took special pains at two different times to tell them plainly I opposed the organ and societies, and gave my reasons. First, they are unscriptural; second, they have caused division throughout Texas, wherever they have gone. I trust that the truth preached at Howe will profit in years to come. I was treated kindly by these brethren, and supported for the meeting. They were not filled with bitterness and evil speaking against the brethren who stand where all stood fifteen years ago, before these innovations came. They seemed to think, even if we are divided, we should love and respect each other, and that bitterness should not exist. If all those who have gone off after these innovations were as kind as the brethren at Howe, and respected those who hold only to God's word as they do, much of the evil speaking, bitterness, and strife that now exists in Texas would be a thing of the past. Brother W. C. Dimmitt is preaching for them half his time, and I learn that almost all are well pleased with his work.

"While preaching at Howe at night, I debated six days at Farmington, four miles away, with J. K. P. Williams, a Missionary Baptist. I must confess that this was the toughest and most ridiculous debate of my life. This was my fourth debate with Williams, and, I suppose, my last, as Williams absolutely refused to conduct a debate on gentlemanly principles or to be governed by Hedge's 'Rules of Logic' for debate. As I cannot come down to the low order on which he desires to conduct debates, I suppose this will be our last." (Gospel Advocate, January 13, 1898.)

Williams was apparently completely off the subject most of the time, arguing first one way then the other on Baptist doctrine, affirming a thing in one speech, denying it in the next, defending positions that no Baptist would accept, and denying things all Baptists believe. There were twelve Baptist preachers in attendance, and W. A. Shultz, Tant's moderator, went to each of them personally asking them to endorse William's position. They all refused. About midway throught the debate, realizing how confused and erratic Williams was becoming, Tant began to make references to heaven, saying, "When Williams and I get to heaven, we will ask Paul what he meant by this statement," or "When I see my friend Williams in heaven, I think he will be ashamed of some of the vile names he has called me in this debate," etc.

After such references as these had gone for three or four speeches, Williams jumped to his feet in the middle of one of Tant's speeches, demanding that the moderators close the debate. They asked on what basis or what grounds he made the request.

"Tant has acknowledged," he replied, "that I am going to be in heaven. You heard him say that when he and I meet in heaven we will ask the Apostle Paul about some of his writings. Now, I am a Baptist. I was born a Baptist, raised a Baptist, and I'll die a Baptist. Therefore it is my

Baptist doctrine that will take me to heaven. If Baptist doctrine will take a man to heaven (and Tant admits I'll be here), then I see no point in continuing the discussion."

Without a moment's hesitation Tant responded, "Why, yes, I am confident J. K. P. Williams will be walking the street of heaven after the final judgment. And I am not alone in that conviction. I believe most of this audience are fairly certain he will be there. For four days now we have been listening to his miserable efforts to make some kind of sensible argument. He has been unable to do so, but has spouted the most non-sense and foolish gibberish I have ever heard from the lips of any idiot in all my life. I feel very certain that when J. K. P. Williams stands at the judgment bar of God, and the books are opened, revealing every deed of his life, and the Lord takes a look at the arguments he has made in this debate, he is going to admit Williams to heaven!

"He is going to poke him in through the fool hole! !"

CHAPTER XI

A TRIP TO OKLAHOMA

Little Maidia Norvell Tant, the premature baby, was not doing well. For the first three months of her life she had grown rapidly, gaining weight and strength with every passing day. But late in December she had taken a slight cold, from which she seemed unable to recover. Along with the cold she had developed a sort of asthmatic wheezing as she breathed that was most alarming. Tant's appointments had been set months in advance, congregations were waiting for him to hold their meetings, and he was torn between conflicting duties — whether to fulfil his appointments, or to stay home with his wife and sick baby.

Nannie assured him, however, that she could "take care of everything, and I'll get in touch with you if anything goes wrong," so early in January, Tant left for a two-month preaching tour. His first stop was at Niotaze, Kansas:

"Our meeting there was largely attended, and three took membership. The brethren decided they had waited long enough on the dancers and the ungodly for repentance, and, as they did not return, the church will shortly withdraw fellowship from a number of them, and will try to do more Bible work than they have been doing. One great trouble at Niotaze is that very few members understand the doctrine of the church of Christ, and, to be on good terms with the sects, have extended their courtesy beyond the truth, and have suffered injury in so doing.

"Brother Charlton has done much preaching there, and baptized the greater part of the church. I learned that he preached about thirty sermons in the Methodist Church house, and as long as he taught morality and said nothing on 'What must I do to be saved?' the Methodists loved him; but the first sermon he

(187)

preached on the gospel, they turned him out of the house.

"One special kindness of the Niotaze brethren was that when they learned I opposed the organ, they set it aside, and song service was nobly conducted by Brother Black; yet I feel sad to think they thought more of me than of my Lord; for it is through Him only that I condemn the organ, and yet they never set it aside for him . . .

"Kansas has been a prohibition state for eighteen years, and while the report has gone abroad that more whiskey is sold in Kansas than elsewhere, yet these people say the report is a lie, that no power could induce them to vote whiskey back again. They say that in many of the larger towns some officers perjure their oath and lie to carry on the whiskey traffic, but still there are many young men who have never visited the saloon and do not know the evil influence of whiskey like they do in states where it is sold at every crossroads.

"Again, I would state that notwithstanding women vote and preach in Kansas, I have inquired and have yet to find the first woman who dips snuff, and I have not found a single store where it is kept for sale. They say some few negro women in Kansas dip snuff, and they look with incredulous eyes when I tell them that in the South thousands of women spend more for snuff than they do for the support of the gospel.

"Negro equality runs high here. Negroes ride in the same coach, go to the same school, eat at the same table with white people, and sometimes sleep in the beds of their white neighbors; all of which, I am glad to say, is not tolerated in 'heathen' Texas." (Gospel Advocate, February 3, 1898.)

From Niotaze Tant went next to Elk City, Kansas, where he found both the Northern Methodists and the Southern Methodists had arranged to run opposition meetings at the very time his was announced. He begged both preachers to divide time with him, but they refused. However, his meeting had nearly twice as many in attendance as both the other meetings combined, so he was not dissatisfied. One thing at Elk City did interest him—he found the members of the church were deeply involved in a political squabble. He says:

> "While I have never yet gone so far on the voting question as Brother Lipscomb and Brother McGarvey, yet in my fourteen years as an evangelist, I have yet to find my first Christian who ever ran for office and came out of politics as good a man as he was when he started in." (Gospel Advocate, February 17, 1898.)

The Elk City meeting was "suspended" for two weeks while Tant returned to Niotaze and Brooks for a couple of debates. The discussion at Niotaze was with Elder J. C. Fogle, a German Baptist, or "Dunkard." Tant was much impressed with Fogle's sincerity. This was a new experience for the Texas preacher, for he had encountered no "Dunkards" in the South. Some curious things happened in the debate:

> "Fogle argued that all religious movements were forward, but we baptize backward; while they baptize forward. I showed that we do baptize 'backward', but that a man then rises 'forward' to walk in newness of life. On the other hand the German Baptists baptize 'forward', and then rise 'backward'; 'and as ye receive Christ, so walk in him'; and that they are walking backward instead of forward.

> "Fogle charged that my brethren do not practice the holy kiss, while they do. I showed that Paul taught three ways of greeting: one with the hand, one by letter, and the last by the holy kiss; and that I did not object to any if I could select the party to kiss; but that the Dunkards are unscriptural by forcing the men to kiss men and the women to kiss women, whereas we were taught by the Apostle that all are one in Christ, and there is neither male nor female." (Gospel Advocate, February 24, 1898.)

Following the debate at Niotaze, Tant went to Hallowell, Kansas, where he preached to a crowded house for thirteen days, baptizing ten people. This was another place, as was becoming very common now, where the church had been divided by the introduction of the organ. From Hallowell he returned to Elk City to finish the meeting there, then returned to his Texas home. He was in Hamilton for fifteen days.

II

The baby grew no better, but worse. There were anxious nights when the struggle for breath went on all through the night, Tant and his anxious wife walking the floor with the babe in their arms for hours on end, using every kind of medication and home remedy of which they had ever heard. The doctor was in frequent attendance and consultation. He finally advised them that the baby ought to "travel for her health." He suggested a trip, any kind of trip, to get the child away from the Hamilton climate for a few weeks.

Tant bought a two-horse hack, loaded his wife and three children into it, and left home on March 24 for a two months' preaching tour of Oklahoma. He had a meeting scheduled to begin at Bloomington, Oklahoma, in about two weeks, so decided he would make a series of one-night appointments enroute from Hamilton to Bloomington. He was widely enough known, and strongly enough in demand that all he had to do was to write ahead and tell the brethren he would be in town on a certain night. They made the announcements, and he was invariably greeted by a large audience. He tried to space his nightly stops about fifty miles apart, as that was the distance he hoped to cover each day with his two-horse conveyance. The first appointment was at the little town of Hico, about twenty-two miles north of Hamilton; the next stop at Paluxy; and the third night he preached at Weatherford, staying there for the Lord's day morning service, and driving on to Whitt on Sunday afternoon.

"I preached to a good congregation on Sunday morning. We once had a large congregation at Weatherford, but Brother Ridgeway, their pastor, introduced an organ into the church one night with a false key, while the elders slept. This divided the church, and the organ party sold out for $1,600.00, which financially crippled our brethren and gave the enemy the advantage of their divided condition. But under the gospel labors of Brother W. T. Kidwell, for almost three years, the church is coming to the front again. Brother Kidwell has recently moved to Fort Worth, Texas, and Brother A. Alsup has moved to Weatherford. He preaches half his time for them.

"I preached on Sunday night at Whitt, some twenty miles from Weatherford. I learned that of the one hundred and fifty members, about fifty were suffering from the society fever and sectarian recognition. Recently they tried to capture Whitt for the Society, but Brother E. H. Rogers of Collinsville, one of Texas' ablest preachers, happened to turn up in time to fight the battle and win the victory for the present; but I fear the same fever will soon break out again.

"The next night I preached at Bethel, twenty-five miles west of Jacksboro. I found a good country church house and the members working together, yet I learned that some had the society fever there also. As soon as this disease takes hold, it will prove fatal, like it has at all points in Texas where they have introduced the organ and society and made them tests of fellowship and demand that all who cannot worship with these things can step down and out . . .

"These law cases over church property are sad, but during the next ten years in Texas there will be very few towns where the brethren have built houses but what they will have to hold them by law, or else give them up to the organ and society faction and build other houses of worship. Law trials over church property were unknown in Texas until the organ and society craze struck the state." (**Gospel Advocate**, April 28, 1898.)

From Bethel the traveling Tant family came to Seymour where, as Tant says, "we once had a large congregation and among the best working churches in the state. I held a meeting there in bygone days and found harmony and love prevailed, but the organ fever told its tale of death there also. The organ was introduced over the protest of some as godly men and women as we have in Texas, and after that I was refused the opportunity of preaching in that house when passing through Seymour. The young pastor in charge gave no other objection to me than that I did not favor the organ." Leaving Seymour early Wednesday morning, the two horses were pointed toward Crowell, county seat of Foard County, some fifty miles away.

It was a hard drive, and Tant kept the horses at a lively gait. The road was little travelled, and the going was rough. Late in the day, as Crowell came in sight some three or four miles away, one of the horses laid down and refused to get up. He was exhausted. All efforts to get him on his feet proved futile, so Tant removed the harness from him, and began to think of what could be done. He saw a ranch house about half a mile away, walked to it, borrowed a horse to take the place of his jaded one, and finished the trip to Crowell in time to preach in the court-house to a large audience. His subject was "The Bible." This was a theme which would not arouse too much controversy. Tant's reputation in Texas was such that many came to hear him, even though there were but a handful of members in the town. Brother S. W. Smith of Lockney, Texas, held a fine meeting in Crowell in June of that year, following Tant's visit.

Next morning Tant traded his worn out horse for one a little fresher, and continued the trip. They stopped that night at an inn just across the Red River. At the dinner table one of the men had some quail which he had shot that day, and which he insisted on offering to the guests. Nannie remarked that she had never eaten any quail, but was very fond of partridge. The hunter and his fellow travelers exchanged amused glances, while Tant explained to his embarrassed wife that partridge was just another name for quail.

The next night, arriving at Maud, Oklahoma, Nannie was too exhausted to get down out of the hack. Tant lifted her and carried her into the house. He put her to bed, left the woman of the house to stay with her, and went on to his preaching appointment. The baby was sick after the service, and Tant walked the floor with her all night, not even removing his clothes. Next morning, however, Nannie was somewhat refreshed, so the Tant family got an early start to Bloomington, where a two-weeks' meeting was scheduled.

III

Those days in the Indian Territory of Oklahoma were strange and vivid ones for Nannie. She had never seen country like this, and had never known the rough, hard life of the frontier. She writes of her impressions:

"We finally arrived at Bloomington, where my husband had scheduled a two-weeks' meeting. While there we made our home with Brother and Sister Ellison Carroll, who at that time were among the largest cattle owners in Oklahoma. During our meeting we had a chance to see the spring round-up. People talked about it for weeks before the day, like they did the Fourth of July when I was a child. I was anxious for the occasion, more to satisfy my curiosity than anything else. Finally, the great day arrived. Sister Carroll took us in her buckboard out on the hills about ten miles from her home. Their chuck wagon accompanied us. We could see people gathering from every direction — men, women, and children, but no dogs. Dogs would have excited the cattle, and so were not welcome at a round-up.

"The broad prairie spread out all around us, and distances were so vast and inconceivable that look where you might, the sky was nothing but a continuation of the vast undulating land. Not a tree was in sight, save, perhaps, an occasional mesquite which looked more like a dwarfed peach tree than anything else I could recall. Other chuck wagons began to arrive, and pots and pans were unloaded. The cooks, who were all men, got busy. Far down the valley, which was not a valley at all but only a slight depression between vast billows of endless plains, we could see the cattle being driven. From every direction we could see them coming, cattle of all ages, sizes, colors, and descriptions. They were being corralled in the valley by the cowboys until all had been rounded up. In that new country there were no pasture fences. All range was open, and every man had as much right to the grass and water as any other. When calves were old enough to be weaned, they were branded and turned loose on the range to be seen no more, perhaps, till the next spring roundup. At this time every rancher was supposed to hunt up all the cattle he could find, drive them to some common meeting place agreed upon, and then each owner would have his men 'cut out' all the stock that had his brand.

"In this particular round-up that I saw there were many thousands of head of cattle. They covered the land for miles and miles, a milling, lowing, stamping herd. The dust rose lazily into the spring sky as old bulls pawed the earth, and young calves frantically bawled and sought their mothers. Finally, the time for 'cutting' began. Men on their 'cutting' ponies, horses especially trained for this kind of work, would ride into the herd looking for a particular brand. Once that brand was spied, the horse was put on that particular calf or cow, and skillfully worked it to the edge of the herd, and out into its owner's bunch. Regardless of how much the cow might try to dodge or turn aside, a good cutting horse rarely let one get away from him, but would skillfully and swiftly counter every move that was made.

"I watched one man and his horse particularly, as he was an expert cowboy, and he had a most beautiful horse, well trained and highly intelligent. But even the best trained horse and the most skillful rider can never be absolutely safe in this dangerous work. And it was my unhappy fortune that day to see an ugly and vicious old steer catch this beautiful horse on the tip of his wicked horn and rip the horse open with an ugly tear from between his front legs extending up into the muscles of his neck. The rider maneuvered the wounded animal away from the angry steer, and saved both himself and the horse from almost certain death. They thought the horse was so badly hurt he would have to be shot, but were going to wait a few days to see if he might possibly recover. It was remarkable, however, that very few accidents occurred, considering the dangerous work that was being done and the reckless abandon with which the cowboys rode into the excited herd.

"At noon we all went to the chuck wagons and were handed a tin plate, a fork, and a spoon. Since my husband and I were guests, the cook brought our food to us; but all the others went to the pot and dipped out their own beans. It was a wonderful dinner — barbecued meat, baked potatoes, frijole beans, canned fruit, pie, and hot coffee. Nothing seems to add zest to a meal quite so much for cowboys as a bawling, dust-caked herd of cattle, the smell of burning hide and hair, and the acrid odor of sweating men and horses." (Reminiscences.)

Following the Bloomington meeting, Tant went next to Cheyenne, Oklahoma, where a once-faithful congregation had now ceased to exist. He reported:

"From Bloomington I went to Cheyenne, to preach the gospel to the people there. We once had a congregation at Cheyenne, but long since had they ceased to keep house for the Lord. Cheyenne presents many interesting thoughts to me. It is on the battleground where General George A. Custer in December, 1876, surprised a band of Indians, and had the famous battle in which fifteen hundred horses and three hundred Indians, and a few soldiers were killed. As I walked over the battle field and secured an old canteen for the J. Robert Norvell Museum, I thought: How different my mission from that of General Custer! It has been only three years since the last Indian outbreak at Cheyenne, in which eighty-four warriors swept down on the town to take 'Red Tom' (a Texas ranger) out of jail to murder him, because he had killed an Indian brave the day before. Many still fear the Indians around Cheyenne; many are living without fear of them; and some are hoping that the United States soldiers will be drawn off to fight Spain, which will leave the Indians without fear, thus causing them to make an outbreak, and this, in turn, will give the citizens an opportunity and an excuse to annihilate the whole race. Almost all Indian fighters claim that that is the only way the Indians will ever be civilized." (Gospel Advocate, June 9, 1898.)

From Cheyenne Tant returned to Bloomington for a twelve days debate with a Methodist, named Smith. He did not know what the six propositions were going to be until he got to the place where the debate was to be held; but this did not worry him as he said, "I am ready to affirm anything a Methodist will deny, as a Methodist, or to deny anything a Methodist will affirm, as a Methodist."

The debate began on May 9, and passed off very pleasantly. Smith was far above the average Methodist preacher of the day in his ability, and made much ado about the wording of the six propositions. He refused to let his opponent affirm "immersion" as baptism, but was adamant in demanding that he affirm "dipping" — which Tant did. One amusing incident marked the discussion, a story that was to follow Tant the rest of his days. Smith had argued that Jesus was sprinkled by John the Baptist, and of necessity had to be, since the Jordan was only a trickle of water at the place of the baptizing, and in the summer time ceased to flow altogether. It was so small, in fact, he said, that "a man could dam it up with his foot, and stop the flow of water entirely, even in the rainy season!"

To this Tant replied: "Brethren and friends, I have travelled from one end of this nation to another, and have seen many marvellous sights in it. I have always had a desire to travel around the world and behold the glories and grandeurs of ancient cities and far places. I have a longing to travel to the country where my Lord lived and died, to stand in old Jerusalem and view the city o'er. I have wanted to visit ancient Egypt, and see the great pyramids and the mighty Nile River. But there is now one thing I'd rather see than all these other mighty wonders combined. There is one sight which I believe would be more awesome, more marvellous, more wonderful than all the seven wonders of the world. Brethren, I want just one time in my life to catch a glimpse of that foot that could dam the Jordan River!"

After the debate several Methodist women brought a big bouquet of roses and put them in Smith's arms (to which Tant commented: "That's right, Sisters; we always decorate the dead with flowers"), and pinned a huge blue ribbon on him. Upon seeing the blue ribbon, Tant got to his feet and made a little speech:

"Ladies and Gentlemen, when I was a young man we used to always have a State Fair every fall. Farmers would bring in their hogs, their mules, their cows and chickens to compete for the blue ribbon. Now in these competitions a jack or a stud or a bull would always be judged in good part by the quality of his colt or his calf. Since I have made no stand along that line in this community, I consider myself not in competition with this good Methodist preacher. But apparently he is well known in Bloomington, and the Methodist sisters feel that he deserves the blue ribbon."

There was an awesome silence — for there had been three illegitimate babies born to ladies in the community that year. And, whether rightly or wrongly, the Methodist pastor was reported to have had more than a nodding acquaintance with at least two of the unhappy mothers.

Tant preached three or four days at Mangum, then loaded his family up in the hack and struck out for El Reno, which was about a hundred miles to the east, very near to the Indian Reservation. He preached in Cameo, nine miles out in the country, for a week, having a very good attendance. One day he took Nannie out to the Reservation and stopped in front of a tepee. Nannie saw a squaw with a papoose on her lap. The old squaw was picking something from the head of the infant, and putting it between her teeth. Nannie asked her husband what the squaw was doing, and Tant told her she was "de-lousing" the baby. Whether this was so, or whether her husband was teasing her, Nannie never knew. But she was much intrigued by other things she saw on the reservation. She wrote:

"The government at that time gave the Indians an allotment of beef at stated times — I believe every two weeks. The day for their allotment came while we were there. It was interesting to watch these people in their savage way tear the raw meat with their teeth and seem to relish it. They appeared to have a particular fondness for the intestines of butchered animals. All the squaws and papooses would seat themselves in a circle, while one big buck stood in the middle of the enclosure with a piece of intestine in his hands. He would give this a sling around his head and throw it, much in the manner of a cowboy throwing a lasso, holding one end of it and aiming the other at one of the people in the circle. This one would catch it, and take a bite out of it while all the others grunted and howled. Then he would turn loose his hold on the intestine, and the big buck would start the performance all over again, this time aiming the whirling intestine toward another. Thus the game went on and on until all that particular intestine was eaten, after which another was brought, and the process began again." (Reminiscences.)

Tant's impression of the settlers in Oklahoma was very good, but he, too, was not very optimistic as to the future civilization of the Indians. He describes his trip to Oklahoma in a series of five articles, entitled "In Oklahoma", in which he says, in part:

"About one-third of the people in Greer County live in dug-outs, that is they dig a hole in the ground as large as they desire, put lumber over the top, and then cover it with about five inches of dirt. They thereby have a cool house in summer and a warm home in winter. The traveler may see a little mound, with five or six children sitting on top of it looking at him. He may know a happy family lives below. Another hindrance to those from the East is the strong wind. Some days the wind blows so hard all day long that it is impossible to walk or to drive a buggy against it. Such was true the first Sunday of my meeting, but a house full of people got to church before the wind began blowing hard, and after they got there, no one could leave; so the brethren took out their horses and braced their wagons and buggies by tying the wheels together so they could not blow away. We had a good time, much dinner, and three sermons that day." (Gospel Advocate, May 19, 1896.)

While in the meeting at Cheyenne, Tant not only visited the battlefield, but also went down to Hammond, where the government had an Indian school and agency. He was not very happy with what he found there:

"The Cheyenne Indians have allotments in that part of one hundred and sixty acres each of as fine land as can be found in the United States. They cannot sell it for twenty years yet, so the land will not be cultivated till after that time. It will then be sold for a trifle to white men and become a prosperous country. At the agency I found two Indian camps, with from three hundred to five hundred Indians in each camp. One camp was led by Chief White Shield; the other by Chief Howling Wolf. They live in tepees, or cone-shaped tents, wear blankets, eat terrapins, rabbits, and dogs; and spend their time in hunting and fishing. They will not work, and have no love for civilization. At the agency I found a small school house, about twelve by fourteen feet, being made of boards, which cost about $15.00, where white children go to school and pay for their schooling, while their fathers were working hard nearby to get a few clothes for them to wear and something for them to eat. Half a mile farther, I found the government school building for the Indians, which cost $13,000.00, with all modern improvements for a first-class college, where two hundred children can find ample room with plenty of books and plenty of clothes (all given by the government) with five or six teachers and directors to control the same. All are paid by the government. There are thirty-one Indian children in school, and I learned from the matron they did remarkably well to get that many to attend. She told me that she had been teaching among the Indians for eight years, and nine-tenths of all who are educated returned to their wild life, wearing blankets, living in tepees, and avoiding civilization after they were out of school. It seems that the teachers of the Indians realize that the only good coming from the government schools for the Indians is to give employment to teachers who direct the schools. No nation can be civilized who will not work. These Indians will not work as long as the government feeds and clothes them; therefore we look for no civilization among them as long as this keeps up. If the Indians were not allowed more than two or three farms together, and let the whites settle among them and work, then let the Indians work or starve, they might, in the course of time, be civilized and Christianized, but they can never be under the present management. I have heard of some converted Indians, but in my travels among them for three years, I have failed to find one." (Gospel Advocate, June 9, 1898.)

IV

In this spring of 1898, the United States found herself at war with Spain. This had a disastrous effect on the interest and zeal of the churches. There had been no general war since the Civil War of a generation before, and the whole nation was swept into a frenzy of emotion by the blowing up of the U.S.S. Maine. This aroused both Christians and non-Christians. Tant contrasted this carnal war with the fight that might have been made if the same energies and wealth were put into preaching the gospel. He wrote:

"For two months carnal war has existed between Spain and the United States, two hundred thousand men have been called into service, and about two hundred million dollars already used, with an estimate that it will take eight hundred million dollars to carry on the war this year . . . . .

"But is this war the work of God or of the devil? If the work is of God, then all are doing God's service to fight in this war; if of the devil, all are serving him who uphold the same.

"In the Christian age we are taught that our weapons are not carnal. The prophet foretelling the Christian age said we should not lift up sword against nation; neither should we learn war anymore. Christ taught that under the former age it was an eye for an eye, a tooth for a tooth; but under this dispensation we should not render evil for evil or avenge ourselves, for 'vengeance is mine, saith the Lord'. Yet we can well say that all this expenditure and loss of life comes under the head of a strict violation of God's word. It is all to avenge the lives of two hundred and sixty men

lost on the Maine. Better would it be to suffer wrong
than to do wrong. While it seems bad to make a comparison between God's work and the devil's work, yet
if the children of God were able to call two hundred
thousand men into actual service for one year, and
devote but two hundred million dollars to preach the
gospel, we could send twenty thousand preachers, with
enough money on hand to keep them preaching for
twenty years at a salary of five hundred dollars each
per year. At the close of this twenty years' preaching, the greater part of the Cubans would be fed,
clothed, and converted to Christianity, and almost all
of Spain would be our friends and brethren, instead
of our enemies; neither would there be so many
widows, nor heart-broken wives and mothers, nor
would there be so many immoral men and women as
shall be found when this war is over.

"In Texas I have been doing the work of an evangelist for fourteen years. For ten years I have received
from ten to fifty calls for meetings more than I could
hold. During the past four years, ending June 20,
1898, I received one hundred and twenty calls for meetings above what I could hold. This year I received
only one call from a congregation in Texas for a meeting, and only a few calls from remote communities,
where they have no congregations, and where they
five too far from town to get the daily papers.

"I have spent most of the year in Oklahoma, as I
find the war craze has not been so great there as in
Texas. Thinking I would have my usual number of
calls for meetings this year as in bygone years, I wrote
a dear young brother in Tennessee, one of our ablest
young preachers, about the work in Texas, and of some
points where I would like for him to preach if he could
come. He wrote me to arrange the meetings. I sent
out letters to sixty-seven congregations, to ask if they
would cooperate with this brother in a meeting. About
one-fourth wrote me they had already made arrangements, one-half were not interested enough to write,
and the other one-fourth wrote: 'Can't tell; no interest here; nothing but war. Don't think the brethren

will hold a meeting this year'. I then thought I would try the preachers, to find out how the war was going on in their parts. I sent out twelve letters to preachers, and learned from them all that war was the order of the day, and Christianity had been driven back." (Gospel Advocate, July 14, 1898.)

Following the Cameo meeting, Tant headed his family homeward. He stopped first at Minco, a little settlement about midway between El Reno and Chickasha. Here he visited the El-Meta Christian College, which he describes as a "mixed school of the highest order, for girls and boys." Of this school he says:

"I found it successfully managed by Sister Meta Chestnut. I learned from her that this school has passed the danger mark of failure, and the prospects of a fine school are now brighter than ever. Board and tuition are so reasonable that I think our brethren of Oklahoma should have at least one hundred boys and girls in the El-Meta Christian College every year instead of sending them to the three or four months' school in the country. I hope many of our boys and girls of the Indian Territory will write Sister Meta for terms, and be ready to enter the next school term there.

"I learned that Brother D. T. Broadus, from Kansas, was preaching for them at Minco, and that they were still satisfied with the Lord's way.

"From Minco we continued south to Cleburne, Texas, and there saw we had been from home seventy-three days; we had traveled in the hack one thousand two hundred miles, and I had been able to speak to the people at eighty different times, and our baby was fifty percent better than when we started.

"Cleburne is one hundred miles from our home, but wife, who can do almost anything, who is one of the grandest women on earth and a preacher's wife from every standpoint, agreed to take the three small children and drive the other hundred miles alone, thus enabling me to come back to my work. There we parted, she to go home, and I to come back to Oklahoma." (Gospel Advocate, July 7, 1898.)

V

Tant's comment on his wife's character as a helper in his work was not unique. Scores of preachers and other brethren visited in the home in Hamilton, and all of them were impressed by the way in which she managed things in his absence. John E. Dunn of Rucker, Tennessee, held a meeting in Hamilton soon after Nannie Tant brought her brood back from the long Oklahoma trip. Dunn got sick during the meeting, and had to postpone further preaching for several days. He stayed in the Tant home. Of that experience he wrote:

"Sister J. D. Tant met me in town and took me to her home, where I stayed and made her house my home while in Hamilton. Her husband, J. D. Tant, is away from home almost all the time preaching the gospel. Sister Tant, with three little children, goes on cheerfully, trusting in God, managing the home affairs, and training the children. I believe she is as patient and faithful as any woman I ever saw, teaching her children the word of God, and to be obedient to their parents and to God; moreover, any one can know by being in company with their children a short time that they are receiving Christian training. Their little boy, Ira, seven years old, I thought was one of the smartest little boys about home I had seen on my travels. He seems as faithful and painstaking as a thoughtful man to help his mother. I was much pleased to see him go out on the prairie after the horses and cows, hitch horses to the hack or buggy, help milk, go to town for his mother, bring in stove wood, and do dozens of other chores; in fact, it would appear to an observer that he and his mother are partners running the farm. Sister Tant is a true Christian mother, who believes one part of her life work is to train her children for usefulness in the service of God while in this world, and for a home in heaven after life is over." (Gospel Advocate, November 17, 1898.)

The Tants' visit to Oklahoma "for the baby's health" was one that Nannie never forgot. She was particularly impressed by the wildness of the country, its great expanse of grass covered prairie stretching to the horizon, the primitive way the people had to live, the ever blowing wind, the sand, the Indians — but particularly the people. She wrote:

"It was Sunday morning. We were all dressed and ready to go to church. Sister Caver remarked, 'It looks like we are going to have a sand-storm today.' I could see nothing unusual in the elements, so thought little of her remark. I had never been in a sand-storm. Our meeting place was a small box-like structure in the country. My husband was up preaching when the wind struck. It came with such a burst of fury that he was compelled to stop, for the people could not hear. Except for the cloud of dust, the heavens were clear. All we could do was to keep our seats and wait for the wind to subside, as no team of horses could have pulled a wagon against such a force; and no person could breathe long in such a sand laden atmosphere. Maidia, my baby, was suffering from asthma, and the dust was almost more than she could bear, even though I kept her head covered all the time. There was a dwelling house about one hundred yards away. I thought if I could take the baby there, perhaps she could breathe easier. We could not see the house, but one of the ranchers said he would help me over to it. After wrapping up the baby, head and all, I took her in my arms and we started. The man was large and strong, and I was small, which, I am sure was to his advantage. He walked behind me with both hands on my shoulders, and literally pushed me through the blinding sand-storm to the house. I was wearing a pretty felt hat with a long ostrich plume on it. The wind took it from my head and I saw it disappear in the distance, quickly swallowed up by the blinding dust. I felt sad for it was the hat I had bought for my marriage.

"We had no sooner reached the house than we saw the barn on fire. We were all frightened for a few minutes, thinking it might blow the flames against the house, but the wind was so strong that even the flames could not survive, and the barn quickly burned to the ground without any flame reaching near to the house.

"It was about the middle of June that we started homeward from Oklahoma. One place we were water bound and had to spend a week in a dug-out with a rancher. He was a very wealthy cattle owner, had no idea how many thousands of head he did own, but had never even given thought to building a house. He had two large rooms, underground, covered over with straw and dirt. It leaked, and everything we had got wet.

"This rancher had a grass-widowed daughter whom I shall never forget. Her proportions were enormous; she must have weighed every bit of two hundred and thirty pounds, and was not over five feet three inches tall. She wore a number seven shoe. While I could see no sign of any other inhabitant in that country for miles in every direction, that charming widow went to a dance somewhere every night. Her escort, the same one each night, came about dark. He was tall and angular, about six feet four, I would guess. It would be hard to determine which was the more pointed, his nose or the spurs that jingled, jangled on his boots. His trousers hung rather loosely from his hips, while the bottom of each leg hung on the top of his boots on the inside while the outside hung lower. He wore a blazing red necktie, and around his waist he carried the customary cartridge belt with a holstered pistol swinging from his hip. The two of them would squeeze into a topless buggy, drawn by a couple of half-broken bronchos, and away they would speed over that level country in a way that would have made Jehu blush for envy. They would return in the small hours of the morning, but that bucking woman seemed never to need sleep. Long before I felt like rising in the morning, I would hear her in the kitchen (the other room of the dug-out) rattling the pots and pans, and getting the breakfast ready, always keeping time with her foot and patting her hands as she shuffled about the room, singing under her breath, and bouncing, jiggling, and dancing as she worked. She was indeed a 'merry' widow.

"The high water went down and we were glad to resume our journey. We came to the Red River, getting there about twilight. The ferryman was gone, so we had to sleep on the Indian (Oklahoma) side of the river that night. I had only one or two quilts or blankets in the hack, which I used to fix up the little ones as comfortably as I could. Then my husband and I took a cushion from the hack as a pillow, the river gravel as a mattress, and the stars of heaven as our canopy, sleeping there until morning. Or, to be more accurate, my husband slept. I watched for old Geronimo. He had been captured in the West and brought to a reservation in Oklahoma. Everybody was in fear for quite a while that he would break forth and lead another wild Indian uprising against the whites.

"When daylight came the ferryman returned to his work, and soon carried us across the river. We had no food for breakfast, and drove all morning and until two o'clock in the afternoon before finding any kind of habitation. Finally, we came to a house; the lady there prepared us a meal, and we spent the night with her. The next day we drove to Bowie, Texas. There one of our horses was too exhausted to travel further, so my husband put me and the two little girls on the train and sent us on to my mother's at Grandview. He remained in Bowie for a day or two while the horse rested, then he and Ira drove on to Cleburne. Because of the slow trip from Oklahoma, he could not go on home to Hamilton, another one hundred miles, with us, as he had to get back to his next appointment. So he put me and the three children in the hack and sent us homeward, while he went on to preach. I drove to my brother's house and spent the night with them. He was furious to see me attempt such a dangerous

trip alone, so quit his work and drove me home."
(Reminiscences.)

This experience helped confirm the Yater family in their
initial unfavorable estimate of Tant as a companion for
Nannie, but apparently affected her not at all except to
bind her even more closely to the man she had chosen.
Whatever his attraction for her may have had or not had,
one of its strongest aspects was unquestionably Nannie's
fervent zeal for the cause of Christ. All the hardships
and sacrifices she endured with and for her husband were
added up, in her thinking, to sacrifices for the cause of
Christ. Her husband had dedicated his life to the preaching of the gospel; she regarded him as one of the greatest
and most able preachers she had ever heard; all she could
do, little or much, to help and encourage him in that work,
to relieve him of anxieties at home, to lighten his burden
in even the slightest degree, to endure with no feelings of
personal mistreatment at all, but rather with joy the hardships of the life she had to lead — these things were the
very essence of a happy marriage so far as she was concerned. Her religion and her marriage were so closely
intertwined that it would be hard to tell the one from the
other. Thus she was supremely happy in sharing the poverty, the arduous work, the physical sufferings of forty-
five years of marriage with J. D. Tant; for in serving him
she was also serving the Lord.

Hamilton, Texas, 1900. Nannie, standing; Ira in rear; Davis in foreground; Zoretta in high chair; and Maidia in her father's lap.

CHAPTER XII

PREACHING IN NASHVILLE

On August 15, 1898, Tant sent in a news report date-lined at Dickson, Tennessee:

"I have closed my first meeting in Tennessee, at Bellview, five miles from this place, where there was a large turnout. I preached the gospel straight and 'comforted' the brethren. The Methodists ran an opposition meeting part of the time, and gave an ice cream supper. But none of this detracted from the meeting. Some of the Methodists got on the warpath. They longed for R. H. Pigue to meet me and show that we were wrong and they were right. So propositions were submitted for me to meet Mr. Pigue at that place, December 12. If this suits them, and no crawfishing is done, by the help of God I hope to meet him then. Brothers Jim Dunn, Gus Dunn, and Logan have preached much in this section. I learned that they are noble young men and grand gospel preachers. May God bless them in their work. There were thirty-nine additions at Bellview, thirty-one being baptized and eight reclaimed. I go next to Bellbuckle." (Gospel Advocate, August 25, 1898.)

On his way to Tennessee from Hamilton he had stopped at Golden Lake, Arkansas, in Mississippi County, for a meeting which was almost rained out. Brother G. G. Taylor of Louisville, Kentucky, had just closed a meeting there with seven additions; Tant remained for fifteen days (and it rained steadily for eight of the fifteen), and felt he had accomplished very little. He declared, "At Golden Lake we have only about thirty members. About ten of them seem to be Christians in faith and practice; the others impressed me as being Christians in faith, but very little practice."

On this Tennessee visit Tant had opportunity to come
in contact with about twenty-five gospel preachers ——
Lipscomb, Elam, Sewell, Brents, and others — and says
that he found only one preacher among them all who was
committed to the society and the organ. He was much
impressed by the unity and harmony prevailing in Tennessee, and by the zeal of the brethren in standing for the
truth and opposing error:

"As to the things which have divided the churches
in Texas, I find they have but little hold in Tennessee.
The organ is seldom mentioned, and many of the brethren were surprised to learn that our brethren in Texas
had departed after such things. Missionary societies,
which have caused so much damage and trouble and
division in Texas, are but little known in Tennessee.
The thousands of members of the church of Christ in
this state and the hundreds of missionary preachers
who have built up the cause and established congregations in almost all towns independently of society
influence are a living demonstration of the falsity of
the old cry in Texas that we will be a failure outside
of 'organized' missionary work. In fact, organized
missionary work in Texas has made its greatest reputation there by going into fields of labor built up by
opponents of missionary societies, and there introducing the organ, frequently after night, dividing the
church, driving out loyal members, taking the property from them, and appropriating it to build up a sister
church among the modern churches. Organized missionary work in Texas has never made its fight for
unoccupied fields in order to preach the gospel beyond,
but has made its greatest fight for church property
that has been built by the opposers of societies. Nine
times out of ten, if they succeed in getting the church
property by any means, they then make their bitterest fight.

"While I stand thoroughly committed on the subject
of baptism, and like Dr. Brents, Brother Hoover,
Brother Dunn, and others, believe that those coming

from denominations into the church of Christ should
be scripturally baptized, yet I am sure more good would
have been accomplished and greater love would now
exist on both sides if all writers on that subject had
been more patient and exercised more love for those
who differed from them and manifested more of the
spirit of Christ in discussing those points of difference.

"As to the subject of 're-baptism', so called, in Tennessee I learned that almost half the preachers I talked with, including such men as R. A. Hoover, Jim
Dunn, John Dunn, and others, preached with all earnestness baptism for the remission of sins; and claim
that it is the exception, rather than the rule, if any
sectarians are scripturally baptized. Many are doing
as old Brother Jesse Sewell did after he gave up Baptist doctrine, and are being baptized for the remission
of sins. They claim that if a man does not know any
more than to become a Baptist or a Baptist preacher,
he does not know enough to be scripturally baptized."
(Gospel Advocate, October 13, 1898.)

During the closing days of 1898, Tant held a rather
unusual meeting in Norman, Oklahoma. This meeting
lasted for four Sundays, and about it he wrote:

"At one time we had a large congregation at Norman — eighty members in all. Granville Jones, some
years ago, held a long meeting there, with many additions. He sowed the seed of discord, built a nice church
house, and left a general bad feeling among many of
the members. Many who had been loyal to the truth
went to other points; some quit; and some went to the
digressives, hoping that by tolerating innovations for
a time, they might convert them from the error of
their way. Along the line of reconciliation they
thought they were progressing well, until the Mormons, who were blowing W. R. Tony, an apostate from
the church of Christ, as a great debater, wanted some
one to meet him. The loyal brethren, to accommodate
the Mormons, made a mistake by sending for Clark
Braden. Braden came, and as soon as the Mormons
ran, he then set in to drive out the anti-organ and

anti-society element. As that element had sent for him, they then turned him over to the digressive element, who heard him gladly. They appreciated his work as much as the digressives in Texas did when they imported Braden to meet Joe Warlick — and then would not go to hear him, after the other side had furnished the house (at Dallas) to hold the debate. So, after the Braden controversy at Norman, the division became greater than ever; and it was by the fifty-four members who oppose innovations that I was invited to preach at Norman.

"We used the Adventist church house till our congregation over-filled it. I then went to the organ party and tried to borrow or rent their house to preach in. I told them plainly I would say nothing of their past trouble, but only desired to preach the gospel in their church house. They said plainly that I could not preach the gospel in their church house. Not to be discouraged, when men and women began to accept the truth, I went again to the same elders and pastor and asked permission to baptize in their baptistery some scripturally converted parties. But they said we could not baptize in their baptistery. The Baptists, however, kindly granted me the use of their baptistery. Of those who were baptized and took membership there were twenty-one.

"Brother J. A. Minton, once an able gospel preacher of Tennessee, but who became entangled with the society work some years past, was with me part of the time, and seemed greatly surprised and disgusted to think that the society element was so bitter against the gospel. I hope, and also believe, that Brother Minton will soon return to his first love, and let his power be felt in Oklahoma Territory as an able gospel minister." (Gospel Advocate, January 19, 1899.)

The meeting at Norman was the last for the year 1898. After it closed Tant traveled south to Sherman, then to Savoy, and Paris, where he preached one time at Lamar Street Church. Then home for Christmas.

II

With the close of 1898 Tant severed his connection with the Gospel Advocate as Field Editor. He makes a frank statement as to his reasons for the action:

"Brothers Lipscomb and McQuiddy: After four years of association with you as Field Editor of the Gospel Advocate, I now come to say, Farewell. So far as my connection with the Advocate family is concerned, it has been pleasant to me.

"It was generally understood when I became connected with the Advocate that I differed from them on sect baptism, and I still believe my position to be the only scriptural one held among us today. I never thought the difference that existed on the subject was great enough to cause the line of demarcation that has been so widely drawn by so many brethren. I think if all on both sides had cultivated more patience, exercised more love, shown a greater desire to teach than to carry their point, all might have loved each other more, been nearer together, and done greater good than we have done. This was the leading thought before me when I became connected with the Advocate. I saw there was a bitterness between the Firm Foundation and Gospel Advocate readers, which, I thought, the differences did not justify. As I was universally known among the Firm Foundation readers, and, perhaps loved by many, I thought my association with the Advocate would have a tendency to bring about a better feeling, and that we would learn to love as brethren, and not think of each other as enemies. As to the good I have done along this line, let others judge.

"Now, it may be asked why I quit the Advocate as Field Editor. To this I make the following reply:

"1. Paul says as we have different gifts, let us wait on our ministry. As a farmer and a preacher, I think I am a success; as an editor, I am a failure from every standpoint. And I am glad that during these four years I have learned the lesson that many like myself never learn; hence, I do not desire to go before the

people as 'Field Editor' when I do nothing to entitle
me to hold this position.

"2. Being released from the Advocate staff, I am
left at liberty to work as a contributor not only to
the Advocate, but to other good papers, and can reach
some by circulating one paper at certain places, and
another paper at other places, and try to impress upon
the brethren that almost all our papers are capable of
doing good so far as they teach the Bible, and that all
should be considered with love when doing good. We
should try to kill out the idea that 'our' paper is the
only paper; our editor, the only Bible editor, and we
only are right and all others are wrong. It is said of
us that we were once known by the Book we read, but
now we are known by the paper we read.

"3. In retiring as Field Editor of the Gospel Advocate, I hope it will be understood that my love for the
paper still remains the same. I have no unkind feelings for any editor on the paper, and shall continue
to contribute to the paper and encourage the circulation of the same as I have in bygone years. I shall
soon commence a series of lessons, twelve in number,
on 'What We Teach, And Why We Teach It', and hope
they will be read with profit by the young.

"4. In retiring from the Advocate, a word of warning to the brethren in Tennessee will, I hope, be in
order. At one time in Texas the Firm Foundation
stood as a mighty wall, with a great host of workers,
against all innovations. Almost all the brethren reported their meetings through said paper, each encouraged the other, all members knew what the others
were doing. But, unfortunately the paper craze struck
our state, and Brothers Nall, Parker, Taylor, Moyr,
Young, and Nichol, and perhaps others, launched forth
on the editorial wave. Few brethren were able to take
half the papers; their knowledge of the brotherhood
was cut to the small circle of the paper they read.
Some of these papers began to struggle against odds
for existence, and I fear the result is that we have not,
in all these papers, done the good we might have done
had all remained together and worked for the Founda-

tion as a strong state paper, contending for the faith of the gospel. I think one strong paper is worth more to build up a cause in a state than a half dozen small papers struggling for existence. I once thought differently, but observation has taught me a few things. I find the Advocate is to Tennessee what the Foundation is to Texas; and as it is already established and occupies the field for good, I hope all will try to preach the gospel through its channel in Tennessee; and not try to build up a half dozen more papers in the same field, to occupy the territory and do the same work the Advocate is doing.

"If, during my four years' work, I have said anything unkind or untrue of any man, I ask his forgiveness. As for the truth I have preached, I offer no apology, for I am sure it will stand." (Gospel Advocate, January 5, 1899.)

Brother J. C. McQuiddy in his "Miscellany" column in the same issue commented that, "We differ from Brother Tant on some points, but we are convinced of his honesty and sincerity, and wish him success in the gospel cause. While he resigns as field editor, he will still contribute to our columns, and his contributions may be looked for from time to time."

Actually, there seems to be no discernible difference in the work Tant did as field editor and the work he did after severing that relationship. He continued to write for the paper as much after resigning as he had written before, and in the first year after terminating his connection even had more articles published than he had in the previous year. Apparently he continued to do what he could to increase its circulation, sending in lists of subscriptions from nearly all his meetings.

III

In the spring of 1899, Tant preached for seven weeks in the city of Nashville, Tennessee, with a total of forty-five

baptisms and seven restorations. The first meeting was
at Carroll Street, where Joe McPherson, a mail carrier, was
serving as an elder, along with J. A. Rose and Owen Henry.
Tant was greatly impressed by the cooperative spirit he
found among the Nashville churches, and also expresses
himself on the "re-baptism" controversy:

"The zeal of the members of Carroll Street Church
soon took effect upon the surrounding congregations.
Brother J. G. Allen, who preaches for the Church of
Christ on Green Street, dismissed during our meeting,
and almost all of their members attended every service,
helping in song and prayer. Brother Moore, who
preaches at South College Street also began to dismiss
all meetings, and he and many of the members became
regular attendants and aided in the interest of the
meeting. We could note from ten to thirty preachers
in the congregation each night, willing to help in every
way.

"It was estimated that more than one hundred
preachers attended our series of meetings in Nashville.
Among Tennessee's noted preachers whom I call to
memory who attended were: F. D. Srygley, F. B. Srygley, F. W. Smith, J. W. Shepherd, J. R. Williams, L. R.
Sowell, W. L. Logan, S. R. Logue, J. W. Grant, James
Dunn, J. P. Grigg, R. W. Norwood, and many other earnest, godly preachers whose names I do not remember.
Added to all these, we also had in attendance David
Lipscomb and J. A. Harding, chiefs among sinners in
opposing the rebaptism hobby. One is now willing to
ask, 'Are you a rebaptist?' To this I answer as did
Paul to the charge of heresy, 'After the way which
they call heresy (rebaptism), so worship I the God of
my fathers, believing all things which are written in
the law and in the prophets,' for it has been generally
known for twelve years that I have been considered a
rebaptist of the rebaptists, even almost spatting with
A. McGary as to which should sit on the cow-catcher
of the hobby and get there first.

"Yes, I had the so-called 'rebaptism' for breakfast,
dinner, and supper; and in almost every sermon I told

where the church was when Alexander Campbell was
born, and impressed upon the people the necessity of
scriptural obedience, and that there was one church
(and only one), one Lord, one faith, and one baptism.
To all of these sermons, so far as I could learn, Brother Lipscomb and Brother Harding said 'Amen'. Some
one is ready to say: 'Harding and Lipscomb were converted and have given up Methodist and Baptist baptism'. No, brother; I want to say with due respect to
all, no one can give up a thing he never held to. I
found that Harding and Lipscomb condemned Methodist and Baptist baptism as bitterly as I do. Here is
where the great trouble has been and how the breach
has been greatly widened: we have tried to force those
brethren to accept and hold a position they have never
believed, neither do they advocate the same. Both
were as willing as I to affirm that baptism as held and
practiced by Baptists and Methodists is unscriptural;
but they claim that all Christians belonging to those
churches are in there through obedience to God's word,
not in obedience to the sectarian doctrine. In this
matter I thought these brethren inconsistent in their
practice, as I claim that Baptists and Methodists do
not mix enough truth with their doctrines to save any
one; but they thought I was extreme in not giving
Baptists and Methodists credit for the good they do.
In all these differences I am now convinced, as I have
been for a number of years, that had all on both sides
had more love, exercised more patience, and been more
careful in words that expressed our differences, the
bitterness, envy, and strife which have existed to a
great extent would have been unknown. Our differences have never been so great as our writings convey
to the world they are, when we understand one another
properly. While it is considered that Lipscomb and
Harding are extreme on the one hand, and I on the
other, yet, after my association with them, I think
they both love me more than before and I can truthful-
ly say that after having more knowledge of the zeal
and godliness and work of those dear brethren, my
love for them is far greater than ever in the past;
and I am sure that many who regard those brethren

today as enemies of the cause and not in accord with the word of God, are greatly mistaken." (Gospel Advocate, June 6, 1899.)

After the Carroll Street meeting was concluded, Tant moved to a big tent erected by the church on Scovel and North Spruce Streets. This meeting was much hindered by rain, the tent being partially blown down three different times. In spite of this, however, and in spite of the efforts of a nearby Presbyterian church and a Methodist church to hold opposition meetings, the crowds continued to come, so much so that Tant began to feel there were even too many there for the most effective work. He suspected some of them might be coming more for the excitement of the big crowd, and to hear the 'wild man from Texas' than because of their interest in the gospel. He wrote Nannie that he thought some of them were disappointed that he did not go into the pulpit wearing a six-shooter on each hip, and with spurs on his boots. It was during this stay in Nashville that Tant made some observations on the "located pastor" system, which he later reported in an article:

"From observations while in Nashville I found the majority of the brethren condemned what they termed 'pastoral preaching' — that is, one man to preach at the same place every Sunday — while most of them practiced the very thing they condemned; only, instead of having one man to preach for them regularly four times a month, they would have four different men, each one having his regular appointment and day to preach. I also found some preaching brethren who opposed regular preaching once a week at the same place, yet they practiced regular preaching at the same place once a month. So far as I am concerned individually, when it comes to principle, I cannot see the difference between a weekly and a monthly pastor. The same verse that teaches it is wrong to have a weekly pastor teaches it is wrong to have a monthly pastor and pay him so much for his work. Brethren, we sometimes get in the habit of condemning, and continue to condemn without ever stopping to think about the position we condemn. While I have ever been opposed to the modern sectarian idea of a pastor, yet when surroundings demand to have some godly man to labor all the time in word and doctrine at any desig- nated place to build up the Master's cause at that place, such is no more a violation of God's law for him to preach regularly once a week than it is for him to preach once a month, or once a year . . ." (Gospel Advocate, July 20, 1899.)

IV

There was one other aspect of this Nashville visit which was to interest Tant for the balance of his life: the Christian college. While he himself had had no opportunity for such an education, he had a deep and abiding interest through all his life in helping poor boys and girls, especially young preacher boys, to attend such schools. He personally gave money to, or paid tuition for, more than a score of young gospel preachers to help them get a start in school, and was as earnest in promoting the interests of the schools as any preacher in the land. In his later years he became especially fond of N. B. Hardeman, and was influential in turning many students to that school. His own daughter, Davis, was to attend Freed-Hardeman College, while his two youngest sons, Yater, and Austin, were to attend David Lipscomb College, the last named also attending Harding College and Abilene Christian College. Tant's interest in the schools, and his efforts in their behalf, caused him to write much on the subject. Keenly aware of his own lack of formal education, he always wanted to encourage others, and particularly his own children, to prepare themselves in every possible way in the classrooms. In the early 1930's G. C. Brewer wrote an article in the Gospel Advocate condemning the practice of young gospel preachers' graduating from various Christian col-

leges and then going on into denomination seminaries or
other graduate schools to get further training. Tant
promptly wrote his son, Yater, who was then a student in
the Louisville Presbyterian Theological Seminary, not to be
discouraged by Brewer's article, that while Brewer was
absolutely right in principle, and that it was a dangerous
and unwholesome practice for most young men to put themselves under sectarian and modernistic influences, he felt
that he, Yater, had sense enough and was well grounded in
the faith enough not to be made a fool of by going to a
Presbyterian school.

In the last two decades of his life, Tant came to look upon
the Christian colleges with considerable misgiving. This
was due not only to his fear that the colleges might be
leading the churches astray from the truth, but also to his
disgust with the attitude of so many churches in demanding "a preacher with a degree," and making the possession
of a college degree the one great desideratum of a preacher, the one supreme qualification, regardless of how good
the man might be otherwise, or how well or how poorly he
preached.

But in the early years of his ministry, he was not critical
at all of the schools as such, as his writing about the
Nashville Bible School clearly reveals:

"While in Nashville, I attended the Nashville Bible
School a number of times.

"Brother F. W. Smith of Franklin, Tennessee, was in
a meeting at the Bible School, and while I heard him
only in his practical talks to the church and to young
preachers, yet I heard enough to pronounce him one
of the safest gospel preachers, and one of the most
godly, consecrated men I ever saw. I cannot understand how any man could go astray under his teaching, and am sure any church would be greatly bene-
fitted by having him give them a series of lessons . . .

"But now to the Bible School at Nashville. Shall I

oppose its work, or shall I help to build it up? I have heard it argued that all Bible schools have been in the front in leading men from the original ground and intent of their organization:

"1. A. Campbell established a Bible School to help young men return to the primitive order of things, which was faithfully carried out for a number of years, and many godly Bible men went out from its walls; but it is claimed not a sound gospel preacher has gone out from Bethany during the past ten years.

"2. J. W. McGarvey started a school for the same purpose, and for a number of years opposed innovations; but long since his pen and voice ceased to move against them, and perhaps not half a dozen preachers have gone from McGarvey's school in the past ten years who oppose organs, missionary societies, and other modern inventions.

"3. Even Texas once had her 'Athens of the South' — Add-Ran College, the joy of J. A. Clark, and the pride of Texas. In those days from three hundred to five hundred Texas boys and girls received godly instruction from a corps of godly men and women; but long since Add-Ran ceased to inculcate the principles she once did. I have not heard of a sound gospel preacher (one who stands as we all stood in Texas before the apostasy of Homan, Clark, and others came) leaving Add-Ran College during the past six years. I have known several sound gospel preachers to enter Add-Ran, such as Ira Adams, McKissick, Simmons, and others opposed to all innovations, only to come out favoring all the modern inventions of men.

"Having these examples before us, some claim that the Nashville Bible School will do likewise, so it is wrong to encourage it now. Upon the same principle I can argue the churches at Jerusalem, Corinth, and Ephesus departed from apostolic grounds, and it would be wrong to encourage the building up of a Bible church now, seeing so many have apostatized . . ."
(Gospel Advocate, July 27, 1898.)

Returning from Tennessee to Texas in the summer of

1899, Tant held a number of "mission" meetings — at Osceola in Hill County, at Itasca, at McGowan Schoolhouse, ten miles east of West, Texas, ("here," he says, "I found more ignorance of the Bible, more prejudice against the truth, and more lies told on me than in any other place I have been lately") and then to Savoy, Texas, for a two-weeks' "meeting" with J. G. Weaver, Methodist. Weaver did not want to "debate", but was willing to enter into a "preach about" arrangement in which both he and Tant would preach on the same subjects.

Following the joint meeting with Weaver, Tant preached a few nights at Cooper, where he baptized two, then went to Elmore (Indian Territory) where for four days and nights he debated D. B. Ray of the "American National Baptist Flag." Ray claimed to have had seventy-five debates with the "Campbellites" — all of which he had most gloriously won. The Baptists told in advance of the discussion that it was becoming very, very difficult for their champion to find any Campbellite who was willing to debate him, as he invariably slaughtered them. The debate was a furious one. Tant early got Ray aroused to a white hot anger, and then relaxed and laughed at him. At the conclusion of the discussion, Tant offered to shake hands with Ray, but Ray refused. Tant then left a standing challenge for Ray to meet Joe S. Warlick at any place in the nation where the Baptists might want a debate. Ray had said he would never meet Tant again; so Warlick was named by Tant as the gospel preacher to meet Ray, since the Baptists had spread numerous stories to the effect that Warlick trembled at the though of meeting their champion.

Tant returned in the fall to Tennessee, where he held a meeting at Bellview, the place where he and R. H. Pigue had debated the previous year. He baptized fifteen during this meeting, and says he found the church in much better condition than it had been the year before. Singing was led by Brother Will Martin, whom Tant commends as one of the finest singers he had ever known. From Bellview Tant went next to White Bluff for a meeting. From this place he reports:

> "I am now in a meeting at White Bluff, and I find indifference, backbiting, envy, hatred, and covetousness are the controlling elements of the church here. I also find the devil has the upper hand with some of the members of this church." (Gospel Advocate, November 23, 1899.)

V

The winter of 1898-1899 was an unusually cold one, and Tant stayed home more than usual. He and Nannie were expecting their second child late in February, and with three children already on her hands, it was impossible for Nannie to do the things that needed to be done about the place. In February the baby came, a girl. She was not named at first, but some weeks later Tant wrote from Brownwood, where he was in a meeting, suggesting the name "Loreta." His penmanship, however, left much to be desired, and Nannie thought he had written "Zoreta." It was an unusual name and a pretty one, so without more ado the infant was dubbed "Zoreta," much to Tant's amusement when he came home a few weeks later. But the name was not changed. This baby was as dark as her sister was fair. Their features were much alike, only the coloring was different. One was a blond of the purest type — azure blue eyes, golden hair, and the fairest, pinkest skin a baby ever had; the other was dark in complexion, deep brown curly hair, and with dark, brown eyes. Tant was the father of eight children, three of them very, very blond, four of them completely brunette, and one (this writer) an "in-between" mixture of blonde hair and brown eyes.

For three weeks following the birth of Zoreta (which

took place on February 26, 1899) Tant stayed home. Then
he left for a meeting in Brownwood, Texas. He was there
three weeks, and had planned to come home briefly before
going on to his next meeting. He expected to come on the
train to Hico, then catch the mail hack on to Hamilton
some twenty-two miles away. The mail hack ordinarily
reached Hamilton about 5:00 o'clock in the afternoon.
Nannie tells the story of that particular day:

"I sent Ira to the post office in the buggy to meet
Papa while I would have supper warm on the table
when he came. The whole day had been blustery, with
heavy black clouds rolling back in the west. But
somehow it did not cast gloom on that day, and the
thunder did not seem so loud, for my husband was
coming, and when I could hide my face on his breast,
and feel his strong arms about me, no storm-cloud or
cyclone could ever worry me very much. With eager
eyes we watched the road for the buggy to come in
sight. At last, we caught a glimpse of it, coming
through the gate about half a mile from the house. I
lifted Davis and little Maidia up into my arms so they
could see the buggy that had Papa in it. They wanted
to go to meet him. I waited till the buggy was a bit
nearer the house, then let them start, while I kept my
vigil by Zoreta's cradle.

"The little girls were nearly to the buggy before
they realized that Ira was alone. Their Papa had not
come. Ira stopped and picked up his little sisters, then
drove on to the house. He had met the hack, but Papa
had not been on it. He had been thoughtful enough
to wait till the mail was up, supposing perhaps Papa
had written a letter, explaining why he had not come.
Sure enough, the letter was there; Ira brought it
home:

"Dearest Loved One:
   My heart is sad tonight because I must disappoint you to-
morrow. We are having the greatest harvest of souls here
I have seen for years. The house is crowded to capacity.
People are coming every night from ten to twenty miles in
wagons and buggies. A large number have already made the

'good confession', and many more seem interested. The brethren will not hear to closing the meeting now. Must continue over Sunday. Don't take it hard, dear. I think you are the grandest little woman in all the world to stay there and take care of my babies while I do my feeble best to try to save souls. If God wills, I'll be home Monday night. God bless you.

Worlds of love,
Your Husband" (Reminiscences.)

For once in her life Nannie gave way to her feelings, fell down on the bed and wept. That excited the children, and soon the three little girls were all crying at the top of their lungs. Eight year old Ira was too much of a man to shed tears, but kept choking them back, and finally spoke up, "Mama, I'm afraid to go to the barn to put up the buggy. It's so dark!"

Nannie sprang from the bed in consternation. She felt shame and self reproach for having weakened. Quickly taking Ira with her she went to the barn and put up the horse and buggy. Even before Ira and his mother reached the house on their return trip from the barn, the wind was beginning to blow with an increasing fury. Soon it became evident to even an inexperienced observer that this was a tornado. The heavy cloud had hung in the west for several hours; then suddenly it began to move — with the ominous funnel shaped finger reaching to the ground. This was a sign no Texan, and especially no West Texan, could misunderstand.

Rapidly gathering her little brood together, Nannie hurried to the storm cellar, a crude affair, some six feet deep, eight feet long, and about six feet wide. Tant had dug it himself, and had left shoulders or ledges all around about eighteen inches off the floor. On these projections he had placed several heavy planks. This was just in case the cellar flooded. In such event, anybody in the shelter could get up on the planks and stay out of the water.

By the time Nannie got the children inside, the water was

already nearing the planks. But fortunately she got everyone into the shelter, and managed to get the heavy door
shut before the full power of the cyclone struck. It was
devastating in its swath, but fortunately missed the house,
taking away only a few out buildings and sheds. It blew
out a few window panes, loosened a number of shingles,
and blew down some of the big trees and some fences.
Otherwise there was no damage.

CHAPTER XIII

"LIPSCOMB DID ME NO WRONG"

"For the past forty years the Gospel Advocate has been looked upon as a sound paper, and Gospel Advocate lovers and supporters are looked upon throughout the Union as those who love God and are striving to keep his commandments. In some particulars I have thought D. Lipscomb and the Gospel Advocate off on Bible doctrine, and on the same items they have thought me the same way; but notwithstanding these differences, I have always been treated with love and kindness by the Gospel Advocate, and cannot keep from being its friend, and desire to see it circulate a hundred-fold more than at the present.

"Yet I must confess the Gospel Advocate of late is bringing some strange things to my ears. Among the things that divide the churches, the Gospel Advocate has always placed societies, instrumental music, and the pastors as the greatest sins on the human side. Yet of late I find such notes as these in the Advocate: 'Hall Calhoun, former pastor at Franklin'; 'George Gowen, pastor at Franklin;' 'Brother Paul Slayden, pastor at Columbia;' 'W. L. Logan, pastor at Murfreesboro;' 'L. S. White, pastor at Gallatin.' Also I hear some of the Gospel Advocate staff claiming this pastor business is the foundation of all our troubles. As I am seeking for truth on this question, and know that sometimes we differ on words without a distinction of principles, I come seeking information on this subject, and ask for help to understand the same." (Gospel Advocate, July 5, 1900.)

These were the opening words of an article by J. D. Tant which focussed brotherhood attention for many months on the "pastor system." Tant propounded a number of questions, which were commented on by M. C. Kurfees in the

(229)

same issue. It was the custom of the Nashville churches for many years to have "monthly appointments" by four different men, (and a fifth in months having five Sundays) each man having his regular Sunday in the month to preach. While doing this, many in the city contended that it was wrong to have one man preaching regularly every Sunday for a congregation. Tant could see no difference in having one man do all the preaching, and having four men divide it up among themselves. If one man doing all the preaching made him a "pastor", then, he opined, four men doing the preaching would make each of them a "one-fourth pastor." If not, said he, why not?

Kurfees was quite complimentary of the courteous spirit and tone of Tant's article, and gave a lengthy comment on it, pointing out the Bible usage of the term "pastor," and showing that it is indeed a scriptural term, and the "pastor" has a scriptural place to fill. He said, "I must leave the **Gospel Advocate** itself to explain the particular use it has recently made of the term 'pastor', and I feel confident that its explanation will fully sustain its reputation for loyalty to the Book, which it has won during 'the past forty years'."

The explanation was not long in coming. R. H. Mc-Laurine carried a lengthy article in the paper two weeks later, taking full responsibility for the matter, and absolving all others. He wrote:

"Upon my own motion, I respectfully submit the following: I have been in the employ of the Gospel Advocate Publishing Company for about two years, and during this period have, the greater part of the time, written the personal matter which appears in the Miscellany page and edited the articles submitted for publication. For the use of the term 'pastor', in connection with the names of Brother Slayden, Brother Calhoun, and Brother Gowen, I accept the responsibility. Brother Lipscomb thought it was used so as to indicate no opposition to the 'modern pastor system', but I did not so intend to use it. I intended by its use what is usually intended by people, religious and otherwise, when they use the term; or in other words, I meant to refer to the brethren mentioned as 'pastors' of the churches at the places named. I used the term advisedly, for, from the information at hand, I believed each of them to be what is commonly called a 'pastor'. If 'pastor' is a misnomer for those brethren filling like places and doing similar work, then by what name shall we call them? It is not sufficient to say they disclaim the name. So far as the brethren named are concerned, I do not think they would engage in that which they believed to be wrong; nevertheless, I believe they sustain a relation to the churches for which there is no divine warrant, whether it be called 'pastor' or something else."

This was a controversy which was not to leave the pages of brotherhood periodicals for many, many years. David Lipscomb wrote at length on the subject over a period of two decades. Tant had little more to say about it, having once broached the subject and called it to general attention. He had made his position clear in that very first article, indicating that he saw no scriptural objection to an evangelist working with one church so long as proper relationship was understood and maintained. His objection to the "modern pastor" was not that such a man preached regularly with one congregation, but that he assumed the oversight and directed the affairs and work of the congregation. He thought there was grave danger in the arrangement, due to the laziness of most congregations in not doing the work they should, and gradually shifting more and more of it to the shoulders of the preacher — almost making him a 'pastor' by default. But if a church was willing to support a gospel preacher, and keep him busy all his time in preaching the gospel, both publicly and privately, then such could scripturally be done, and should be done. This position through thirty years of controversy has gradually come to be generally accepted among the churches.

II

The Tant-Oakley debate in West Nashville began on June 11, 1900. It was to stir up quite a bit of controversy in Nashville, which would not subside for many months. John T. Oakley had debated a number of gospel preachers, and had a rather unsavory reputation for dealing unfairly, and striving for advantage and victory rather than truth. His tactics had become such that even many of his own brethren felt it was unwise for the Baptists to use him in discussions. But during Tant's meeting on North Spruce Street in late May and early June, the Baptists had become so aroused that they had challenged Tant for a debate; and friends of Oakley had managed to get him the endorsement of the Baptists as their champion.

The debate attracted huge crowds, and tension ran high. The Gospel Advocate had carried two or three announcements of the discussion in advance of it, but gave no report of it when it was concluded. This was taken by the Baptists (and some brethren) to mean that the Advocate brethren had been disappointed in Tant's work, and did not feel that he had maintained the truth in the discussion. The Baptist and Reflector carried a lengthy report of the discussion, making wild charges against Tant, and claiming that the "Campbellites" had been utterly routed. The editor of that journal reported:

"Brother Oakley was champion not only of the Baptists, but of Methodists, Presbyterians, and all who believe in the simple, old-fashioned gospel of salvation by grace through faith. This he preached with remarkable plainness and earnestness, and he had the sympathy of everyone in the community, with the exception of the 'Campbellites'. Of one thing we feel sure: Campbellism is dead in that community for years to come."

Brethren were not slow in letting Lipscomb know their displeasure at the Advocate's failure to carry any report of the "victory" they felt Tant had won. Lipscomb gave an explanation:

"A brother writes to know why there was no mention of the Tant-Oakley debate in the Gospel Advocate last week, while the Baptist and Reflector crowed so lustily over it. These debates with Oakley, Whitlock, Estes, and others, have become so frequent of late that we could only announce them. Brother Srygley, Brother White, Brother Pullias, Brother Byrd, and others have frequently met them in discussion within the past few months. This discussion, as the others, was several times announced in the Gospel Advocate. None of the writers for the Gospel Advocate attended the discussion. Most of them were away from home. I have not been out at night for several months. Brother Tant or any of these brethren mentioned can easily maintain the truth with these men. Indeed, in the discussions, these men really make no effort to maintain Bible truth, but to trap their opponents and create a laugh. Numbers attend, and a preacher of the gospel who will not be led off by them has an opportunity to teach the truth to those willing to learn it.
"The first man attending this debate that spoke to me of it is a Baptist. He said Oakley was not meeting Tant's arguments. He noted the scriptures used by each, and after attending through the debate, still says Tant 'downed' Oakley. Some brethren who heard him did not approve of some of Tant's positions. He took the rebaptism position, which they think a partisan view, and that he suffered from it in the debate. All whom I have heard speak of it condemn severely the personalities and coarseness brought into the discussion. So far as I have learned, Oakley led, but both indulged in it. This tends to bring discussions and the Christian religion itself into reproach . . ." (Gospel Advocate, June 28, 1900.)

This article by Lipscomb led to a stinging reply by Folk, editor of the **Baptist and Reflector**; and this, in turn, caused Lipscomb to write a two page editorial exposing the tactics of Folk in all his editorial work. Meanwhile, some brethren had been trying to stir Tant up against Lipscomb, but without too much success. Letters from his Texas friends commended him for teaching the truth on the "rebaptism" question, and were harshly critical of Lipscomb for not backing Tant in the debate, and for not reporting it in the **Advocate**. His long-time and intimate friend, A. J. McCarty, was one of those who wrote.

> 1008 West 10th St.
> Austin, Texas
> July 12, 1900

Dear Brother Tant:

I read with much interest your piece, "Who Will Help?" in the July 10th issue of the F.F. I was indeed glad to hear this from you, and I now congratulate you and do it in good faith. Coming from you, it will have a good effect and influence for the cause and for the paper.

I also saw your article in the **Advocate** on the "Pastor System", to which Kurfees replied. I am sure you are right in your opposition to this "pastor" business. The **Gospel Advocate** is raising and educating a lot of men who are semi-digressive, and some turn to the digressives out-right. There is only one place for us to stand, and that is flat-footed for the truth — God's word. And that means opposition to error in all its forms.

I was glad to hear that in your debate in Nashville with Oakley you took a square and firm stand for the whole truth, and condemned sect baptism, even if old Brother Davey et. al. were against you.

If you reply to Kurfees, I hope you will come out strong and make a good fight for the truth. I will read your written discussion with Brother Harding with much interest, and hope it will do much good.

Write more and oftener for the F.F., and do all you can to increase its circulation, for you are a good solicitor. I suppose you are at Lott now in a meeting, but am not sure, so will send this to Hamilton, and your wife can forward to you. I trust you will have good success in all your meetings. We have some excellent brethren at Lott. Give them my love. I have work booked till the middle of November. My next meeting is at San Marcos, and begins the last of this week. Pray for me and mine. Wife and mother join me in Christian love to you, Sister Tant, and the children.

Your Brother in the one faith,
A. J. McCarty.

McCarty was in Austin when he wrote this letter. It is apparently obvious that he had been in consultation with A. McGary about Tant's work in Nashville, for the very day after McCarty mailed his letter, McGary also wrote Tant:

Austin, Texas
July 13, 1900

Dear Bro. Tant:

Although I am in the midst of many duties today, preparing for a trip into Blanco and Hayes Counties to hold some meetings, I feel like appropriating a little time to express my congratulations and good wishes for you in the bold, brave stand you took in your Nashville debate with Oakley.

I have seen nothing of it save Bro. Lipscomb's meager mention of it, but from what he said I know you took a flat-footed stand for the whole truth. It seems strange to me that a man like Lipscomb would allow his prejudice against the truth on the baptismal question to restrain him from giving a fair account of the debate. But such is life — or, rather, such is the spirit possessing many men.

Again, I wish to assure you that I duly appreciate your words in the F.F. about your intention to do what you can to assist in building it up and enlarging its field of usefulness.

I tell you, that in a short while I am going to open
the most earnest canvass and campaign that I have
ever undertaken to widen the field of the paper's
work, and I will be glad indeed to have your cooperation in the good work. And unto this end I would be
glad to meet you and have a long talk with you. I
am to begin a meeting at Cleburne the first Lord's
day in August. Should you be near there during the
progress of that meeting, I would be pleased to have
you drop in, for I would like to talk with you. But it
may be that you will not be in that part of the country
during that time. If not, I hope we may find it convenient to meet sometime between this and the 1st of
September.

In conclusion I desire again to assure you of my
kindly feelings toward you, and my wishes for your
welfare.

Yours for the truth

A. McGary

Letters like these two embarrassed Tant. He received
scores of them, from brethren (particularly Texas preachers) whom he had known and loved for years. He felt
humbly grateful for their love and confidence, but he
thought they were being unfair to Lipscomb. He was fearful that in their loyalty to him, and their suspicion of Lipscomb on the baptismal question, they might be injuring the
unity of the church as a whole. He was passionately eager
to heal the breach that had existed between the Firm Foundation and the Gospel Advocate, and had worked for four
years as a Field Editor of the Advocate with that very
thing in mind. He regarded the loyal defense of his Texas
brethren as a threat to whatever progress might have been
made toward developing better spirit between the two sides.
So he wrote an article about the Oakley debate:

"For some time I have been watching Brother Lipscomb's spat with the Baptists over my debate; and

having received several letters about the same, I now make a few statements for the benefit of all:

"1. Lipscomb did not treat me unkindly, as some think, about not reporting the debate. He was not there. No one sent up a report of the debate; and then it is no honor to the Gospel Advocate to have any debate reported in it with John T. Oakley.

"2. Lipscomb did me no wrong in publishing his regret over personalities in the debate. I deplored such, and pleaded with Oakley and his moderator for two days not to use them; but to no avail. So I went down after him; and as no man can kill a polecat without smelling bad, neither can one meet Oakley without stooping to his low order to expose the same.

"3. Lipscomb is not my enemy, neither did he make a thrust at me on my position on rebaptism.

"John T. Oakley claimed (a) that he had converted two people at some town; (b) they both confessed that God for Christ's sake had forgiven their sins; (c) they were both baptized because of remission of their sins. Then Oakley said that Elder E. A. Elam went to that town and took them into the Church of Christ. He asked me if they would be saved. I told him plainly persons having such conversion, experience, and baptism, would go to hell, and Elam did wrong in accepting such into the church.

"Brother J. W. Grant and others, I hear, became offended by my taking such a position; but I still feel sure I was right. While Lipscomb, Harding, and I differ on those things I love them both. I do not think I have better friends in Nashville; and I feel sad to think some believe we cannot differ and still be brethren. So much on Lipscomb.

"As to John T. Oakley, he is below the ordinary as a debater. He does not regard his word like J. N. Hall and W. A. Jarrel, and other Baptist debaters do. He misrepresented Campbell, Anderson, Wilson, Brother Sheffer, and others, which was proven on him in the debate. Even the Baptist Church in West Nashville refused to endorse him to represent them in debate.

His strong power is in appealing to Methodists and Presbyterians for sympathy.

"As to editor Folk's statements in the Baptist and Reflector: (1). 'Tant claimed only those baptized by himself or brethren can be saved.' Untrue. (2). 'Tant claimed that all Methodists and Presbyterians are children of the devil and will go to hell'. Untrue. This was one of the questions I asked Oakley that was never answered. (3). 'Tant claimed that boards and conventions among his brethren are matters of liberty'. Untrue. (4). 'Elder Tant claimed God was a material being'. Untrue. (5). 'Elder Tant claimed he was perfect'. Untrue.

"Now, had Folk qualified this last statement as I did, his report of it would be true. Oakley asked me: 'Do you claim to be perfect?' I said: 'Yes, just like Noah and David were perfect. God said Noah was perfect, yet he got drunk; God said David was perfect, yet he committed murder and adultery. I, in the scriptural sense, am perfect as they were, but sometimes sin, as they did'. No one knew better than Folk that I placed these qualifying terms in my answer; yet he states it to create a false impression.

"Excepting the above five untrue charges, the most of Editor Folk's article was correct. I, like him, deplore personalities in debate, and he knows how hard we begged Oakley to keep them out; and, as Editor Folk remembers, Logan had to force him to rule on such. As Folk claims the debate did a world of good in Nashville, and as I am coming back to Nashville next spring to do good, and as I am sure Folk and Lofton can hold a debate without personalities, I, therefore, challenge either or both of them to meet me, with their home congregations, for an investigation of the differences between us. If Folk thinks the Baptists won in the Tant-Oakley debate, this will be accepted; if he does not, this debate will never come." (Gospel Advocate, August 16, 1900.)

The debate with Folk never did materialize. But there was a rather amusing aftermath of the debate with Oakley. After these two men left the debate, they each went their separate ways, and rather lost track of each other through the years. But they were destined to have at least one more brief encounter. It happened at the Freed-Bogard debate which was held in Nashville in the winter of 1926-27. Tant and Oakley both happened to be in attendance, and came face to face one night in the aisle of the old Lindsley Avenue Church of Christ building, where the discussion was being held.

Both men recognized each other, though they had not met in more than twenty-five years. They shook hands cordially.

"Well, well," said Oakley affably, "so it is J. D. Tant in the flesh. Why, I thought you would have been in heaven long before now."

"John Oakley," responded Tant with equal good humor, "I am glad to see you. I had no thought, of course, that you would be in heaven by now, for I knew that would never happen . . . But I did think you had left this world!"

III

The Tant-Harding written debate on the rebaptism question was a highlight of 1901. It had been planned for 1899, but had been postponed. Tant prefaced his first article with a brief "Note of Explanation":

> "Last year Brother Harding and I agreed to debate the baptism question — three articles each in the Firm Foundation and the Gospel Advocate. Without the fault of either, said debate miscarried; and now we desire to renew the same, in five articles each, to be published in the above papers. Each article is to contain fifteen hundred words. We hope all will carefully read the arguments introduced by each." (Gospel Advocate, May 30, 1901.)

There was no formal, stated proposition. Both men

knew wherein their differences lay; both understood exactly what the point at issue was, and each was perfectly willing to enter the debate confident that the other would offer no quibble about some side issue, but would come to grips with the real problem. The debate continued, week by week, in both journals, each of them carrying Tant's article one week, Harding's reply to it the next. The spirit of the discussion was exemplary. Both men were unfailingly courteous in all their references, neither accused the other of trying to dodge the issue or evade the question. It was simply a matter to be decided by Bible teaching.

Probably this discussion did as much to promote harmony and to resolve the "rebaptism question" as any single thing throughout the entire controversy. Tant was a recognized champion of the "rebaptizers"; while James A. Harding, co-founder of Nashville Bible School, and one of the greatest evangelists in all the church, was held in utmost esteem and veneration by all. Those who held to his position would have been as willing to trust their cause to his hands as to any man whom they might have found.

The Tant-Harding debate said about all that was to be said on either side. It was carefully studied by thousands of readers, both in the west and in the east. Gradually, it began to be evident that there was no fundamental differences in the convictions of the men. Both believed that baptism was essential; both believed that it was for the remission of sins; neither believed that Methodist doctrine or Baptist doctrine, or Methodist baptism or Baptist baptism, would make a man a Christian. Each believed that if a man were thoroughly taught, and understood what he was doing, it might be possible for a Baptist preacher or a Methodist preacher scripturally to baptize him. Tant held that such an occurence would be a rare and phenomenal exception; Harding believed that it would happen very often, and that probably a vast number of people in the denominational churches had been scripturally baptized.

While the controversy was to continue for many years (and even now, more than half a century later, is occasionally referred to), yet this discussion probably turned the tide, and assured that there would be no general division over the matter. Tant and Harding demonstrated that brethren could differ, could discuss their differences as Christians, and still fellowship one another. The bitterness and acrimony which had marked the Lipscomb-McGary debate a dozen years previously was markedly absent this time. Perhaps the brethren were growing up.

CHAPTER XIV

THE BEGINNING OF SORROWS

That year, 1901, was one of sadness and tragedy for Tant. He was distressed that his dearest and closest Texas friends were angry with Lipscomb because of the slight they felt Lipscomb had done him in failing to report the Tant-Oakley debate. He was becoming increasingly unhappy with the failure of his farm at Hamilton to produce any kind of paying crop. The land was poor and thin, and the rent was barely sufficient to pay the taxes. And his only son, Ira, was sick — sick unto death.

The doctors had diagnosed Ira's trouble as pericarditis, and had told his parents that he might live for several years, or, on the other hand, might go quite suddenly at any time. It was a heavy burden on the heart of both Tant and Nannie from the time they knew of the diagnosis until the August night, five months later, when Ira died. Since his condition was so very uncertain, it was impossible for Tant to remain at home all the time with him. As it chanced, he was away from home, in a meeting at Midway, Madison County, Texas, when the end came. Phone service was very poor, and repeated efforts to reach him by telephone were futile. Finally, a telegram was sent him, telling of the boy's death.

The undertaker felt he could not postpone the burial long enough to permit the father to come; so Nannie told him to go ahead with plans for the interment. Meanwhile, the telegram was delivered to Tant. He immediately got in touch with some of the brethren who were leaders in the Midway church, and told them he must close the meeting and go to his wife. One of them offered to drive him to Lovelady, the nearest railroad connection, that he might

catch a train. When they got to this place, and while waiting for the arrival of the train, Tant managed to get a
telephone call through to Brother W. M. Sparkman, an
elder in the Hamilton church. Sparkman told him that apparently the telegram had been delayed in reaching him,
and that Ira was to be buried that very day. He could not
possibly reach home in time for the funeral. Tant then
went to a drug store in Lovelady, got some paper from
the druggist (J. W. Skipper, Dealer in Drugs, Medicines,
Toilet Articles, Soaps, Etc. — according to the letter-head),
and wrote to Nannie:

Lovelady, Texas

August 16, 1901

Dearest Love:

It is now 5:00 p. m., and Sparkman has just told me
over the phone that you are to bury Ira at this very
hour. No one on earth can know the sorrow I feel to
think you are having to bear all this grief alone, and I
am in a strange land, among strangers, and can not
come to you. I should not complain, but it does seem
that I have had my full share of sorrows in trying to
save others. As soon as I am out of the present engagements I shall stay at home, and let others do the
work for a while.

I cannot understand why I did not get word before
today, as the telephone line comes to Midway. I could
have left yesterday, and been at home now if I had gotten the call before 1:00 P. M., but such is life. I got
the telegram at 11:00 A. M. today, and came over here
at once to come on home. Then when I talked to Sparkman, he told me that Ira is being buried today — right
now. I could not possibly get there in time for the
funeral. I have now decided, therefore, not to come
unless you call me. I'll go back tomorrow and continue
the meeting. But if you get sick, call me at Midway,
and I'll come at once.

In all these things no woman has done, or could do,
better than you have done. I have prayed for you

much, and I know I love you better and more than ever in life. I shall try to prove to you, and show you through the rest of your life how grateful I am for the kindness and love you gave to my boy in his last sickness. I am truly glad Ira is out of his pain at last. Write me all about his dying. How did he die? And did he know he had to go?

Yours in Love,

As quickly as Tant had mailed the letter, he returned to the place where the hack was waiting for him, got in and drove back to Midway in time for the service that night. Since there had been no opportunity to announce that the meeting would close, the house was crowded again.

The next day Tant wrote again to his wife:

Midway, Texas
August 17, 1901

Dearest Love:

I got back from Lovelady, 21 miles from here, in time to preach last night. It was a furious race back in time to make it for the service, and we were a little late; but we made it. I preached last night to a large hearing, and had one confession. I am waiting for time to preach again this morning; and perhaps no one in life is more miserable than I am at this hour, trying to fight the great battle between love and duty. I know, dear, I love you supremely, above everybody and everything on this earth, and I feel like I should be by your side in this great trouble. But I see all things are ready here, the hearts of many fathers and mothers are troubled over their children; some are dying out of Christ, and the gospel is their only hope. I believe if the Savior were here, he would tell me to stay and continue the meeting. I must give way to duty, and try to drive back the scalding tears that keep coming to my eyes, and hope that time will heal our broken hearts. I pray that the sun of happiness may shine in our home again some day. Job was once afflicted with a loss of all his property and all his children, and he

was a better man than I. Yet God made his life happy
again; and by God's help perhaps you and I can come
through this greatest of sorrows.

I realize how lonely you are, and I know many would
think me cruel to leave you all alone. Yet you could
not love my boy more than I. And if I can submit to
this blow, I know you, too, can bow your head to the inevitable and pass under the rod with me. If God loves
us as a father loves his own children, as the Bible says,
then surely he will not let this awful cloud hang over
our home so long without letting the sun shine once
again. Our troubles are great, but so many of earth's
people have suffered so much worse than we that we
should not complain unduly. We can only wait and
pray that time will dry up the fountain of our tears,
heal our wounded hearts, and help us to understand
that "He who doeth all things well" will sustain us.
And this may be only a beginning of sorrows for us,
for it may yet come our lot to stand over the graves of
all three of our dear girls. We do not know. And if
so be that even greater sorrows are in store for us,
let us be brave, knowing the end will soon come for us
too. As soon as you feel like it, I want you to write
a short notice of Ira's death and send it to both the
Gospel Advocate and the Firm Foundation.

God only knows what our future will be, but let us
trust and serve him, for surely he knows best. And it
may be that the present grief will be for our good. If
true, let us receive and profit by it.

Love to all,
J. D. Tant

True to her husband's request, Nannie wrote a tender
obituary of the boy whom she had loved, and sent it to the
two journals Tant had named:

TANT

"At ten o'clock on the night of August 14, our dear
Ira ceased all pain. With bleeding hearts we watched
till the last ray of hope had faded and the sweet spirit had returned to God. For three months our darling

boy had been sick, and loving hands did all in their power to restore him to health, and some of the ablest physicians in the state assisted; but all to no avail. Through all his weary weeks of suffering I cannot call to mind one time that he ever complained. Ira was a sweet, innocent boy of ten bright summers. He was full of life and joy, and often by his loving deeds and cheering words, dispelled the loneliness from our hearts. I have often heard it said that he had as much judgment in practical things as the average man. Ira's dear mother had been dead for over seven years, and for four and one-half years I have tried to guide his tender feet aright on life's rugged pathway. In his last sickness I thank God that I was able to nurse him to the end. In my arms he breathed his last, and I closed his sweet blue eyes forever. His father remained at home much to help nurse Ira, but his sickness was of such a nature that he had no warning when the end was near. The doctors thought he might live six months or a year, and upon this advice Brother Tant. had been away from home three days, preaching. God only knows the pangs of misery that filled his father's heart when three hundred miles away he received the message: 'Ira is dead.' Ira was his first-born, his only son. I think that he loved his child with a tenderness and a pride that not many fathers know. But Jesus said, 'Of such is the kingdom of God.' Our hearts are sad, our home is desolate; but heaven has another prize." (Gospel Advocate, September 12, 1901.)

II

After a residence there of fifteen years, late in the fall following Ira's death, Tant decided to pull up stakes and move from Hamilton. He had many ties there; his father, mother, sister, first wife, and son, were all now buried in the old Hamilton cemetery. He was loved and respected by the whole town. But he became convinced that so far as he was concerned, Hamilton was a dead-end street, and he must move. Nannie explains the matter:

"Our home on the hill was a nice place to live, but did not contribute anything to our bank account. The land was poor and rocky, broken by gulleys and washouts. We usually rented it, but the rent no more than paid for the upkeep. True, we had our chickens and cows and hogs and horses, as well as a garden and an orchard. But we could have all that, my husband thought, on good soil as easily as on poor. He got a bee humming in his ear that kept saying 'trade for something better.' The years were rolling by faster now than they used to; our family was growing, and my husband argued that a man's years to accumulate were between thirty-five and sixty. As he was knocking at the door of forty, and had not accumulated much for our children, or for our old age when he could not keep steadily at work, he decided it best to try some other locality. This was perhaps the saddest mistake we ever made.

"At that time South Texas was an inviting field. The rice industry had just been launched there, but was yet in the experimental stage. We had opportunity to trade our home and farm in Hamilton for four hundred and eight acres of rich farming land on the Guadalupe River in Victoria County, Texas. We had to assume an indebtedness of $4,500.00 to make the trade — an enormous debt for the turn of the century.

"The trade was closed, and preparations were made for the move. My husband was off in a meeting just before moving time, but he had given me careful instruction by letter as to how to go about the job. He told me whose wagons to engage to haul us to the railroad station at Hico, and how to have everything in readiness. He was to reach home on a Tuesday night, and we would begin the move the next day. For two weeks prior to the day I was busy packing and sorting things, and making all sorts of preparations.

"On Sunday I taught my Sunday School class for the last time. Many were the sad farewells and many were the tears that were shed that day. These friends had been with me in those first difficult years when I came as a bride to Hamilton. They had nursed me in sickness and had wept with me in sorrows. They had sus-

tained and comforted me in Ira's last long sickness;
and when the end had come for that sweet child, and I
was alone, they had stood beside me. And now came
the grievous hour of parting. Brother Sparkman, one
of the elders, at the close of the worship service had
asked me to stand in front of the pulpit while they
sang several songs and let all the congregation who desired to do so pass by and shake hands with me.

"A terrible ordeal! But that was the way they did
things fifty years ago. The congregation then numbered about two hundred members. I took my stand
with Zoreta in my arms, Maidia clinging to my skirts,
and eight-year-old Davis standing beside me. The
children all behaved nicely in the beginning, but soon
many sisters began to cry and hug me, and I cried,
too. This frightened the children, and they began to
weep and wail unrestrainedly. Our parting was a sad
one — and a wet one!

"More than fifty years have passed since that trying
day, and only one of the friends of that day have I
ever laid eyes on again.

"Our move was like all moves — things torn up and
much lost or destroyed. But we finally became settled
in our new home at Nursery, Texas, a tiny settlement
about ten or twelve miles northwest of Victoria."
(Reminiscences.)

Tant had high hopes that his move to Nursery would
enable him to achieve some sort of financial status which
would provide for his family, so that he might get back into
full time preaching without too much worry and anxiety
about them. He writes from Nursery:

"After seventeen years of continual travel as an
evangelist, never being out of a meeting as much as
two weeks at any one time, and spending eight-tenths
of my time away from home, I am now resting from
preaching, and am working on the farm for a living,
as I did in bygone years . . .

"I hope the brethren will note that I shall not be out
preaching any more for the next three years; so they

need not write me for any more meetings. If the Lord
wills that I shall prosper and get out of debt during the
next three years, so that my wife and little ones can
make a living without my help, I will then be in the
field doing the work of an evangelist as in the past.
This seems to be my expectation at the present, but
no one can tell what the future may bring. So I shall
patiently wait, trusting the Lord's will to be done in
all things." (Gospel Advocate, October 31, 1901.)

As quickly as he could get his household goods even half
way in order, Tant headed for the fields to begin his life
as a farmer again. He had a natural love for the soil, and
was eager to get his hands on the turning plow and set his
feet to following in the furrow as the rich, black soil was
turned. He expected this fertile country to provide abund-
antly for his needs. And if hard work and determination
were any factors in such a provision, he would not be found
wanting.

III

The brief residence at Nursery, one year, was destined
to be a bitter and frustrating one. All the high hopes with
which Tant had gone there were doomed to wither and die.
And he came very near to losing his own life, as well as losing the lives of his wife and new-born babe, in that sorrowful time. Nannie's description of both events shows it from
her point of view:

"My husband went into his farming at Nursery with
that unbounded energy and enthusiasm with which he
attacked everything in life. It was a challenge to him,
and he was all eagerness to get going. Scarcely were
we settled in the farm house until he was off to the
fields to plow. He had not given up the idea of preaching at all, but was determined to get a little bit ahead
financially, so as to provide for me and the children.
The land he was plowing lay along the Guadalupe River. The stream there was deep, with a high bluff

across the river, and the land on our side, our farm, coming right to the river's edge, just a few feet above water level. I could not see the field from the house, and my husband took his dinner with him in a lunch pail, as he only wanted to stop plowing long enough to rest the horses a bit and let them eat, and then back to the plow.

"Late in the evening, as the sun was near to setting, I began to look for the preacher-turned farmer and his team to come in from the field. He did not come. As darkness came on I grew apprehensive. I knew he would not have stayed out so long unless something unforeseen and serious had caused it. There were two Mexican families on the place, their yards adjoining my own back yard. I could not speak one word of Spanish, and the Mexicans pretended they could not speak English. Nevertheless, I went to them and asked them if they had seen my husband. All I got was a 'No sabby,' and a 'No spik Englice.' I then made signs and pointed to the field. Same result. I knew I could not leave my babies with these savages; but I also knew I must try to find some way to get to my husband. He was undoubtedly in trouble.

"Finally, I decided to try another plan with the Mexicans. I went to the house, lighted a lantern, and took it to one of the Mexicans, and said, 'Go, hunt my husband.' I spoke firmly and with authority — at least as much 'authority' as I could summons up. The man understood me perfectly, took the lantern, and started for the field. He met my husband on the way, soaking wet and so weak he could barely manage to walk. At sundown, he had unhitched his team from the plow and taken the horses to the river to let them drink before starting to the house. One horse, the largest I ever saw, had plunged into the stream and gone out of sight in twenty feet of water. Apparently this creature could not swim, a most unusual thing for a horse; for with most of them swimming comes as naturally as with a dog. When my husband saw the horse go out of sight, and not come up, he dived in after him. For an hour and a half he had struggled to get that horse's head out of the water long enough to tie him to a big limb that extended out over the river. He had finally managed to do this when almost completely exhausted himself. He then swam to the bank, managed to roll a big log into the river, and by some means I never have understood, was able to hold the horse's head above water with that log while he maneuvered him to shallow water so the creature could reach bottom with his long legs. Husband was in the water for a full hour and a half, and came very near to losing his life in the struggle.

"We hired a man, and he and my husband worked early and late, putting in over two hundred acres of corn and cotton. The land was heavily sodded with Johnson grass, and their labors were almost wasted. The season was rainy, and the corn had to be planted over the third time before we ever got a stand. It seemed all nature had conspired against us that year. The cotton crop was a miserable failure — three bales from fifty acres of land. The corn yielded six hundred bushels from a hundred and fifty acres — a magnificent crop of four bushels per acre!

"My husband had weighed 175 pounds when the season started; he went down to 140 before it ended. In that country cotton is ready to pick by July. By June it was evident that our crop was a failure. We had spent a thousand dollars on it, and would not make enough to pay the hired man and feed the stock. We were expecting our third child in July, hoping and praying, of course, for a boy this time. We did not see how it would be possible for us to pay a doctor to deliver this baby, and since I had had no trouble at all with the first two children, my husband said that if I were willing to try it, we would forego the doctor this time. At first I was frightened at the thought. I could have more easily consented for the first one; but now that I had had two babies, I had some idea of what the ordeal was. But I knew the Mexican women never thought of having a doctor for their confinements; and in view of the fact that our doctor lived seven miles away, and might come too late to help with the baby anyhow, I finally agreed to the plan. But with considerable misgivings. A big German woman who lived nearby gave birth to a fine baby about two weeks before mine was due. She got up and cooked breakfast for her entire family the next morning. Knowledge of this cheered me up much; but still I had hours of sheer terror. But we really saw nothing to do. We considered it a sin not to pay the doctor's bill — and we had no money with which to pay.

"At last the day arrived, July 5, 1902. I was suffering too much to think or care about a doctor. I cannot describe the misery, as no woman ever could. But my boy was born, and he lived. He was a fine, healthy baby; and my husband and I were overjoyed at his arrival. Having lost our precious Ira less than a year before, we felt this son was an answer to our prayers. God had heard us, and was going to let the sun shine once again upon our home.

"I seemed to be doing very well, and on the sixth day thought I was strong enough to get up and do a little work. This was a mistake; but my husband was working so hard all day long in the fields, and having to come in and prepare his own meals, besides caring for me, and trying to tend the baby, I felt he needed help. We were getting so low on groceries, too, that I knew my husband would very shortly have to go back to holding meetings to provide something for the family to eat. I thought if I'd sit up, it might give me strength; and I would gradually build up my strength, doing a little bit more each day, until the 17th of the month, at which time my husband could leave for his meeting. I tried this for four days; but when J. D. Jr. (we named him for his father) was ten days old, I had to go back to bed. I tried to think it was not for long, for I knew that Husband had to go. We were in debt, the crop was a failure, no money was coming in from any source, and we had bills to be paid.

"About six miles across the river was a girl who agreed to come and stay with me. She was a member of the church, and while we did not know her, she was recommended to us as being reliable in every way. The hired man and his wife, as soon as it became evident the crop was a failure, had left the place. My husband left for his meeting. The girl he had secured

to stay and care for me remained three days. Then
she left. The baby was having colic all the time, day
and night. I could not stand on my feet at all without terrific pain; and had I tried it, even for a few minutes, would certainly have fainted.

"This left the entire responsibility of the household
on Davis, my precious little helper, only nine years old.
She was as sweet as an angel, doing all her childish
heart could think of to lighten my load. She would
look after her two little sisters and the baby; would
light a fire in the cook stove, bring me every needful
thing to make the bread, and then I would sit on the
side of the bed and make up the dough for the biscuits. Davis would cook the bread, set it on the table,
and then feed her two little sisters and herself, and
would bring me something to my bed. Sometimes the
biscuits would burn, and sometimes they were soggy.
But it was the best we could do.

"Oh, how I missed the dear neighbors at Hamilton,
and the beautiful live-oak trees in the yard.

"To add to my misery, I had the toothache for several months before the baby was born, and for two
months afterward. I could not find any doctor who
would extract the tooth, as they told me it was a violation of the law to pull a tooth from a pregnant woman.
I never heard of such a silly law (if it was one), and
argued with them about it. One day a woman came in
to visit me, and seeing how I was suffering, told me
that if I would put snuff in the 'holler' tooth, it would
ease it. By this time I was willing to try anything anybody suggested. So she measured out some of her
snuff, and showed me how to put it in. I obeyed to
the letter. It was my first experience with snuff —
and my last! I soon became deathly sick at my stomach, was thrown into a hard chill, and got no relief
from the toothache either. (But in justice to the noxi-
ous weed, I really think the chill was caused by malaria, for that was a damp country, mosquitoes were
plentiful, and I suffered from malaria all the time we
lived there.) When my temperature went high, however, the tooth did quit aching temporarily.

"There were two white families who lived some distance from us. They heard of my condition, and were very kind. Would often bring us baskets of cooked food. Maidia was having much trouble with her tonsils then, and one lady took her home with her and treated her for tonsillitis for a week. My husband was gone the latter half of July and most of August. In writing him I made no mention at all of our direful condition, for I knew he had done all he could for us before he left home, and he could do nothing but worry now that he was a thousand miles away. Any letter telling of our condition would only have grieved him and caused him anxiety and distress. He would do what he could for us when he came home from the meeting; until then, we would tough things out as best we could.

"Little Davis tried to do the washing for the family. One day she brought me a bunch of diapers she had washed, and said, 'Mama, I think these diapers need boiling. I'm going to make a fire around the wash kettle and boil them.' It was a dry, hot day in August, and I felt she could not hurt anything by trying, so told her to go ahead if she wished. After building the fire and putting the diapers in the boiling pot, she happened to come too near the fire and stepped on a live coal with her bare foot. It burned so deep that the coal was still sticking to her little foot when she came screaming to my bedside. Poor child! She was wild with pain. But with a few first aid remedies which I managed to keep always on hand I soothed her as quickly as I could. But she could not walk on that foot for several days.

"My husband came home early in September. He washed all the dirty clothes, which, save for the few Davis had washed, had accumulated for six weeks, thoroughly scoured all the floors, and began to get things in order around the house. I stayed in bed for another month after he got there, and then was strong enough for him to take me to my brother's home in Cleburne, Texas. My brother was a physician. He gave me some repair work which should have been done at the time of the baby's birth; after spending a month with him, I was able to walk and could do most of my work by sitting most of the time. Brother also cured the baby's colic, and from that day on he was the best baby I ever had.

"While I was recuperating at my brother's, Husband was out on another preaching tour. This time he found a place to trade, by which we could leave the disastrous farm at Nursery, and try to get out from under the heavy debt which was soon coming due. Or, rather, the interest on $4,500.00 was coming due. The property for which he traded was located at San Marcos, the most picturesque little town I have ever seen. He made a good trade — twenty-four acres of land in the suburbs, just outside the corporate limits. There was a very large, beautiful building on it that the former owner had used for a small female college. There were twelve large rooms, one being twenty by thirty feet. This had been used as a class room by the former owner. We assumed a debt of $2,000.00 which was against this place, and the man with whom we traded took over our $4,500.00 debt along with the farm at Nursery." (Reminiscences.)

IV

After the disastrous year at Nursery, Tant was ready to go back on the road as a gospel preacher. He announced this (and his sale of the farm at Nursery) in language somewhat more cheerful than the spirit of his wife would warrant:

"After one year's work on the farm, I have an opportunity of selling the same at a financial gain, which enables me to enter the field again as an evangelist. From now on our home will be at San Marcos, Hayes County, Texas, on the head waters of the San Marcos River, twenty-eight miles south of Austin, and forty-five miles north of San Antonio. This is one of the most beautiful and heathful locations in Texas, and considered the leading educational town of this section." (Gospel Advocate, January 8, 1903.)

Selling at a financial gain? Well, it depends on how you look at it. He traded a $4,500.00 for a $2,000.00 debt; and in that way it was a "gain". But from this time until just

a few short months before his death, Tant was never again
for more than a few days at a time entirely free of debt.
At San Marcos Nannie decided to enter again into the
school room. She writes:

"The city schools were crowded, and every year a
number of free school pupils were transferred to our
district, and the teacher received the money. This
amounted to about $75.00 per month. My husband and
I talked things over, and decided that it would be good
for me to try to teach again for a year or two to re-
coup some of our losses. I had not fully regained my
strength, but we moved in December, 1902, and since
they already had a teacher for that year, my work
would not start until September, 1903. This would
give me nine months to recuperate. So the decision
was made, and I applied for the school.

"When we moved from Nursery to San Marcos we
had a very fine white woman who went with us as
'house-keeper', and to do the heavy work while I tried
to rest as much as possible and regain my health.
Her name was Murphy. She agreed to stay with us
through the next school year and help with the work.
So Husband felt free to take up his evangelistic work
again." (Reminiscences.)

This was not too hard to do, for Texas was in desperate
need of preachers, and Tant had had many letters during
his year at Nursery begging him to come for meetings. He
had turned most of them down until mid-summer, when he
realized his crop was a failure. But as he plans to take up
full time work again he writes:

"As to myself, I know of no change, moral or spiritual, that I desire to make. I shall preach the gospel
straight, being satisfied with what is written in the
word of the Lord. In addition to my preaching I hope
to be able to write more often for the Gospel Advocate.
I still love the truths it teaches, and I think its lessons
were exceptionally grand during the last year. It
makes me sad to think that Brethren Lipscomb and

Sewell are so near the end of life, with still so much work to be done. I hope the brethren who have written me, and who count on my holding their meeting this year, will write again at once, so I can form my plans for the year." (**Gospel Advocate**, January 8, 1903.)

Soon after getting settled in San Marcos, Tant held a meeting for the congregation there. He reported it, along with some memories of the past:

"Since moving to San Marcos, Texas, I have just closed my first meeting for 1903, with four additions to the congregation. Twenty years have gone into history since I last preached at San Marcos, and there have been many changes in Texas during that time.

"Twenty-two years ago I bought a home near San Marcos, and for four years lived happily in this country. I was then only a boy. Father, Mother, Sister, and I were the family. Only a few miles from here I learned the truth, under the teaching of W. H. D. Carrington, and came out of Methodism which I was then preaching. I began to preach the truth. Not far from here I baptized my only sister, my first convert, many years ago. Brother Carrington, who was one of God's noblemen, now sleeps in the old church-yard at Austin, awaiting the final call. My father, mother, and sister are all sleeping, side by side, in the old Hamilton graveyard, which is far, far away. San Marcos is the place where I joined the noted C. M. Wilmeth, when we started out to evangelize the great state of Texas — he to be a Paul, and I to be a Timothy. Wilmeth now sleeps in a foreign country — in Mexican soil. I lived near San Marcos when I wrote to the old soldier of the cross, Dr. Carroll Kendrick, to come and help me in some meetings. He came from California. This proved to be his last trip to Texas before he went to his reward. All these events cause me to feel sad, to think that even I have passed my forty-first mile-post on the road of life, and will soon start down the hill on the other side.

"Many have been the changes in Texas during these

twenty-two years. At the beginning of that period the church in San Marcos was considered among the leading congregations in the State. We have the oldest church building in town. The lumber with which it was built was hauled on wagons from Bastrop, more than forty miles away . . .

"San Marcos is the place where the organ was first introduced into the church; and like all congregations where it has since gone, the church was divided. Dear old Grandma Driskill, a mother in Israel, in the goodness of her soul, thought she would put an end to the organ wrangle in San Marcos; so one day she took a hatchet (as did George Washington when he cut down the cherry), went into the church and demolished the organ. But even that did not stop the trouble. Grandma Driskill has long since gone to her reward, and her son, Brother J. A. Driskill, is about the only one of the old time members who still stands firm. For fifty years he has stood on the Lord's side. He has done much preaching and has probably baptized more old persons than any other preacher in Texas. Through his influence we can still claim to have a sound congregation in San Marcos. Long ago the organ people withdrew, built a house of worship, and have done as the organ people at other places have done — joined the great denominational army of the town and become a sister church among the many human churches of our time". (Gospel Advocate, February 12, 1903.)

Back into the swing of things again, Tant resumed his heavy schedule of debates and meetings. In late February and March he went to Uvalde and Bracketville. He reported a few scattered members in these places, and pleaded with brethren to help him buy a tent that he might keep it busy all the year round in preaching in such mission points. He offered to donate $50.00 a year himself to any gospel preacher who would go into that section to spend his time trying to build up congregations. He evidently got the tent, for the next year he reports a number of meetings in which he used "my tent."

Tant was often criticized for his plain preaching. This seemed to bother him not at all. Of one such criticism he wrote:

"A short time ago a brother was lecturing me on account of my plain preaching. He said he knew the people of a certain town better than I knew them, and he knew they would not come to hear me preach. I told him that I was plain, and that I preached the gospel straight; that during the last seventeen years more than 3,000 people had come into the church under my preaching, and that more than fifty of the boys who were among that number were now preaching the gospel. He had lived there for fifty years and had been a Christian for thirty years; so I called on him to tell how many he had led to Christ. I was not surprised to learn that he had converted not a single soul during all those years." (Gospel Advocate, April 2, 1903.)

Tant's debates with the digressives were a constant and continuing thing during these years at the turn of the century. He was in a better position than most brethren to know who was, and who was not, faithful to the church in those uncertain years of confusion and division; and he frequently wrote notes of warning to the religious journals, cautioning against certain digressive preachers who were trying to tear up churches and control church properties. In May, 1903, for example, he warned against brethren sending money to build a church at Quinlan, Texas. The man soliciting the funds was a digressive, and he was trying to build a house for the digressives. A. D. Rogers had recently held a meeting for the Quinlan church, which had been reported in the Gospel Advocate of May 7, 1903. This caused Tant to feel justified in giving the story of Rogers' departure from the faith, which he did:

"A. D. Rogers, formerly a member of the church of Christ, but now a convert to the organ faction, is giving the church trouble at many points. Some years ago he held a meeting at Godley, Texas, and baptized a large number of people. Having great influence, he was instrumental in building a church there. The brethren held him in high esteem until he joined the Society. He is employed as 'district evangelist', and is making the organ and the society tests of fellowship, trying to force them on all the churches. The digressive element at Godley, seeing his work, and thinking that he was the man to help them to force the organ and the society at that place, arranged for him to hold a meeting. The elders then wrote him a long letter, begging him, for the sake of peace, not to come, as he would create strife, and perhaps divide the church. He gave no heed to their letter, but went to Godley and held the meeting. After his departure two of his admirers became so bold in advocating his divisive work that the church withdrew fellowship from them. Posing as a saint and a martyr, Rogers went back to help these excluded members and the Baptists and Methodists tear down the church of Christ, if possible.

"Before returning to Godley, Rogers sent the following message to his loyal brethren: 'I will meet any man whom the opposition party will furnish who will affirm this proposition: The Scriptures teach that the use of an organ as an aid to singing is a sin.' He told me that the reason he worded it that way was that he did not believe there was a man in the United States who would affirm it. I told him it was unfair, but that I would affirm anything to show up his ungodly work before the church. The debate lasted two days.

"Rogers preached in the Baptist Church at night. On the first night he declared that the most pitiful sight to him in life is a man who will not work to help save souls in other churches when he sees that he cannot save them in his own church. On the next night he gave an invitation to the people to come and accept Christ, saying that he did not want them to join any church or faction; he wanted them to accept Christ. He called on the Baptist preacher to lead in prayer, and was helped by the Baptist organ and choir.

"During the debate Rogers declared that anything might be right in itself, yet if any man believed it to be

wrong, to him it was wrong. He said that, on the
other hand, anything might be wrong in itself, yet if
any man believed it to be right, to him it was right.
He stated that he had not changed on the organ question or the society question in twelve years. He said
he entered the Nashville Bible School with the same
views that he now holds; and that of nine preachers
who were there with him, he had led seven from under
Lipscomb and Harding.

"For twelve years Rogers spent his time in preaching
for churches who were opposed to all innovations, and
was supported by them. He kept his real faith and
purpose in the background until he had gained a great
personal influence over these churches; then he went
to Corsicana, Texas, and got a job under the State
Board, after which he began to run over the earnest
desires of the elders and to hold meetings and divide
the churches at all points where he had gained an influence. He has been requested by the elders not to
come to Collinsville, Rio Vista, Godley, Rosenthal, and
other places in Texas; but no man who departs from
God's word cares for the request of elders when he can
push his divisive work.

"Rogers is a weak debater, and spends much of his
time in crying and begging for sympathy. The Baptist preacher at Godley, Mr. Tarrant, who acted as
chief moderator, seems to be quite gentlemanly in his
bearing. He has far more sense than Rogers, using
Rogers as a cats-paw to tear down the church of Christ
— which he should do if the Baptists are right and we
are wrong. Rogers, however, could not see that such
was the work the Baptists wanted him to do.

"I have written this to show up Rogers in his true
colors before the churches, so that all can beware of
him. I am ready and prepared to meet Rogers at any
place where he is doing his divisive work, and will
deny anything Rogers will affirm and will affirm
anything that Rogers will deny." (Gospel Advocate,
May 28, 1903.)

As Tant resumed his work, being gone again from home
a good part of the time, he reflected on the value of a

home, and on the sacrifices men are called upon to make when they preach the gospel:

"After many years of continual travel and mixing with different families on earth, I have now been at home the greater part of a year; but today all things are ready. God is giving the call, 'Go . . . preach the gospel'; and Duty says, 'Go'. To home, then, I must say, 'Farewell.' As I start, I think of the dear old home, where loved ones dwell; I think of the little children without a father's care, and of the wife who has so bravely stood by me in all the troubles of life — of her double work, her loneliness, her responsibility, and her sacrifice in being a preacher's wife . . .

"Often in life's work I have almost become discouraged by seeing life's failures and hearing evil speaking, lies, false representations among brethren, discord, and hate. Even when life's pathway would seem to be crossed by dark clouds and the storms of persecution gather, when the vivid lightnings of jealousy would flash, and the deep-toned thunder of falsehood could be heard, I have often stopped to ask myself the question: 'Is this the reward that I am to get from those who should be my friends for life? Is it not better to let them alone and never try to save them?' But through all the mist and fog and gloom, I could think of home and remember that there is always the lamp of love and welcome burning brightly for me there, and that anxious ones are looking for my coming. Then I knew it was all worth while." (Gospel Advocate, June 11, 1903.)

CHAPTER XV

TROUBLE AT McGREGOR

In the fall of 1903 the Southwest Teachers' State Normal opened at San Marcos. About three hundred teachers were enrolled that first year. A few small dormitories had been built, but not enough to accommodate all the students. Tant's house was large and well arranged. It occurred to them that they might make a little of the money they so desperately needed by taking in a few girl boarders. Mrs. Murphey was going to be there to help with the work, anyhow, and it would be a simple matter to arrange the rooms and accept a few girls.

Nannie spoke to the Superintendent of the Normal School about it, and he helped her secure eight young ladies to board with her. They paid $15.00 per month each for board and room. With the school teaching salary of $75.00 per month plus the money cleared above the food for her boarding girls, Nannie's income that winter was about $125 per month—far more than her preaching husband was making, or ever had made, or ever would make, in the evangelistic field. Mrs. Murphey kept the three Tant babies; Davis, the oldest girl, was in school; and Nannie was in the school room eight hours a day for five days each week.

Tant was gone almost constantly in his preaching work. On September 5 he closed a meeting at Ben Hur in Limestone County, Texas, with forty-seven additions. The Baptists had become so stirred up here that they challenged for a debate; so he arranged to return and meet Elder Blankenship on November 9. From Ben Hur Tant went to Rosenburg, where he met J. M. Howell, a half-way Russellite, in debate. Tant wrote:

"He (Howell) was once a Christian; his father is a Christian preacher and is one of the best men I ever knew. I feel sad to see his son side-tracked and wasting his useful life on such foolishness as Russell teaches. I have been in the debating field sixteen years, holding from three to ten debates each year, and have debated along the line of twelve different channels, but I find less comfort and less good in the 'Millennial-dawn' theory than any other which I have met; it is hard for me to understand why so many of my brethren become so much concerned about these outside matters." (Gospel Advocate, September 24, 1903.)

Tant was home for one week following his debate with Howell, then went to Roswell, New Mexico, for a tent meeting. The church there numbered less than twenty members, and they were discouraged and about ready to give up. But Tant baptized a few and put new life into the others. He reported that this was a fine country, but not nearly so fine as the advertisements going over the country would lead one to believe. He advised that all who might be contemplating a move to New Mexico should make thorough investigation before they moved. He felt there were such great drawbacks in the climate and natural circumstances of the country that it would be many, many years before much progress could be made in the state.

From Roswell he moved the tent to some other little place in northwest Texas which he describes only as a "mission point", without giving it a name. After two weeks there he came back to San Marcos for a few days before going off to another debate.

II

One of the most famous law-suits in Texas religious history was the controversy between the digressives and the loyal church at McGregor, Texas. Tant held several meetings at McGregor both before and following the suit. Early in 1904 he was there for his seventh meeting. He gives a full account both of the meeting and of the law-suit:

"I recently closed my seventh meeting at McGregor. Four persons were added to the congregation, and the attendance throughout the meeting was the best I have ever seen. The song service was conducted by Brethren Acuff and Everidge, two excellent singers.

"As the litigation in regard to the church property at McGregor has been for some years a topic of interest with the brethren of Texas, I believe a short history of this trouble will be of benefit to many struggling congregations.

"After the brethren had been informed that they had lost their property (which was a mistake), I met D. A. Leak, a digressive preacher, in debate on the organ question. The discussion was held at McGregor, and Leak was defeated. The digressives then sent for B. B. Saunders to come and 'preach Tant's funeral'. Saunders and Mrs. Dowthit are the persons who divided the church at McGregor. As I had returned to Hamilton, the digressives decided to send Mr. Dowthit there to kill me; but, unfortunately for them, Tom Smith, another digressive preacher, disclosed their purpose, and I was not killed. Then a letter to Dowthit and a proposition from me in the McGregor paper offering to prove all that I had said caused them to think there was another side. So after all this trouble, I was glad to know that I could go back there and hold a meeting for the brethren — the best one that I ever held for them.

'At the close of my debate with Leak the ungodliness of the digressive element of Texas was shown up so plainly in the case of their stealing the church property that the sentiment of the better element at McGregor was turned against their outrage; and four hundred and seventy-five dollars was raised toward building a church. In less than sixty days a beautiful, well-finished church building was ready for occupancy. The building cost one thousand dollars, and at my last meeting the final two hundred dollars was raised; and now the church is out of debt, is doing fine work, has the largest attendance of any church in town, and the members are at peace with one another.

"But the loyal brethren of the McGregor church did not lose the old building. In the lower court and the Court of Appeals the case was decided in favor of the digressives, but it was carried to the Supreme Court on another appeal. When the time came for trial, our lawyer was sick; and two days before the trial he informed W. K. Homan (digressive preacher and lawyer for the digressives) of his condition, and the latter agreed that he would not go before the court, but would let the matter stand until our lawyer recovered. Much to the surprise of our lawyer, two days after this agreement, Homan appeared in person at Austin and declared that we had no case, else we would have a man there to represent us. He did not ask for the house; he pleaded only that the minority be allowed equal rights in the house. The judge, believing Homan sincere in his plea, granted the digressives not the house, but equal rights in the house. Homan, however, telegraphed the digressives that they had gained the house. Believing this, our brethren turned over the keys to the digressives. Our brethren continued in this belief that they had lost the house until the Baptists became involved in a similar church law-suit at Paris. At this trial one of the Baptists called the attention of the same judge to the fact that he had decided in favor of the digressive Christians at McGregor, and demanded a like decision there. Whereupon the judge made the following statement, which may be found in the Southwestern Reporter:

In support of the judgment of the District Court, the plaintiffs in error cite the case of Peace vs. church of Christ, in which this court refused an application for a writ of error from the judgment of the Court of Appeals of the Third District, as found in the Southwestern Reporter, Volume 48, page 534. The trial court in that case found that the majority of the congregation permitted only its principles and doctrines to be taught and its customs and usages to be followed, and would not permit those adhering to and holding a doctrine with the 'progressive' faction (the minority) to hold religious services, or preach their principles and doctrines, in the church building; that on September 23, 1897, defendants, G. A. Trott and R. M. Peace, elders of the aforesaid church (of the majority) locked the church house and took possession thereof for themselves, and for the other defendants, all of whom adhere to the Firm Foundation faction (the majority), claiming that they are the original church of Christ at McGregor, and said defendants now hold exclusive possession of the church property, against plaintiff corporation. The court also found that the minority organized a corporation, naming it 'The First Christian Church of McGregor'. Those constituting the minority were the plaintiffs in that case. On examining the application for writ of error, without regard to the differences of opinion which prevailed between members of the congregation, it was the opinion of this court that the majority had no right to exclude the minority from the use of the building so long as the latter were not dismissed from membership in the church, and that the effect of the judgment in favor of the corporation was to restore the building to the use of the whole church. Upon this ground the application was refused, and not because this court approved the opinion of the trial judge which was approved by the Court of Appeals, holding that the majority had departed from the faith, and that, therefore, the minority constituted the original church. We may have been in error as to the effect of the judgment in this respect, because it may be true that the action of the minority in that case amounted to an abandonment of their membership in the original church, by which they lost their rights to the property, which was deeded to the original organization, and that the corporation did not include the majority. If so, the writ of error should have been granted; but that case is not authority upon the question involved in this.

"From this statement we see that the judge claims that he did not give the property to the digressives, as they claim; that he only gave them 'equal rights' with the loyal brethren to meet in the house. He admits that he might have been wrong in so doing, and refuses to recognize his former decision as a legal precedent, and in a similar church trial he makes a contrary ruling.

"As soon as this statement was published, our lawyer told me that on account of Homan's outrage on him in promising to wait until he got well, and then secretly going to Austin and arguing the case, he would bring the case before the same judge and gain the suit, free of charge, if I would get the other members of the church at McGregor to bring the suit. About the time he and I arranged the papers and got all the members to sign for a second trial, the Tant-Leak debate was held. We were sure we could gain the case, yet were just as sure Homan would keep the case in court for five years, so we decided to abandon the suit and build a new house, which we have done, as before stated, and are now doing well.

"The digressives at McGregor have been practically dead since the debate, meeting only part of the time; and they are now trying to get their church under the State Board as a mission point." (Gospel Advocate, February 4, 1904.)

W. K. Homan was furious when he saw Tant's article in the Gospel Advocate. He wrote a blazing statement to David Lipscomb, demanding that Lipscomb give it space in the Advocate, on threat of a libel suit. Homan was an able, albeit somewhat unscrupulous, attorney, as well as a digressive preacher and editor of the Christian Courier, digressive paper of Texas. He couched his statement to Lipscomb in the legal jargon of the day:

"The publishers of the Advocate are notified to publish in that paper, without delay, in as conspicuous type and place as that in which libelous statements appear, a full and unequivocal retraction of each and all the statements regarding myself, above pointed out, and of every other intimation or insinuation in said article contained reflecting upon me, or in any way questioning my integrity or the propriety of my conduct as a lawyer and a man in the matter referred to." (Gospel Advocate, February 25, 1904.)

Lipscomb published Homan's statement in full, and then responded:

"We publish the above. We know nothing of the facts; did not see Tant's article until it was in print. We take it that Homan's statement of facts is true, inasmuch as he had personal knowledge of them. We do not think Tant intended to misrepresent Homan or others, but he allowed himself to look at them from a one-sided standpoint and heard only from one side. I doubt not he will be glad to correct all wrong impres-

sions made. The easy way for them to get an understanding in the matter is for them to confer together
and understand all the facts. Homan, doubtless, will
say this should have been done before publication.
This would have been better, and have avoided any
wrong. But all are liable to make mistakes." (Ibid.)

Lipscomb's statement reflects the calmer and easier
course of the division in Tennessee, in contrast to the
explosive and bitter nature of the Texas split. In Tennessee the loyal churches were considerably in the majority,
and the digressives with a few notable exceptions made
very little effort to steal the buildings. But in Texas it was
different. The digressives were greatly in the majority
here, overwhelmingly so. When the final separation had
been completed, it seems probable that between eighty and
ninety percent of Texas Christians followed the digression.
Texas was a new, raw country. This was the frontier,
where violence was common, where tempers flared, and
where quarrels and differences were often as not settled
by a blasting six-gun. Tant knew his Texans. And he
knew that his facts were not in error. He had seen the unscrupulous way in which Homan had "bulled through" his
Society at Austin in 1886; he had known of many instances
of deceit, falsehood, and every kind of trickery by which
the digressives had contrived to steal the buildings in Texas. He personally knew Homan; and Lipscomb did not.

But Tant was not inclined to try to defend himself, or to
correct the false charges Homan had made against him, or
even the implications of Lipscomb's statement. He very
wisely saw that there would be no point in pursuing the
thing further, as it would involve the Gospel Advocate in a
suit for slander, which they would win, but which would be
a costly and acrimonious battle. Lipscomb's whole nature
shrank from such a brutal encounter. Tant was not particularly averse to such a controversy, but he could do lit-

tle in this case without Lipscomb's moral support. So he made no reply to Homan.

The brief exchange, however, led to several questions in the **Gospel Advocate** concerning lawsuits among Christians. And although Lipscomb was right at this period involved in the long drawn out litigation over the Newbern, Tennessee, church property, he nevertheless gave his strong advice against all efforts to retain property by law. He advised rather that the brethren surrender their houses and build new ones. This was contrary to the feeling and conviction of many Texas preachers and brethren; but Lipscomb's advice was sufficient to weaken their position with the members generally, and for several years all over Texas houses were surrendered to the digressives "without a shot being fired."

Whether the policy was a wise one is still debatable. Certainly it proved tremendously discouraging to the faithful in Texas for more than a generation. From the early 1900's to the late 1930's, they labored under terrific handicaps, and under great difficulty, because of the debacle occasioned by losing their buildings and many of their members. There can be little question that thousands of members, untaught and scarcely realizing what was happening, "stayed with the building." Whether rightly or wrongly, they had come to identify "the church" with those retaining the meeting house; and could not bear to leave the meeting house, regardless of what happened there. This is a problem which Christians have had to face, and will face perhaps forever.

III

Bracketville and Del Rio were two southwest Texas towns where Tant held tent meetings in the spring of 1904. The former is about 170 miles southwest of San Antonio, and was the site of Fort Clark, which garrisoned from six to

twelve hundred soldiers. The work there had been started
by T. S. Sweeney, a government employee, who had come
to Fort Clark in the early 1890's. He had gathered together a little group of six people, and gradually had built
a fairly good congregation. Tant baptized six in this meeting, and declared that "according to their financial ability,
the brethren supported me exceedingly well."

Del Rio was thirty miles farther West. Here Tant preached for twelve days under his tent. Three young ladies were
baptized and two wanderers were reclaimed. There were
about twenty members at Del Rio, but they had no one to
lead them. Tant wrote numerous appeals in the papers for
someone to go there, without any guarantee of support, and
help these people.

The last of May and the first of June found A. J. Mc-
Carty in a good meeting with the San Marcos church. Tant
was out of town, so did not get to attend at all. He continued to hold meetings in Texas through the summer and
early fall. Late in October he returned to Houston, where
he had held a meeting the previous year. In this meeting
nine persons were baptized, bringing the total membership
to forty. Tant writes:

"One year ago there was no church of Christ at that
place. Brother Crain and family separated themselves
from the digressives and were soon joined by Brother
A. A. Lucas and family. They rented an old store-
house, and are now doing a great work. Houston has a
population of 60,000, and I do not know of any greater
mission field or a better opening for work. The brethren need some strong young man who can live among
them and teach them for a year, and in that time I
think they can become able to build a house and become
self supporting. A young man is also needed to take
up the work at San Antonio, and an able preacher to locate at McGregor. One who is looking for a 'pastor's'
job, where they will support him, cannot succeed at
any of these places; but any one willing to 'endure

hardness, as a good soldier', and help build up the
Master's cause will find a happy welcome. I am now
in Paris for a month's meeting, and I hope to be instrumental in doing a great work here." (Gospel Advocate, November 10, 1904.)

Meanwhile, back in San Marcos, Nannie was having some
difficulty in her school work. She writes:

"When my first school term closed, Mrs. Murphey informed me that she wanted to go into business for herself, and could not help me further. That was a terrific set-back to me. I knew nobody else with whom I
was willing to trust my babies, and who would take the
interest in my house that she did to keep everything in
order. Always gentle and kind, never too tired to relieve me, she was one of the most completely honest
and fairest persons with whom I ever dealt. She had
asked my husband to baptize her into Christ, and she
was a most devout and faithful Christian. When she
wanted to open a millinery shop, I was glad for her
sake, for I knew it would be much to her financial advantage to do so. But it did leave me with a great
problem.

"I had grown much stronger through the year, with
Mrs. Murphey relieving me of the house-work; so I decided that for the next term I would not keep so many
boarders, and would try to do all the work myself, as
well as continuing to teach. We were so very anxious
to pay off the $2,000.00 indebtedness against the home,
and keep the place. I liked San Marcos very much and
hoped our children could grow to maturity there, and
go right on to college without having to leave home. I
kept four boarders the second school year (beginning
in September 1904), did all my cooking, house cleaning,
laundry, sewing, and other work. In addition to this,
I taught school eight hours a day for five days each
week. I was also put on the Board of Examiners by
the County Superintendent, and that took up one full
Saturday each month. But, withal, it was a happy and
pleasant fall. The work was hard, and I had overesti-
mated my strength; but the sweet girls I kept helped

me out, and everything was going along very well. But
I realized the burden was gradually sapping my
strength; and I began to try to think of some plan by
which I could continue to teach, and keep the girls also. I turned it over daily (and nightly) in my mind.

But my husband had plans, too. He was hundreds
of miles away on one of his preaching tours, and came
home about Thanksgiving to inform me that — we
were going to move! He had found a man in Quanah,
Texas, who wanted to move south. My husband had
traded our lovely home in San Marcos for seven hundred and ten acres of land in Hardeman County, Texas
and a nice six-room house in Quanah, a town of about
three thousand inhabitants. It was a good trade; the
pasture and farm on that Hardeman County property
would easily support a nice herd of Hereford cattle
(which also had gone with the place as part of the
trade), and the residence in town was convenient to the
school, and better suited to our family than the large
rambling house at San Marcos. The life in Quanah
would enable me to give all my time to my family;
Brother Tant would go on with his preaching — and
the Herefords would supply the necessary funds to
keep us all alive, and fed, and clothed.

"So we moved in December, 1904.) (Reminiscences.)

IV

Quanah was originally an Indian town, named for Quanah Parker, a son of Cynthia Parker. In 1836 the Comanche Indians, most war-like of the Texas tribes, had
made a raid on Fort Parker (now Groesbeck) in which Silas
Parker, father of Cynthia Ann, was killed. Cynthia Ann,
nine years old, and John, a younger brother, were captured
by the Comanches. All efforts to rescue them proved futile. Cynthia Ann grew to womanhood and became the
wife of an Indian brave, Nicona. She became the mother
of four children, two boys and two girls. In 1860 Sul Ross,
who later became governor of Texas, in company with some
Texas rangers, gave battle to the Comanches, who had

their camp in Medicine Mound, four miles from where the town of Quanah now stands. Pete Nicona and his fifteen-year-old daughter were killed. The two younger boys escaped. Cynthia Ann, with her two-year-old daughter, Prairie Flower, was captured. She had no desire to return to the Indians, for her husband had been killed. But she pined for news from her two boys. She never heard from them, however, for she died at the home of her brother in Anderson County, Texas, in 1864. Her boys were still living the life of wild Indians on the frontier.

In 1905 when Teddy Roosevelt and some hundred of his friends came to the "Big Pasture" in Oklahoma to hunt, Quanah Parker rode horseback by the President's side and showed him the best hunting ground. Quanah was now an elderly and honored chief among the Indians, having made peace with the whites. Tant happened to be in a meeting at Frederick, Oklahoma, at the time of Roosevelt's visit, and was in the crowd nearby when Roosevelt made a short talk, Quanah Parker being mounted on his horse meanwhile beside Mr. Roosevelt.

Medicine Mound, the place where Cynthia Ann and Prairie Flower were captured, was located on the farm for which Tant had traded in Hardeman County.

Tant was eager to get a congregation started in Quanah. He tells of his efforts to that end:

"I found no church of Christ here. There has been a digressive church here for ten or twelve years, and I found some members who had been faithful elsewhere had gone in and worked with these digressives, because there was no church of Christ here. I also found that the unscriptural things which were first tolerated by said members with a protest were now almost fully accepted; for it takes only a few years for a man to accept any innovation if he will only work with said innovation. Here is where many members are deceived. They think if they will go in and work with members who have accepted innovations, they can convert them. They might as well pour water into the river to make it run upstream, or hire a saloon-keeper to run his bar to try to reform him, as to endorse the work of the digressives in order to reform them. Many of the prophets and apostles were considered kickers, yet none of them ever engaged in heathen worship to reform the heathen.

"After coming to Quanah, I begged for the house to hold a meeting in, offering to pay all expenses and pledging myself to preach nothing but the Bible. But when they learned I would preach nothing but the Bible, they evidently decided Bible doctrine preached in their house would cause division in their church; so they absolutely refused to let me preach the Bible in their house. I then got the court-house and held a meeting, after which we rented a schoolhouse to meet in, and now we have a small band of faithful brethren, meeting for worship each Lord's day, trying to do the will of God." (Gospel Advocate, March 2, 1905.)

That meeting held in the court-house was a most difficult one. The weather was bad throughout. It was in January, 1905, only a few days after reaching Quanah that the meeting took place. Nannie recalls it:

"For three weeks after we arrived in Quanah the ice and snow covered the ground. It kept snowing at night, melting a little bit when the sun came out, then freezing again and snowing at night, until a solid sheet of ice covered the ground to a depth of several inches. One of the neighbor women said it was thirteen inches thick, but I doubted that.

"My husband had planned to hold a meeting in the court-house, as we did not have a building then. Sister Coffee, who was a good singer, had come up from San Marcos to help in the meeting. Our only conveyance to and from the court-house was a two-horse wagon. The ice was so solid on the ground that at no place did it crack or break through under the weight of this big wagon and team, with the wagon full of people. Sister Coffee seemed to enjoy her visit. But

notwithstanding the very bad weather, we had large
crowds and a fine interest. We succeeded in establishing a church in Quanah. After the meeting we rented
a school-house, and Brother Bozeman and I used to go
every Sunday and take our children and as many others as we could get, to teach them the Bible." (Reminiscences.)

When Tant came to Frederick, Oklahoma, for a meeting
in April, 1905, he was getting back into familiar territory.
He had been all through this country, off and on, for ten
years. But this was his first time to preach at Frederick.
There was no church meeting there; but he managed to
round up fifteen or twenty people who had at one time in
life been members of the church, and after about three
weeks of work and preaching, left a congregation meeting
regularly there. From Frederick (where he had had his
brief sight of Quanah Parker and President Roosevelt)
Tant went to Altus. He reports:

Six persons were baptized and two others were added to the congregation. We have a good house and a
splendid working congregation at that place. They
supported me well in the meeting, and I must say that
this is the only congregation that has asked me this
year to hold a meeting outside of July and August —
though I have more than one hundred calls for those
two months." (Gospel Advocate, June 1, 1905.)

These July and August invitations were a source of constant concern and irritation to Tant. He felt that ten
months of the year were being wasted, while every congregation wanted a meeting either in July or in August. He
wrote repeatedly on this problem, typical of such articles
being the following:

"I find seven-tenths of the country churches in Texas spiritually dead; and ninety-nine one-hundredths of
them have gone out of business except in July and
August.

"In June I had one hundred and seven calls for meetings in July and August; another brother told me he had·one hundred and forty-three calls for the same time; yet I have found only one church in Oklahoma Territory, and not one church in Texas, that had life enough to hold a meeting outside of July and August.

"I have long since decided that our system of July and August preaching, and baptizing twenty to forty and leaving them to a set of so-called 'elders', who have not a single qualification as an elder, is a failure. Nine-tenths of the outfit are dead by the next July or August, and all wait for the preacher to come back and warm them up and baptize a few more, and thus it continues from year to year. Up to June I held four mission meetings this year; also two debates at mission points, for the Texas churches want neither debates nor preaching except in July or August. To more than a dozen churches who wrote me for July and August, I replied, 'I can't come then, but can come in April, May, or June.' Soon the reply would come back, 'We don't want you then. . . .'

"I would suggest that all preachers begin to advertise their work for another year, and advertise for ten protracted meetings — four of these meetings to be held at some strong churches during July and August; four others to be supported by these churches, at some place selected by them, and at a time set by the preacher. Then let every preacher hold two mission meetings at his own expense. These ten meetings will take us up to August; and all churches who call for July and August meetings — just let them wait until fall, as you are already engaged for July and August!

"If the preachers will study this matter and refuse to hold July and August meetings for churches unless said churches will hold one mission meeting at some other point and time, this will soon educate our strong country churches that they can do mission work. Hundreds of ordinarily strong churches who are able to hold one meeting, and frequently fail if they cannot get it in July or August, will soon learn that all preachers are at work in July and August, and that they will have to take another time or quit. As soon as they take another time, and learn that the Lord can work from September to December, as well as he can in July and August, they will arouse more people and churches to more work and better work." (Gospel Advocate, November 9, 1905.)

All through the late summer and fall of 1905 Tant held meetings in Arkansas. He contracted malaria, and was constantly bothered with chills and fever; but refused to go to bed or quit preaching. He came home in December so weakened as to bring genuine alarm to his wife and family. Through the months of January and February he was hardly able to get around, although he insisted on trying to preach each Sunday for the little congregation meeting in the school house.

LECTURESHIP AT DENTON, TEAS, 1906

Back Row, left to right: W.H. Owen, Foy E. Wallace, C.R. Nichol, J.W. Chism, Price Billingsley, George W. Savage.

Center Row: W.E. Morgan, R.L. Whiteside, J.C. White, O.H. McGavock, D.S. Ligon

Bottom Row: Mrs. Foy E. Wallace, Mrs. C.R. Nichol, Mrs. Price Billingsley, Mrs. Goerge W. Savage

CHAPTER XVI

CALIFORNIA

In the spring of 1906 Tant made his first visit to California, just in time to experience the great San Francisco earthquake. Throughout the winter he had suffered much from fever and chills, and had lost much weight. Nannie was unable to prevail on him to seek medical attention, and by March he was so weak he was hardly able to walk alone.

Nannie became genuinely alarmed, and decided she would have to take a hand in affairs at once, or else face the prospect of early widowhood. Carefully searching the news reports in the Firm Foundation, she found the name and address of a gospel preacher in California. She wrote to this brother, told him the situation, and asked his help in arranging two or three meetings for Tant in California. She knew her husband well enough to know he would never consent to going out there unless his work called him. Brother G. W. Winter of Forestville replied that he would gladly arrange the meetings, and for Tant to come on. Only after she had completed all the arrangements did Nannie tell her husband of what she had done. She writes:

"On March 23 I took him to the railroad station, and he was so weak that I had to half support him as he walked out to the train. I saw the brakeman help him aboard, and with a heavy heart drove back home, praying that he might be strong enough to make the trip, and that his health might be restored. He had an awful time reaching California, and the first week he was there was so weak he had to preach sitting in a chair. But almost from the first day he began to improve, and within a very short time he was back to his normal health." (Reminiscences.)

Tant wrote a series of four articles, describing his first trip to the Golden West:

"On March 23 I bade adieu to wife and children and started West for my next meeting at Aromas, California, twenty-two hundred miles away. . . ."

"After leaving El Paso, Texas, we spent all day in south New Mexico, traveling over beautiful table-lands skirted by the mountains, passing towns every forty miles or so, with no one living between the towns. This is the dry district, and will never be settled up.

"At Benson, Arizona, I dropped off the main line and ran down into Old Mexico to look at some land in Sonora, with a hope that some day I might colonize fifty or one hundred Christian families there. Sonora is one of the finest countries on earth, near the Pacific Coast, beautiful, and in a few years will be thickly populated by American farmers. If we could induce a few hundred families from the older states, who are Christians, to settle in there and get cheap homes and build up good schools, they would add much to the fighting force of primitive Christianity in a few more years.

"From Old Mexico I came back and dropped off one day in Tucson. I met some brethren here whom I had baptized twenty years ago, and learned there are a number of Christians in Tucson, but they are not meeting nor trying to work for the Master. I hope in years to come I may be able to drop my tent there and hold a month's meeting and help build up the church of Christ. Tucson has a population of about 20,000. It is a mining district; much drinking and gambling are going on here . . .

"Going west for three hundred and fifty miles from Tucson, we are in California, at Salton and by the Salton Sea. . . . After leaving Salton, we came next to Palm Valley. We learned that five miles out is the noted resort, Palm Springs, in a very beautiful Palm Valley. This valley was discovered by the Spaniards more than three hundred years ago; yet the nation that planted those trees and lived off the fruit had perhaps been gone for more than a thousand years. For the trees were very, very old even when the Spaniards came.

They had been planted in perfect order; the Indians who occupied the country when the Spaniards came in could give no account of the nation that had planted the trees. . . .

"My first meeting in California was held at Aromas, one hundred miles south of San Francisco, and near to Watsonville. Watsonville contains about 4,000 people. We once had a good congregation there, but the digressives came in and introduced the new order of things, divided the church, gained the property, and now they have a thirty-five-thousand dollar house and are the leaders in all societies and worldly entertainment of the day. I did not hear of a single Christian left in the town to contend for the ancient order of things. The gospel is as unknown in Watsonville today as it is in any other denominational town in California. As soon as all turned to the popular way, there was an old brother, named 'Mann', left like Elijah of old, who could not go the gaits; so he refused to go with them, and built a small meeting house in the country, where a few faithful met for years.

" But in time Brother Mann sold out and left; and his mantle fell on Brother J. W. Snyder, who got able to build the small house at Aromas, which cost $600.00. He built it all at his own expense except for forty dollars which was given him by Brother Mann. It is a beautiful house; it is small, well seated and lighted, yet large enough for our present use.

"I preached two weeks at Aromas and stirred up the church, I trust, to more active work. Aromas is a fine fruit country, and one of the most beautiful parts of California. Ten acres is considered a good-sized farm.

"Brethren moving to California, and desiring to locate near a church, will do well to write to J. W. Snyder, Watsonville, or to W. A. Canse, Aromas. You can get finely improved homes in Watsonville valley from two dollars to eight dollars per acre. The meeting at Aromas brought me up to the San Francisco earthquake, of which I may speak in my next." (Gospel Advocate, May 31, 1906.)

The meeting at Aromas closed on Sunday night, April 15.

Tant was scheduled to start at Colony Center, near San Francisco, on Wednesday night. He planned to spend a couple of days in San Francisco, taking in the sights of the city, before going on out to Colony Center. Arriving on Monday, he spent the rest of that day and all of Tuesday wandering around the city, asking questions, going from place to place as friendly policemen or strangers he stopped on the street might direct him. Tired out by the endless miles of walking the streets, he caught a train late Tuesday night on out to Colony Center, some eighteen miles from down-town San Francisco. He got there, found a room in a small hotel, and was fast asleep when the first tremors of the great earthquake struck about 5:00 o'clock in the morning. The shock was so severe that Tant was rolled out of bed and halfway across the room before he realized what was happening.

As quickly as daylight came, Tant made his way back into the city, which by now was a scene of wild confusion and disorder. The great fires which were to destroy the city (for it was fire rather than the quake which did the damage) were just beginning to take hold. The tremor had broken many of the water mains, and once a fire got well started there was no way to control it or fight it. Everything the hungry flames could reach went up in a roaring inferno of smoke and fire and terrific heat. Tant spent all of that day wandering about the city, trying to help as best he could, but being careful not to go into any of the restricted areas. The city had been quickly placed under martial law, and the soldiers and officers were authorized to "shoot on sight" any whom they saw burglarizing the stores or stealing from the bodies of the dead.

Back in Quanah, Texas, the news of the quake came swiftly. Nannie knew that her husband was to be in San Francisco on that day, for he had written her his schedule. She was frantic with worry, but soon managed to calm herself and await word from him — or of him. It was four days in coming. All the telegraph and telephone lines were tied up, and no messages could get either in or out for many hours save those that were most urgent or on government business.

But Tant had other things on his mind than an earthquake. He continues his story of the California trip:

"From San Francisco I went to Colony Center, where I found Methodist, Presbyterian, and digressive churches; but all refused to let me preach the Bible in their houses. Mr. Lackey, the digressive preacher, told me they had a perfect unity in practice among the three churches; and since they did not discuss the doctrine of either church, in a short time the Methodists and Presbyterians would learn his doctrine by 'absorption', and then all would be one. I found twelve to twenty faithful members at Colony Center, meeting for worship at the home of Dr. W. H. Pardee. I preached for them a few days.

"I then went to Fresno, and there found Brethren E. C. Love, Paul Hays, and Fred Hays — all loyal gospel preachers living in that area. Unfortunately, however, they have adopted the idea that it is wrong to have church houses, or to meet on Sunday in a Sunday school to teach the Bible. I found the moral character of these men spotless. I preached for them two nights in the Adventists' building and begged them to build a house of worship and to teach the Bible. Brother Love had a tent, and if he will abandon these items and impress the brethren with the essential things, I am sure he can do much good.

"I am now in a meeting at Madera, the county seat of Madera County. We once had a splendid church house here and a good congregation; but the digressives introduced an organ, division came, and the digressives captured the house and sold it to the Baptists. Now, after many years of hard work and struggles, Brother C. F. Bonner with the help of a few faithful ones has built up a good congregation with about forty members. . . .

"This is a farming country, and it is a good country if a man has from five to ten thousand dollars to start in with; but not much country for a poor man. People will not go to church in California, and unless a quest for health would lead a man to this country, if he has a family of children to rear, I would advise him to remain in the East." (Gospel Advocate, June 1, 1906.)

"From Madera I came to Forestville, the home of Brother G. W. Winter. Forestville is in the northern part of the State, and perhaps is better known to the eastern brethren than any other place in California. Brother Winter is one of our ablest preachers. I think we have at Forestville the largest congregation in the state, there being over 100 members in the band here. Brother Winter baptized twelve people during April. Several others have been baptized since our meeting began, and the attendance is large. Forestville is a small country village on the electric car line. Here the digressives are very different from what they are in the East. If there is an enemy on earth to God and the church of Christ, it is the 'digressive' of California. Brother Winter was forced to leave Forestville three years ago for his wife's health, and he had been gone only a short time when the digressives ran their 'State Evangelist' into Forestville in an effort to capture the church. This man finally got in his work by capturing fifteen or twenty members; but as he failed to capture their house, the church withdrew from the fallen members, and the effort failed. Yet the effects are strongly felt in the church.

"In this connection, I am glad to note the digressives are showing up in their true colors in Nashville and in other parts of Tennessee. I am glad Tennessee is seeing the work as it is, and as we have had it in Texas since 1887. In California, I have learned, the digressives have watchmen out, looking after each move made by the church of Christ, to try to overthrow all Bible work and to capture all gospel churches started. I am sorry to say that many who come to California, at least nine-tenths, soon get discouraged and go off with the digressives or quit the church entirely." (Gospel Advocate, June 28, 1906.)

Tant closed his Forestville meeting with fifteen baptisms, and returned to his home in Quanah on June 17. He had been gone for nearly three months; his health was fully restored, and he was eager to get back into some of the places where he had been. He reports:

"I will remain at home only three days, then off to central Texas for a meeting; then one month in Oklahoma, one month in Mississippi, and one month in Arkansas, then back to Texas for two debates. After that I will make a short visit home; then off again." (Ibid.)

II

That "one month in Mississippi" in the late summer of 1906 was to mark a milestone in Tant's life. For it was while preaching there that he made up his mind to move again — this time away from Texas and to Tennessee. He describes his reason for the change:

"I am glad to announce to the Gospel Advocate force and to all workers in the Lord that I am now located among you, and hope my work may be for good while I live in Tennessee.

"While I have been interested in Tennessee work and intimately associated with the Advocate during the past twelve years, yet Texas has been my home. During the last year, while holding meetings in North Mississippi, I saw the great need of more preachers being located in West Tennessee and Northern Mississippi, and thought that some of us should scatter out rather than to concentrate like preachers are doing around Nashville and Denton and other points.

"I have made a deal for a home in West Tennessee, and am now located on the farm thirty miles east of Memphis, five miles from Williston. I have my gospel tent with me, and shall spend the summer in protracted meeting work. I want to say especially to Brother John R. Williams and Brother N. B. Hardeman, as well as to other faithful workers in Tennessee: Count me among your workers, and I hope our combined efforts in the vineyard of the Lord may result in much good during the coming year . . .

"I shall be glad to correspond with brethren who desire to change locations, and tell them of this country and help them get homes, so all can work together in building up good schools and churches of Christ in this part of the country.

"I want to hire some Christian man to work on the farm and to stay with my family while I am out preaching. I have a fine library and if there is any young brother who wants to work and study and prepare himself for a useful life, wife and I will be glad to give all possible help in his studies, and will pay him good wages for his work. I believe we could be of great help to any young brother who is looking forward to the time when he hopes to preach the word." (Gospel Advocate, January 3, 1907.)

Of that trade and move to Tennessee Nannie says:

"Our ranch in Hardeman County, Texas, and home in Quănah were traded for an old southern plantation, thirty miles east of Memphis, Tennessee. This was another good trade, perhaps the best trade we ever made. We were now out of debt, and had five hundred acres of land, mostly very fertile, and an old ante-bellum mansion, built some sixty years previously, but still in a splendid state of preservation. The house was built by a shipbuilder, and every detail of workmanship and material showed his skill. Even the plastered walls had not cracked nor crumbled in the sixty years the house had stood. The cypress-shingled roof had never been replaced and did not leak any place. The large front porch with its beautiful white columns, the wide hall with its winding stairs, and the large rooms, each with its own fireplace, were all indices of the time and style of the age in which the house had been erected.

"Macon was the name of our little village (but we got our mail on a route from Williston). It had once been an educational center, supporting two colleges, a male and a female; but the schools were no longer in operation, and the old buildings were condemned and in decay. Nearly all the old, aristocratic families who had controlled this country had moved away from their plantations, and the country was now populated by a different class of people. As had been the case at Quanah, we again found ourselves in a community where there was no church. I began to feel like perhaps I was a missionary unawares and unintentionally. Our first effort in that section, of course, was to establish a faithful congregation." (Reminiscences.)

The editors of the Gospel Advocate were more than willing to help in this endeavor, and inserted the following notice in the Miscellany column of January 20, 1907:

"Brother J. D. Tant of Williston, Tennessee, is anxious to learn the names and locations of the members of the church of Christ living in Fayette and Shelby Counties, Tennessee. We request those who can to give Brother Tant the desired information."

This request was granted by some scores of brethren. But the number of disciples in Fayette and Shelby counties in 1907 could be numbered by the scores rather than by the hundreds or the thousands. There was one small congregation in Memphis, and it was not even able to build a meeting house without outside help. Brother A. M. St. John, in the Gospel Advocate of January 31, gives a list of the brethren and churches who have contributed funds for the building of a house in Memphis. The total came to $555.74. He expresses deep appreciation to Brother E. A. Elam for his help, and says that had it not been for Elam's help in soliciting the funds, they never could have built the house at all.

Tant soon got his spring farming under way, and late in March gave notice of his schedule for the next few weeks:

"I will soon be off the farm, preaching all the time. I will be at Whiteville on the first Sunday in April; at

Toone on the first Sunday in May; at Williams' Chapel
on the second Lord's day in May; then off to Nashville for a meeting at Green Street, beginning Thursday evening, May 16. I will hold a tent meeting at
Macon, my home, beginning on July 23. While this
will be wholly a mission meeting at my own expense
(for there is not a church of Christ in the county), yet
I will gladly take care of all scattering brethren who
may desire to come to the meeting. I am trying hard
to induce brethren who live at a distance away from
church opportunities to come and attend my meetings,
look at this country, locate here, and help to build up a
strong church. This is a fine farming country, also
healthful. Some brethren are writing me from Texas,
Illinois, and Mississippi, wanting to attend this meeting. I would be glad to hear from others, and have
them come and look at our country. By another year
I hope to be able to make a strong fight for Bible religion in West Tennessee." (Gospel Advocate, April
11, 1907.)

In July Tant held his tent meeting in Macon. Large
crowds were in attendance, many of them visiting brethren
from Kentucky, Alabama, and Mississippi. Since there
were no hotel accommodations, and since they were brethren, most of them stayed with the Tant family for the entire course of the meeting — three weeks.

On his forty-sixth birthday Tant was old enough to look
back over his life and reflect on how times were changing.
He wrote:

"I am today (June 28, 1907) forty-six years old; and
knowing that I have ascended the hill of life and am
now fast passing down to the river below, my mind
runs back with a vivid memory for forty years, and
it seems the changes have been so great that we are almost separated five hundred years from that time in
all we do. Then we had the loom, the spinning wheel,
the old-time water mill, the cradle-cut wheat, the home
raised boy, and the many little things that made home

happy. But things have changed, and old things have
passed away. With them has passed, also, the old-time
preacher.

"In those days we had many godly men who would
work on their farm until Friday night; get on their
horses on Saturday and ride from twenty-five to forty
miles, preach on Saturday night and three times on
Sunday, and do some baptizing; and then off for home
on Monday morning. These were not big preachers —
only godly men. They were not paid ten to twenty
dollars a trip, but went at their own expense; and when
they went, they knew but little of grammar and history, but were full of the Bible and of love for the children of men. These men were welcome everywhere.
All religious people in the community went out to hear
them. None became tired at the two-hours' sermon;
all were anxious to shake hands with the preacher and
have him go home with them. The preacher in those
days was not looked upon as the professional man that
he is today, but all recognized him as a messenger of
God.

"I am now preaching in the hills of Alabama, and I
often hear members speak of the old-time preacher.
We had no ambitious schools and colleges to make
preachers; yet we had the preachers any way. We
cannot claim that we had such big preachers as we
have today, but they were men of God; and today we
have members and a few congregations all over Alabama, Mississippi, Georgia, Tennessee, and throughout
the South that were built up by the old-time preachers.
But as times began to change, many brethren began to
seek the preacher that could entertain their neighbors;
and as these old brethren were not so well up in smooth
language and good manners as the college boys, many
of them were relegated to the background to make
room for the big preacher. As many of the big preachers must have money and are wanted at big places,
I find that at many of the interior points, where the
church is not able to send for the big preacher, the
cause is now dead; and men and women are dying without the knowledge of Christ and the gospel. The old-
time preacher has gone, and these places are not able

to employ the young and able preachers. Would to God a spiritual wave could come over the church to-day, and hundreds of brethren who have homes and ordinary intelligence could give up the great desire for money-making and fast living and move far back into the country, build up homes among the people, preach to them the plain simple gospel, which is God's power to save, reinstate the old-time preacher and gospel preaching, and preach more to save and less to enter-tain and please the sects! If this could be done, in ten years time thousands of good people all over the coun-try could hear the gospel and be saved; but under the present surroundings they are bound to be lost. May God help us to think on these things." (Gospel Advo-cate, August 29, 1907.)

All through the summer and fall of 1907 Tant kept writ-ing pleas in the gospel papers for brethren to come to West Tennessee and try to build up faithful churches. He de-clared: ⁻

"Few sections are better blessed with gospel men and women than Middle Tennessee, and few sections are as far behind and need the gospel as much as West Tennessee. So I hope, brethren, you will hear me pa-tiently, and think seriously of our condition. I live thirty miles east of Memphis, and in my county there are not only hundreds, but thousands, of men and wom-en who have never heard a gospel sermon. We have not a single working church in Fayette County. In many communities we have found from one to six mem-bers, uneducated in the gospel, spiritually dead, and their children herding with the sects. We also have many towns with from five to ten members that are doing no good. We have a few congregations — per-haps a dozen in eight or ten counties — that are just existing and depending on the annual meeting, while thousands around them are dying for want of gospel food.

"Our first great need is to get this country before the brotherhood and persuade our members to come here and buy homes and live among us. After thirty years in Texas, I am fully convinced that, all things considered, West Tennessee furnishes more inducements for a poor man than Texas. Thousands pass Memphis each year, going to the far West, who could do far better here. Our country is beautiful, and our lands are productive and cheap. If three or four hundred families of Christians who live in Middle Tennessee, where lands are high and where each congregation has five or six brethren who are able to lead the services, could sell their homes there, they could with the money buy four times the amount here, which in a few years will more than double in value. Let each of these members come with the determination to preach the gospel. Let each man and woman come, as we used to go, with a New Testament well studied and marked, and let all, both men and women, preach the gospel in their own communities, and in the way God has ordained, that their neighbors may learn the truth. . .

"We want four or five young men who will go, like the Mormons, from house to house seven days in every week and preach the gospel everywhere. A young minister in this part could hardly stop at any man's house to stay all night without getting one or two families to come over after supper, and he could tell them of Christ, and his church, of our object and work, of our differences from all human churches, and point out the advantages in being nothing but a Christian." (Gospel Advocate, September 19, 1907.)

It was a beautiful dream Tant had. But in practical application it proved disastrous — to him and his family, at least. A part of that disaster can be traced to Tant's own emotional makeup. He had a tremendous sympathy for, and tenderness toward, the unfortunates of earth. The poor, the illiterate, the sick, the crippled, the orphan and widow in any circumstance in life would receive quick (and sometimes unreasonable) help from Tant's hand. He had not the ability to discriminate between the deserving and the dead-beat, between the case of one genuinely in need and one who was "on the make". His tender concern for the orphan child was to lead him, in later years, into an association with Tennessee Orphan Home, and cause him to spend much time and energy in promoting that institution. He felt every helpless child ought to have protection and shelter until Christian people could be awakened to their obligation to take such into their homes, and wrote frequent articles of criticism against congregations for not caring for these children. It is probable that his own poverty-ridden childhood contributed to his naturally sympathetic feelings for the underprivileged.

Nannie tells how this sympathy got the Tant family into trouble:

"Previous to our moving east, my husband's work had been largely in the western states. But now he had many calls from eastern churches to help them in their meetings. While holding a meeting in Huntsville, Alabama, he observed the hardships of some of the brethren who worked in the cotton mills there. The same summer (1908) he was called to the hills of Kentucky for a meeting. He there came in contact with some good brethren who were hard pressed financially, and with their large families were barely able to eke out a rather miserable existence on the poor, hilly soil they were trying to cultivate. Educational advantages for the children were non-existent; the land was thin and unproductive. Life was a hard and bitter struggle for all. They were good people, honest and God-fearing, but were living on the ragged edge of starvation.

"All this made a deep impression on my husband's heart. When he came home that fall, he told me he believed God would not hold him guiltless unless he did all he could to relieve the distress of some of the poor people whom he had met. We had made a marvelous cotton crop that year, the land being rented out to a number of good negro tenants who were 'share-cropping'. Most of the negro tenants on our farm had far more to their share that fall than many of the white families my husband had encountered through the summer. He saw that the negroes for the most part squandered their money on whiskey and gambling, and took little thought to better their lot. This was the final straw that made up his mind. He decided he was going to reserve one hundred acres of land adjoining our home-site for us, and then divide the remainder of the farm into fifty-acre tracts. He would then sell these fifty acre farms to poor, struggling brethren — on credit, and with no down payment.

"I was never one to object to any business deal my husband proposed, but this time I did interpose a few mild protests. I could see the blight of some of my fondest dreams. I called his attention to the fact that our farm was well provided with good tenant houses; we had as responsible negroes as could be found to work the land, we had an adequate supply of teams, and all the farming equipment necessary; and we had just completed a beautiful, big barn. I told him it looked to me like we were just now in the position he had been trying to bring us to ever since we had married — a position in which he could feel perfectly free to go anywhere and everywhere and preach with never a moment's thought as to the support either for himself or for his family. Under our arrangement there I could easily manage the business end of the plantation, the negroes would do the work, and we would have far more security and a far better living than we had ever had in our lives. Not only so, but we would very easily be in a position to support at least two, and probably three or four full time preachers of the gospel to go into needy areas, as well as himself. Furthermore, our oldest daughter, Davis, was about ready for college; and we needed to consider the fact that one by one our children would now be growing up and reaching college age. We needed to provide something for those forthcoming expenses.

"But my husband had an answer for all of that. He said he would sell the eight small farms to eight honest and reliable brethren; and let each one of them pay him $100.00 per year for fifteen years. He would have them make out the notes for the full amount, non interest bearing, and that would be their annual payments on the farms they were buying. In this way we would have $800.00 for certain each fall, plus what we made off of the 100 acres we were reserving for our own use, plus anything that he might receive from his preaching. I was finally convinced.

"He selected eight brethren (from the scores who had written him or who had visited when his scheme became known), and explained the full plan to them. They all eagerly accepted; they would have been simpletons to have turned down such an offer. All eight men made out their notes, and we drew up eight separate deeds to the various tracts of land. Each man agreed to pay $1,500.00 for his fifty acres, the payments to be spread out over fifteen years. We agreed to furnish lumber for each man to build a three room house, and the men were to do the carpentery work in putting the houses up. All things were now ready for our brethren to begin moving in and taking possession of their small farms.

"The moving began. As each family reached the railroad station, some ten miles away, my husband would send our hired man with a wagon to meet them and haul them out to the farm. Those who had houses already built (the tenant houses) moved into them at once; but most of the families would spend from one day to three weeks in our home, until their own houses were ready. At one time we had twenty-seven people in the house with us. That was just one month before my fifth baby, Yater, was born. But these ladies were very considerate of me, and did the greater part of the work. It was in December, hog-killing time, so I turned all my sausage making and lard rendering over to them.

"To make a long and tragic story into a short and tragic story, only two of those families knew anything at all about farming. Several of them were from the cotton mills, and were totally inexperienced in farm work. Most of them arrived at our home with not enough money to buy even a week's supply of groceries. My husband stood for them at the store, expecting they would pay him in the fall. With full and unlimited credit some of these brethren went on fantastic buying sprees, living far more opulently than they had ever dreamed of back in Alabama or the hills of Kentucky.

"At the end of the first year, only two of those eight families paid their accounts at the store; those same two paid their notes on the land. The other six paid neither their store bills nor their notes to us.

"But it had been a bad year, climate wise, so everybody thought the next year would be better. My husband went to the various stores and told them to let the people have groceries and supplies for another year, and he would stand surety for their debts. But the second year was a repetition of the first — two families paid their bills and their notes to us; six paid neither. This year the climate had been fine.

"But my husband was determined to help these six poor families get a start in life. He felt that they were good and honest people, but simply inexperienced, and that surely with two years' experience behind them, they would make a good crop the third year! So once again he went to the stores and stood surety for these six families.

"End of the third year — same sad result. We became convinced then that of the eight families who had bought our land, two were good farmers and honest men, and would pay as promised; four families were honest enough, but simply failures as farmers; and two families were strictly dead-beats. These two families bought more groceries and more clothes, I am sure, than they had ever had in their lives before. Frequently one of the ladies would sit by me in the church house with her baby in her lap. I noticed the baby would be wearing white kid shoes, lace cap, and the very choicest and finest of little dresses. My baby would be bare-footed, and have nothing on but a diaper and the very cheapest of little cotton dresses. All the fine clothes had been charged at the store — with my husband promising the merchant he would get his money.

"My husband was away preaching at cotton picking time, and it was by sheer accident that I saved even one bale of cotton that one of these families sold. I had an officer follow the man to the market and garnishee the cotton as it was sold. One by one the failures and the dead-beats left us, leaving huge charge accounts behind them, never having paid a dollar on the land they had bought or the houses they had built. We took their notes to the bank and tried to discount them to get money to pay their grocery bills. But the notes were non-interest bearing, and no bank would have them.

"We had to sell our beautiful home in the country to pay the debts these six families had piled up on us, and it took us ten long years to get all the merchants in Macon finally paid. We got a smaller house in town, took back some of the tracts of land which we had sold to the brethren, and were fortunate enough to get back some of our original negro tenants who had worked these acres for many years.

"While all this was happening we sent Davis away to Freed-Hardeman College (it opened in Henderson in the fall of 1908) for two years. And came very near to losing our oldest son — J. D., Jr."

**Macon, Tennessee, 1909. Zoreta at left; J. D. Jr. at right;
Davis and Maidia standing at rear; Mozelle in her father's
lap; Fanning yater in his mother's lap.**

CHAPTER XVII

TUMBLE-BUGS, PIGS, AND BULLS

In February, 1908, a debate was scheduled between Joe S. Warlick and Elder Wyatt, one of the Apostles of the Mormon Church. The discussion was to be held at Bethany Church, about four miles northeast of Cottage Grove, Tennessee. The Latter-Day Saints were rather numerous in the community, and were filled with exuberant confidence to have one of their really great men, an Apostle, meet the champion of the "Campbellites." They freely predicted that this would be Warlick's last debate with a Mormon, and some even offered to wager that Warlick would not show up for the encounter. Just a few days before the scheduled discussion, Wyatt wrote Warlick, telling him that since he, Warlick, was a man of such ungentlemanly reputation and character, the debate was off. He wrote: "You can go on to Tennessee and blow your horn and holler 'back out!' if you desire; I'll not be there!" When Wralick received this letter at his home in Texas, he dismissed the debate from his mind, and remained at home with his family, some of whom were sick with smallpox at the time.

Not knowing that the debate had been called off, J. D. Tant went to Bethany Church on the appointed day, hoping to enjoy a discussion as an auditor — a rather unusual experience for him. When he got there he found that Warlick was not there — and Wyatt was! The Mormons were having a field day, proclaiming that, as they had predicted, the "Campbellite" champion had taken cold feet and failed to show up. There was loud laughter, hilarious singing, hand-shaking and back-slapping going on all over the place as the Mormons were congratulating one another on their great victory. Knowing smiles gradually gave way to sneers and taunts as the time kept going by and Warlick did not appear. Neither did anybody know where he was, nor had anyone heard from him as to whether he could be expected.

About noon time, after two hours of suffering under the Mormon "victory parade", some of the brethren came to Tant and asked him if he would be willing to debate in Warlick's place. Tant readily agreed. The audience was called to order, and was told that the Church of Christ leaders had asked J. D. Tant to represent them in the absence of Warlick; and the debate would get under way and proceed as scheduled.

Brother A. O. Colley reported the affair:

"Each affirmed the church question. Brother Tant so clearly presented the truth on his proposition that Wyatt did but little against him. When the church of the Latter-Day Saints came under criticism, it was a real enjoyable time for the Christians. Brother Tant had no books with him, but, like David of old, slew the great giant with a few well-chosen stones from God's Book." (Gospel Advocate, March 5, 1908.)

Wyatt made many references to Warlick's "cowardice" in failing to show up for the discussion. He had the audience in an uproar a good part of the time, the Mormons laughing uproariously at his sharp jabs aimed at the "Campbellites," and the Christians writhing under his sallies and muttering under their breath. Tension was mounting by the moment. Tant repeatedly called on Wyatt to get on the subject, and to stop dealing in personalities. All to no avail. Wyatt's ridicule and sarcasm seemed to grow sharper and more cutting with each passing speech. Finally, Tant decided to put a stop to it. He began to turn Wyatt's witticisms back on him with devastating ef-

fect, countering blow for blow, jab for jab. Wyatt finally
began to grow obviously agitated and uncomfortable under
the onslaught. The Mormons grew silent. At length
Wyatt began to complain.

"Elder Tant has shown himself even less of a gentleman
than Warlick," he complained in one speech. "He has
called me every kind of belittling and ridiculous thing a
man could think of. I can't call to mind any kind of animal
he has failed to compare me with unless it be a tumble-
bug. I guess now that I've mentioned it he will be calling
me a tumble-bug in his next speech."

"Not at all," responded Tant when he got the floor.
"Why, before God, friends, I thought everybody recognized
what is happening in this debate — J. D. Tant is the
tumble-bug, and Elder Wyatt is the stuff the tumble-bug
is rolling down the road!!"

Shortly after the Tant-Wyatt debate, Tant moderated
for Joe S. Warlick in a debate with R. H. Pigue at Hazel,
Kentucky. This was Warlick's third discussion with Pigue.
About twenty gospel preachers were there, and only three
Methodist preachers. These three stayed only a short
time, then left. Pigue made much of this, claiming that
the "Campbellites" had to send a thousand miles to get
their great champion, then he had to have fifteen or twenty
of their strongest men to help him, while he, Pigue, just
a poor, ordinary circuit-riding pastor, could whip the whole
bunch of them single-handedly, meanwhile sending his own
Methodist brethren out to preach the blessed gospel while
he was doing it.

Tant reported the debate:

"At times the debate was too tough to come under
the head of a religious discussion; but a man can no
more meet Pigue successfully and occupy a high plane
than one could kill a polecat with a yardstick and not
smell bad. Joe S. Warlick is a strong man, and, I

think the most adept I ever heard at meeting a man on all points, and turning every argument against him." (Gospel Advocate, March 12, 1908.)

II

In the summer of 1908 A. G. Freed was rapidly completing plans to open Freed-Hardeman College at Henderson in September. In this endeavor he found a faithful and energetic backer in J. D. Tant, who wrote:

"At one time we had at Henderson, Tennessee, a Christian school that sent its students into all parts of the country, filling their mission and teaching the gospel of Christ. But innovators captured this school, and turned it into sectarian channels. And as the sectarian field was already occupied by larger and better schools, this school had no distinctive field to occupy, and in the course of time died a natural death.

"About this time A. G. Freed, who once managed the Georgia Robertson Christian College successfully (before it departed from the truth), came upon the stage of action again at Henderson, and sought to establish in West Tennessee a high-grade normal college for the purpose of developing first-class teachers and other professional men and women for the higher walks of this life and that above. Brother Freed, knowing the whole duty of man is to 'fear God and keep his commandments', has added a Bible department to this school, so that all persons going from this college may be able to teach the gospel plan of salvation to those with whom they may come in contact in all the walks of life.

"Associated with Brother Freed in this work is his former student, his Timothy, and also his long and tried companion in the gospel, N. B. Hardeman, a man who was reared at Henderson and who for some time has been County Superintendent of Public Instruction, and who holds the respect of the entire town. I have been more or less associated with our teachers and preachers for the past twenty-five years; and I am sure we have not two more loyal preachers in the

church of Christ than N. B. Hardeman and A. G. Freed.
And as teachers, they have no superiors in the South.

"We want this school to be to West Tennessee what
the Bible School has been to Nashville, and what the
Lockney Christian College has been to West Texas.
When I call to memory that twenty years ago nothing
like the Nashville Bible School was known, and now
when I can see and hear of our boys in more than
half the states and in Canada, I realize what great
things can come from small beginnings." (Gospel
Advocate, April 9, 1908.)

Throughout the summer of 1908 Tant wrote a number
of articles for the religious journals, pleading the worth
and value of such schools as Freed-Hardeman College. He
told of the beginning of the Nashville Bible School, and
how it had grown to the point that they were unable to
accommodate all who desired entrance there; then how J. A.
Harding had gone to Bowling Green, Kentucky, to start
another school. Shortly thereafter J. N. Armstrong, Harding's son-in-law, had gone to Odessa, Missouri, to start
still another school. Cordell, Oklahoma, was also in the
list of places where Christian colleges were being developed. All this Tant approves and encourages in his articles.
He has no idea that anyone will ever think of these schools
as taking the place of the church, or as competitors of the
church. They are simply high-class educational institutions, operated by faithful Christian men, in which boys
and girls can receive the very finest cultural and professional training in the land. The Bible will be taught in
these schools, and thus the students will be encouraged
in moral and spiritual values along with their secular education. He hopes that such schools can soon be started
in Memphis, Chattanooga, Martin, Knoxville, "and at all
other points where we must fight the enemy." (Gospel
Advocate, September 10, 1908.)

In September Tant entered his own daughter, Davis, as

a student at Freed-Hardeman College. Although he was
never a man of any wealth, before his life ended he was
to have the names of twenty-seven young men and women
whom he had personally helped through one or the other
of the Christian colleges. His writings were often an
enigma to many brethren, for in the same articles in which
he urged brethren to support these schools he would speak
in the plainest and strongest terms of their shortcomings.
He was particularly critical of the tendency on the part
of many churches not to engage a preacher unless he came
from a Christian college. His disillusionment with the colleges was a thing of slow and gradual development, and
did not reach fruition until late in life.

It was in 1909 that Tant began to voice his first real
alarm as to the "drift" which he thought he saw taking
place within the brotherhood. This "drift" coincided with
the years in which the fight with the digressives began
to subside, and brethren began to try to build a "new approach" to the denominational world — an approach in
which debating and discussions would have an ever de-
creasing emphasis. In an article entitled, "Where Are
We Drifting?", Tant wrote:

"While in Texas I have received many calls for
meetings I could not fill. Some came from churches
and some from mission points. I have talked with
these brethren, telling them I cannot hold their meetings, and have wanted them to get such men as J. Q.
Pringle, John S. Newman, Brother Hicks, or Brother
Calloway, who are grand, godly men, and gospel
preachers who work on the farm for a living and hold
meetings each summer. They are making sacrifices
for Christ. But with one consent all have refused to
get them because they are not 'big' preachers, telling
me plainly that if they could not get a 'big' preacher,
they would not have any. This impresses me more
and more that preaching every year is becoming a
profession, and with our present rate of progress noth-

ing but the professional preacher from a Bible College will be allowed to preach in any pulpit twenty years from now.

"At one time the lamented F. D. Srygley was talking to me on the Bible College preacher, and said that by hearing any man three times he could tell which college ground him out, as each college had a different machine to turn their preachers on. And, knowing the working of each machine, he could tell where the man came from . . . .

"Twenty-five years ago many of our churches had young men in them who would study and go out each summer, hold four or five meetings at school houses, baptize fifty to one hundred, go home and tell of this grand work. All would rejoice and give God the praise and say this is only church work. But I find the churches have gone out of the preacher-making business today. There is no home talent being developed. All our young men have decided that it is just as essential for them to go to college to learn how to preach as for the doctor to go to medical school; for he must be a professional or none. This idea is killing the usefulness of hundreds of good men who are not able to go to college, and who realize they are not wanted because they are not 'big' preachers.

"Another thing I have carefully noted: not a single Bible College in my knowledge has turned out an ordinary or second-class preacher for fifteen years; but each preacher is said to be 'the ablest of them all'. I would be glad to get the picture of just one second-class preacher turned out by the Bible Colleges. I want to put the picture in my museum as a curiosity. As soon as the professional preacher comes in, not only must the old-time and little preacher go, but God's ordained eldership, commissioned of God to feed the flock, will go too. I may not live to see it, but, brethren, I sound the word of warning, and say that on this line we will have much trouble in the next thirty years.

"I believe strongly in education. But Christ never did establish colleges to make preachers, and I have tried to sugar-coat and swallow that preacher-college

pill half a dozen times; but so far it has vomited me
and I spew it up. I would like to get something to
make it stay down if there is anything on it in the
Bible. Remember, no church today wants, or is satisfied with a gospel minister to preach for them if he
is not a 'big' preacher.

"My position is quite unpopular, and it forces me to
go in a crowd to myself. But Elijah had to go on that
way, and as my life work is almost ended, I am not
trying to please the world, but the Lord. He is the
one to pass on my record at the last day." (Gospel
Advocate, November 2, 1909.)

Tant was again much concerned about the failure of
both preachers and churches to do more work. He wrote
a lengthy article under the caption, "What Does It Mean?":

"I notice in the Firm Foundation six preachers out
of work and calling for more work to do. Also an
able brother here today has only one more meeting,
then he will be up with his work, and without the
promise of another meeting until next May. I also
learned from two congregations in Oklahoma that they
had letters from one of our ablest preachers and debaters in Texas asking them to let him hold meetings
for them this winter. But they do not want him as
churches of Christ can work only in the summer time.

"Early this year Joe Warlick was at my home, and
told me he then had sixty calls for meetings more than
he could hold in Texas this year. While I was in Texas
a few months ago I had fifteen or twenty calls that
I could not fill — all wanting their meetings in July
or August.

"Two more meetings and one debate will close out
my work for this year; and while I put myself up as
one of our ablest preachers (in fact, I don't know any
better!), still I don't have any idea of another call
for a meeting before next May. So I can go home and
loan out the money I made this year preaching, and
have a good time until next year. Will have plenty
of money to pay all my lodge dues, and were I like
some of my brethren, I could also have good tobacco

to chew on all winter.   But I don't even cuss yet, much less use tobacco.

"In looking over my books I see I have held twelve meetings this year, and have been paid $560.00, or $46.00 for each meeting. However, two of the churches paid me $100.00 each for their meetings; but three of the meetings held were mission meetings, so the average was $46.00 per meeting.

"To hold these meetings I have had to run all over Tennessee, Kentucky, Louisiana, Texas, and Oklahoma, and my railroad fare has been about $100.00.   This leaves me $460.00 to support my family and speculate with.   Still my salary compares favorably with what I always got when I was in Texas preaching all the time, and I am sure it is far above the average salary of my preaching brethren . . . . .

"My dear preaching brethren, you are up against a hard proposition.   Nine out of every ten will, in old age, have to become beggars just like poor old Brothers Harris, Polly, and McIntyre.   In their younger days they were abler preachers than most of us, yet they had to beg.

"I am paid for preaching less than $800.00 a year; out of that salary I hold from one to four mission meetings each year.   I know churches worth $20,000.00 to $30,000, with from fifty to one hundred members, yet from $40.00 to $50.00 a year for one meeting is all they can do.   Paul teaches that one should not be burdened and another eased.   Let us think on these things." (Firm Foundation, November 23, 1909.)

This same issue of the Firm Foundation carried an article from Brother A. A. Hartsell somewhat critical of the preachers for being too money-minded.   He wrote:

"It seems to me of late years some of our preachers expect too much pay for their labor.   I call to mind one circumstance.   A preacher with whom I am well acquainted (and he is a good preacher too) held a meeting at a place where there were only a few members.   They paid him $16.00 for one week, and he would not preach any longer.   He said that would not pay his expenses. His railroad fare was only twenty cents. I have read of others getting as high as $75.00 and even $100.00 for a meeting of two or three weeks. That is more than I can make in four or five months of hard labor; and it seems the preachers are hunting just such places as that and neglecting the by-ways and hedges. At least, many of them are."

Since Tant was generally recognized as one of the most sacrificing preachers in the church, and had never turned down a call anywhere because of money considerations, G. H. P. Showalter wrote him, enclosing the Hartsell letter, and asking him to comment on it. Tant did:

"I have read with interest what Brother Hartsell says, and comment that he may see the other side. I have held two meetings this year (one was for a month) where they paid me $100.00 for the meeting; also my books show three mission meetings held at my own charges, and I start to Kentucky tomorrow for my fourth mission meeting this year. Also my books show that for January this year I was paid $5.50; for February, nothing; for April nothing. Then when we count that three-fourths of all mission work is done by the preachers, not by the churches, and when we count that there are three to five months each year when the preacher is not paid railroad fare, I don't think the poor preacher is to blame for hunting a place where they will pay him $75.00 to $100.00 for a meeting. Four years ago in winter time I preached five months, and received for all that time only $47.00; my railroad fare for that time was $63.00. I have a wife and six children to support, and many of my preaching brethren have as many. If we don't get a few $100.00 meetings to hold, our families will suffer, and we will be worse than infidels, and will die and go where most of our brethren are going who do not give as they have been prospered. No, brother, our preachers are good men. They are not out for the money. They are all anxious to have the by-ways saved, but are not able to save them unless the churches will help . . ."   (Firm Foundation, November 23, 1909.)

III

The Tant-Pigue debate was held at the Oldfield Methodist Church in Crockett County, Tennessee, in 1910. It was the first discussion between these two men (they were to have two more in following years), and was notable for many reasons. A huge throng of people had gathered for the opening session. Pigue was there, dressed to perfection, in elegance and style. As the time drew near for the discussion to open, Tant was nowhere in evidence. After a delay of some little time, waiting for Tant to make his appearance, Pigue got into the pulpit and made a short speech about the "Campbellites." He said that they were long on boasting, but short on everything else; and that since Tant was obviously too scared to make his appearance, the debate would have to be called off.

Just at that moment a figure arose from the back seat of the assembly, a lanky, dirty, unshaven farmer, dressed in the ragged overalls and dirty sweat-stained shirt of a field hand. All eyes began to turn toward the farmer, and when Pigue saw that he had not the attention of his audience he stopped his speaking. The farmer then spoke up:

"My name is J. D. Tant, and I am ready for the debate to start."

Pigue commented with some disgust on the "uncouth and sloven" appearance of his opponent, and opined that the dignity and importance of the occasion demanded a more respectable presence than Tant offered.

"I grew up on a farm," Tant responded with his nasal twang even more pronounced than usual, "and my old pappy always told us boys to dress for the kind of work we had to do. I come down here to do a hog-killin' job

on a fat, over-grown, over-stuffed 'pigue', and I dressed
for the occasion. Let's get on with the job!"

That set the tone for the discussion. It was sharp and
bitter from the opening session. Pigue was a master at
sarcasm and ridicule, and began to punctuate his arguments with a sing-song ejaculation: "Tant just can't cut
the mustard; he can't cut the mustard."

After this sort of refrain had extended over two days,
Tant put a rather sudden end to it by saying,

"Elder Pigue keeps shouting that 'Tant can't cut the
mustard'. Well, I don't know so much about cutting the
mustard — but I've had plenty of experience in the hog-
lot, and before God, brethren, I claim to be an A number
One champion when it comes to cutting pigs!"

The years 1909-1912 were years of deep personal tragedy
and sorrow for Tant. His troubles multiplied beyond measure. These were the years when he was losing his farm
at Macon to brethren who were failing in their promises
to pay him, when his son, J. D., Jr., developed the illness
that came near costing his life, and when the Gospel Advocate barred his writings (and for a while even his name)
from its pages.

This last was a cruel blow to Tant, for he had long been
one of the staunchest backers and helpers the Advocate
had ever had. He had sent in thousands of subscriptions
to the paper, urging the brethren both publicly and privately to read it. He had come very near to alienating
many of his life-long Texas friends by his loyal support
of the Tennessee journal. But 1909 was the year in which
the Gospel Advocate came out with a new format, much
smaller pages, neat, attractive, and much more "literary"
in style. The character of the writings shows a marked
retreat from the aggressive "fighting" spirit of the paper
during the years when Lipscomb was in his prime.

And this was the year, 1909, when Robert H. Boll of

Louisville, Kentucky, became front page editor of the journal. John Straiton wrote of R. H. Boll:

> "For grace of literary style, depth of insight, true spirituality, there are but two writers with whom I can compare him. These are Dr. Robertson Nicol, and our esteemed English brother, H. E. Tickle, of Glasgow, Scotland." (Gospel Advocate, October 21, 1909.)

Tant had no "literary style". He did not fit into the company of Boll, Nicol, and Tickle. He was a son of the frontier, with all the blunt "earthiness" and plainness of speech which characterized the age and the people from whence he came. The new Gospel Advocate could not carry on its pages a man who was likely to shock its more cultured and effete readers. "Bulls", "polecats," "tumble bugs", and castrated pigs might be fit subjects for parlor conversation or pulpit eloquence in the wilds of Texas, but they were obviously not proper topics for the cultured sons and daughters of the "Athens of the South," and not for the literary style of R. H. Boll.

Tant's exclusion from the Advocate was contrary to David Lipscomb's judgment and wishes, but he yielded here, as he did in many things in his declining years, to the desires of others. He loved Tant, and had complete confidence in him; but Lipscomb was growing old, and more and more he left the management of the Advocate to other and younger men. Too, the spring of 1909 found him in one of the gravest and most prolonged illnesses of his life, an illness from which he never fully recuperated.

In spite of this exclusion, however, Tant continued to work for the interest of the paper. He still urged brethren to read it, and continued to subscribe for it himself. He still sent in a list of subscriptions from almost every place where he held meetings. Most of the men on the editorial

staff (E. A. Elam, M. C. Kurfees, E. G. Sewell, J. C. Mc-
Quiddy, and David Lipscomb) were all his long time
friends. He had met R. H. Boll, but had had very little
acquaintance with him. Tant was particularly close to
F. W. Smith of Franklin, Tennessee, who for many years
was one of the Advocate staff of writers. When Tant's
articles were again accepted by the Gospel Advocate some
ten years later (1920), J. C. McQuiddy wrote an apology
for the years of his exclusion, saying it had been caused
by "false reports" of Tant's pulpit language. Evidently
some of the brethren had brought greatly exaggerated
accounts of the Wyatt and Pigue debates and of Tant's
preaching in general. Tant had twice offered to pay the
travel expenses of his accusers if they would meet him
in the Advocate office and make their accusations face
to face and give him an opportunity to be heard in his
own defense. This they refused to do.

IV

His exclusion from the Gospel Advocate caused Tant to
increase his writings to both the Firm Foundation and the
Christian Leaders. He also sent in many subscriptions
to these papers, and the Firm Foundation particularly carried frequent notices of receiving lists of subscriptions
from him, and expressed gratitude for his loyal support.
Early in 1909 he wrote an article entitled "Big Things"
which appeared on the front page of that journal:

"The same disposition that prompts men to go with
the big crowds also decides men in their religious dis-
positions. They seek for popularity; they can not bear
to be alone. They seek to mingle with the big crowd;
they go to hear the big preacher; they are always
found at the big meeting; they will go to church on
big days; but when the faithful few meet to worship
God and gain spiritual strength these people are never
there. They little consider what injury they do them-

selves in seeking to follow the multitude." **Firm
Foundation,** January 19, 1909.)

Tant also gave a series of eight long articles in the
Foundation that year under the title, "Reviewing The
Past." In these he told of his early struggles for the truth
in Texas and elsewhere, and gave many interesting reports
of the various experiences of a gospel preacher in the closing years of the nineteeth century. (Much of the material
in those articles is to be found in the earlier chapters of
this book.)

In the sping of 1909 Tant had a brief exchange through
the Firm Foundation with W. S. Vickery on the subject of
"Valid Baptism." Vickery wrote a series of articles, pur-
porting to prove that a full understanding of the design of
baptism was not required of the penitent sinner. Tant
responded to him:

> "The Scriptures teach that a man must believe and
> understand that baptism is for the remission of sins to
> make it valid.
> "Brother W. S. Vickery, in April 27th issue, claims this
> position is untrue, and calls upon all to show him he is
> wrong. Ten years ago nineteen-twentieths of the lead-
> ing preachers of Texas held this position as true. All
> the little preachers and almost all of the big preachers
> hold the same position today. But as it is not popular
> in some papers, I notice some of the popular preachers
> now tell how many came from the Baptists and Meth-
> odists. But to help Brother Vickery I write this let-
> ter. . . ." (Firm Foundation, May 18, 1909.)

Tant then gave a long summary of the arguments made
on the "rebaptism" question, and urged all brethren to be
content with Bible teaching on the subject.

Meanwhile, preaching and traveling were continuing as
usual:

> "Brother J. D. Tant will begin a meeting at Briar,

five miles west of New Ark, Texas, August 17th. All
who can are requested to go and camp and help in the
meeting". (F. F. June 22, 1909.) "Brother J. D. Tant
has closed his meeting at Waxahachie, Texas, with
twenty additions to the congregation, seventeen baptisms and three restorations. Brother Tant is now at
Longview, Texas, in a meeting." (Ibid, June 29, 1909.)

It was in this meeting at Longview that Tant began his
life-long friendship with John W. Akin, a poor, but extremely hard-working farmer who lived a few miles out of
town. When the meeting was ready to close, Tant announced, "John Akin will preach for you next Sunday."
Akin had never made any attempt toward public work in
the church at all, and was more than a little agitated at
the thought of trying to make a talk. But he accepted the
challenge, made his talk, and for the rest of his life was
an active teacher, and for many years an elder, in the
church. The discovery of oil in east Texas brought a rather
considerable fortune to Akin, and he became one of the
heaviest contributors of his generation toward the support
of the gospel. In addition to contributing hundreds of
thousands of dollars directly toward gospel preaching, Akin
was a very liberal supporter of the work of educating young
preachers, and gave generously to some of the Christian
colleges to assist in that work. He remained on the closest
terms with Tant for the rest of Tant's life, and on several
occasions made small loans to help him in some financial
emergency. Tant was always very careful to repay these
loans when due.

He was buried in a suit which had been given to him by
Akin.

Concerning his Longview meeting Tant wrote:

"I have just made a fight for Bible Christianity at
Longview, Texas. I find Brother John T. Poe and the
few loyal members with him have been greatly out-

raged and hindered by the digressives, who captured
their house fifteen years ago. I find the few members
altogether worthy of help. A house and lot will cost
us about $1,200.00. Old Brother Poe only owns his
house and lot. Brother John Akin the same. They
will each give $100.00 for a house, and the other mem-
bers there will give accordingly. I examined the whole
grounds, selected a lot, appointed a building committee,
and we will have a house there in sixty days' time.
Brethren, I ask you in the name of our blessed Master,
help us save the cause at Longview. Will not all
churches take note of this and take one Lord's day contribution and send it to Brother John T. Poe, Longview,
Texas? I preached at Dike yesterday (July 7), and began a meeting last night at Nelta. The brethren have
everything in readiness. The meeting is being held
under an arbor." (**Firm Foundation**, July 20, 1909.)

While Tant made no specific reference to his exclusion
from the pages of the **Gospel Advocate**, it is obvious from
his writings in the other periodicals that the hurt went
deep. In the **Christian Leader And The Way** he wrote an
article entitled, "Union, Not Likeness"

"In the prayer of the Son of God, Jesus prayed that
all might be one. Paul told the church at Corinth to be
of the same mind and speak the same thing. (1 Cor.
1:10.) In the twelfth chapter, Paul represents this
oneness by the body, showing that in one body we can
have eyes, ears, mouth, hands, feet, etc., and at the
same time all be one body, and fitly joined together,
each member filling its ordained office in the house of
God.

"I find some brethren who forget this principle, and
argue the law of likeness. If they are hands, they
want all preachers to be hands. They decide the kind
of language the preacher must use in the pulpit, the
kind of words he must use in conversation, the kind of
people he must travel with, his manner of dress, and
all things else he must do in order to be in accord with
their way of thinking. And when it is not, instead of

trying to help said preacher, they will get behind his back and try to pull him down.

"Some people forget that each man occupies just as distinctive a place in the Church as each member does in the body.

"I can go to any town where our ablest ministers live, and reach a class that no other man can reach; and if five or six more preachers follow me, each of them can reach a class that none of the others could reach.

"Yet some brethren conclude that they only know how to reach all classes, and if a brother doesn't carry out their idea in word, in conversation, in manner, then they work not to strengthen him in his channel, where God has ordained he should work, and where some would be lost if he did not work, but they do all they can to injure him in his own heaven-ordained sphere. They seek to destroy him because he is not a foot-channel, or an eye-channel, or a hand-channel of the one body, where these members happen to be at work."

CHAPTER XVIII

BIBLE COLLEGES

In January, 1910, a number of well known brethren in West Tennessee sent out a call for a meeting of all elders and preachers who would come to convene at Henderson, Tennessee, on January 25, to discuss ways and means by which a number of churches might cooperate in the support of a full time evangelist to preach in the weak places of West Tennessee.

Tant had had no small part in stirring up the sentiment for such a preacher. He had repeatedly pleaded with the brethren, both through the journals and in his private letters, as well as in gospel meetings to do more by way of supporting faithful men to preach the gospel. This Henderson meeting, the invitation to which was signed by J. W. Dunn, G. A. Dunn, G. Dallas Smith, John R. Williams, N. B. Hardeman, W. Claude Hall, T. B. Thompson, F.O. Howell, and D. A. Parish, was to convene "that the brethren might get better acquainted; learn from one another more of the conditions of this great field of labor; mutually encourage and inspire one another for the work of preaching the gospel, and gain a more intimate knowledge of the Henderson school."

The meeting was held on schedule, and attracted a great number of visitors. David Lipscomb, however, looked upon the meeting with more than a little apprehension. He wrote:

"Some of the brethren last week called for a meeting of preachers and elders in West Tennessee. We do not doubt that these brethren intend only the best for the churches, for themselves, and others. But I have been through and under these meetings so much it surprises me to hear of such meetings . . . I have seen much evil come out of them to the preachers and the people. I never saw any good come out of them to anyone. It is scriptural to call one man in to teach the members aright. But I never found an inspired man called in at a council of elders and preachers. Let us all individually and collectively try to stand on solid ground." (Gospel Advocate, February 3, 1910.)

Lipscomb's editorial stirred up a considerable controversy, some approving, others disapproving what had taken place at Henderson. The final plan of the Henderson meeting, according to a report by G. Dallas Smith, was for the Henderson Church to send out an evangelist into the destitute places of West Tennessee, and for other congregations to help by sending their money to the Henderson elders who, in turn, would oversee the work done. This was the old, old plan of "receiving, managing, and disbursing church" which had been tried in Texas some thirty years before, and which had led finally into the formation of the Texas Christian Missionary Society at Austin in 1886.

J. D. Tant attended the Henderson meeting. He did not participate in any of the discussions, and was there more as a visitor than anything else — although it had been his work, as much as that of any other man in Tennessee, which had stirred up the brethren and caused them to want to do something. But Tant was wary of the plan that was introduced. He was suspicious of the whole idea of "mass meetings." He finally made one brief speech, in response to rather urgent invitations that he do so, and told the brethren that:

"This meeting can't do anything; it cannot vote on anything; it cannot pass any resolution; it cannot reach any decision! The Lord's plan is for each church to operate, and any kind of organization (even a meeting like this) which makes decision for church work is without Bible authority."

Although he had worked under, and had encouraged the old system of the "receiving, managing, and disbursing eldership", which was now apparently to be re-activated at Henderson, Tant showed considerable reluctance to becoming involved in that kind of arrangement again. Any kind of cooperative arrangement which would activate the "church universal" (i.e. furnish a method, mode, plan, arrangement, or means by which the whole church could function as a unit) was highly suspicious to him. This was the basic error Campbell had made which had led to the establishment of the Missionary Society. Tant had been wounded with an incurable hurt by the evil which the Society had brought to the churches of Texas. Like a burned child avoiding the fire, he would steer clear of anything that even looked like it might be headed in the direction of such.

About a decade after Tant's death there was much discussion among the churches over what came to be known as the "sponsoring church" type of cooperative action. This was the plan by which one congregation would select a particular field, or project, considerably beyond its ability to support, "assume" the control and oversight of this project (perhaps supporting a group of missionaries in some foreign field, or conducting a national radio or television program for the general good of all the churches, or some other such general work), announce to the brotherhood that such and such was now its own exclusive work, and invite all congregations everywhere to send their funds to the treasury of this "sponsoring" church, that the work might be accomplished. Tant's name figured in these controversies, some claiming he would have favored, others that he would have opposed, such schemes.

There can be little doubt, in view of his long and bitter fight against the digressives, that had he lived when the "sponsoring church" controversy was raging, Tant would have been adamant as ever he was for the integrity, autonomy, independency, and all-sufficiency of the local church. He would have bitterly fought any kind of amalgamation of churches, or the pooling of resources, influences, or power of many churches under any kind of centralized directing power, whether an eldership or a society. He had seen at first hand how the working of such a machines could split the church asunder. If he recognized anything at all in any project as tending in that direction, he would have been opposed to it. This was why the Henderson meeting got scant encouragement from him, in spite of his oft repeated pleas that the brethren and the churches "get to work."

II

The late summer of 1911 saw further trouble come to the Tant household. The family was now complete, consisting of four girls and three boys, the last child, Marcus Austin, having been born on December 4, 1910. Davis, the oldest girl, was now finished with her schooling and was at home; the three youngest children, Mozelle (born April 9, 1907), Yater (Born December 30, 1908), and Austin, were not yet old enough to be of school age.

On August 12, J. D. Jr., nine years old, came in from play and told his mother that his ankle was hurting. She bathed the foot in warm water, applied some liniment to it, and told him he had probably sprained it and that it would be all right tomorrow. But the next day the whole foot and lower leg were so painful that the boy could not bear his weight on it at all. A little swelling had begun to appear. All through the day the pain increased, and the swelling began to appear all the way up to the knee and even higher. The local doctor was called, and gave his diagnosis — inflammatory rheumatism.

For a full week J. D. stayed in bed, and the pain increased almost by the hour. Spots of pus began to appear. An-

other doctor was called in. His diagnosis: "general tuberculosis." For another two weeks every kind of treatment
was tried. All to no avail. It was obvious the boy was
rapidly approaching death. The two doctors had a consultation about the case, and told Nannie that the child could
not possibly live. They thought six weeks would probably
be as long as he could last.

In a final desperate move Nannie called for Dr. Robert
Mann from Memphis, a great bone specialist, to come and
take a look at the boy. Dr. Mann came, made his diagnosis (osteo myletis) and said maybe an operation could
save the child, but it would have to be at once. Tant was
in a meeting in Kennett, Missouri. Nannie called him on
Sunday afternoon, and Tant caught the very next train
home. Dr. Mann operated on Monday morning, opening
the leg from the knee to the instep, scraping the bone deeply all the way, leaving only a thin sliver of bone intact. As
the doctor had to return to Memphis at once he left the patient in care of the local doctor to dress the wound and
keep down all infection.

J. D. began to improve at once. The fever abated; he
was much stronger, and by the third day seemed well on
the road to recovery. Tant wanted to remain a few days
longer at home, but he had interrupted his meeting at Kennett, and since his child seemed now out of all danger, he
felt obligated to return to the meeting. Another thing that
pressed heavily upon him was the tremendous financial
debacle he was facing; he desperately felt the need for
whatever support or income his preaching might bring in.
So he returned to Kennett.

Two days after his father had left, J. D. Jr. took a turn
for the worse. The pain returned to his leg, intensified and
multiplied. He became delirious, and his agonizing cries
were such as to alarm the neighbors. Nannie was just debating whether to call her husband again, or to take the

task on herself and call Dr. Mann for further treatment
when a letter arrived bearing the post-mark of Kennett,
Missouri. She opened the letter and read:

> Kennett, Missouri
> September 18, 1911

Dear Mrs. Tant:

I believe it to be my duty to inform you that your
husband left this place last night for parts unknown
with the most disreputable woman ever known here.
If you desire further information, write the elders of
the church here.

> Signed: A Friend

As Nannie let the letter fall from her numbed hands, she
heard a scream from the bed-room. The letter was forgotten as she rushed to the side of her suffering child. For
two days she was constanly by the bedside, barely leaving
the room for more than a minute or two at a time. She
did take out a few minutes, however, to write a brief note
to the elders at Kennett, Missouri, enclosing the letter she
had received, and assuming they would know who wrote it,
asked them to deliver to her anonymous "Friend" the following:

Sir:

Your unkind letter received. Wherever my husband
is, I am sure he is about his Father's business. Go
thou and do likewise.

> Signed: Mrs. J. D. Tant

Nannie knew that her husband's next meeting, after closing at Kennett, was Alamogordo, New Mexico, but that he
could not reach that place for two days, as the train connections from Kennett to New Mexico would require at
least that much travel time. She tells of her feelings and
fears in those dark hours:

"In substance I told the Kennett elders that I could

inform them as to the where-abouts of my husband if necessary, and as to the 'disreputable woman' he had taken with him, I was only too glad he could be of some help to her, for I felt sure she must be some one in trouble whom he was trying to help. I told them I was enclosing the anonymous letter, hoping it would help in identifying the author so they could disabuse his corrupt mind, for I felt that such a letter could not have originated except in one who was depraved and evil.

"I called my husband in Alamagordo, and he started home immediately, arriving on the second day at noon. We called Dr. Mann again, and he arranged for us to bring the boy to Memphis and put him in the Presbyterian Hospital there. This we did on September 21. Dr. Mann operated the next day. As we were taking the lad to the operating room, I heard Dr. Mann tell my husband that he felt the leg must come off to save the boy's life. My husband replied that he would rather bury his son whole than in pieces, and for him to do what he could, but NOT to amputate. Dr. Mann told me later that he actually felt his patient would die anyway, and since the father was so antagonistic to amputation, he decided to forego such and do the best he could anyway.

"The operation required nearly two hours, and ended at 7:00 P. M. Do I believe in prayer? Why should I not? On bended knee that night I kneeled beside my darling's bed and pleaded with God to spare him. I vowed, like Hannah of old, to give him to the Lord all the days of his life if he should live. We had a special nurse with him, and both my husband and I were in the room. At 9:30 the floor nurse came and told us one of us would have to leave, as it was against hospital rules for that many to be in the room. My husband told her we would both stay with our boy. The floor nurse called the head nurse. She was insistent that one of us leave. Husband told her we were staying. She got angry and said she would call a policeman to take one of us out. My husband told her not to call one, but four, as he didn't want to waste him in whipping just one policeman.

"She let us stay.

"It was midnight before we could determine for certain that our boy was reviving. By five o'clock in the morning he was conscious. At that time I had to leave, for I had a nursing baby back at Macon (Austin) with the neighbors, and I must get back to him. Our faithful nurse and my husband would do all for J. D. that could be done by mortals. But I know the hardest battle I ever fought, the one that tore my very heart strings, was when I bent over the bed to kiss my son good-bye, and knew that I might never again see his big blue eyes look into mine.

"I spent the day back at Macon, and made arrangements with a good sister there to keep my baby. He was old enough now that I could wean him from the breast, and I felt he would be in safe hands. I got back to the hospital at Memphis at 7:00 o'clock in the evening. At my first glance at the pale face on the hospital pillow my heart leaped for joy. For I could see a remarkable change. The boy was not suffering now; his eyes were clear and bright. For five days we kept him there, and both of us stayed with him, day and night. There was a time or two when he seemed to turn for the worse, but always he rallied, and at the end of a week, Dr. Mann told us he thought the child would live. We kept him in the hospital for still another week; and at the end of that time moved him to a rooming house nearby and dismissed our nurse. I then returned to Macon and my husband stayed in Memphis with J. D.

"Oh, yes, the 'disreputable woman'. It has ever been one of my husband's greatest works in life to try to raise the fallen — both men and women, boys and girls. I don't think I could begin to count the number of unfortunate girls we have taken into our home, kept them till their babies were born, and then helped them find homes for themselves and for their babies. And more than once my husband has gone to the jail to go bond for some boy who was in trouble, and brought such into our home, helping him to get his life back on the right track. I was certain this was the situation at Kennett when the anonymous letter came.

"My surmise proved true. My husband had found an unfortunate orphan girl, who had become a mother under the promise of marriage from her sweetheart. When the man found out that a child was coming, he fled the community and abandoned the girl. She lived with her uncle, an elder in the church, who felt the disgrace keenly — but not in a Christian way. The girl was a member of the church; and after her fall had had the courage to make confession of her sin, and ask forgiveness. The whole church had forgiven her — except her uncle! He would not forgive her, but made her life miserable and intolerable by endless persecutions. When husband came to Kennett for the meeting, this poor child went to him and begged him to help her get away to some place where she could start her life over. Husband happened to know of a fine Christian man in Amarillo, Texas, whose wife was ill, and who was in dire need of some good, Christian girl to live in his home and keep house and help wait on this sick wife. He got in touch with the man by phone, told him of the girl at Kennett, and asked him if he would take her. The man gladly agreed to do so, and asked my husband to bring the girl immediately, as he was going on his way to the Alamogordo meeting. It was not out of the way, so this plan was carried out.

"The girl made good in her foster home, and nursed the man's wife through a long illness, staying with her and comforting her in her dying hours. She won the love and affection of the whole family, and after the death of the sick woman, the sorrowing husband and his orphaned children begged her to stay on as housekeeper. This she did; and about a year later married the man for whom she was working. Many years later I had a sweet letter from her, telling me of her happiness and of her undying gratitude to J. D. Tant who had befriended her in the darkest hour of her life. I also later had good reason to believe that the anonymous letter I had received had come from the girl's uncle, with whom she was living. He was actually making a slave out of the girl, and resented losing her services." (Reminiscences.)

The stricken boy, J. D., Jr., had a convalescence lasting over five years; but finally recovered fully, and even played quarterback on his foot-ball team in high school. Tant had spent endless hours bathing the boy's leg in warm salt water, day and night, over a period of three weeks. Dr. Mann credited this constant care with being the deciding factor in saving the boy's leg, and probably his life.

III

Tant's dissatisfaction with the Bible colleges began to find fuller expression in 1910. He wrote an article in the Firm Foundation calling in question some of the things being done by the colleges. He particularly objected to the apparent willingness of some to let the Bible colleges supplant and make unnecessary the church's teaching of the Bible. Brother O. A. Carr, President of Carr-Burdette College (where Nannie Yater Tant had received her college training) replied to Tant in a rather sharp article, asking just exactly what it was he was objecting to? He dwelt at length upon the good work being done by the schools, pointed out that such institutions had been characteristic of the disciples since the days of Alexander Campbell, and criticized Tant for trying to cause good brethren to turn against the schools.

To this Tant responded with an article entitled: "To Brother O. A. Carr":

"I am glad to note your criticism of my letter on Bible colleges. If I am wrong, I want to know it; if I am right, all should know it.

1. Remember, I believe in education.
2. I believe the Bible should be taught in all schools.
3. I believe each church should be a Bible college, and teach the Bible all it can.
4. At Henderson, Tennessee, we have the largest school managed by our brethren anywhere. More young men study the Bible there than in any oth-

er school I know of, yet it is not a 'Bible College'. At Cleburne, Texas, we have the same kind of school. Both of them I endorse.

"Then why do I condemn 'Bible Colleges'?

"1. The 'Bible College' is a church institution, belonging to the church, controlled by the church, owned by the church, operated by the church — has its president, dean, secretary, with four or five societies in each school. Then, inasmuch as said societies belong to said colleges, and said colleges belong to the church of Christ, no man can condemn missionary societies, endeavor societies, ladies' aid societies, and at the same time endorse church college societies.

"2. Church colleges have been the hot-bed of innovations, and have led all churches from their original ground without an exception.

"3. If it is right to build church colleges, and call on all the churches to help run the same, because it is a 'church' school or 'Bible' college, why not have a brother in each community to start a church hog farm, or a church cow farm, or a church horse farm, and call on all the churches to help him support his farm, because he is running a church farm instead of an ordinary farm like his brother on the other hill, whose hogs, cows, and horses are not church property?

"4. God knows only two institutions, the church and the family; and all history shows that when man begins to create, the thing created soon gets larger than the creator. The creator will eventually be controlled by the thing created. . . .

"The digressives created their missionary societies. Today their societies are controlling the churches. The church of Christ created the 'Bible Colleges'. In twenty-five years the church will be under complete control of the colleges. No preacher will be wanted if he does not come from the college. At many places it is that way now.

"5. Law schools turn out professional lawyers, medical schools turn out professional doctors; and our Bible Colleges are turning out professional preachers; and when preaching becomes a profession, it will soon cease to be spiritual.

"6. By their fruits ye shall know them. Campbell started Bethany, a Bible College. But I have not heard of the machine turning out a gospel preacher in twenty years. McGarvey and Grubbs started Lexington. I have not heard of this machine turning out a gospel preacher in ten years. The Clarks started Add-Ran College. She became a 'church' institution, and the whole thing, buildings and all, departed from God's law. . . .

"Brother, I do not object to a good school, and the Bible being taught. But for God's sake, do not make the school a CHURCH institution, and beg the churches to support it because it is a CHURCH institution.

"These are a few of my objections to 'Bible Colleges'. The whole principle is wrong. I do not condemn the thing done (the teaching of the Bible), but the way it is done. I endorse the gospel work done by the society, the way it is done is what I condemn." (Firm Foundation, March 1, 1910.)

Repercussions to Tant's article were not long in coming. One of the first was a response by Henry E. Warlick of Cordell, Oklahoma, whom Tant had baptized, a number of years before, and who was a close friend:

"Brother Tant always writes 'singularly'. Well, he says he is in 'a drove to himself', and has been for fifteen years.

"No, Brother Tant, you do not need to start a 'new paper' to ride your (?) hobby. Just drop by and see Daniel Sommer, and he will give you ample room in his 'Octographic Review'. I remember that when Add-Ran University at Thorp's Spring fell to pieces by reason of the Clarks going digressive, J. D. Tant appealed to the brotherhood of Texas to buy the school property there, and establish a good Christian school (Bible College?). Some time after that Tant purchased some school property at San Marcos, and started a school in which young girls could get the advantages of a Christian education under the tutorship of Sister Tant (whom Tant married out of a good Christian school). Later Brother Tant came to Oklahoma, and while in a meeting at Granite, sprang the subject on the brotherhood of this western Oklahoma country that we should establish a good 'Bible School.' And just what little Brother Tant said about the matter then caused the brethren to go to work and establish just such a school at Cordell — the Cordell Christian College." (Firm Foundation, March 28, 1910.)

In the months following this exchange, a lengthy discussion on the subject of colleges, orphan homes, and congregations filled the papers. Brother L. S. White of Dallas pleaded for many orphan homes and good schools. Brother John T. Poe of Longview took issue with him. Others joined in, and soon a full chorus was joining in, some for, some against, some arguing one point, some another. The Gospel Advocate was having problems of its own, particularly the "Henderson meeting", and for the most part paid little attention to the Texas furore.

C. R. Nichol and N. L. Clark took issue with Tant in separate articles. Not many of the brethren seemed to know exactly what Tant was criticizing, so he tried to clarify his position:

"I notice Brother Nichol and Brother Clark of Texas are a little troubled over myself and others because we are arguing against the 'Bible Colleges'. They misunderstand me. I do not condemn Bible colleges except when they are conducted as church colleges or church institutions.

"1. Brother Nichol claims they are fought by men who never had opportunity of attending them. I am glad this is true in my case. Jesus did not steal or get drunk, yet he condemned both. I did not know it was necessary for a man to have experience in anything to enable him to see the evil.

"2. Brother Nichol claims that Christ, while on earth, schooled the apostles for three years. True; but how? By sending them out to preach, instead of buying a $75,000.00 building and saying, 'This is a church college', and then begging all the churches to help pay for the building to start a preacher factory to help turn out preachers.

"We all condemn digressive women for giving church suppers to do the Lord's work. What is the difference in giving a church supper to do the Lord's work and in starting a church college to do the Lord's work? We condemn the digressive preachers for organizing a missionary society, with its president, secretary, and board of directors, and begging money from all the churches to help run their missionary society to enable it to preach the gospel.

"What is the difference in organizing a church missionary society and a church college with its president, dean, its secretary, and its board of directors, and then begging all the churches to give money to help pay this college out of debt, to make big preachers out of young men to enable them to preach the gospel?

"Brethren, before the God of heaven, I can see no difference. For thirty years we have fought the digressives on one society, and now it seems we are trying to build another!

"Brother W. F. P. in Christian Companion of March 24, makes the following statement: 'A school is private property, and not a church work, and must not be chargeable to the church. The church has no auxiliaries, such as societies, schools, bible readings, and printing plants. Nor is she in need of such in performing the work given her. To say she is, impeaches the wisdom of the Lord who gave her no such ordinances to keep, yet declared she was perfect'. This tells my position on the Bible college. Brother A. B. Barrett has such a school at Cleburne; Brethren Hardeman and Freed have such a school at Henderson, Tennessee. For these schools I work. But when I find authority for running a church farm, a church hog ranch, a church medical school, a church law school, a church paper, then I'll be found working for our church Bible colleges, owned and operated solely by the church of Christ . . .

"The Texans' war cry was 'Remember Goliad; Remember the Alamo!' Then to these good brethren, I say, 'Remember Bethany; Remember Lexington,' Remember Thorp's Spring!' Brethren, when we make our colleges church institutions, not only is the principle wrong, but the creature will soon be larger than the creator, and in twenty-five years the church will be as much under the church college as the digressives are today controlled by the Missionary Society.

"I am not your enemy because I tell you the truth, and would be glad if you would carefully study these matters. Remember, church colleges have been the hot-bed of innovation in all churches." (Firm Foundation, May 17, 1910.)

Brother N. L. Clark, one of the editors of the Firm Foundation at this time (the others were W. T. Kidwell, J. E. Lane, Early Arceneaux, G. W. Savage; and G.H.P. Showwalter as Managing Editor) was president of Gunter College. He quickly reacted to Tant's article:

"Brother Tant's remarks in last week's Firm Foundation, whether he intended them so or not, have all the force of an advertisement for the schools at Cleburne and Henderson. At the same time he directly slaps all the other schools in the face ... But I am teaching. I have been a teacher for twenty-four years. Teaching is my profession. By it I earn an honest living while using my every influence to uplift humanity. Brother Tant's thrusts at me are thrusts at my personal business. This is why I speak out at this time. Brother Showalter's reply to Brother Tant is all that is needed from a logical viewpoint to silence Brother Tant's objections forever. But Brother Tant is not the only man who has misrepresented me on the school questions. For reasons partly unknown to me the Gunter school seem to have suffered more from the opposition of brethren than any school among us. This may not be true, but it appears so to me. Why is it thus? What evil have we done? Wherein do we differ from the schools Tant endorses? This school has never by the authority of its directors or its faculty asked any church as a church for a contribution. It has been our position from the beginning that this school is NOT a 'church' school. It belongs nominally to the eleven men composing its board of directors.

"For Brother Tant's special information, let me say what I have often said before. I would not teach a day in any school run either by a local church or by the church in general. The church is not in the school business, the mercantile business, the newspaper business, or any thing else of the kind. This is exactly why I am opposed to your 'Sunday School', Brother Tant. Its advocates claim either that it is an adjunct to the church, or that it is the church at work. The church of God needs no such adjuncts; nor does it need any such name as 'Sunday School' or 'Bible School' to designate it when doing the Lord's work. Thoughtless or ill-informed brethren still persist in trying to put the 'Sunday School' (so-called) on a par with Gunter Bible College. Such brethren are always prating about Clark's inconsistency. My position is that God has made a very marked distinction between what the church may do and what the individual Christian may do. When I am convinced that there is no such distinction, I shall be ready to join with Chalmers McPherson on his party. . . ." (Firm Foundation, May 31, 1910.)

Brethren W. W. Otey and G. H. P. Showalter got into the dispute, along with a host of others. J. N. Armstrong made a lengthy reply to Tant, asking specifically for Tant to describe the difference between those schools he endorsed and those he did not endorse. He charged that Freed-Hardeman College and the school at Cleburne "solicited gifts", just as did the other schools. He asked Tant if he thought it was right for one man to own a school, but wrong for nine men (a board of directors) to own the property. He then refers to the school operated at Beamsville, Ontario, Canada, by Brother Jones, and says that Jones owns the school — but that the school is conducted in property (the building), which is actually owned by the church of Christ. Armstrong sees nothing wrong in this if good men run the school and the elders of the church have enough confidence in them to let them use the church property.

This was a controversy that was not to be settled in Tant's life time; nor has it yet been settled. For while none of the schools are apparently willing now to solicit funds from the churches, it seems quite apparent that this attitude is one only of policy, and not of conviction. And it appears probable that within another generation this whole question will erupt into another violent controversy among the churches of Christ. With the general softening of opposition to various 'church connected' institutions, such as elementary schools, hospitals, recreation centers, youth camps, etc., it would be unrealistic to think that the promoters of the colleges will indefinitely defer a strong fight to have their institutions put into the church budgets.

Tant did not let this controversy, however, deter him for a moment from his preaching of the gospel. Through it all, he was as busy as ever in gospel meetings. From Paragould, Arkansas, he reports:

"I am in a fine meeting at Paragould, with thirty-five added up to date and the meeting continues. The Baptists do not like my preaching, and have sent for Ben Bogard to show up the other side. So he and I will meet in debate here, commencing next Tuesday, May 31."

CHAPTER XIX

NEW MEXICO — LAND OF ENCHANTMENT

During the years 1910-1912 Tant's financial condition steadily worsened. Six of the eight brethren to whom he had sold his small farms defaulted completely on their payment, year after year, not even paying the interest. Meanwhile, all six families were running up enormous bills at the local stores, buying clothing, groceries, and household necessities — and charging them to J. D. Tant. On top of all this was the immense medical expenses growing out of J. D., Jr.'s hospitalization. It seemed that financial disaster was inevitable.

Under the burden of these anxieties, however, Tant slackened his preaching activities not at all. In the closing weeks of 1910 he preached for a full month in Waco, Texas. G. H. P. Showalter was a visitor to the meeting, and reported his impressions:

"It was my pleasure to visit the church at Waco last Saturday and Sunday, and preach on Sunday night, at the close of Brother J. D. Tant's meeting, which had been in progress since the 20th of October. I found Brother Tant fully up to his usual physical vigor, and in first class condition for preaching the gospel. He says he is 'twenty pounds heavier and ten years younger' since he left Texas. Brother Tant goes next to Bay City, Arkansas, for a meeting, and then to Tennessee for a debate. In January, he expects to conduct a Bible reading at his home congregation, Macon, Tennessee. None were baptized at Waco, but the brethren were much pleased with the meeting. The church withdrew from fourteen disorderly members and deserters; the faithful ones seemed encouraged, and there is a brighter outlook for the future." (Firm Foundation, November 22, 1910.)

A month's meeting without a single baptism was indeed a rarity, but Tant reported it as "one of the best meetings in the history of the church in Waco. No additions; fourteen subtractions."

In the fall of 1910 and summer of 1911 Tant held meetings at Ardmore, Oklahoma; Waco, Texas; and Terrell, Texas, persuading all three congregations to undertake building programs. He also reports a meeting from Paragould, Arkansas, and has something further to say about the "college fever":

"I have been opposed at some places this year where they had the college fever. Good brethren will say, I know Brother Tant preaches the gospel, but he does not favor 'our colleges'. In twenty years from now gospel preachers will be turned down by loyal churches if they don't favor the church Bible colleges, just as loyal preachers are turned down today by society churches because they don't favor societies. Brethren, think, and don't go to extremes on these things." (Firm Foundation, June 13, 1911.)

Two months later another report from Greenfield, Illinois:

"I am now in a fine meeting near Greenfield, Illinois. This is the boyhood home of the noted John S. Sweeney, and there was a loyal congregation here for about fifty years but the spirit of apostacy struck them and they departed from the Bible, introducing all the late innovations. They robbed the church of their house. And the mean things they have done against the church of Christ are too bad to believe, even if I should publish them. However, their last digressive preacher who did the church of Christ much harm here is now in jail, and the digressives are fearful the State of Illinois is about to give their pastor a permanent job; if so, he will not be able to help them further in their work against the church.

"Illinois is a great mission field; don't think we have

more than thirty loyal preachers and more than sixty loyal congregations in the entire state. Almost all the digressive preachers try to teach the people here that the church of Christ is dead. Would to God that we could locate about ten aggressive, loyal Texas preachers in Illinois for one year to help the loyal preachers here in their fight for Bible Christianity."   (Firm Foundation, September 26, 1911.)

II

J. D., Jr. had now been sick for well over a year. He was able to hobble about on crutches, but gained very little strength. The doctor said he must have a change of climate, and suggested going to the higher altitude and the dry air of the Southwest, perhaps New Mexico or Arizona. Tant recalled his meetings in New Mexico, and decided he would try to make some sort of trade to get his family to that state — a state later to be known as "The Land of Enchantment", but which proved anything but that for the Tants. Nannie tells the story of those years in the West:

"We traded everything we had left in Tennessee for a house and lot in Anson, Texas. But we never moved to Anson. Before the time came to move, my husband had traded that property for two sections of land in Andrews County, Texas. This trade was made 'sight unseen', wholly on the description of the property given by the owner, a man named Kincade. We were trying to find some way to trade for property in Alamogordo, New Mexico; but repeated advertisements in the various farm journals brought no opportunity to trade the Andrews County property for anything there. So we bought for a very nominal sum (and on credit) 160 acres of land near Alamogordo. It had a barn-like house on it, and was located about one mile east of town.

"We shipped all our household goods by freight car. Husband rode the freight train all the way to New Mexico with our goods, while the six children and I took the passenger train. By this time the two older

girls, Maidia and Zoreta, were big enough to help with
the three babies; and J. D., with the kindly help of the
conductor, was able to get about by himself. Davis,
the oldest girl, had married Joe Rauch and remained
behind in Memphis. We arrived in Alamogordo on
Christmas Day, 1912. We were met at the train by my
husband, who had already arrived, and by Brother Oliver, one of the members of the little congregation at
that place.

"Alamogordo is an oasis in the desert. It is a beautiful spot, located in the valley between the Sacramento
Mountains on the east and the San Andres Mountains
on the west. The Sacramento Valley is sixty miles
wide and three hundred miles long. Being protected
by these mountain ranges, the valley does not suffer
from the high winds like other parts of the state. In
the summer the days are not so hot, due to the low humidity. And the nights are delightful. One needs a
light wrap as soon as the sun goes down.

"When we arrived here there were a number of fine
orchards and alfalfa farms in production in the valley.
An irrigation company had been formed to develop the
area, and several large springs at the foot of the Sacra-
mentoes furnished an abundant water supply. The
land we had bought was not irrigated from the ditch,
but we had a very fine small orchard, about one-half
acre, which was irrigated from the city water supply.

"Brother Lundy Dale, a dear friend of ours at Macon, Tennessee, had preceded us to Alamogordo by a
few weeks. His wife had tuberculosis, and the doctors
had told him to take her to a higher climate. So he
had sold his lovely home in Macon, and had moved to
Alamogordo. She lived for three years in New Mexico, but was bed-ridden all the time. My husband and
Brother Dale rented an orchard and an alfalfa farm
from the irrigation company, and worked it together.
Irrigation was a new experience to both of them, and
they had some difficult times with it. The orchard
had been neglected for several years, and almost all
the terraces were broken down and had to be re-built.
The trees had to be pruned and sprayed, and a general

cleaning up of the whole farm was necessary. Sometimes in setting his dam-sheets my husband would have to get into the big ditch in water up to his waist (and sometimes he slipped and went under, head and ears). He never stopped to put on dry clothes, but worked day and night when it came time to irrigate. The water was furnished by the company on an hourly basis; and if a farmer did not take his water when the time came, he had to wait two or three weeks till his turn came up again. Such a delay might have seriously damaged the crop. So at irrigation time, we were under much pressure. I have known my husband to come to the house with his clothes frozen stiff. Many times I've stayed up all night to keep the room warm, and to keep his coffee hot, so he could run in for a few minutes after setting his borders and try to warm himself before going back to the ditches. He was always too wet to lie on the bed, so would lie down on the floor by the heater, sleep a few minutes, and then go back to change his leads for the water.

"Both my husband and Brother Dale worked terribly hard that year, and made a good alfalfa crop, and fair fruit. But they realized no profit at all from their labors. The costs of irrigation, plus the expense of getting the orchard cleaned up had simply absorbed all the profits.

"This caused my husband to consider the possibility of putting down his own well, and thus saving the great expense of buying water from the irrigation company. The place we had bought was too near the mountains to attempt a well there. We would have to go perhaps 1500 feet to find a sufficient supply. But land was cheap. So we borrowed $2,500.00, and bought 160 acres of land west of town, in a very fertile area. Husband bought a well drill, an engine, and a pump. He decided to dig the well himself. He went down 165 feet, and struck an abundant supply of water, enough to fill an eight inch pipe.

"But, Oh! the drilling of that well is like a nightmare in my memory. Husband called in all his meetings, and for eight straight months gave himself to drilling the well and working on the farm. Some days everything went smoothly, and they went down several feet. Then some of the machinery would break, and there would be a stop until a new piece could be ordered or made. Since he planned to use a centrifugal pump, it was necessary to dig a hole some four or five feet in diameter. He had a boy hired to help him, and day after day they dug, my husband in the bottom of the hole, digging with a pick and shovel and filling a big fifty gallon can full of dirt, the boy with a windlass, drawn by a mule, pulling up the can when it was full. The boy was a dreamy, listless youngster, who only paid half attention to what he was doing.

"One day this boy had a heavy bucket full of dirt near the top, let it slip, and the whole load of mud and rocks came crashing down on my husband. Fortunately the bucket did not hit him squarely on the head, else it would have killed him instantly. It did strike a glancing blow, however, knocking him unconscious, and cutting a huge gash in his forehead. It split his lower lip wide open. He laid in the well unconscious for several minutes; but finally revived, called out to the boy on top to pull him out, and managed to get into the bucket, and hold on to his consciousness till the boy got the mule to wind the windlass and pull him to the surface. Then he fainted again.

The well was four miles from where we lived. About the middle of the afternoon I saw Eugene Dale, the fourteen year old son of Brother Dale, coming toward our house as fast as the two-horse surrey could bring him. He stopped the loping horses in a cloud of dust and gravel, called out telling me what had happened, and said my husband wanted me to get some bandages and come dress his wounds. I wanted to get a doctor, but knowing husband's aversion to such, did not do so. I went on to him, thinking I could decide when I saw him whether he needed a doctor or not.

"He did. But he refused to let me call one. I had stopped at the drugstore on the way out, secured bandages, adhesive tape, antiseptics, and all the surgical

dressings necessary. I had also taken my scissors, and
a pan to boil everything in. The wife of Moses once
said, 'A bloody husband thou art to me'. My husband
was all of that, and more too. When I saw him I
could not tell whether he was living or dead. He was
lying on the porch floor of the little house on the
place, all the upper part of his body bloody and muddy,
with blood still ozzing from the horrible gash on his
forehead. As quickly as possible I prepared an anti-
septic wash, bathed the dirt and blood from his
wounds, and tried to pull the sides of the gash together. If I had known how to sew a wound, I would
have tried to take some stitches, as it was obvious
that several were needed. But he tried to belittle the
whole matter, and told me he would be all right within
a day or two. He was too weak to work any more
that day, or for two days following.

"Finally, the well was finished. But, meanwhile,
all our money was gone. Zoreta, the second girl, had
had a very serious appendectomy, during which she
nearly died; and while we had managed to exist, our
resources were absolutely at the vanishing stage. The
property at Anson had been traded for two sections
of land in Andrews County. Upon investigation it
developed that Mr. Kincade did not have legal title to
the Andrews County property, so he could not give
us a deed to the place. He refused, however, to give
up the deed to our Anson property. We had to sue,
and finally recovered the property, but had to pay an
attorney $1,000.00 to do the work for us. We had
lost everything. The Anson property was hardly
worth enough to meet the attorney's bill for regain-
ing it for us. I got a job sewing; Zoreta quit school
and got a job waiting tables in a hotel; Maidia got a
job in a millinery shop. Carl Nichols, a fine young
Christian man, came to me and said that if we would
not let Zoreta wait tables at the hotel, he would pay
us $25.00 per month till the end of the year. She was
a beautiful girl, only fourteen years of age, and he
thought she ought to continue in school. I am not
opposed to charity when it is necessary; but when

people are able to work, and can get work to do, I
see no reason for it. So we declined young Nichols'
offer — and I've regretted the decision a thousand
times since." (Reminiscences.)

Tant, meanwhile, continued his keen interest in planting
the cause in New Mexico. He might be reduced almost
to starvation himself, but he would do what he could to
help some other man preach the gospel. Brother J. W.
Dunn of Tennessee had been advised by the doctors to
take both himself and his wife to a higher and drier
climate. He was a long time friend of Tant; so he wrote
him in Alamogordo asking his assistance. To Tant this
seemed a wonderful opportunity to help Dunn, and at the
same time to get a strong gospel preacher located in New
Mexico. He wrote out a form letter, and sent it to some
seven hundred churches and individuals, asking them to
give $1.00 per month each toward Dunn's support.

He sent repeated appeals through the papers, as well
as a constant stream of letters to people he knew, begging
for their support for Dunn. His appeals began to be productive. He reports:

"I am glad to inform all who have had fellowship
in Brother Dunn's work in New Mexico that it has
gone beyond our expectations. Up to date, there have
been established under his work six new congregations; almost one hundred baptized; fine meetings held
at Hope, Artesia, and Roswell, and a church building
erected at Roswell.

"Brother Dunn has spent two months in mission
work in El Paso, Texas, with the membership increased
from thirteen to seventy; and a lot has been bought.
He will spend the remainder of this year in El Paso,
helping them build a church house there. I have received and paid to Brother Dunn $700.00. My books
show $408.00 promised toward his support which has
not yet been paid. Hope those making the promises
will take note and send in the amount at once.

"I am now trying to get the churches at Roswell, Alamogordo, Artesia, and Hope to support a man all the time in their territory next year. If this can be done, we want to put another man out in the new field Brother Dunn has built up, to push the work. We will need outside help in his support. Brother J. W. Dunn is one of the finest workers, one of the ablest preachers, and one of the purest men I have ever met. All are pleased with the work he has done." (**Christian Leader**, October 20, 1914.)

III

After two years in Alamogordo, Tant saw he must make some sort of move in order to live. He still had the two tracts of land in the Sacramento Valley; but he owed almost the complete purchase price on each of them. He was receiving no income from preaching, and the situation was growing more desperate by the day. He had held meetings at Hope, across the Sacramento Mountains to the east from Alamogordo, and had found a member of the church there who had a beautiful orchard and alfalfa farm, and who was willing to trade, sell, or rent. This man told Tant to come over to his place at Hope, and they would work out a satisfactory deal on his place one way or the other; he could buy it if he wanted to, or rent it if he preferred not to buy. The deal was made late in 1914, and Tant went back to Alamogordo to bring his family over the mountains to Hope. "Hope" was about all that was left for the Tant family to live on by now — and even that was soon to be dashed. Nannie tells of that trip across the mountains:

"It was now December, and our only means of travel was a two horse wagon, for we had no money to ride the train. Even if there had been a train across the mountains. Which there wasn't. We did manage to borrow enough money to ship our household goods to Cloudcroft, a summer resort town, some 9,000 feet

above sea level. This was twenty-eight miles from
Alamogordo. We planned to load all the family, with
our personal effects, into the wagon, make the trip
across the mountains to Hope; then husband would
make two or three trips back to Cloudcroft with the
team and wagon to get the things we had shipped
there.

"After much work and worry we were ready to
start. My husband had a large tent that he used in
the summer time for meeting work. It weighed several
hundred pounds. He also had a hay frame, a very
large one, that he wanted to take along. These two
articles were so heavy they would cost too much to
ship, so he decided to take them on the wagon with
the family. He first took off the regular wagon bed,
put the hay frame on the running gear of the wagon,
then put the regular bed back on top of the hay frame.
The hay frame was several feet longer than the wagon
bed, and this formed a very convenient place to put
the tent.

"Husband got this part all arranged, and we put
everything in the wagon which we had not already
shipped to Cloudcroft. We were about as full as we
thought we could make it over the mountain. We
had four horses hitched to the wagon, to help us up
the grade to Cloudcroft. We had no spring seat, but
husband did have a large revolving library chair. This
was set up in the wagon to provide a seat for the
driver. I had a low chair behind him, and all the
children were distributed around and among the gear
and household goods as best they could be. It was a
cloudy morning when we started. We had no wagon
sheet to cover us, but were riding in the open air.

"We had not driven more than two miles when a
cold, slow rain set in. We tried to pull parts of the
tent into the wagon to protect us, but it was rolled
up and tied down so we could not get to it. The
weather was not so very cold when we left Alamogordo,
but as we climbed into the mountain, it got steadily
colder and colder. I had cooked a tub full of provisions
for our trip, hoping it would last most of the way.
At noon on that first day we stopped under a bluff

that overshadowed the road and formed a nice spot for us to get out of the rain for a few minutes while we were eating. A dead horse was also under the bluff, but it was so cold he didn't smell very bad. Not real bad, anyhow.

"The hay frame gave us trouble from the very first. Going up steep grades, the wagon bed would slip back and nearly push the tent off the hayframe. In making short curves in the road, the frame would rub against the bank on the side of the cut. The horses were fractious and hard to manage. Two of them were a young team, frightened, nervous, and skittish. As the hill got steeper and steeper, husband finally decided that we would never make it to the summit with the hayframe, so determined to remove it, leave it beside the road, and come back later and retrieve it. So, in the drizzling rain, we got out of that wagon load of junk, unloaded everything in it by the side of the road, and husband tugged and pulled and strained with almost super-human effort (he could never have done it at all had he not been a man of almost incredible physical strength) until he finally got that wagon bed off the hayframe, the hayframe off the running gear, and the wagon bed placed back on the wagon in proper position. Then we loaded everything back in it, including the tent, and then all the family climbed back on (not in, because the wagon bed was now piled much too high for anything or anybody to get 'in' it), and tired, cold, and miserable we continued the wearisome journey.

"We had gone about twelve miles, and it was getting dark. Fortunately, we were near a vacant house, so we stopped for the night. Some other wanderers were there before us, but they were kind, and shared their fire with us. Husband got the axe out of the wagon and cut enough wood to last us through the night. It was a good fire and we dried out all our wet clothing. I made pallets on the floor for the children; but as I could never sleep on a floor, I sat in a chair before the fire place all night, dozing as I could. Husband was always a good sleeper, so he stretched himself out before the fire-place and was soon fast asleep.

Poor soul! He needed it. It had been a miserable, heart breaking climax to two miserable, heart-breaking years at Alamogordo.

"Next morning I warmed us some breakfast, and we were soon on the road again. The rain had changed to snow. The road was slippery and very dangerous. At one place it had been cut from the sheer side of a cliff for nearly half a mile. To our left the mountain rose straight out of sight into the clouds; on our right, just beyond a flimsy protecting chain, a vast chasm yawned for a thousand feet below us. As our fortune would have it, this happened to be the very spot our lead horse chose to balk. Perhaps the horses had become frightened by looking over the edge of the road into a thousand feet of empty nothingness. A wagon was meeting us, coming down the road at a fast clip. We saw the driver was in trouble, as he kept see-sawing his lines, trying to control his team as his heavily loaded wagon kept bumping against them. It looked momentarily like he was about to lose control of both team and wagon, and all of them would come hurtling down the hillside like an avalanche, and most certainly crash into us. In such an event, all of us, together with wagons, teams, and everything else would have ended up in the bottom of the chasm. At this instant, Zoreta, always swift and agile, jumped down off the wagon, and ran to our lead horse. Seizing his bridle she gently coaxed him into putting his shoulders into the harness, and we barely got under way in time to avoid a disastrous collision. It was a narrow escape for all of us!

"The higher we ascended the mountain, the deeper the snow became. When we came within two miles of Cloudcroft, our horses simply gave up; they seemed completely exhausted. But again our necessity was met. A man came by with a strong, fresh team, pulling an empty wagon up the mountain side. Husband hired him to hitch his team on to our wagon, and take us on into Cloudcroft. We found a very nice room in a boarding house, and spent the night there.

"Next morning, my husband bought a spring seat, some wagon bows, and a wagon sheet. Better pre-

pared now, we started out from Cloudcroft on the
perilous descent toward Hope — ninety long miles
away. The snow was blinding at times. The road
was rough and dangerous. But we made it to May-
hill, a tiny settlement, an hour or so before dark. We
spent the night with Brother Bell, a man who was
wonderfully kind to us. Early next morning, we started again.

"This was now our fourth day of travel. We had
hoped to make the entire trip in three days; but our
plans had not worked out as desired. The fourth day's
travel was terrible. The snow was from twelve to
thirty-six inches deep. We had nothing to guide us
or keep us on the road, except to judge where the
trees had been cut out, leaving a lane through the
thick woods. Occasionally we would see the top of a
fence post, or a leaning telephone pole. There had
once been a telephone line through here; but it was
long since out of operation. While driving through
the snow we would suddenly go into a deep hole, or
get caught on a projecting boulder. Husband and
J. D. Jr. (by this time largely recovered from his
awful operation) would get out and pry the wagon
loose. Some times we would run over stumps or logs
or large rocks. We did not travel far that day, and
spent the night again in an abandoned ranch house.

"The fifth day found us on a slightly better road,
and the weather had moderated slightly. But I was
getting very, very tired. I was about five months
pregnant, and all day long I kept feeling uneasy pains
shooting through my abdomen. I knew I should stop,
and not continue the vicious cruel jolting of the wagon.
But there was no place to stop. There was no help for
the situation. We must go on.

"That night we came to a very pleasant place. It
was a nice home; the lady had fixed it up for Christmas, and had a beautiful Christmas tree ready for her
children for the next day. Her husband was not at
home; but she took us in like an angel of mercy, and
fixed us up for the night. Six-year-old Yater was so
tired and sleepy that he went to sleep on his feet in
front of the heating stove, toppled over on it, and

burned the whole side out of his coat. He was frightened, but not hurt.

"I spent a restless night. All of us were travel worn, and near to the breaking point. But my darling husband said nothing. There are some circumstances in life so appalling that silence is more eloquent than speech. I knew he was suffering agony to have his family in this condition; but he was doing the best he could. He uttered no word of complaint or self pity for the grievous turn our fortunes had taken. He was blaming himself for it all, of course, but we were so far gone by now that there was little point in any kind of blame or reproach; even self-reproach would have been to no profit.

"The next day we crossed the 'Devil's Backbone', a ridge rightly named. It was fifteen miles across, and each vertebra stood up in such projecting points that at times our wagon would nearly turn over, then would slide off that boulder and come down with a jarring thud that would throw all of us against the opposite side. That night we reached the "Y" crossing of the river, only fifteen miles from our destination. We spent the night in a hotel.

"The next day was Sunday, the seventh day of the trip we had expected to complete in three days. Our teams were as tired as we were, but we journeyed on. At noon we drove up to the house of Brother Riley, the man whose farm we were going to rent (or buy). His family had gone to church, but in a short while all were back. They soon had dinner prepared for all of us. I could eat nothing, for by now I was deathly sick. I went to bed, and a doctor was called out from Hope as quickly as possible. He came very soon, and worked with me all night; but on Monday morning I lost my baby. I have prayed that God will not hold me guilty for undertaking such a trip in my condition. Life can be hard and cruel, sometimes, and it seemed for us at the time that there was no alternative other than for me to make the trip.

"I remained at the Riley house for one week. He had four rooms, but only one heater. His family of eight and my family of eight all had to stay in the one room where the heater was, and that was the room where I lay so sick abed. It was cold and snowy weather. Mud completely covered the floor. Once a day the floor was swept, and I covered my head under the sheet to escape the choking fog of dust.

"On Saturday we borrowed a discarded coal-oil stove from a neighbor, borrowed a bed from somebody, and went on to our home on the farm near Hope. I will never forget how Maidia and Zoreta tried to cook on that smoking stove, and to take care of me in my weakness, and to look after the smaller children.

"It was a nightmare which I still shudder to remember." (Reminiscences.)

CHAPTER XX

THE PASTOR SYSTEM

Those three years in New Mexico, years of sorrow and tragedy for the Tant family, still found the head of the house forging ahead in his life's work, preaching the gospel. From Alamogordo soon after arriving he wrote:

"We have about forty members of the church of Christ, and hope to increase our membership to 200 and build up a good school here during the next three years, where the Bible can be taught as a regular text book in the school.

"New Mexico is almost four times as large as Tennessee or Kentucky, still we have only about one dozen loyal preachers, less than twenty small congregations, and only two church houses in the State.

"I came here mostly from the health standpoint, and to build me a home." (Firm Foundation, January 21, 1913.)

In April of that first year in Alamogordo, he persuaded a number of faithful and well known gospel preachers to sign a joint appeal with him for brethren to assist the congregation in Roswell in building a meeting house. Dr. C. M. Yater, Nannie's brother, was one of the leaders in the Roswell work. Signing the appeal with Tant were G. H. P. Showalter, Foy E. Wallace, Sr., N. L. Clark, Jesse P. Sewell, J. S. Dunn, J. Early Arceneaux, T. W. Phillips, Liff Sanders, T. H. Etheridge, W. F. Ledlow, and Joe S. Warlick. This appeal was successful in bringing in enough outside help to enable the Roswell congregation to go ahead with a modest building. Tant, meanwhile continued his preaching activities from across the mountain in Alamogordo. Tied down to the farm through the week, he still found time to preach nearly every night somewhere near his home. The religious journals for those two years at Alamogordo contain frequent reports of his preaching in little country school-houses, riding his horse sometimes twenty-five or thirty miles through the snow to reach a Sunday appointment, or conducting tent meetings through the summer. Although at this time the religious journals were filled with a great deal of controversy about socialism, secret societies, and the work of the Holy Spirit, Tant had very, very little to say about any of these hot issues. Instead his writings were nearly always in the nature of appeals for more brethren to become interested in preaching the simple gospel and saving the lost and unsaved. He returned to Texas and Oklahoma for a few, a very few, meetings:

> "I spent August in meetings at Nugent, Jones County, Texas, and Hermleigh, Scurry County, Texas. Both meetings were too short. Only held long enough to get up an interest among outsiders. I found good members at both places, but spiritually dead, having an idea that to meet on the Lord's day for worship and to hold one protracted meeting each year is all God demands." (Firm Foundation, September 22, 1914.)

The congregation at Nugent invited Tant to return the next year for another meeting. He declined (with a statement he used more than once in turning down return engagements with dead churches) saying, "No, thank you; I never like to view the corpse but once."

While Tant did not enter into the warm discussions on socialism and the secret societies, he did have his vigorous say about another problem then coming to the front — the "pastor system":

> "I hail with gladness the articles of Henry Warlick and U. G. Wilkinson opposing the new hobby of A. W.

Young's, in which he seeks to relegate to the background the eldership in the churches of God, and substitute young preachers in the place of those who have borne the burden and heat of the day. I notice C. E. Holt of Alabama is also giving warning on the same problem in the east.

"I am also the more rejoiced to see Henry Warlick coming back to his right mind. It has only been a short time since Henry got in the swim, pulled up and left the old farm and country where he was appreciated, and went to Cordell, where was located one of our Bible Colleges that is turning out young preachers — of whom Henry now complains. But changes come; and when the Lord and Special Providence began to run the Cordell school, Henry came to his own mind, went back to the farm, and is now trying to see things as they are.

"Years ago, when the church at Commerce, Texas, decided that old Brother Booth (a godly man and a fine gospel preacher for over fifty years) and Brother Gough were no longer able to lead them, one of the women stated, 'We never can get our girls married off with these two old men to lead. We must have a young man to draw young people'! So they hired a young pastor at $8.00 per month (all any of those boys is worth) to build up the church of God and sit as 'minister', not pastor, over the house of God. Soon trouble came. J. W. Denton and I were sent for to settle the same. We then and there saw that our next great fight in Texas was going to be over the young professional minister, doing the same work and occupying the same position as the modern digressive and denominational pastor or hireling.

"Recently I noticed a report from one of these young ministers, not yet twenty-two years old, pastoring for one of our oldest congregations, stating that his time would be out in April, and he could be secured to hold meetings or labor for any good church wanting him. For this same congregation, I called to memory, I had held seven protracted meetings, baptizing more than two hundred at that place; had also held one of my best debates there. But that was in the long ago, when the elders ruled the house of God, and the evangelist was only invited to hold their meetings and persuade their neighbors to become Christians.

"Now, I notice in each issue of the **Firm Foundation** from four to ten calls from preachers, begging for work; but most of our leading churches are supplied with pastors, many of them made by our Bible colleges. So they can't call them. The few poor struggling congregations out in the country are not able to support a man, so the change must come. Then many of you preachers, like myself, are getting old, and cannot please the people. We have worked in the gospel harness too long. I saw the change coming years ago. My calls for meetings were getting fewer; I took the pains to enquire at many places where I went, and found that many of these churches had letters from two to four of our leading preachers wanting to arrange meetings.

"After I have spent thirty years studying to learn what and how to preach, before I will become a beggar to my brethren and beg them to let me hold their meeting, I'll shave the hair off the top of my head and sit on buzzard eggs for the rest of my life for a living!" (**Firm Foundation**, April 6, 1915.)

G. H. P. Showalter, C. A. Norred (whom Tant had baptized), Isaac E. Tackett, A. W. Young, C. D. Crouch, A. O. Colley, and a host of others joined in the discussion and wrote on the subject. Tant wrote two more articles, entitled, "Young Preachers And Elders":

"When Henry Warlick, U. G. Wilkinson, Rawlins, C. E. Holt, and I saw the danger and gave the signal, I did not know at that time that such would make us sinners above all men, or put us down as 'preacher haters'. One brother declared it was only envy and jealousy that made us write such.

"If said brother could call to memory that for twenty years I stood as the great helper of young preachers in Texas, keeping one or more in my home from one

month to five years at a time, and that my book of
diagrams and sermons has been more help to young
preachers than all our Bible colleges combined, he
would feel ashamed to think that I was envious of any
man preaching the gospel in Texas.

"U. G. Wilkinson, Warlick, and myself are all friends
to the young preachers, but we want them to stand
on gospel ground. They are not doing it today, and
we shall continue to raise our voices along this line.
It was God's law that the church should train the
preachers, and nineteen-twentieths of all our old self-
sacrificing preachers were made in the churches. But
the church became tired of her work, turned her
preacher-making job over to the Bible colleges, and
now you can hardly find a boy who has courage enough
to want to preach if he does not go to a Bible college.

"Sometime ago I wrote to the president of the Board
of Regents of a Bible College, telling him that the
digressives had their missionary society with its president, secretary, vice-president, treasurer, board of directors, etc., to collect money from the churches to
teach the gospel and do other good works. He and I
agreed that this society was unscriptural. Then I told
him the church of Christ has its Bible college society
with its president, secretary, treasurer, board of directors, etc., to collect money from the churches to teach
the gospel and do other good works. Then I asked
by what process of reasoning could the digressive missionary society be unscriptural and our college society
be scriptural.

"The great trouble, brethren, is that we got off on
the wrong foot when we started our Bible Colleges.
We made them 'church institutions', and set them up
to do the work of the church. And now we are turning out Bible college boys that are going to hunt jobs
among the old established churches, and time only can
tell where the end will be.

"Don't misunderstand me, and think I condemn educational institutions of a high order. I am working
for one right now. And if I live at Hope for five years,
we hope to have a $50,000.00 house and four hundred
students in school. But it will NOT be 'our Bible col-

lege', or 'our Christian school'. It will simply be an educational institution in which all parties, Baptist, Methodist, and all others, are interested; and my brethren will be in the midst of them as the salt of the earth." (Firm Foundation, June 8, 1915.)

The "trial sermon" was also a source of irritation to Tant along with the "pastor system." He wrote:

"U. G. Wilkinson is slow of speech, deep, logical. He is an able teacher, yet it takes him about one hour to preach a sermon. But you have heard something when he is through. David Lipscomb is on the same order. Each of these men has forgotten more than I'll ever know; yet I can take them through Texas, let each preach a trial sermon, then take two twenty-year-old boys with me, and let each of them preach a twenty-minute sermonette, give the churches their choice, and nine out of ten of them will want the sermonette boy! Brethren, whither are we drifting? To my mind it seems funny, when you get sick, to send for a doctor to give you some 'trial doses' of medicine to see whether or not you want him to practice on you; or, if you get in trouble, to get a lawyer to give you a 'trial case' or two to see if you want to employ him. Yet I do not know of a church wanting a preacher which does not send for him to preach a 'trial sermon'. Don't forget, brethren, we are drifting." (Firm Foundation, June 15, 1915.)

II

The year at Hope proved to be as disastrous as had been the two years at Alamogordo. Nannie tells the sad story:

"This was an irrigated farm, but the water was supplied by a dam across the Peneasco River, which usually went dry in summer. The forty acres of orchard was beautiful to behold. We had several acres of Stamen and Winesap apples — an orchard whose fruit had taken first prize at the State Fair at Santa Fe the year before. We gathered nine car loads of fruit that fall. Shipped five car loads to El Paso, Texas, and the only return we ever got was a statement from the railroad company that we owed them $1.50 for freight. The apples had lacked that much of selling for enough to pay shipping charges!

"While we made no money, it was a joy to see such beautiful fruit. There were piles and piles, and tables and tables, with men and women grading the fruit and packing it in boxes. Some were Grimes Golden, some Jonathan, some Winesap. In addition to the apples, the orchard had a variety of other fruits — peaches, pears, apricots, plums, cherries in abundance. But we had no market for these things. There was nothing to do but to use what we could, in whatever way we could. Wood was scarce in the valley, and the mountaineers would sometimes bring down wood from the mountains to exchange for fruit — a wagon load of wood in exchange for a wagon load of peaches, pears, or apples. The children and I canned all we could, and dried some. We traded one lady enough fruit to get a practically new hack from her.

"I had thought while we lived at Alamogordo that we had had our share of TB people to visit us; but we had more at Hope. Husband seemed never to be able to resist the plea of anyone who came to him asking for help. In his meetings over the nation he ran across many, many people who were sick — often with tuberculosis. I think we must have had at least a dozen to come and visit us in Hope. Some stayed for a few days; a few, who were broke and friendless, stayed for weeks or months.

"My dear husband worked very hard that year, just like he did at Alamogordo. But at the end of the year we had no money to show for our labor. He held a few meetings in the summer, one being in the town of Hope. Many came from Roswell and Artesia to attend, two of them being my nieces, Xanna Yater, daughter of Dr. Charles Yater, and Minnie Lee Yater, daughter of Dr. Lee Yater of Cleburne, Texas. We got a congregation started in Hope.

"After our apple crop was gathered, we sent Maidia and Zoreta to Waco, Texas, to live with my sister, Mrs. Kanna Gebhart, and to go to school. She was kind enough, and financially able to board them without cost, and to buy clothing for them, something they had not had the last three years.

"But the year finally ended, and the time came for settlement with Brother Riley. The agreement had been made that we were to trade farms, our farm in Alamogordo for Brother Riley's farm at Hope. We got our title without trouble, but Brother Riley could never get a clear title to his property (a situation not unusual in those early unsettled days of the West), so the trade was not made. We just paid our rent, and my husband started looking for a new location for us." (Reminiscences.)

Thoroughly discouraged and disheartened with his adventure in the far west, Tant turned his thoughts toward Texas, his old home, and the place where he had so many friends. He located a farm at Cleburne, Nannie's home town, which he thought would make an ideal home. Once again, his natural optimism and hopefulness surged over him. He quickly completed the agreement for the trade, and wrote his family to make all things ready for the move; they were coming back to Texas, back to the "promised land." Nannie recalls that move:

"Artesia was our shipping point, thirty miles from Hope, over deep muddy roads and long stretches of open prairie with no road at all. We borrowed Brother Riley's team and wagon, and with our own wagon managed to load everything. J. D. drove one wagon and my husband the other. They drove off to the railroad, while I remained behind in the home of Brother A. J. Cox with eight-year-old Mozelle, seven-year-old Yater, and five-year-old Austin. I was to wait there till my husband telephoned from Artesia and told me to come on. The hack we had traded for was still good, and the team which had been so young and frisky when we came to Hope were now well broken and subdued, and perfectly safe for me to drive. A neighbor man went with husband to help put our stuff on the train and to bring the Riley team and wagon back to Hope. The two wagons had left Hope in the gray dawn one morning, and about four o'clock in the afternoon I got the telephone call telling me they had reached Artesia, and for me to come on; the freight car would be loaded and everything would be in readiness for us to leave Artesia the next day. Husband wanted me to get to Artesia in time for him to put the team and hack on the freight car; he planned to go through with the train to take care of the livestock, and the rest of the family would take a passenger train and meet him in Cleburne. I bundled up the children well and left the Cox home about 4:30 in the afternoon, December 21, 1915.

"I had never been over the road, but my husband had give me full directions. For six miles the road was well travelled, and I followed it easily. After that, however, the road gradually faded out into a mere cow trail, and I struck out across the open prairie. My three sleeping children were in the bed of the hack. It was not the most pleasant feeling in the world to be out on this lone prairie on a winter's night, trying to find my way across the great stretches of open country to a strange town. The moon was shining brightly, and only occasionally did we run into mud. At rare intervals we would pass a ranch house, but for the most part the drive was long and lonesome, with only the occasional howl of a wolf, or, more likely, a coyote, to break the stillness of the night. I finally managed to catch the reflection of the lights from the town, as they reached into the sky, and turned my horses' heads in that direction and kept going. Shortly before 11:00 o'clock that night I drove up on the main street of Artesia — thirty miles across an unknown prairie was not a bad bit of driving for a night trip! My husband was waiting for me, and stepped out in front of the team almost as soon as I got inside the town. When I was a girl and he used to come courting, I was always thrilled at the sight of him; but never in my life was I happier to see him than that moment he stepped out of the darkness to stop the horses that night in New Mexico.

"We got a room and I put the children to bed as soon as I could. Husband left on his freight car the next morning at 6:00 o'clock. I planned to go on to Roswell and spend two or three days with my brother, Dr. C. M. Yater, and give my husband time to get to Cleburne and have the household goods unloaded and somewhat straightened up before I got there. This we did; and my children and I finally arrived in Cleburne on Christmas Eve. My husband was there and had our junk (for that is about all it could be called by now) all in the house and the place pretty well straightened out.

"The house to which we came was comparatively new, having been but lately built by a wealthy cattleman — who, incidentally, had more money than good taste. It was about a mile south of town, on Gatewood Hill. The house was a two storey structure, built of cement blocks, with eight large rooms besides a huge center hall. There were numerous closets and bûilt-in features, including an ice box. All porch floors as well as pantry and kitchen were of cement. All other floors and all interior wood-work was in a beautiful shade of dark oak. All the walls were plastered and were snow white, except for my husband's library room, which was tinted pink. The place was lighted with carbide lights with electric lighters in beautiful chandeliers. The rooms were huge, one of them being 18 by 24 feet. Beautiful cabinet mantles above cream colored fire places with inside chimneys gave the place a look of elegance in sharp contrast to the primitive homes we had had in New Mexico. The house had cost $14,000.00 to build; and in addition there were two smaller houses on the place, a magnificent barn, and two huge siloes.

We had traded our Jones County property for a 200 acre farm near Glen Rose, in Somerville County, Texas. This we had now clear of all debt. Purchase price for the Cleburne farm was $18,000.00, which we were to liquidate over a period of several years. My husband agreed to borrow $5,000.00 on our Glen Rose property to make the down payment on the Cleburne farm. But after trying several different banks and loan agencies, he was unable to get that much of a loan. Mr. Whit-field, the man from whom we were purchasing the Cleburne place, told us he had a wealthy brother in east Texas who would lend the money, provided the Glen Rose property were put in his (Whitfield's) name. He told my husband to deed him the farm at Glen Rose, he would secure the loan for us, and then he would immediately deed the property back to us. This looked rather odd to me, but my husband was never one to be suspicious of anybody; so we made out the neces-sary papers. Whitfield now had a quit claim deed to our Glen Rose property (which was valued at about $10,000.00) and also had a vendor's lien against the Cleburne property for $18,000.00. Once he had all the papers, and had them recorded, he announced that he was unable to get the loan from his brother, and that he was satisfied to let things go as they were!

"Husband had to take the matter to court to recover our Glen Rose property. This was done easily enough; but it nevertheless added to our financial woes. We had hoped to put in a first class dairy at Cleburne; but once again we ran into trouble. The 100 acre farm was heavily sodded with Johnson grass, and fit only for pasture. The banks refused to advance us the money to buy dairy cows, so once again we were fac-ing a blank wall — an $18,000.00 property with no re-sources and no income at all to meet the notes that were coming due.

"It seemed we just must do something; and since we had failed in getting a dairy, I decided to start a poul-try farm. I talked with our county agent, and with his help our State Poultry Husbandman, F. W. Kaz-meier established a demonstration farm at our place, and taught me how to manage a poultry farm. The poultry industry was then in its infancy in Texas. I borrowed $50.00 from my long time friend, C. R. Nichol, and with that money bought two 140 egg ca-pacity incubators, two brooders, and enough single comb White Leghorn eggs to fill the incubators. Mr. Burton, the man from whom I bought the eggs, was kind enough to sell me eggs for two more hatchings, and wait till I had sold enough chickens to pay for them. By working almost night and day, carrying baby chicks from the house to the cellar, and back to the yard, gathering them in when rain threatened, fighting off our chicken-eating sow, as well as hawks and rats, I succeeded in raising enough chickens to pay Mr. Burton all I owed him, repay the loan to C. R. Nichol, and ended the season with eighty fine pullets, which I planned to keep for breeders for the next year.

"Husband was preaching all the time. Maidia, our oldest daughter, had now returned from Waco, and was able to get a job in the millinery department of one of the largest stores in town. She learned rapidly and was soon being paid $20.00 a month for her work. She was quite proud of this, for it enabled her to buy a few clothes, and to help me get a few things for the smaller children which they needed so desperately. Of course, everything my husband received from his preaching was now being used to pay off debts in New Mexico and in paying lawyers' fees and interest on the money we owed. Then, too, we had another bit of misfortune in Cleburne. One of the elders in the congregation was in the real estate business. He agreed to help my husband try to work out the deal with Whitfield, and to borrow money on the Glen Rose property. My husband finally borrowed $1,000.00 from a good friend of his who lived several miles away. As he was just ready to go off on a meeting when he got word that the money was available, he asked his agent (the elder in the Cleburne church) to go out and get the money for him, and deposit it in our account at the First National Bank. The elder agreed to do so.

"My husband went on to his meeting, and was gone for several weeks. While away he wrote a check on his account at the First National Bank in Cleburne. The check bounced. Investigation revealed that the elder had received the $1,000.00 all right from the friend who was lending it to us, but had deposited it in his own name, and then had checked it all out, and had concealed it some where. This caused some serious trouble. Some of the good brethren in the Cleburne church, incensed at this brother's theft from us, brought him before the church, and demanded that he

pay the money back. He admitted his guilt, pleaded
that he had been hard pressed himself, and only meant
to take the money temporarily, and that he would
repay every cent of it. He was removed from his office
as elder in that congregation, but continued a member
there in good standing.

"He never paid back one penny of the money. he
stole from us, and died in that condition.

"There was no way at all we could remain at Cleburne. So the Tant trading proclivities were again
brought into play. The two places we had left in New
Mexico were now traded — one for a $5,000.00 interest
in the Johnson Nursery at Dallas, Texas; the other
for the old Morris Sheppard home in Delta County,
Texas. Our Glen Rose property was sold to Dan Smith
for a little money, plus 160 acres of land in Midland
County, plus a house and lot in Mineral Wells, a few
old Oliver typewriters, and numerous shares of stock
in various mining and mineral companies — none of
which ever profited a penny. The nursery stock in
Dallas proved to be worthless. We traded the Morris
Sheppard place to a man named Frank Corn, a millionaire cattleman of Texas, for $8125.00 worth of
stock in a cotton seed oil mill at Mineral Wells. He
represented the property as being clear of debt, but
six months after completing the trade we received
notice that the mill would be sold at a sheriff's sale on
a certain date to satisfy a $25,000.00 mortgage against
it. There followed then four long years of litigation
with Corn. Our attorneys, Horton, Barwise, and
Thompson, a law firm of Fort Worth were confident
we had won the case — but the judge refused to let
it go to the jury and decided it himself in Mr. Corn's
favor. It was some slight consolation (but no money)
to us later to learn that this judge was removed from
office under scandalous charges. Our lawyers were
certain he had been bribed by Mr. Corn, but we had
not the money to fight the case into the higher courts.

"Just about this time my husband met a fine old
man in Southwest Texas named Gus Noys, a multi-
millionaire rancher, who had a fine irrigated farm at
Menard, Texas, that he wanted to sell. The farm of

some 400 acres was bought by my husband for $13,-
000.00. Mr. Noys agreed that we should only pay him
the interest for the first three years, and then should
start paying off the principal. He also had another
fine farm nearby, and he offered to knock off $2,000.00
from the price of our farm if we could find him a buyer
for the other farm. Husband soon found the buyer,
Brother John Keeney, a life-time friend of his, and
thus our purchase price was substantially reduced."
(Reminiscences.)

Menard, Texas, 1917. Ranch house built by Gus Noys. Appearing in the picture: Mozelle at left; Austin, mounted on horse; Zorete, at gate-post; J.D. Tant; Nannie Yater Tant (with sombrero); J.D. Jr., and Fanning Yater Tant, leaning against mulberry tree.

CHAPTER XXI

DEEP IN THE HEART OF TEXAS

The farm at Menard was well located, on the beautiful San Saba River. This stream formed the entire northern boundary of the farm. The banks of the river were shaded with large pecan trees; the water was clear and deep, affording an abundant supply for irrigation. The crops were mostly alfalfa, cotton, wheat, and corn.

Gus Noys had built and for some years had lived in the house which he sold to Tant. It was in a beautiful setting, about two hundred yards back from the highway, approached through a lane of large mulberry trees, whose limbs overlapped to form a leafy canopy over the driveway. The house was a large, two-storey, frame, painted white, with old style bay windows in front, covered with Martha Washington roses. It looked well enough from the exterior, but the interior was filthy — as the Tants soon found out. Nannie explains why:

"Mr. Noys had had a family of tenants by the name of White living in the big house. It looked and smelled like a hog pen. Worst of all, the Whites had not yet moved out when we moved in, and for three weeks we had to live together. Then they moved out to a tenant house on the place. They continued to pasture their stock on the farm. We had in about fifty acres of wheat, and it was so green and tender that the Whites' cows kept breaking through the fence into the lush field. My husband asked White several times to put yokes on his cows, as the land was wet and muddy and it would be most injurious to have cows grazing the field in that condition. White would always promise to yoke the cows, but did not. One day we saw the White cows out in the field, so one of the boys went out and drove them all off except one, which we put in a stable in the barn.

"White came in from the saloon about 4:30 in the afternoon. His wife must have told him one of the cows was missing, for he soon came looking for her. Husband was out in the yard cutting wood. White came to my kitchen door, his face red and flushed from the whiskey, and obviously more than a little drunk. His tongue was so thick he could hardly be understood. He was carrying a club, about four feet long and three inches in diameter. In an angry and belligerent tone he demanded, "Whar is Brother Tant?"

"I pointed out my husband to him, only a few yards away cutting wood. White then went to the barn, turned the cow out, and started to the place where my husband was working. Husband saw him coming, and realizing that White was angry and drunk, put his axe on his shoulder and started toward him, saying pleasantly as he approached,

"Hello, John."

"White began to tremble. 'Lay down that thar axe,' he bellowed. Husband glanced at the axe, reached over and stood it against a tree, and kept advancing toward White. White threw his hands in front of his face, began to back off, and to beg piteously that husband not hit him. Of course no such thought had even entered my husband's head!

"The Whites' cows all had yokes from then on.

"But that family tormented us in every conceivable way for a whole year. Their grievance was that Noys had sold us the place, and the Whites did not want to move out of the big house in which they had been living, and into a smaller tenant house. My hens were laying many eggs, and one morning I went out to the barn to find the horses literally covered with broken eggs. One of the White boys had found a hidden nest, and had amused himself by hurling the eggs at the horses. I was then selling eggs for fifty cents a dozen.

"Another day, late in the afternoon, I went to the hen house to take feed, and while there counted the eggs in the nests. There were forty-five. About an hour later I went back to gather the eggs, and not

one could I find. I had seen the White boys down at
the barn with their team, so I told my husband what
happened. He told me just to stay quiet, and he would
see if he could find out what happened.

"When it got good dark, husband slipped out of the
house, and went noiselessly down to the river. Presently he caught a glimmer of fire light shining
through the trees, and coming closer saw a bunch of
boys having a picnic. They were having a fish-fry
— with boiled eggs as an added delicacy. Husband
stepped out of the darkness and spoke to one of the
boys. There were about seven or eight of them there,
mostly the White boys, but with one or two neighbor
boys also. One of the boys, Russell Rambo, son of
our neighbor on the north side of the river, greeted
my husband, and asked him to join them in the fish
fry, and to eat a few eggs.

"How many eggs have you?" my husband asked.

"About eight dozen."

"Where did you get them?"

"Henry White said he bought them from Sister
Tant," replied Rambo.

"How much did he pay her?" asked Tant

"Don't know; it's his treat." Then, as the light
slowly began to break on Rambo, he asked, "Brother
Tant, were these eggs stole?"

"Yes."

"Then I'll pay you for every one of them," said
Russell.

"Husand refused to accept the money. Henry seemed penitent, and promised to pay for the eggs. But
he never did. Neither did he stop stealing them."
(Reminiscences.)

There was no church at Menard when the Tant family
arrived. But this was nothing new or unusual for them.
Within a few weeks a little congregation was meeting regularly for worship — at first in the little school house
adjoining the Tant farm, and then very shortly in the
town of Menard. Tant reported his move to Menard:

"I hope all will note my changed address from Cleburne to Menard, Texas. This move was not through desire, but through forced circumstances. Some time ago I went back to the farm to try to buy me a home before I got too old to work, and that I might not be forced to beg for a living, as many of my preaching brethren are forced to do. I was not so well up in the business world as I was on preaching, and made some mistakes and have been a servant of debt for four years past.

"When I bought at Cleburne, I hoped and prayed that I could pay for the farm, and be through with moving. But we made a complete failure on dry land farming, I was unable to meet the first payment, and with heavy loss I turned the farm back to the original owner. But as Paul teaches, 'All things work together for good to those that love the Lord', I am sure my failure was best for me.

"We have no church here at Menard. Wife, son, and I are keeping the ordinances in our own home each Lord's day. I hope soon to hold a meeting here and build up a church." (**Firm Foundation**, March 27, 1917.)

David Lipscomb died on November 11, 1917. In far off Texas Tant read the news with sadness. Lipscomb had been his friend for more than twenty years. He grieved to see him go.

But his sorrow over Lipscomb's death brought again to his mind the whole question of "Bible Colleges", and caused him to re-think and re-study the problems involved in it. He came up with some new ideas on the subject:

"Some of our Bible Colleges are having 'preachers' meetings' every year. From the time such things started at Nicea in 325 A.D. until the present these meetings have led from God instead of building up his kingdom. There have been no exceptions to the rule." (**Firm Foundation**, February 12, 1918.)

"Among the past mistakes that have brought wreck and ruin to the Alabama Christian College at Berry,

Alabama, has been the idea that this was one of 'our Bible colleges' — a church college, something God never heard of.

"For twenty days I have been trying to build order, system and life out of the wreck. I have urged the following changes:

"First: Cut out the habit of calling it 'our Christian college,' or 'our Bible college'. The church of God has no Bible colleges.

"Second: Show that it is an educational institution, to help prepare boys and girls for the duties of life along both literary and commercial lines. Have the Bible taught only as a class book, the same as it is now.

"Third: Attach an industrial department. Select 200 acres of land near the school, get a first class agriculturist to manage this farm; raise tomatoes, put up a small canning factory, get twenty to thirty milk cows, and set up some incubators. Provide work enough to put fifty to one hundred boys to work half their time, supporting themselves while they go to school." (Firm Foundation, January 1, 1918.)

Contributing in no small measure to Tant's uneasiness about the Bible colleges was the kind of preaching he saw being encouraged in some of them. He wrote:

"Brother A. W. Young thinks we must change our manner of preaching and 'skinning the sects', else our days of usefulness are over. When God's children went into Canaan, the denominations, seven in number, occupied the field. God said, 'Thou shalt make no covenant with them, nor show mercy. Thou shalt not make marriages among them.' But he said, 'You shall destroy their altars (churches) and break down their images and burn them with fire'. (Deut. 7:2-7.)

"God ordained they should 'limb-skin and jaw-hawk' (these are Brother Young's words; I don't know what they mean) the sects. As long as they did that, they obeyed God's commands and prospered; when they quit it, they lost their identity as the people of God, became one among the great churches, married and inter-married until they were driven out of the land. I am sure Brother Young is right about our preachers' losing their influence among many brethren if we preach the gospel plainly as we did twenty-five years ago.

"An elder in the church of Christ, a grand and godly man, told me recently that one of our leading presidents of one of our leading colleges had been preaching in their congregation twice a month for six months and not a single time had he preached a gospel sermon, neither could any man tell from his preaching to what church he belonged. During the time the Methodists gave a big blow-out, and as their preacher was not big enough, they had our (?) big president of one of our Bible colleges to preach their big sermon. They were all 'brethren' together, and the Methodists even called him 'DOCTOR'. This same president held a meeting for one of our leading churches last year, and some time ago I asked an elder of said church, 'Did he preach a single gospel sermon?' He said, 'Not one, but he gave some fine lectures'. I said, 'Why did you get him again this year?' He said, 'Because the Methodists and Baptists wanted him and we could not resist the pressure. . . .'

"Brethren, while we are gaining some in numbers and in wealth, are we gaining in Bible knowledge, and are we seeking to please the Lord? Or, is it not true that many of us are seeking to please the denominations!" (Firm Foundation, September 24, 1918.)

The Tant children were growing up. Both Ira and Davis, Tant's son and daughter by his first wife were now dead; and the six children of the second marriage ranged in age from twenty-year-old Maidia to eight-year-old Austin. Menard was still in the frontier western stage, and cattle rustling, horse stealing, and an occasional duel with six-guns was not unknown. Work on the ranch was hard and monotonous. The Tant children all went to the fields to ride the plows, or to chop cotton, bale hay, or do the innumerable tasks required of a farm or ranch family. Riding calves or racing the cow ponies provided the usual diversions.

Nannie records the passing years:

"Our two years at Menard were full of varieties: high water, courtships, weddings, war, a cattle stampede, to mention only a few.

"When we left Cleburne, Maidia remained there, for she was drawing a good salary, and to have gone with us would have stopped that. She boarded with a cousin in Cleburne. Zoreta was still in Waco.

"As the warm weather of summer came on, Maidia's health began to decline somewhat, so we urged her to come on to Menard and quit her job. She came, looking thin, pale, and tired. She soon began to mend, however, and the roses returned to her cheeks. She decided to teach school there in Menard; but since school did not start until fall, she had nothing to do except help around the house. But that was plenty! In June Zoreta's school was out, and she came home. All my brood were at home once more, and I was very happy.

"But girls are an uncertain quantity. Brother John Keeney, who had bought the other farm from Mr. Noys, had a very handsome son, Clide; his visits to our home became more and more frequent. Zoreta was the attraction. It took them only a few weeks to become engaged. But soon Clide had to go into the army, and he left for Camp Travis (at San Antonio) early in October. American boys were being given only the briefest kind of training, and rushed swiftly to the fighting fronts in Europe. The allies were hard pressed, and American soldiers by the thousands were being hurried into battle with very, very little preparation or training. Six weeks after Clide was inducted into the service, he was told to prepare to go overseas, and that his outfit would be going to France in December. Before leaving for the war zone, he tried to take out $10,000.00 insurance from the government, naming Zoreta as beneficiary. But he was informed that he could not name her as such, since she was neither his wife nor a relative. So that was their excuse. He

came home on December 23, and they were married
on December 24. She was too young; only eighteen.
But I suppose hardly any mother ever thinks her
daughter is ready for marriage.

"Maidia's sweetheart was in Fort Morgan, near
Mobile, Alabama. Of course she was much excited
over Zoreta's wedding. She had been engaged for
several months, and she and her sweetheart, Elmer
Franklin Smith of Rio Vista, Texas, had planned to
marry the previous October, but his going into the
army had caused them to plan a delay of a few months.
But when he came home for a Christmas furlough,
spurred on by the war hysteria, and the fear, no doubt,
that they might soon be parted never to meet again,
they abandoned all thought of waiting till that un-
predictable day when the war might end, and decided
to marry immediately. They were married on January 4, 1918, less than two weeks after Clide and
Zoreta had been married.

"The interest on our debt at Menard was $880.00
annually. The first year we made it without any
trouble. But the next year, 1918, Was a different
story. It seemed like everything went wrong. Boll
weevil ruined the cotton crop. The wheat harvest was
far short of expectations; labor was high for nearly
all the men had been drafted into the army. When
the fall of the year came around, it was obvious that
we would not be able to pay our interest.

"But husband was never one to give up. If one
avenue failed, he was always ready and resourceful
with something else. He found a man in Falls County,
Texas, who wanted to trade his 160 acres of land there
for our Menard farm. On account of the war, I suppose, property had become much inflated in value;
and our place was now valued at $24,000.00. The man
deeded over to us his 160 acres and we deeded to him
our 400 acres. He assumed our debt of $11,000.00,
and we assumed an indebtedness of $5,000.00 which
was against his place. But there was just one hitch:
he would not trade unless we paid the $880.00 interest
then due on our debt!

"That was the very thing we felt we could not do.

But the trade looked like too good a deal to miss, so we agreed to raise the $880.00 and pay our interest. It was due on February 1. Husband was away in meetings, as usual, and Mr. Noys served legal notice that if the interest was not paid by March 1, he would foreclose. We had about 2,000 bales of hay in the barn, but could not sell at any price. I went to the bank and tried to borrow the money. No luck. I knew a very wealthy man, a millionaire, who was a member of the church. Tried to borrow from him. The answer was "No." The days were going swiftly by, and it seemed I was not making any progress at all toward raising the money. Finally, I wrote to my beloved brother, Wilk Yater, in Cleburne, Texas, and borrowed $500.00 from him. I had a lady friend in Menard who owned some oil wells in Oklahoma. I told her of my plight, and she loaned me $200.00. To make up the other $180.00, I sold chickens and managed to get a few local people to buy a few bales of hay each. Two days before the deadline I went to Mr. Noys' agent and paid him the $880.00. Three days later my husband came home with $600.00 he had borrowed from Brother George Birchfield in Fort Worth, Texas. Of course I took $200.00 of this and repaid my friend in Menard. My brother was in no hurry for his, so I did not pay him till several months later. This left us $400.00 — with which to move." (Reminiscences.)

II

The 160 acres of land in Falls County with nothing on it was soon traded for a house and lot in Rogers, Arkansas, together with 26 acres of land. Twelve acres of this was a fine orchard of Jonathan and Grimes Golden apples; there was a one acre cherry orchard, and there were several acres of strawberries, raspberries, and blackberries.

Tant, as usual, chartered a freight car for the moving of his household goods, farm implements, and a few head of stock. He went along to water the stock, taking J. D., Jr. and Yater with him in the box car. They had a nice place fixed up on a mattress, deep in the end of the car, and rode in true comfort as "knights of the road." Nannie, with Maidia, Mozelle, and Austin, went through on the passenger train, reaching Rogers some thirty hours before the freight train with the household goods arrived. She spent the first night there in a hotel, but was quickly moved out of that place the next day and taken to the home of Brother Jim Elder, one of the faithful members of the Rogers church, a groceryman, who had a lovely home. He insisted on keeping the Tant family as his guests until their own house could be set in order and made liveable. Brother Elder's son-in-law, James Arthur Warren, was the song leader for the Rogers congregation. They had originally come from Kentucky to Arkansas. Nannie describes the arrival of the Tant family in Rogers:

"Husband and the boys arrived in Rogers during our second night at the Elders. He telephoned me as soon as he could, because he knew how anxious I would be about them. He said they were too dirty to go to anybody's house, so they all three slept in the box-car until daylight, got breakfast at a nearby cafe, and then began unloading the car and hauling our things out to our new home. Rain had started falling during the night, and the weather gradually turned colder and colder, finally turning into a freezing sleet. The streets were paved, and passable, but frightfully slick. Sister Elder sent us out to our home as soon as we had had breakfast. Husband was there already, and had brought one wagon load of our things. He had a heater up, and a fire going. About the time I got there our wagon arrived from the freight yard with the second load of the morning.

"I was all eyes for my precious little boy, Yater. He was then ten years old, too fat for his age, shy and retiring. He was always the most easy going of all my children, never one to stand up for himself or assert himself very much; he would suffer endless abuse and impositions from his playmates before striking back. But, oddly enough, when he did get into a fight, as he did a few times, he fought with a fury and a determination that almost frightened me. The weather being so wretched made me more than a little worried about him.

" 'Where is Yater?' I called to J. D. as he was backing the wagon up to the porch for unloading. Without a word Yater raised his head up from among the rubbish piled high on the wagon, and I saw his muddy old 'overseas cap' pulled down over his head. He began to climb down from the wagon, wet, muddy from head to toe, and shivering all over, but not uttering a sound.

" 'What on earth happened to you?' I cried, as I saw the dumb suffering on his face. Then I realized why he had said nothing. He was literally so cold he could not speak. I took him into the room beside the roaring fire in the heater, and soon had him thawed out. J. D. then told me that as they were driving home, one of the wagon wheels had hit a mud-hole, throwing Yater from the top of the wagon to the ground, under the wagon wheels, and right into the middle of an ice-filled mudhole. The loaded wagon had passed over him, the wheels mashing him down into the mud. The ground was freezing, but not frozen so hard that it would not give. It might have hurt him seriously had he not been in a mud-hole. J. D. had quickly jumped down from the wagon and pulled him out of the mud. I never saw a more miserable looking and forlorn child. His little fat hands were so chapped they were cracked and bleeding; railroad cinder dust was ground so deeply into his skin it took me days to get him clean. I wrapped him in a blanket and put him by the heater till I could warm some water and get the room warm. Then my first job was to give him a bath and put him in a warm bed and try to prevent pneumonia. In a few days he was quite himself again.

"Of course in our move over the Sacramento Mountains our furniture had been ruined; but I had repaired and varnished it a little and tried to make myself believe that it was tolerably nice again. But now it was all to pieces and broken up once more. But Maidia was adept in the line of "making over," and with the aid of a few screws, tacks, finishing nails, concentrated lye, brush, polish, paint, and varnish, we soon had the furniture back in shape.

"We had a splendid church at Rogers, and that was a wonderful experience for us. Some of the dearest friends of a life-time were made there. On Monday after our arrival all the children started to school — sometimes I think this was the best schooling they ever had. Especially was the grade school good." (Reminiscences.)

In July Tant held a tent meeting in the park in Rogers. It was attended by considerable audiences, and stirred up much interest. He writes:

"For two weeks I have been bombarding Rogers, Arkansas, with the ancient gospel. Songs ably led by J. D. Bowles, the digressive preacher here.

"There were two baptized, and more excitement and Bible preaching on the streets than ever known here before. Four sectarian churches started a union meeting to keep people away, but still they came.

"I got many questions, one calling in question two statements I had made about John Wesley, demanding I furnish the books and meet a committee and prove my charges, or else correct them. I furnished the books, and went twice to meet the committee at their appointed place. But they failed to come.

"Then they challenged me to take a three-day public examination in Greek and Hebrew, as preparatory to a debate they said they wanted on baptism — provided I can pass the examination. This challenge I gladly accepted, and added that I would not only take the examination in Greek and Hebrew, but also in Choctaw and Comanche, if they were afraid to debate in English. I also asked them to extend the examination to penmanship and the unknown tongues. Am to be examined in October. . . . .

"A letter in our daily paper of Rogers from the Methodist Episcopal preacher tells why they cannot stoop to meet the church of Christ in debate. This calls for a public challenge, which I am making to-day in the paper. There is something doing in Rogers. The church of Christ at this place came to hear me preach because I preached the Bible, and in so doing I did not please the sects." (**Firm Foundation**, August 3, 1919.)

On September 26, 1919, A. J. McCarty, Tant's beloved friend, died at his home in Killeen, Texas. The friends of his youth were now beginning to cross over, and an increasingly melancholy tone is found in Tant's writings from time to time. He recalls quite often the days of the past, and tells of the experiences he had with many of these preachers in the early days in Texas. But his preaching continued without interruption. In the fall of 1919, he reports:

"I have just held a tent meeting at Grove, Oklahoma. Grove is where I preached earlier this year and left a small congregation of ten members to work. We had the largest congregations to hear the gospel ever seen in Grove. The digressives, after working a month against my meeting before I ever got there, sent two of their preachers to meet me on the organ question. After two nights' investigation, I am quite sure I will never get to meet them again. Their argument was: 'Where there is no law, there can be no transgression; and there being no law on instrumental music in the New Testament, we have the right to use it!" While we have only five male members at Grove, and all poor, they love the Bible and are hoping to reach heaven later. . ." (**Firm Foundation**, October 7, 1919.)

"I spent the first Lord's Day in January with Brother W. W. Slater of Fort Smith, Arkansas, and preached for the church of Christ there. Less than one year ago, thirty-three members pulled off from the church and moved several blocks away, and commenced meeting in an old store building. Now they have a splendid cement church house, well heated. They are working in peace and love. There were more than one hundred

and twenty-five out for Bible study the morning I was
there.   One sister had fifty-four in her Bible class.
The only trouble confronting them now under Brother
Slater's able leadership, is that the house will be too
small in less than one year, and they will be forced
to divide again, or else to enlarge their church house.
I regretted to learn that there had been a little fric-
tion in the old church before the thirty-three members
left.   All the congregation favored Sunday School literature such as song books, chapters and verses in
our teachers' Bibles, and the references in our Bibles,
all of which are nothing but human literature; also
they were reciting four different classes in the church
at the time, in that they were teaching the Bible in
song, carrying four different parts.   Some of the members wanted to extend this literature and use printed
literature; but the others wanted nothing but oral literature, gotten up by themselves in asking questions
in the class.   I hope soon to hold a meeting for the old
church in Fort Smith, and show them that printed or
written literature is just as good as oral literature.
Then we will all work together in love.   I wonder what
has gone with all the 'anti-printed literature' brethren?
For years I have kept this proposition before them
that I will affirm: First, Sunday Schools are scriptural; Second, Sunday School literature is scriptural."
(Firm Foundation, February 3, 1920.)

Settling Church Troubles

'I suppose it is because I live in Arkansas, and because I am on the Lord's side, and care but little what
my brethren think of me, or what they say about me,
that I have received near fifty letters during the last
year, asking me to come back to Texas at some selected
place and go in with a gang of preachers and sit in
judgment on some more preachers and condemn their
conduct and expose them to 'our brethren'.

"As I lived in Texas long enough to know that no
preacher lives in Texas without doing wrong, and as
my Savior said for the guiltless to cast the first stone,
I feel like I am disqualified by my own conduct to sit
in judgment on these preachers.   I also notice that

'turning preachers out of the church' (whatever that is) has become a fad in Texas.

"As some preachers are better off out of some congregations than they are in them, and as some congregations are better off with some preachers out than in, I don't feel like stopping or interfering with the good work.

"I can call to memory five different occasions where preachers have gone in and tried to assume authority over some local congregation, without a shred of Bible authority. They have always made bad matters worse. I feel like it is not the thing to do.

"On two occasions preachers have come together and tried me, and became judge, jury, and witnesses, and decided that in some things I had acted 'indiscreetly'. Now, as that word can include everything in the catalogue of crimes, and at the same time can mean nothing, I would much rather they would accuse me of drunkenness, adultery, or stealing, than to say I am 'indiscreet'. At both times when I was tried, convicted, and.condemned by an outfit of jealous preachers, without being permitted to speak for myself, like the heathen allowed Paul to do, I was hundreds of miles away from the trial, preaching the gospel of the Son of God.

"If certain preachers have done wrong, I am sure if their brethren (other preachers) will go to them and show them the wrong, they will correct it. If they will not make correction, then let the charges be made in the congregation where said preacher belongs. If the congregation 'turns him out', he can find plenty of company with other preachers on the 'outside'. But if said congregation will NOT turn him out, then I think it safe to leave this preacher and the congregation in the hands of God 'who doeth all things well'. Other preachers have little business trying to interfere.

"I might also mention that I have received a number of letters asking, 'Have you heard of the new paper that is to be started at Dallas?' When they tell me of the able brethren who are to run this, the only sound and loyal paper in the brotherhood as soon as it starts, and when I know these able brethren so well, and know if all the paper brains they have were put in the hollow of a mustard seed they would have as much room to wiggle around as a tad-pole in the Gulf of Mexico, it amuses me. Some men's egotism and brains are far apart.

"I once worked for the **Gospel Outlook**, so I could kill off the **Firm Foundation**, but failed. I then tried to help George W. Savage run the **Christian Monitor**, the only sound paper, to kill the Foundation, but failed. As the **Firm Foundation** is already committed against sect baptism, and in favor of Sunday School literature (I mean J. D. Tant's Bible Studies), both positions I endorse; and it is only shaky on 'our Bible colleges' and located ministers. But as this new 'only loyal paper' is to cover the same territory as the Foundation, only they want bigger schools and closer state affilia- tion, which will lead them farther from the word of God, I shall try to content myself to live in Arkansas and preach the gospel and occasionally tell Showalter how to run the Foundation.

"As soon as I get out of debt, and get money ahead, I want to start a Bible College, provided I can be presi- dent, to educate scriptural elders on how to feed the church of God, and send out scriptural evangelists to preach the gospel, and to oppose the located pastors. Then I shall want to start a paper to tell what great things I am doing. But until that time I do not think I am in favor of more papers." (**Firm Foundation,** March 2, 1920.)

CHAPTER XXII

AN APOLOGY OFFERED AND ACCEPTED

On October 7, 1920, the following notice appeared in the Gospel Advocate, page 977:

"Some years ago J. D. Tant was shut out of the columns of the Gospel Advocate on what was thought to be reliable evidence, but further developments proved this to be untrue. For the injustice done him I offer my apology, and deeply regret the occurrence. The Advocate never charged nor believed him guilty of any criminal conduct, and only thought his plainness of speech often amounted to bluntness, which offended some people. The management of the Advocate was only anxious for him to prove himself innocent; but when his accusers refused to meet him in Nashville, J. D. Tant offering to pay all railroad expenses to and from Nashville, he had no way left to exonerate himself. It now appears clear that there is no truth in the accusation."

To this Tant responded:

"Brother J. C. McQuiddy: I am glad to note in the Gospel Advocate of October 7 that you consider one, J. D. Tant, worthy of an apology from you on account of certain treatment given him by the Advocate in the long ago. While said treatment caused some of my friends and myself to lose respect for the Advocate, for we felt I did not have fair treatment, yet I assure you with all love that I accept your apology in full, and we will rub out the past and be brethren, as we were in the long ago.

"It it also quite true that my language is blunt and plain; having been reared in the West, where we all use plain speech, and being an Irishman (for I'd be ashamed to be anything else), we all use language out there that can be understood. When I heard many of my brethren, especially among the pure-hearted preachers, claiming that my language was offensive because I said 'bull' in the pulpit, I hardly knew what to do.   After all, a preacher must try to please the Lord instead of men in preaching the gospel.

"David could not wear Saul's armor to fight Goliath, yet he won the victory.   Paul's brethren said his speech was contemptible; yet he fought a good fight. Also, Paul said, 'To the pure all thing are pure; but to the defiled nothing is pure'.   Many of my brethren who are shocked at my speech, I believe can not show up a better moral life than I can.

"I shall not quit preaching to go to college now to learn smooth language that will please my brethren, but shall continue to preach the gospel straight and keep in touch with the Lord, and keep myself unspotted from the world.   I will work and pray for the salvation of all men I may influence, for I am more anxious to fill heaven than I am to get a college education so I can use language that will please my brethren.   I well know that I must soon give an account of my stewardship to God, and I think if I have preached the gospel and lived right, God will give me one hundred percent on language.   And Freed and Hardeman will give me one hundred percent on penmanship, and then I'll be on the safe side."

> In love, J. D. Tant
> (Gospel Advocate,
> November 30, 1920.)

II

In the spring of 1921 Tant went on a three-month preaching tour into North Carolina, coming back through Alabama.   On the way to this work he stopped for two days in Nashville, Tennessee, and visted a meeting at Green Street Church being conducted by R. V. Cawthon.   He was invited to preach the night he was there, and did so. He also visited David Lipscomb College, and spoke at the chapel service:

"I learned that the students had a college dog that

was worthless, and that they had voted to give it to the biggest fool who spoke there this year. They not only gave me the dog, but begged me to take it home with me. But as F. B. Srygley and F. W. Smith had both spoken there, and as C. R. Nichol was soon to follow me, I realized it would be unfair to them for me to take the dog." (Gospel Advocate, May 12, 1921.)

The trip to North Carolina was an eventful one. Tant held meetings at Statesville, Boyer, Warner's Chapel, and a number of other places, baptizing quite a few people. He had some pretty sharp encounters with some of the "no literature" brethren and the "no Bible class" brethren. After two months in this state, he came back home by way of Alabama, where he held two meetings:

"My last two meetings were in Alabama. Held one meeting at Bear Creek, Alabama, with ten baptized and two restored. Don't think I ever found a congregation so little in accord with the word of God as Bear Creek. Envy, malice, evil speaking, evil surmising, adultery, whiskey drinking, no love, and neglect of worship, seemed to be the order of the day. No laying by in store upon the first day of the week, as God ordained, was once thought of among them. As a result they were unprepared to support the meeting, and failed by half to fulfill God's command to support the preaching of the gospel.

"Some of my brethren think it no wrong to call a man 600 miles from home to hold them a twelve to twenty day meeting, and then declare they would like to support him, but do not have the money. At the same time they are buying their tobacco on mule credit, for if they are not responsible for their debts, they will put a mortgage on their mules to buy their tobacco. At the same time these brethren seem to think they are doing God's will and will get to heaven. For such I have no hope.

"From Bear Creek I went to Barnes' Creek and preached ten days, baptized five; one hundred mem-

bers who had been running with the devil made a
strike against him, and confessed their wrongs, coming back to the Lord and promising to do better work
for him. One day during this meeting I went down
to White House congregation, eight miles away, and
persuaded seventy-five members there also to quit
the devil and confess their wrongs and go to work for
the Lord. I started them to work in a good Bible
school at each place, and each congregation hopes to
have a Bible class taught this fall to learn more about
the Bible that they may be able to do more good.

"Never in my life have I found as much ignorance
of the Bible as I found on this trip. Faith, repentance,
baptism, and skin the sects, seems to be all they know.
At Barnes Creek, with two hundred members, I put
the question to the entire church: Did God make
Abraham or Adam first? They were unable to tell.
Yet they were sure the Baptists and Methodists would
go to hell because they had Sunday School and taught
their children the Bible, and could not see like we see.
Brother Willcut and Brother Wyley, both able preachers and among our best men, made this meeting a
success by their continual work and help in the same."
(Firm Foundation, July 26, 1921)

III

Three years at Rogers saw the Tants on the move again,
this time to Quitman, Arkansas, a small town in the southwestern corner of Cleburne County, some sixty miles north
of Little Rock. Again the move was made by a chartered
freight car, J. D., Jr. and Yater going along to take care
of the stock. Nannie took the other two children, Mozelle
and Austin, on the passenger train to Conway, the nearest
railroad connection to Quitman.

But there was trouble ahead for the family:

"We had a beautiful house, splendidly built, and of
the very best lumber and workmanship. It was set
well back from the road, on a little hill or knoll over-
looking the town, and directly across the road from
the village cemetery. The place had a $3,000.00 mort-

gage against it, which we assumed. After three years'
effort in clearing titles with releases, paying back
taxes, settling with minor heirs, etc., we managed to
get a federal loan for $2,250.00. The former owner
of the property, J. J. Kane, the town banker, moved
into another and larger house in town.

"But a great calamity was just ahead of us. In the
summer before we left Rogers, Austin had begun suffering with his right leg. I had him under treatment
of different doctors, but none seemed able to help
much. There was no particular pain, but the leg became stiff and started to swell. Two or three doctors
diagnosed it as "rheumatism"; but I learned it was
common with them to diagnose anything they could
not understand as "rheumatism," just as they always
said a crying baby was "spoilt." About two weeks
after we became settled at Quitman, I noticed a black
spot on Austin's leg just above the knee. Pressing it,
I discovered pus. He had been on crutches for four
months, and I knew that some dread disease had been
doing its deadly work all this time. In five days the
black spots became so large, and the swelling so great
that the leg was in a strut. I was fearful it might
burst open.

"What was I to do? A stranger in a little backwoods, country town, with no doctor whom I could
trust, my husband hundreds of miles away, and with
only $14.00 to my name, and a very sick child?

"I had two brothers in Cleburne, Texas, who were
excellent doctors. I would go to them.

"I managed to borrow a hack from a kind old man
who was a neighbor, and fixed up a bed in the back
of it for Austin to lie on for the trip to the railroad.
I had no money with which to buy railroad tickets,
but felt I might secure something from Brother J. C.
Dawson, a faithful gospel preacher and business man
in Conway. After J. D. had driven me to Conway in
the borrowed hack, I went directly to Brother Dawson's office, laid my case before him, and received the
money — although, as he later told me, he was considerably reluctant to let me have it, as he had been
the victim of more than one 'hard luck' story by down

and out brethren. I sensed his attitude, and was
deeply embarrassed by it; but my child was slowly
dying, and I was willing to swallow my pride and beg
for the money on my knees if it had taken that to get
it. Brother Dawson let me have the money, and we
went on to Cleburne on the train. As quickly as I
could get a letter off to my husband, I told him how
humiliated I had been by Brother Dawson's attitude,
and asked him to repay the money at once. He did.
He also showed Brother Dawson my letter. But J. C.
Dawson was a fine, Christian man, and long before
his death he offered apology for his brusqueness with
me. He and the Tants remained the closest of friends
through the remaining years.

"On December 16, 1921, my brothers operated on
Austin, removing about seven inches of decayed bone,
leaving only a thin sliver of bone tissue to maintain
the length of his leg. When new bone formed, they
planned a second operation in which they would remove that section, and thus, in the two operations,
remove all the infected bone from the leg. Both operations were successful, and Austin, after many weary
months of convalescence, made a complete recovery.
He is strong and healthy now, a robust six feet tall,
and shows no signs of his close brush with death save
the long cruel scars on his leg." (Reminiscences.)

Meanwhile, Tant was busy in his meetings in Texas,
Arkansas, Oklahoma, Alabama, Tennessee, and North Carolina. He writes:

"I closed my last debate with J. N. Clark in West
Tennessee on December 10, and started home. As we
had located at Quitman without any church there, and
wife had been writing me how lonely it was for her
and the children to worship alone in our own home on
Lord's Day among strangers, I had thought, if it was
the Lord's will, I would get to spend one month at
home with wife and children; but when I reached
home, I found that wife had been gone two days under
a rush call to carry our youngest boy to a sanitarium
in Cleburne, Texas, to be operated on for tuberculosis

of the bone. The next day a telegram from wife stated that the Yater doctors and Dr. Self, of Cleburne, had taken several inches of leg bone out of my little boy's leg above the knee. So all our expected happiness was turned into sorrow. While wife is patiently watching our little darling, Austin, in the sanitarium many miles away, three other children and I are keeping house at home.

"On the last Lord's Day in December I preached to a large congregation in the Methodist church house at Quitman, cut wood all Christmas week, and started the new year by preaching the gospel to the church of Christ at Searcy, Arkansas. . . . .

"So our fondest hopes and greatest desires are often blighted. But all will be well in the end. The day dawns after the darkest night, the longest lane will turn, and I have only a few more mountains to climb, only one more river to cross, and all will be light and happiness 'over there'. It is grand to be a Christian!

"Wife will remain in Cleburne with our boy for some time yet, perhaps three months, as the doctors tell her they will have to do a second operation in March.

"As soon as possible I shall get into the work again. If I can find some brother who is blessed with money, who will lend me two hundred dollars to bridge over and meet present emergencies till I can get into the field again, I shall be glad. If I do not, I shall fight it out alone, and let those I owe wait till I get on my feet again. God only knows what is best, and I am willing to wait, fight, and pray, and leave the results with him." (Gospel Advocate, February 2, 1922.)

The last Sunday in February, 1922, Tant went to Berry, Alabama, for a two weeks' meeting. He had preached there before, and had been quite active in promoting the "Berry Christian College," which had been in operation there, but which had run into considerable financial difficulty. Eleven were baptized during the meeting; and Tant worked hard, but unsuccessfully to try to find some way out of the financial morass into which the school had fallen. He reports some months later that his efforts were in vain:

"Quite a number are asking about 'our Bible college' at Berry, Alabama. I will state that it is a thing of the past. At the time of my last meeting there, Brother Shepherd agreed to cancel his sixteen-thousand-dollar mortgage against the school property, provided the brethren there would build a dormitory. An outsider promised to give the lumber with which to build it if the brethren would cut and haul the logs to the sawmill; but they were not interested enough to do so.

"But Berry is not the only little town that has made the same sad mistake, and many brethren have lost all they had by breaking up and moving to a school. Lockney, Denton, Cleburne, and Sabinal, Texas; Odessa, Missouri; and Rector, Arkansas, can all tell the same sad tale. Thousands of dollars were lost in building school houses, and many went school crazy and worked harder to build up 'our Bible college' than they did to build up the church of Christ.

"In fact, I sometimes doubt if our so-called 'Bible colleges' have ever been any benefit to the upbuilding of Christianity. A very large percent of our finished-up preachers who come out of our Bible colleges come out as professionals, hunting to 'take charge' of some church, and set the eldership aside, filling the place of a modern sectarian pastor.

"If our Bible college is God's ordained institution, instead of the church, to make gospel preachers, why not start one to make scriptural elders? I am sure the greatest hindrance we have today is the inefficient eldership. Eight out of ten who act as elders have the work forced upon them by the church. They declare that they do not want it, and Paul says they must desire the office. Many have neither time nor inclination to prepare the food to give to the church of God, as Paul instructed them in Acts 20:28. They give out so many tin cans, raw bones, and so much spoiled meat that a goat would starve to death on such feed. They claim they do not have time to do this work, and must hire a pastor to do it; yet, if the eldership

of the church of Christ carried a salary of five dollars a day, three-fourths of all the men and two-thirds
of all the women who are added to the church would
qualify themselves and want to be elders.   Brethren,
let us think seriously of the services we offer God."
(Gospel Advocate, June 28, 1922.)

Through the summer of 1922 Tant held meetings at
Quitman, Arkansas, with four baptized; at Albion, Oklahoma, with thirty baptized; at Strawberry, Arkansas, with
twenty-six baptized; at New River, Alabama, with an un-
specified number of baptisms; and held a debate at Ozark,
Arkansas, "to fill Brother C. R. Nichol's date with Steward
on the infidel doctrine of a future kingdom and soul sleeping."   One of his most interesting meetings was at Liberty,
Arkansas:

"Five years ago we had a good church at Liberty,
but some introduced the organ and tore it up.   Then
the organ lovers went to other parts, and the church
building has been standing idle.
"Through the efforts of W. C. Evans and J. B.
Martin, I was called there for a mission meeting.
During the meeting we had more shouting and rejoicing than I have seen in the church of Christ for
twenty years.   Quite a number were baptized, and
with those who came back from the devil's side and
confessed their wrongs, we had sixty-seven additions
in all.
"One good man who had preached in the Freewill
Baptist Church for forty years heard me one week,
and he seemed to be surprised to know that there was
a church of Christ which taught Bible doctrine.   He
said he had been teaching the same for forty years,
contending with the Baptists that there is only one
church, and that, the church of Christ; and that baptism is for the remission of sins.   He begged to have
fellowship with us.   He said he did not come changing
his faith, as he had been teaching the Bible as I was
teaching it for forty years.   He and his whole family
took a stand with the church of Christ at Liberty,

and as they all have good records, I am sure they will do much good." (Gospel Advocate, October 19, 1922.)

IV

As Tant passed his three-score years, he found himself being called more and more often to try to arbitrate church wrangles. He had preached now for more than forty years, had established scores of churches in many states, and was respected generally as one who was fair and reasonable. Typical of the work done in settling these church fusses was the trouble at Anson, Texas, as reported by Dew Womack:

"Twenty-seven years ago J. D. Tant held the first protracted meeting in Anson. As a result there was a house built which served the church until last year. We now have a new house, and Brother Tant has just finished the first meeting in it. He came and found us all divided over different matters, the church almost ruined. But he got us all together and left us in working order. He gave us an awful whipping, but we love him just the same. Two very fine young men obeyed the gospel. Tant is so strong and plain in handling the word of the Lord that you must appreciate his efforts. If there is any trouble in any church, send for the one and only J. D. Tant; and if he can't settle the trouble, you might as well shoot the whole outfit and stop them." Gospel Advocate, April 19, 1923.)

Tant's methods in dealing with church troubles sometimes lacked a delicacy of touch, but they were often very effective. In a meeting at the little Texas town of Belcherville, about this time, he was staying in the home of a Brother Smith, who was the "leading elder", and who was passionately opposed to what he called "the class system" of Bible school work. Smith had a large family, ranging in age from a six-month-old infant who was nursing at the breast to grown sons and daughters. After preaching there a week, and realizing that Brother Smith was holding the church back by his stubborn opposition to the classes, Tant spoke out on Sunday morning from the pulpit:

"Before God, brethren, if Brother Smith had as much sense as his wife has he could make a fine church out of this outfit here. As I have been living in his home all week I have observed how Sister Smith feeds her family. As you know, their young ones are like stair-steps. Sister Smith fed some of these children meat and beans; some were eating mashed potatoes, some were eating various kinds of fruits; and the baby was nursing from its mother's breast. Now, if Brother Smith were trying to feed those children instead of his wife, and if he treated them like he treats the church of God, he'd have every last one of those children sucking from the same teat! I wish he would show as much sense in feeding the church of God as his wife shows in feeding her family!"

The little congregation at Sayre, Oklahoma, had had a terrific fight, and had come to a glaring impasse; both groups continued to meet in the auditorium, but at different hours of the day. And to further underline their irreconciliable differences, they had divided everything in the building in halves, and had even taken up one half of the benches and turned them around to face the rear of the one-room building. They had built a makeshift pulpit at the rear of the auditorium, and for several months had continued in this incredible condition.

Tant came for a meeting. He was called by one side or the other, but because of his former preaching in the section, and because of his reputation in the church generally, the house was filled to overflowing. Most of the early comers got seats, but many had to stand. Tant got into the regular pulpit, preached one half of his sermon, then deliberately walked down out of it and to the other end of the house, mounted the make-shift pulpit and finished his sermon. He said:

> "I am doing something today that neither Jesus Christ or the devil would do — I'm preaching for this ungodly outfit at Sayre. It is clear that Jesus Christ is not here, as shown by this silly seat arrangement. He will not abide where sin is, and if there ever lived a bunch of sinners, these benches would show you are that bunch. It is also clear that the devil is not here. Why should he be? He has already got you — lock, stock, and barrel! There is no point in his hanging around here; he can be off somewhere else trying to drag somebody else down to hell. He doesn't need to worry about you!!"

His sixty-second birthday found Tant in a reminiscent mood. He wrote on that day:

> "This is the twenty-eighth day of June, 1923. I am at Locust Bayou, Arkansas, preaching the gospel of the Son of God. I am sixty-two years old today, weigh one hundred and ninety pounds. My physical and mental strength have not abated. I am in the best of health, know more about the Bible, and know that I am a better preacher than ever before; yet I realize my life's work is almost finished, and I am nearing the end." (Gospel Advocate, August 16, 1923.)

Some years after Tant's death, Ulrich R. Beeson, then of Little Rock, Arkansas, wrote a description of that Locust Bayou meeting:

> "Locust Bayou, a peaceful little village, located midway between Hampton and Camden, Arkansas, on a well-traveled road, consisted of four stores, two blacksmith shops, a lumber mill, and a gin. A church of Christ has existed there for many years, having been established presumably by Brother Henry G. (Dick) Cranford. Some of the best people to be found anywhere were members of this congregation; but, like

many other churches, they had become contented with the 'status quo', and had gradually been dying for years. In their complacency, these good people had let their meeting house go unpainted within and without, despite their prosperity. Some had become dissatisfied with such a state of affairs, and had recommended that Brother J. D. Tant be asked to hold a meeting.

"It was during the hot days and dusty roads of 1923 when Brother Tant arrived and sized up the situation. His powerful sermons, his reputation as a preacher, and his Irish mannerisms began to draw good audiences for each service from far and near. Among the preachers who attended were W. T. Breedlove, John Medley, and Hugh Hogg. Things went smoothly the first week; but toward the end of the meeting Brother Tant began to point out the weaknesses of the church, getting a little bit harder and more pointed in each sermon. Some were beginning to flinch, until the climax was reached the last Sunday afternoon of the meeting.

"At the morning service, Brother Tant had hung on the wall behind the pulpit a rather large canvas displaying a crude drawing of the Locust Bayou meeting house, with its spacious grounds and its ramshackle out-buildings. He depicted the church as being on wheels, moving 'upward and onward', and its members, according to their respective short-comings and sins were roughly sketched upon and around the building. The morning worshippers were filled with wonder and curiosity; and some of them with ominous forebodings and premonitions as to what the afternoon sermon would be. At the close of the morning service, Brother Tant announced his intention of preaching from the chart that afternoon, and urged all members to be present. When the time came for the afternoon service, the house could not contain the people.

"The church property was aged and in a bad state of repair. A huge dug well at the rear of the building had an old frame curbing, beneath which a gaping chasm had been washed out, permitting surface water to flow freely into the well. The old well bucket was rusty and dirty. The out-door rest rooms appeared unsightly and indecent, with their doors sagging on rusty hinges, and leaves from Sears and Roebuck catalogues littered the premises. Hogs rooted and grunted around the church building during the services. The house had no class-rooms, and the Sunday School was generally a bedlam of squeals and grunts from the pigs underneath the floor mingled with the pious admonitions of the teachers — and the bored inattention of the urchins who were anxious to be out on the ground playing.

"Time came for the afternoon service to start. It was one that Locust Bayou has never forgotten. Several songs were sung, among them one of Brother Tant's favorites, 'Where He Leads Me I Will Follow'. After the prayer and the reading of the text, Tant took up his long pointer and started his sermon. He gave a name to each of the figures on the chart, and described his spiritual character. Behind the imaginary stalled church, pushing mightily and trying to get the building to move forward were pictures of Tom Priddy and Buddy Bridges, with their shoulders against the wheels. On top of the house sat Holden Sims fast asleep; right behind him, also asleep, and in the act of falling off the house to the ground was J. Ponder Hollis. Several faithful sisters were named who had hold of the rope and were trying with all their strength to pull the church forward; one brother was poking a tree limb through the spokes of the wheel; another was throwing a huge boulder under a wheel. Others were looking on indifferently, some walking off the ground and going in the direction of the Sunday picture show, others trying to light their cigarettes, and one surreptitiously trying to sneak a nip from his whiskey bottle.

"As Tant went through the chart, naming the characters one by one, the air was electric with tension. But occasionally the speaker would throw in a humorous touch that would bring a roar of laughter from the audience, even from those who were squirming and suffering most acutely under his barbs. It was a sermon that was never forgotten.

"It is not hard to judge the results of that afternoon's sermon. Many did not know whether they should quit or go on. However, a wonderful change came over the congregation. Locust Bayou was completely shaken out of its lethargy. The house got a coating of paint outside, and a thorough clean up job inside; a new well-bucket was bought, and the well curbing was repaired; the hogs were fenced off the church property; some provisions were made for adequate Sunday School rooms — and Tant was invited back for another meeting!"

Back home in Quitman in September Tant reported:

"I have just held two two-weeks' meetings at Fowlkes and Gates, in West Tennessee, with four baptized and two reclaimed and both churches put to work. During the Gates meeting I debated with the noted "Wild Bill" Evans, a Methodist preacher, who claims fifty. thousand converts. I have held two hundred debates, and I do not think I ever met a man who knew less about the Bible. The debate was attended by two thousand people, and I knocked "Wild Bill" out in the fourth round with the word of God. He declared publicly that he would never meet me again." (Gospel Advocate, September 27, 1923.)

V

After two years at Quitman, Tant began to count up some of the disadvantages of the place: it was thirty miles from the nearest railroad at Conway, and his constant traveling meant that he had to leave always a full day earlier than would have been the case had he lived in a railroad town, also was a full day later in getting home from his meetings; the tenants (share-croppers) to be had in that community were simply not dependable, which meant that Nannie and the children had to work the farm. This necessitated taking the children out of school several weeks for cotton picking each fall. The interest on the indebtedness each year took nearly all the farm produced. And it looked like there was no future to farming in Arkansas. So Tant tried to figure out some way to trade the Quitman farm.

He put an ad in several farm journals: "To trade, a 300 acre farm at the foot of the Ozarks. Address, Box 187, Quitman, Arkansas." He got scores of answers, and after several months of negotiation worked out a trade with a man at Mercedes, Texas, in the Lower Rio Grande Valley. But before the time came to make the move, he had traded the Mercedes place for a cotton plantation at Greenville, Mississippi.

The move to Greenville was made in January, 1925. This time there were no horses or cattle to go on in the freight car, only the household goods. Everything was taken by wagon to Conway, then loaded on the car. When the final items had been stacked inside the car, Tant took the wagon and team with which he had hauled the things to Conway, and traded them for a used Ford touring car. It was a used 1922 model that he finally got.

Sending all his family except Yater on to Greenville on the train, Tant declared that he and Yater would drive the Ford through. There was just one slight problem — neither of them knew how to drive. But Tant declared that there was "nothing to it", and got the car dealer to show him how to start and stop the car, explain the intricacies of the three pedals under the steering column (forward gears, brake pedal, and reverse gear), and set the spark and gas levers about where they ought to be.

And the Tants, father and son, were off!

Everything went fine for a while. Coming to Little Rock, however, brought forth some complications. At an intersection Tant nervously jammed his foot down on the forward gear instead of the brake pedal. The car went into low gear, and slowly but inexorably moved out into the intersection, and banged into the left rear fender of a car in the crossing. But it did not kill the engine, and since Tant still had his foot pressed hard against the low gear pedal, the car continued to move forward for fifty or a hundred feet, until the pedal was suddenly released. This threw the car into high gear, and killed the engine. Tant told Yater to "get out and pull that fender up from the wheel." (The car had no bumpers.)

Yater did so, and then climbed back into the front seat. But by now Tant was a bit flustered, and had forgotten how to start the car.

"What did that man say you stepped on down here to start this thing?" he asked.

His son pointed to the starter button, which on that model was on the floor about where the driver's heel would ordinarily rest.

Tant pushed hard on the starter button; the car began to jump and sputter as the battery turned the engine over (it was still in high gear, as Tant had failed to pull up the lever to put it in neutral), rolled about ten feet down a slight incline, and suddenly came to life as the engine fired and began to run. It jerked and bounced for a few yards until the proper speed had been attained, then ran smoothly.

The accident, minor though it was, had served to shake Tant's confidence a bit, and make him a bit more cautious about his driving. He did not drive quite so fast, although he still had not learned to slow down for corners. Between Little Rock and Pine Bluff, Tant saw a log wagon about a mile down the road coming toward him. Very intent on avoiding a collision, he kept his eyes fastened steadily on the approaching wagon — and quite easily and gently pulled the Ford off the road and into a ditch, never taking his eyes off the log wagon.

When the Ford rolled into the ditch, it lazily turned over

on its side. Tant and Yater, unharmed, climbed out and
began to survey the damage. There was little hurt done
to the car; but they found themselves unable to turn it
up on its wheels again. After about five minutes, however,
the driver of the log wagon came along, put a chain on
the back axle, and dragged the car out of the ditch and
back on to the road. Tant thanked the man, tried to pay
him but without success, and prepared to resume the journey.

"Let me drive a while," said Yater. He was sixteen
years old, had never driven a car at all, but was confident
he could do no worse than his father.

"I'll drive the rest of today," said Tant, "and you can
drive tomorrow."

The next day Yater rather fearfully took control, managing to drive several miles without mishap. Finally coming to the Mississippi River at Luna Landing, Yater drove
the car down on to the ferry boat, hugely enjoyed crossing
the great river, and with mounting confidence drove off
the ferry and up the levee on the Mississippi side of the
river.

Coming down off the levee, Yater saw that the road
forked. Not knowing which branch of the road to take
he picked one, then saw a huge mudhole in it, and tried
swiftly to swerve the car into the other lane. But too
late. Inexperienced in handling a car, he jerked the wheel
too sharply, and the Ford, rather precariously perched on
the slanting side of the levee already, slowly began to
turn over on its side — the opposite side from that on
which it had turned the day before when Tant was driving.

Neither Tant nor Yater was hurt; both climbed out, and
began to try to get the car upright. Some men in the cars
behind them stopped, righted the car, and told them which
road to take. Yater drove on to the new home, a few
miles east of Greenville. Driving into the yard, he was

too upset over the wreck to remember how to negotiate the foot pedals so as to stop the car — so pushed the gas lever up as far as he could get it, and tried to push all three pedals at the same time. The car was barely moving when it bumped head on into a tree and killed the engine. Damage to the car was negligible.

That night as the Tant family were gathered around a roaring fireplace in their new home the group was strangely quiet after the first burst of conversation died down. Not a word had been said about any of the car mishaps.

Finally, Tant turned to Yater and said, "Son, why don't you tell the family about how I turned the car over?"

"Well," replied Yater, "I hadn't planned to say anything about that. I thought you'd tell them if you wanted them to know."

"Oh, no," Tant roared, as his whole body shook with laughter, "you hadn't planned to say anything at all to them about it — not one single word! Why, you were so anxious to get home and tell them about it you could hardly wait - - - - until I let you drive and you turned the car over, too! That was the time you decided not to say anything about my wreck, wasn't it?"

Yater looked at his father with growing wonder. Was it possible that his father had let him drive the car actually anticipating that he would have some mishap, and so be in no position to tell off on his father's driving?

It was possible!

CHAPTER XXIII

"AN ORPHAN HOME TO MY LIKING"

Tant remained in Mississippi two years, one year at Greenville, and one year at West Point. His old-time Texas friend, P. J. Taylor, came with his wife and son, Paul, to Greenville in the summer of 1925 for a two weeks meeting. He preached in a tent in Leland, the little town eight miles east of Greenville where the Tant family worshipped. When school started in September, Yater, then sixteen years old, went to Texas to stay with his oldest sister and finish high school there. It was hoped that the Texas climate would help him to overcome a persistent cough which had lingered for many months. Nannie correctly surmised that she was bidding "farewell" to her son insofar as his ever living at home again was concerned. She grieved over it; but there seemed nothing else to do.

The practice of calling sectarian preachers "brother" was particularly distasteful to Tant. He wrote:

"I notice in the Gospel Advocate that Brother A. McGary is writing what he thinks of a gospel preacher in Tennessee who calls sectarian preachers "brother", and calls on them to lead prayer. McGary thinks such is hypocrisy, and that preachers who do such, not believing these sectarian preachers are Christians, are hypocrites. I know of more than twenty 'big' preachers in Tennessee that people tell me are guilty of the same.

"For instance, Billy Sunday is not my brother in Adam, for I have come out of Adam. He is not my brother in Christ, for he has not come into Christ. There were religious churches when Christ was here. Sadducees and Pharisees were more in accord with the word of God than any of the sects of our time, yet Christ never did talk about his Sadducee brethren or his Pharisee brethren, like many of my brethren talk about their Methodist and Baptist brethren.

"In the long ago, when I was in debate with J. N. Hall, he urged me to call him 'Brother'. But his god was not my God, even he being judge. Therefore, I could not compromise the word of God in calling him 'brother'. (Gospel Advocate, February 5, 1925.)

Tant's meetings and debates continued to come in rapid succession. From Bay, Arkansas, in the summer of 1926, he wrote:

"The meeting is being largely attended. I go from here to Illinois for a debate, then back to Tennessee for four meetings and one debate, then back to the farm. I regret that financial failures have forced me out of the preaching field; but if Paul of old could afford to quit preaching and make tents for a support, I suppose I should not complain when I have to quit the pulpit and go back to the plow." (Gospel Advocate, July 8, 1926.)

The Illinois debate took place on schedule late in June. J. W. Moore was the Baptist who opposed him. Brother C. L. Overturf moderated for Tant and reported the discussion to the papers.

On August 13 Tant sent in the report of another meeting:

"I have just closed a fine meeting at Mount Moriah, eight miles south of Camden. We have a good church house there, but all the members had quit the Lord and gone to working for the devil. They had quit the worship of God. Fourteen came back and confessed their wrongs, one was baptized, and seven were withdrawn from. They paid me eighty cents a day for the meeting above actual cost to me in going." (Gospel Advocate, August 19, 1926.)

This little country church invited Tant to return and help them in a meeting the next year. He told them he would not do so unless they were willing to support him. They said they felt like they could not pay what they would like to, as they were "just a bunch of poor farmers." Tant then made them a proposition:

"I will come back next year on this condition: there are twenty-five or thirty families of you farmers here. If each family will set aside one baby pig out of the next litter of pigs born on your farm, and will give that pig the slop from your kitchen until I come back next year, I'll come in a truck and take those thirty pigs back home with me, and that will be all the pay I'll accept for the meeting."

There was a fast bit of calculation with a stubby pencil and a piece of paper by some of the brethren, then one of them said:

"Brother Tant, thirty full grown hogs, at market price, would be five times as much as this church has ever paid for a gospel meeting."

"Before God, brethren," Tant replied, "if you aren't willing even to give the slop off your kitchen tables to support the gospel of Christ, then you can keep your slop and go to hell with it, and I'll go back home to Tennessee."

Although many meetings were thus poorly supported, not all of them were of this kind. Meetings at Lawrence Avenue Church and the Joe Johnston Church in Nashville, Tennessee, in the spring of 1927 were well supported. The Lawrence Avenue meeting was held in early spring (April), but in spite of this the weather was unseasonably warm. One day Tant took off his coat while preaching and hung it on the back of a chair in the pulpit. He had on a pair of suspenders that had seen better days. Two or three of the ladies in the church thought it would be a nice gesture to buy him a pair of suspenders. This they did. One of them made the presentation to him, saying, "Brother Tant, some of us noticed that the suspenders you were wearing yesterday were pretty old and frayed, so we decided we would like to give you a new pair. Here they are."

"Thank you, sisters," said Tant as he took the proffered package. "But really these suspenders I'm wearing are plenty good enough for me. I've only had them three or four years. But I do appreciate your gift."

"Well," replied the lady with a mischievous twinkle in her eye, "some of the folks were getting pretty worried, afraid those might break and you'd lose your trousers right in the middle of the sermon; and that would break up the meeting. We did not want that to happen."

"Now, you don't need to worry about that at all, sisters," Tant came back. "If I should lose my pants during a sermon, this house would not hold the people that would be here the next night!"

The summer was a hot one, and when Tant came back to Joe Johnston Church for a meeting in June, the whole city was sweltering. Once again, and nearly every day, he removed his coat when he started to preach. This was entirely too informal and "country" to suit one of the good sisters of Joe Johnston church; so after three or four days, she told Tant she felt it was somewhat beneath the dignity of a gospel preacher to remove his coat in the pulpit and preach in his shirt sleeves.

Tant very carefully looked at the woman, beginning at her feet and letting his eyes slowly and deliberately travel from sheer-hosed legs, to sleeveless, extremely low-cut dress, made of the frothiest kind of material then he intoned with a slow nasal twang:

"Why, sister, I could pull off my pants right now and still have on more than you are wearing!"

Although Tant for several years had been sounding the alarm against "our Bible colleges", he still felt there was a rightful place for the existence of schools in which the Bible could be taught. His complaint was against these schools

as "church schools," soliciting and accepting money from
the churches, and against the inordinate emphasis so many
of the brethren were putting on the "degree" craze among
the churches.

"I am in a great meeting near Union City, Tennessee.
Brethren John R. Williams, W. R. Hassell, and Cole-
man Overby, noted preachers, are all attending to learn
wisdom from me.

"I learn from John R. Williams that we have only
about six preachers who are big enough to hold meetings at certain places. I also learn from the Gospel
Advocate that we are soon to get another preacher
from the 'digressives', who holds two degrees, who is
now waiting for a call from some big church. Also,
news comes to me from Cordell, Oklahoma, that in a
meeting there an able college preacher stated that
within five years no gospel preacher would be admitted into a Christian pulpit if he did not hold a degree. Again, a letter comes to me from a sweet Christian girl in Washington, D. C. She will contribute five
hundred dollars to me to go to any Bible college long
enough to get a degree. Brother Hassell offers to support John R. Williams if he will go and get a degree.
And while I think John R. Williams and I have held
more mission meetings and built up more Bible
churches than any twenty college preachers I can
name, yet we must meet conditions. If the time has
now come that a man cannot preach the gospel of
Christ acceptably without a degree, just as soon as
Williams and I can arrange our business, the brethren
may find us both in some Bible college getting a Christian education and hunting for a degree. All churches
who can help us will please send their contributions to
John R. Williams." (Gospel Advocate, September 30,
1926.)

But only a few months later we find him writing on the
other side of the picture:

"I spent one week at the closing exercises of the
Freed-Hardeman College. For nineteen years this

school has been in operation, yet we have had the largest attendance at the closing exercises that has ever been known. Our visitors were all the way from St. Petersburg, Florida, to Detroit, Michigan.

"Seventeen boys and girls graduated from the college and quite a number from the high school. I learned that peace and harmony prevailed among the teachers and students throughout the year without a jar or discord, and that there had not been any criticism of the deportment of any boy or girl in the town this year.

"Brother Hardeman, his wife and daughter, associated with other teachers, are doing one of the greatest works that can be done in the church of Christ in educating boys and girls. There have been twenty-four young men in attendance studying for the ministry.

"They have the best equipped buildings in the brotherhood. They have a fine dormitory that will accommodate eighty girls, under as fine management as can be found. They will need about fifty more students to make it self-supporting.

"There were more than one hundred visitors one day, who made talks and expressed their unbounded confidence in N. B. Hardeman, and renewed their zeal and determination to stand behind the school. On account of its location and safe environment, I think it one of the grandest schools in the brotherhood to which to send boys and girls to be educated under proper protection.

"Every student, preacher, and visitor who was there to see the work of the school is pledging himself to work more earnestly to make up a number of students for next year. The Freed-Hardeman College has met the difficulties, has fought the battles of adversity, but is now on top of the hill, with the brightest future before it that has ever been. Its success is bound to come, and we hope, trust, and pray that God's blessings will attend the school at Henderson, Tennessee." (Gospel Advocate, June 2, 1927.)

Meetings and debates continued at a fast pace:

"On Tuesday, November 15, I am to meet A. J.

Sloan, Missionary Baptist, in a four-days' debate at Union Hill Baptist Church, four miles from Gallatin, Tennessee.

"On Tuesday, November 29, I am to meet C. B. Massey, Missionary Baptist, at Mount Pisgah Baptist Church, near Yuma, Tennessee.

"On Monday, December 12, I am to meet J. B. Hardy, Primitive Baptist, at Whitehurst, two miles from Denver, Tennessee, in a five-days' debate.

"I have calls for three other debates this year, but time not dated." (Gospel Advocate, September 15, 1927.)

II

As the year 1927 came to a close, Tant looked back over the past twelve months with some satisfaction and some regret:

"I have just closed out my year's work with twelve protracted meetings, four debates, and preaching done at eight other points, most of which was done at my own charges, and five months spent working on the farm and helping to support my family.

"I find that there are three stages in all religious movements: The first is the fighting stage, when people are few and humble, and lean on God for support. At that stage they all fight and try to overthrow the teachings of men, as the Jews did as recorded in Deut. 7.

"The second stage is the stage of greatness; we become strong and respected and want fine houses and big schools like the sects around us. The Jews reached that stage when they rejected God and wanted a king, to be like other people.

"The third stage is the age of compromise, when we don't want the differences between the church of Christ and the denominations debated, for fear we will hurt somebody's feelings. I fear the church of Christ is in the third stage today, and will be followed by spiritual death if some change does not come." (Gospel Advocate, January 5, 1928.)

Early in 1928 Tant moved back to West Tennessee.

"In the long ago West Tennessee was our home, but changes came and we went to far-away New Mexico, and for many years have been wandering. But we are now moving to a forty-acre farm north of Memphis. Lucy, Tennessee, will be our post office. I am fed up on big farms and negro plantations, and hope on this little farm in a few years to be able to pay all back debts, continue to preach the word as occasion demands, and finally come down to the grave able to meet Paul's requirements to 'owe no man anything but to love him'.

"Memphis and West Tennessee hold many sacred memories to me. My oldest daughter and her husband sleep side by side in the Memphis cemetery. When I left there in the long ago, John R. Williams, Tom Smith, G. Dallas Smith, Brother Parrish, and old Brother Haskins, were all on the firing line as grand gospel preachers; but they have reached the end, and have exchanged their cross for a crown. Also I remember Brother Barnett, A. O. Colley, Jasper Dunn, and Gus Dunn, faithful West Tennessee preachers. All are now preaching the uncompromising gospel in Texas.

"I am glad to note that N. B. Hardeman is still doing business in the same old stand. Hardeman is somewhat older, much stronger, and a far abler gospel preacher than he was when I left Tennessee. While the Freed-Hardeman College was never started as a preacher incubator, yet I know of no school that has taught more Bible and turned out a grander set of young gospel preachers than Freed-Hardeman. While the school has had some ups and downs, I rejoice to know that it is fast gaining ground as an educational institution." (Gospel Advocate, January 29, 1928.)

Tant's writing so vigorously in criticism of "our Bible colleges" and then almost in the same breath commending them, as in the above statements, was most puzzling to many of his brethren. How, they asked, could he complain about "degree" preachers, write so sharply of "our Christian colleges" as preacher incubators, and "our Bible chairs" as departures from the simplicity of Christ, and at the same time help young people financially to attend the schools, and pledge himself to use his influence to help promote such schools as Freed-Hardeman College?

The answer is easy to arrive at; apparently the difficulty lay in Tant's strong manner of expressing himself. He was not opposed to "our Christian colleges", as such, but was violently opposed to their being "church" schools — that is, soliciting and receiving money from the churches, attempting to do the work of the churches, exerting undue influence on the churches, and being regarded by the membership generally as "our" (the church's) institutions. If his articles are read in that light, there is no inconsistency at all in them. He loved the schools so long as they maintained their status as independent, secular, educational institutions, owned and operated by brethren in Christ; he despised them wherever he saw any hint at all that they were encroaching on the work of the church, or were being regarded either by their own forces or by brethren generally as having a "church relationship."

III

This same thing is apparent in Tant's connection with the orphan homes. He was a strong supporter of such work, and was a frequent visitor at the various orphanages in operation. He wrote letters urging brethren to help support the Belle Haven Home at Luling, Texas, and in later years was much interested in Tennessee Orphan Home, Boles Orphan Home, and the Sunny Glen Orphan Home. He visited Columbia, Tennessee, in 1928, and wrote:

"I have just carried an orphan boy to the Tennessee Orphan Home at Columbia, and was invited by Brother

Ben Harding to preach for the First Church of Christ both morning and evening.

"I seldom find as nice a church house as we have at Columbia. I found a most excellent, loyal congregation, three hundred in Sunday School, and best of all, the church working together in peace and harmony and love. I have known Ben Harding from childhood, and I see in him the same unselfish disposition and love for the truth I knew in his father. Among all the preachers I ever knew, James A. Harding, the father of Ben, was the most untiring, unselfish, and devoted. I found Ben walking in his father's footsteps. I praise God for such men.

"I found the Tennessee Orphan Home, managed by John W. Fry, more to my idea than any other orphans' home I have ever known. It is not tacked on to the church, under elder management, as God knows nothing of church orphan homes or church schools. The home is used only as a clearing house to find homes and locations for orphan children. When my brethren come back to the Bible from where we have drifted to be like the sects, then every local congregation will be an orphans' home to care for three or four children. We will have a thousand orphans' homes in Tennessee, caring for three or four thousand children, instead of one Home caring for one hundred. When each church becomes a Bible college to teach young men and women the Bible, then we will have a thousand Bible colleges in Tennessee, where we now have two; and from four thousand to ten thousand boys and girls can be taught the Bible each year instead of four or five hundred as we now have at Nashville and Henderson. But I fear too many of my brethren have gone crazy over Bible colleges and too few are enough interested to arouse all the churches to Bible study to ever get out of our present channels back to the Bible." (Gospel Advocate, May 3, 1928.)

In August, 1928, the Board of Directors of Tennessee Orphan Home employed Tant "to travel and tell the churches of our work, solicit help, and ask their cooperation in the care of the orphans and the neglected, as the religion of the son of God teaches us to do. We commend him to this work, praying God's blessings upon him and begging all the churches to receive him as our messenger and help him in the work he is now out to do." (Gospel Advocate, August 30, 1928.)

Tant did tell of the needs of this institution wherever he went, and was able to interest many individuals in giving to it; also several churches, at his urgings, made contributions to the home. He felt that the criticisms that were made against the Home for placing orphan children in a few instances in denominational homes were most unjust. His concept of the Home was that it was a "clearing house" to be used only as a temporary shelter, an emergency arrangement, until unfortunate children could be placed in the care of people who would provide for them.

"Since I have been selected to travel for the Tennessee Orphan Home, I have heard some adverse criticisms on the management of the Home, because in rare instances they let people who are not members of the church of Christ take children from the Home . . . I do not believe an orphan home is any more scriptural than a Bible college. Both should be operated as independent institutions. But I do believe that every local congregation should be a 'Bible college' to teach the Bible to their young members, and that each local congregation should be an 'orphan home' to support and care for all the orphans they can. The management of the Tennessee Orphan home believes just as I do.

"As we are only using the Tennessee Orphan Home as a clearing house, to take up the homeless children and get them good homes where they will be clothed and fed and educated, are we to be condemned for getting them homes elsewhere, if our brethren will not open their homes to them? The argument that is sometimes made that the sects will make sectarians of them has another side. Joseph was sold into the hands of the heathens; Moses was reared in a heathen home.

Naaman's little Jewish maid did good in telling him how to be saved. Esther saved her people in being the wife of a heathen king. Samuel, at the age of eight years, was put under Eli, whose sons were profligate. If all these people came out good, who knows but what these children from the Tennessee Orphan Home may go into the families who are enemies of God and convert the whole family?" (Gospel Advocate, September 27, 1928.)

Some years after his death, Tant's position relative to the "orphan home" question became a matter of interest, and was discussed off and on for several years. His teaching concerning the "all-sufficiency" of the church, his undying hatred of the Missionary Society, and all such human organizations to do the work of the church, were well known to all. But, at the same time, he was employed by, and diligently worked for, a benevolent organization, Tennessee Orphan Home, which, in effect, was fulfilling in the realm of benevolence exactly the same place and work that the Missionary Society had in the realm of evangelism. It was an organization, outside of the churches and independent of them, through which the churches could work in discharge of their obligation to care for the needy.

How, and why, could Tant reject the Missionary Society and at the same time accept the benevolence organization?

To understand his thinking on this, it is needful to keep in mind his own emotional feeling for the poor, the distressed, the unfortunate of the earth. Perhaps growing out of his own poverty-stricken childhood, and perhaps as a part of his inherent nature, he had a compassion for the down-trodden that led him to work in every way he could, far beyond his financial ability, and often contrary to all reason, to relieve their distress. His giving away his great farm at Macon, and impoverishing his own family for the rest of his life, is but one instance, of hundreds that might be cited, to show his compassion for the needy. The sight of an orphan child, hungry, neglected, bereft of love and care was something that moved him to his very depths. So eager was he to see such a child receive a "home" that he was willing to see him go into a denominational home, where food, and love, and care would be his, rather than see him suffer without such. The institutions, such as the one he worked for, were simply "clearing houses", to expedite the placing of helpless children in homes that would care for them. Since there would always be needy children, there might always be a need for some such agency to place them; but no child should ever be kept in an institution a single minute longer than was necessary to find for him a home — a Christian home if possible, a denominational home if no Christians would take him.

G. C. Brewer, in commenting on Tant's teaching and practice, gave his explanation. He wrote:

> "The editor of the Gospel Guardian . . . quotes J. D. Tant as opposing the orphan homes as an unscriptural method of caring for orphans even at the time he was connected with the Tennessee Orphan home. Thus J. D. Tant was shown to condemn as unscriptural that which J. D. Tant was practicing.
> "This was not at all new to some of us oldsters. We know that J. D. Tant did that very thing on more than one point, but we would not, now that Brother Tant is dead, tell these things on him. They were overlooked when Tant was living on the ground that J.D. Tant was J. D. Tant!" (Gospel Advocate, December 20, 1951.)

Brewer thought there was an inconsistency between Tant's teaching and Tant's practice. In the light of later years, and as the true nature of the modern orphan homes has become more clearly defined, it seems clear that Brewer's criticism is to a degree justified. Tant's teaching was simple and positive; the implications of it as applied to the orphan home he probably never fully realized.

A more charitable view than Brewer's, and probably, all

things considered, the correct one, is set forth by James A. Allen, who was editor of the Gospel Advocate at the time Tant worked for Tennessee Orphan Home:

"Brother Tant favored orphan homes just like all the rest of us did when such a system was first sprung on us. We all had a deep and heart-felt sympathy for the orphans, and wanted to do anything in our power to help them.

"W. T. Boaz, who recently passed away, was the father of the present-day orphan home. The Fanning Orphan School, and possibly one or more such institutions, were not in this class, and did not raise the issue that is now tearing asunder the church of the Lord. . . .

"The only way to form an opinion of what a man would do, if he were living today, is by what he did when living. The powerful preaching of J. D. Tant in repudiating and warning against all institutions and organizations, other than the church, is an unerring indication that if he were with us today, instead of rebuking 'Tant's son, Yater', he would give him every encouragement, and rejoice to know that he had a son with the conviction and courage to stand up against the ambition and wealth of presumptuous men, who have already carried many of the churches into the beginning of an apostasy." (Gospel Guardian, January 30, 1958.)

CHAPTER XXIV

"MY IDEA OF A BIBLE COLLEGE"

"Of late years I have said the time will come that we will go so far from Bible Christianity we can well say, 'We had a prophet among us, but did not know it'." (Apostolic Review, December 7, 1939.)

These words in an "Open Letter" to Daniel Sommer only two months before Sommer's death show that in spite of his feeling that Sommer had gone to an extreme, Tant nevertheless believed there was an equal danger of extremism on the part of those promoting the colleges. The writings of the last fifteen years of his life reflect a growing concern as to the place and influence of the "Bible college" among Christian people. He continued to visit the schools as he had opportunity, made speeches in their chapel services, and wrote commendatory things of them. He approved of much of the work they were doing, but was increasingly critical of their "church connection," and apprehensive as to their future influence on the churches. There was a gradual lessening in the general demand for "degree preachers" among the congregations, and Tant welcomed this. He felt that perhaps his own writings had contributed somewhat to putting the brake on the swift downward course that so many were taking toward reducing the Lord's church to the status of a mere denomination. His fears were allayed somewhat, but never fully dissipated.

Late in 1931, after having moved from Memphis, Tennessee, to DeQueen, Arkansas, Tant wrote under the caption, "Shall We Expel C. R. Nichol?":

"For some time I have been thinking that C. R. Nichol has not been equalled in presenting gospel knockout

drops against all innovations since the days of A. Mc-
Gary. I had made up my mind to accept his exposition,
which hurt many of our good brethren who were connected with the ministerial associations in our cities.

"Now I notice that he comes out boldly and states in
the Firm Foundation of August 11 that our schools are
not church institutions. That it is unscriptural to
graft money from the church to teach mathematics,
grammar, history, and athletics in the school. If they
are not church institutions, then to whom do they belong? When Brother Jesse P. Sewell, who had been
president in Abilene for ten years, resigned, why did
he publish a letter to all the churches, telling them that
he took their school under certain conditions, and spent
his time and ten thousand dollars, and then returned
it to them?

"If the Bible College is not a church institution, why
did a Bible College send out agents to get church
elders to make a twenty-year pledge for the church to
give so much each year for twenty years to keep up our
colleges? If they are not church institutions, then
why were the churches of Christ called upon recently
to raise two hundred thousand dollars to keep our
school from going to the wall? Why did a certain
church raise two hundred dollars at once to save our
school? If our Bible Colleges are not church institutions, why was a brother selected at a salary of $4,-
000.00 a year and sent out to beg churches for a million dollars to endow our Bible College? . . .

"Not only has C. R. Nichol ruined himself before our
brethren in coming out with the Bible on these things,
but I notice Foy Wallace, whom I had given up as gone,
because he had gotten up on a higher plane of journal-
ism where discussion is not permitted, but I see that
he comes out in the Gospel Advocate of August 6th and
takes the same position that Nichol does.

"I saw this unscriptural thing fifteen years ago and
lost all interest in our so-called Bible Colleges, and am
glad that such men as Foy Wallace and C. R. Nichol
are coming to their right mind. But I fear they have
done like J. W. McGarvey. They have run on the
wrong road so long until the brethren they have

worked with will now refuse to hear their voice, and will put them out of their company, and will continue to beg the churches for large sums of money to build up great colleges like the sister churches around us.

"Don't forget, brethren, we are drifting." (Firm Foundation, December 16, 1931.)

Tant's matured judgment as to how to solve the problem of the Bible College, with its great power either for good or for evil, was set forth in a series of articles under the caption: "My Idea Of Bible Colleges":

"For twenty years I have, at times, had my doubts as to the scripturalness and good that 'Bible Colleges' are doing the church of Christ. I have no condemnation for a religious education, and will rejoice when the Bible as a text-book will be taught in every school. I think I will live to see that day. I believe the Bible should be a part of the education of every young person. But have we not put the Bible education beyond the reach of ninety percent of our children by lugging in the entire system of secular education and forcing the child to pay for all of this in order to get a Bible education? In other words, we have commercialized the gospel, and hid behind it to give our boys and girls a secular education when we are taxed to pay for such, and it is given free by all the states. What have we done in order to teach the Bible? We have educated and forced the church to spend more than $2,000,-000.00 in school property in order to teach one thing — the Bible. Not only is this true, but there is Lockney, Thorp's Spring, Sabinal, Odessa, Harper, Bowling Green, and Berry, Alabama, where several thousand dollars worth of property now stands idle which was built by the sacrifices of the brethren. All because those buildings and locations do not fit into the modern idea of worldly education. . . .

"If our claim in having the Bible Colleges is to correct infidelity, and we put three hundred boys and girls from Christian families together, ninety-five percent of them being Christians, how can they fight infidelity when none of the world is there to come in contact with them?

"Then I suggest:

"Instead of raising five hundred thousand dollars to build fine school houses to teach secular subjects, with the Bible classes added, let us take this five hundred thousand dollars as a down payment and build five hundred school rooms, a thousand dollars each, in reach of every state school in the nation. This will give us five hundred Bible colleges instead of one. Let the state teach all the secular branches, where our boys and girls can go and get their secular education in buildings provided by the state with all modern equipment and under state supported teachers. We who are Christians can then employ some strong men to go to each place and teach nothing but the Bible, having their classes come each day to the class-room we have provided, and cut out this foolishness about state "standardization." In doing this we can throw the same safeguards around our boys and girls that they get at the Bible Colleges. Furthermore, this will instill in our boys and girls a working spirit, and they can get one hundred or two hundred of their classmates at each state school to fall in with them to study the Bible — young people who do not have the opportunity to study the Bible under present conditions. Thus, coming in contact each day with infidelity as taught in secular schools, our Christian boys and girls will have material to work on to weed it out. Ninety percent of my brethren who are now unwilling to pay teachers to teach secular subjects in our Bible schools (knowing such subjects are taught free of charge in the state schools) will gladly support these Bible teachers to teach nothing but the Bible. These teachers with their association with the State teachers will have far more influence over them than they would if sidetracked off in some Bible College five hundred miles away. Our young people, coming in contact daily with thousands of boys and girls whom they would never know if they were segregated in a Bible College, will, in a few years, have the 'Bible college problem' solved. And it will be at a cost of ninety percent less than we pay for our Bible Colleges as now operated, and will reach ninety percent more people with the Bible than are being taught now.

"Brethren, what do you think of this suggestion?" (Firm Foundation, June 23, 1931.)

Response was not long in coming. Batsell Baxter, then president of Abilene Christian College, took exception to the article, and replied to it in the same journal, pointing out certain weaknesses in it. To this Tant replied:

"Brother Baxter criticizes my idea of Bible schools. He claims such would be a failure because Brother Robertson's Bible Chair at Austin failed. His logic: The Bible Colleges at Denton and Lockney both failed: therefore, the Bible colleges at both Abilene and Nashville will fail. Second: Brother Baxter should remember that Brother Roberson's 'Chair' failed because it was a farce from the beginning on account of his seeking standardization of Bible teaching in order to get state accreditation. The State furnished him the things that he must teach about the Bible, and prescribed also what he must not teach. Any student can get this kind of teaching from the Baptists and Methodists. Third: Brother Baxter claims that Jesus 'segregated' his apostles for three years to teach them, and sent them out; therefore, my idea of Bible Colleges is against the Son of God. I deny that Jesus ever grafted his people for five hundred thousand dollars to teach his disciples grammar, arithmetic, science, and the foolishness that many of our Bible Colleges are teaching today. On the other hand, Jesus went everywhere doing good, and taught his disciples daily in the word of God." (Firm Foundation, August 11, 1931.)

Early in January, 1933, Daniel Sommer of Indianapolis, Indiana, made a lengthy tour throughout the south, visiting Louisville, Kentucky, spending ten days in Nashville, Tennessee, where he made about a dozen speeches, and spending some time also at Henderson, Memphis, and Austin, Texas. He visited both David Lipscomb College and

J. D. TANT

(At age seventy-five)

Freed-Hardeman College, having lengthy discussions with many brethren connected with these schools and with leading preachers whom he met on the trip. In Austin he stayed in the home of G. H. P. Showalter, and while there wrote an article setting forth some of his impressions of the trip. Inasmuch as Sommer had been the leading opponent of the Christian Colleges, his views after his visit were of keen interest to brethren generally. Sommer wrote:

"1. Neither David Lipscomb College, near Nashville, nor Freed-Hardeman College in Henderson was listed as church property to avoid taxation, for no schools in Tennessee, nor many other states, are taxed. Hence, reflections in the Review on that subject have been erroneous, and should not have been made.

"2. Those schools were listed as 'church property' because established and supported chiefly, if not wholly, by members of churches of Christ. But since attention has been called to the fact that the church, as such, is not authorized to go into any secular business, the disposition now is to regard the colleges as an extension of the home as an educational institution. As an evidence on this subject, I mention that the Central Church of Christ in Nashville, for a time, had a cafeteria as a part of its equipment. But some one said the church had no right to enter into that domain of business. As a result, the cafeteria was turned over to an individual, and is no longer any part of the work of that church. On the same principle the schools at Nashville and Henderson are now being considered. . . .

"4. The college at Morrillton, Arkansas, and at Abilene, Texas, I am informed are both more pretentious than the Nashville and Henderson schools. They both have a four year course and bestow diplomas and degrees. But even such schools, if managed as individual enterprises, or as an extension of the homes as educational institutions in caring for children (either their own or other) may be considered in the light of Romans 14th chapter. I have no right to say how far in education another man may go, nor another home may go, while I am not thereby judged. But if I am denounced as not in favor of education; or am denounced as 'a slacker in the Lord's army' or a 'traitor to the Lord's cause', or am threatened with 'perdition' if I do not give to establish and support such an institution, then I appeal to Romans 14th chapter for protection.

"5. But some one may be disposed to inquire about churches as such establishing or supporting such schools by their treasury. This has already been answered by the remarks thus far offered. Yet additional remarks are in order because such treasury from a legal view-point would be regarded as a joint-stock company-fund._ As a result every one that has even one cent in that fund should be consulted in regard to its use. If some one questions this and says it is 'the Lord's money', then the question arises, What does the Lord say should be done with it? The answer is found in Acts 11:29-30; I Cor. 16:1, 2; Gal. 6:10; Phil. 4:15.

"6. In conclusion for this time I state that the question of the church treasury is connected with the question of church government. That question was closely contested years ago in a formidable lawsuit. Expert witnesses testified, and the court decided, that the government of the churches of Christ is not authorized to be executed by the elders only nor by the churches only, but by the elders and the churches as such conjointly. That decision was endorsed by the Supreme Court of the State in which the lawsuit was introduced and urged. I think those courts were right."
(Firm Foundation, February 7, 1933.)

The interest stirred up by the Sommer visit to the South was widespread. His statement concerning the colleges was read with eager concern by all. James A. Allen, former editor of the Gospel Advocate, but at the time of Sommer's visit editing his own paper, Apostolic Times, wrote:

"Brother Sommer is not illiterate and unlearned, but is highly educated, a graduate, as above mentioned, of

Bethany College, over which A. Campbell was president until his death. He contends that running a college is a private enterprise, just like running a printing office or a religious paper, and that we have as much Bible authority to ask churches to finance a printing office as we have to ask them to finance a college. In other words, the church is not in the college business any more than it is in the restaurant business; but the business of the church is to concentrate all its resources to preaching the gospel and taking care of the afflicted and the poor.

"Brother Sommer has no objection to a school as an adjunct and auxiliary to the family, and says that fathers and mothers have the right to send their children to any school they may choose. He has no objection to fathers and mothers, as individuals, donating to the support of schools. But the point is, a church school, or a school that looks to the church for support, upsurps the work of the church, and not only robs the church of its honor and glory, but drains it of its resources. . . .

"I could name many of the leading brethren of the South and safely say that their views of Bible colleges and the views of Daniel Sommers are basically the same. F. D. Srygley, the old-time, able and brilliant first-page editor of the Gospel Advocate, was as much opposed to Bible colleges as is Daniel Sommer, when run as anything else than individual and private enterprises. The only difference was, Brother Sommer had a paper of his own and could say what he pleased, while Brother Srygley was not allowed to say anything the management disapproved.

"Knowing that some of the ablest brethren in the South, while not allowed to speak out through the papers, are not satisfied that human organizations to take care of widows and orphans are any more Scriptural than missionary organizations, I asked Brother Sommer what he thought about orphan homes, etc. He replied that he had not thought much about them, as they had no such things in the North, because all such work was amply and well done through the local congregations. It cannot be denied that this is the

way in which the Holy Spirit guided the apostles in doing such work, and this fact alone explains the conspicuous absence of such organizations from the Bible."
(Apostolic Times, February 1933, as quoted in Firm
Foundation, March 7, 1933, with note of editorial approval by T. H. Etheridge.)

Tant attended the Abilene Christian College lectureship early in 1933, and there met Daniel Sommer. He reports his reaction to the lectureship and to his visit with
Sommer:

". . . I spent three days attending the lectureship at
Abilene Christian College. After learning of our four
congregations in Abilene, and seeing the large school
buildings there; I can hardly realize that thirty years
ago J. D. Tant was called to Abilene by Price Billingsley and lectured one week in a small frame building to
about fifty members, and persuaded old Brother Childress to give his home and thirteen acres of land to
build a Bible college, then known as Childress Insti-
tute. No one then present could imagine what changes
thirty years would bring . . .

"At the lectureship I met Brother Daniel Sommer,
perhaps the oldest preacher in the church. He has always fought Bible colleges as church institutions'. I
think ninety percent of the church of Christ hold his
position if he were understood. I think many of our
differences are only imaginary, and will vanish once
we understand each other. Brother Sommer delivered
a fine lecture, was greatly appreciated, and I am glad
he was treated so kindly in the South. Hope he will
come back again. I am sure many of his supporters
do not know he was educated at Bethany College, started by A. Campbell, the first Bible college among us,
and the first to drift. Others have followed. Which
makes me feel like those today who have gone crazy
over degrees, and standardized affiliation to turn out
big preachers only, may yet forget God. But I was
educated under Peter and Paul who did not give degrees. I am often condemned for speaking out on

these things. I fear many of Brother Sommer's readers will drop his paper when they learn he has a Bible college education.

"After all, I had a fine time; but I feel like Uriah of old. Should preachers spend money to have a good time when thousands are going to hell for want of the gospel? The thousands of dollars that was spent by brethren going there would have supported some gospel preacher in the mission field for a whole year; and one hundred converts in heaven would mean more to me than a good time here." (Firm Foundation, March 21, 1933.)

This was the first, and only time, in his life that Tant ever attended the Abilene lectures. On the day he was ready to leave, he was standing on the steps of Sewell Auditorium, taking his leave of several of the brethren. Turning suddenly to J. P. Crenshaw, and thrusting forward his hand for a final handshake, Tant said,

"Well, Brother Joe, I am about to do something this day the devil himself has never done, and wouldn't do."

Crenshaw stood for a moment in speechless astonishment. Then with great curiosity asked,

"What on earth is that, Brother Tant?"

"I'm leaving the city of Abilene. Goodbye." And with that Tant picked up his suitcase and walked down the steps and toward the street.

II

From Springdale, Arkansas, in mid-summer of 1933, Tant sent in the following report of his work:

"I am at Springdale, Arkansas, in my seventh day of an eight days debate with C. A. Smith, Baptist.

"My physical health along all lines is as good as it was thirty years ago, and my mental powers have made some progress since that time. I mean to continue in the debating field, meeting any man the enemy may put up, for the next eight years. I am booked for three

more debates this year.   Then I shall resign debater-
ship, and let one of my preacher boys take my place.
As to my preaching, I hope to continue fifteen years
longer.

"This is June 28th, and I am seventy-two years old
today.   I have been thinking of the more than 8,000
people I have baptized during the past fifty years.
Away over here in Arkansas, where I am preaching
the gospel to many Baptists (by way of debate) who
never heard it before, I am reminded of the old days in
Arkansas, and of how their customs stack up with present day practices.

"Those were the days when game hunting was good,
and people depended more on their guns for a living
than they did on their brains.   They could get by with
hunting and fishing, and very little work.   Often they
would meet and recount their hunting adventures.
Some one would tell of what a good marksman he was;
another would boast of the power of his gun to kill.
Another would tell of what good times he had on the
hunt, and another would tell of how many coons he
could kill.   He would brag that the coons seemed to
hunt him up and actually came up to the camp and
begged to be shot.

"Some listener, hearing such a yarn, would doubt
his veracity, and would offer to count coonskins with
him.   All of which reminds me of some of my brethren.
They keep bragging of their great capacity crowds, of
how their houses are continually filled, and of how the
other churches love to hear them preach.   They try to
raise themselves in their own and their listeners'
opinions by running down other more successful
preachers than themselves.   This has recently been
brought to my attention by several little incidents.

"A few days ago an old brother, after hearing me
preach three times in Houston, Texas, came to me and
said, 'Brother Tant, I am glad to have heard you
preach.   You are not the type of man that I had expected to meet.   It has been told on you by certain of
your preaching brethren that you are vulgar in the
pulpit.   They said that you are rough and abusive; un-

refined and uneducated; that you are so plain in your preaching that refined people could not listen to you. Since hearing you I have decided that such reports are preachers' lies, prompted by jealousy, and not by the love of God'.

"As a further illustration, I have recently had a letter from a good sister, saying, 'We are dead here and doing no good. Many of us would like to have you hold a meeting, but our elder says that you are too tough on the brethren, too hard on the other churches, and that we must have a man the denominations like to hear'.

"A letter from a Baptist preacher who wants to meet me in debate in a town where one of our leading Bible colleges is located says that he has talked to several of our younger preachers there, and they say, 'Brother Tant is too old to debate; and he doesn't have a college education'.

"Well, I'll admit that I have not the good English that N. B. Hardeman has. Neither can I measure up to G. C. Brewer's law of culture and refinement because I frequently go barefooted when I am asleep. I preach in my shirt-sleeves, and put my pencils in my outside coat pocket. And if my brethren don't like it, they can go on to the devil, and I'll stay here and preach the gospel to people who want to hear it. Neither have I the refined disposition of Brother Sam Pittman. I am just an old-fashioned, plain gospel preacher from the frontier . . . but I am now ready to count coonskins with any of our modern, college educated, women-pleasing pastors!

"I have this month rounded out fifty-two years of plain gospel preaching. I have baptized approximately 8,000 men and women. More than one hundred of the boys I have baptized in by-gone years are now out preaching the gospel. I wonder if God will reject all these souls I have been instrumental in leading to him merely because I am not refined'? Because I do not wear my coat all the time?

"Count my coonskins, brethren, before you get too hard on me.

"One of the ablest preachers we have in Arkansas

lost his located job, not because he was not preaching
the gospel, but because one of the influential sisters in
the church could not bear to listen to his old-fashioned
language.   She did not like his Arkansas grammar,
and thus could not invite her denominational friends to
hear him.   I doubt if the poor thing could tell whether
or not Jesus Christ was crucified at Calvary or shot
on Bunker's Hill . . .

"I have tried to do the best I could to serve God in
the backwoods and out of the way places where a college degree is not so important.   When brethren condemn me on account of my rough manners and plain
speech, I shall not be too upset about it, but shall
speak kindly of them and pray for them.   And after
life's battle have been fought and we all come before
God to be judged, I may not be able to produce much
refinement and education, but I shall say, 'Lord, I have
done the best I could among the common people'.

"I may go to hell on account of some meanness that
I have done, but even so I shall be happy to know that
some of the souls I have helped save are in heaven because of my work.   And when I meet some of my
brethren in hell who have consistently violated God's
law as found in Romans 14:13, we can at least have
some satisfaction down there in counting coonskins
and telling of the work we did while on earth.   Each
one of us should strive to fill his own corner, and not
throw rocks at his brother in another corner.

"Don't forget, brethren; we are drifting."   (Firm
Foundation, August 8, 1933.)

Brownsville, Texas, Christmas, 1936; the last time the children were all together with their parents. Standing, left to right: Zoreta, J.D. Jr., Mozelle, Austin, Maidia, Yater.

CHAPTER XXV

"I'LL RETIRE AT NINETY"

When David Lipscomb was in his seventies he wrote a friend, "As I grow older I find I have less and less interest in the world around me." That was an attitude that Tant never reached. When he was seventy-five he said to a group of friends who were visiting in his home:

"I intend to preach for fifteen more years. Then I'll retire at ninety and spend a few years here on the farm getting acquainted with Nannie before I leave this country. She says she'd sort of like to get to know something about me before she dies, because she is pretty sure she won't be seeing much of me in the place where she hopes to go."

This gay, almost debonair spirit never deserted him. Even at an age when most people turn their thoughts inward, and begin to lose interest in worldly affairs, Tant lived with an intensity and a zest each day that was contagious to those about him. People enjoyed having him in their homes in meetings, for he made himself completely at ease; and would tie paper shoes on the cat, tease the colored cook about her love affairs, and tell simply incredible tales to the children with grand impartiality. He seemed to enjoy his debating in the last years of life even more than he had in his early years, if possible. At the time of his death he had three debates scheduled, and was trying to negotiate more. There was a flavor of humor and good-natured banter in his daily conversation that kept his little home near Los Fresnos filled with company.

One day James W. Adams, preacher for the San Benito church, drove up in front of the house. From his rocking chair on the porch Tant recognized him, and hailed him:

"Get out, Adams; come in and tell me all you know. It won't take you more than a couple of minutes!"

In the late nineteen-thirties, Roy E. Cogdill held a meeting at San Benito. Tant drove over to hear him, and at the close of the service sought Cogdill out:

"Roy, I've come to take you home with me for dinner. Nannie will have it ready when we get there. I want to catch up on all the latest gossip."

"I'm sorry, Brother Tant," Cogdill replied, "but I can't go with you today. I am scheduled to go home with Clarence and Eunice Gist for dinner."

"Well, Eunice can take you some other time," responded Tant imperturbably, "You're going home with me today."

At this point Sister Gist broke in on the conversation to announce that her dinner was waiting, and that Cogdill must go home with her. Tant refused to yield, and only laughted at the vain protests that Cogdill's would-be hostess was offering. Ignoring her obvious displeasure, he got Cogdill into his car, and drove down to the drug store where Clarence Gist was at work. Parking the car in front of the store, he and Cogdill got out and went inside. Sister Gist had driven up right behind them, and followed them into the store, still fuming.

"Brother Tant," she said, "I almost hate you for taking my company away from me today!"

"Now, Eunice, I'm glad to hear you say that," came Tant's reply in a loud stage whisper, "And especially in front of Clarence. You know, I sort of got the feeling that Clarence might be getting to the point he was thinking you were becoming entirely too fond of me!"

Cogdill ate dinner with the Tants, and spent the afternoon there.

One memorable event of those final years in the Rio Grande Valley was the great storm of September 3, 1933.

Tant had been at Los Fresnos only a short time when the
event occurred. Nannie writes the story:

"The day had been warm and cloudy. Many shifting
clouds and winds were in the skies. About 4:00 P.M.
Brother E. D. Kraner, superintendent of the local
school, came to our house and suggested that we go
with him to the schoolhouse, which was the strongest
building in town. It was of brick construction, and was
one story high, spread out over the ground. Many people were leaving the Valley and were going upstate to
escape the storm. But my husband said, No, we would
not leave the house. If the wind blew it away, he would
be there to pick up the pieces. Kraner insisted, and so
did I. Finally, Husband said for me to go along with
Kraner, and if he saw the storm getting too bad, he
could come on over and join us. The school house was
about three hundred yards from our home. I wanted
to go, but did not want to leave my husband. He insisted, and I finally reluctantly yielded. By 6:00 o'clock the
wind was furious. By 7:00 o'clock darkness as black as
midnight covered the earth. I could see the light in
the window of our house, and knew Husband was still
in there alive. But I was frightened and worried.
Why did he not come?

"Presently by a flash of lightning I saw the house
next to ours swept from its foundations. Very quickly another house was unroofed, and the roof went sail-
ing through the air, end over end. But the light was
still on in our window, and I tried to calm my uneasy
fears. But suddenly the light went out. My heart almost failed me. Was he, too, blown away? I suppose
that if I had not been so busy doing all I could to save
the life of Sister Kraner's unborn baby, I might have
gone beside myself with anxiety. People who know
those Gulf storms know that they are not like our West
Texas tornadoes, soon ended; they last for hours. This
one blew with a velocity at times of 110 miles per hour
for twelve straight hours. About dawn, as the winds
began to subside a bit, we saw dimly in the lightning
flashes a figure coming toward the school. Some one
opened the door and admitted my husband. He said he

had stayed in the house till the chimney fell in and the
front porch blew away; then he had taken his big cat
(he was always extremely fond of cats), crawled into
the back seat of the car which was parked in front of
the house between two huge palm trees, and gone to
sleep. He seemed proud of his feat, but I was a little
bit aggravated at him for staying out there all night
and worrying us to death.

"At daybreak we waded home through water sometimes three or four feet deep. I think it was about
twenty persons we housed for several days till we
could help them find places to stay. Their homes had
all been either destroyed or too seriously damaged to
live in without extensive repairs. I knew our children,
scattered from the Gulf of Mexico to the Great Lakes,
would be concerned about us, so I tried to get messages
to them. Could not do so for several days, as all the
wires were down. I wrote letters by the first mail.
Zoreta and Austin were the nearest to us — only 500
miles away. They came to the Valley the next day,
not knowing whether they would find us living or dead.
But this, like other calamities, soon passed away. Husband built back the porch, and hired a man to rebuild
the chimney, and life moved on as before." (Reminiscences.)

Tant wrote a brief article to the Firm Foundation saying
he had received a great number of letters inquiring as to
whether or not he or his wife had been killed or injured in
the storm, and he took this means of letting all who were
interested know that they had come through in fine shape,
and thanking them for their concern. But he described the
Valley as being a scene of appalling desolation and ruin.

II

Tant's sermons during his latter years, and all his life
for that matter, were never long. At an age when sermons of one or even two hours duration were not uncommon,
he rarely spoke more than thirty-five minutes. His words

came rapidly and with force. His sermons invariably had elements of wit and humor, and sometimes were so hilarious as to bring an audience into laughter they could hardly control. But Tant himself never let his droll stories or observations on human nature get out of hand as far as he personally was concerned. He was better able to control his humor than he was his more somber emotions. Often in illustrating some point of a sermon, or telling of the love of Christ and his sufferings for us, he would be swept by an intensity of emotion that would almost choke his voice, and leave him struggling for words. This feeling would quickly pass, but it would always be reflected in the audience, and would be shared by them. He was not a "crying" preacher, but he could bring an audience to a point of great tension as he so obviously felt the emotional impact himself of that which he was speaking. Perhaps one reason for the explosive hilarity with which audiences so often greeted his witticisms was that they afforded a relief from the great tensions that had been developed in the sermon.

Tant returned again and again to his teaching on sectarian baptism:

"The Son of God said, 'Except ye become converted, yet shall in no wise enter into the kingdom of heaven'.

"Is denominational conversion scriptural? Brother C. E. W. Dorris, one of the elders in the Central Church of Christ in Nashville, Tennessee, tells of a Baptist, conversion: A still small voice told a man to crawl into a hollow log. He did, but saw nothing. But the same still small voice told him to crawl farther back. He did so, and met Jesus far back in the hollow log, who told him he was saved. That experience was voted on, and the man was baptized into the Baptist Church.

"Years ago, southeast of Austin, Texas, a poor man was praying under a tree one evening. He heard a peculiar sound, got up shouting, and related his experience that night at church. He was voted on by the Baptists, and baptized the next day. For three

days he continued to go to church, rejoicing each day
that God had saved him and had spoken peace to his
soul. The fourth day he went back to the same tree to
pray, and heard the same sound. By examining he
found that the noise he had heard was June bugs
coming in to roost. He claimed that if he had not
gone back there the second time, he would have gone
through life on June bug religion.

"Another man near Dripping Springs, Texas, saw a
light in his corn crib one night, related his experience,
was voted into the Baptist Church and baptized. A
year later he was in the same crib saw the same light.
By examining he found it was the moon shining
through a knot hole. He claimed that if he had not
gone to the crib the second time, he would have gone
through life on a knot-hole moon-shine religion.

"These are fair samples of Baptist conversion. Yet
I notice in our papers many brethren preach so little
gospel that people come up on their conversion and say
they are satisfied with their baptism and are welcomed
into the church of Christ without scriptural baptism.

"In 1894 I became associated with the Gospel Advocate. As they had been accepting sect baptism all
along the line I had great hopes of showing them the
truth. Joe McPherson was the only one I found in
Nashville then holding tenaciously to the one baptism.
It was in a great measure through his influence that I
was called to hold thirteen meetings in Nashville and
three debates. In all I baptized two hundred and thir-
ty-four people, fifty of whom were good men and wom-
en who had come into the church of Christ satisfied
with their baptism, who, after learning the truth, demanded baptism by divine authority.

"During that time I was called upon to debate the
baptism question with Brother J. A. Harding in his
Bible School, which I did, and later he and I debated it
through the Advocate and the Firm Foundation.

"Baptists today are no more intelligent and do not
preach any more Bible than they did thirty years ago;
they relate the same experiences, tell the same yarns,
and get into the Baptist church now just like they did
then. Yet how my brethren can claim to preach the

gospel so as not to teach them the truth, and report so many additions coming from the Baptists and Methodists satisfied with their baptism, I can not understand. I noticed some time ago a Texas preacher seemed to be elated over a Methodist preacher asking him to preach in the Methodist church house. When I lived at San Marcos, Texas, the Methodist church there lost their $3,600.00 a year preacher. I offered to preach for them for $1,800.00 a year, but they informed me they did not want my preaching even if it was free of charge! I am sure such is true with all my preaching brethren who preach the gospel. But when brethren preach in such a manner that all the churches love to hear them, and call in their meetings to hear our preachers, and ask them to preach in their houses, I feel like my brethren are not preaching the gospel. The sects usually start two or three meetings to keep people from coming to my meeting instead of calling in their meetings to attend mine.

"Brethren, don't forget; we are drifting." (Firm Foundation, March 29, 1932.)

His many debates with the one-cup, no-literature, no-class brethren had given Tant a full understanding of their position, and the reasoning by which they sought to sustain it. He was responsible for converting scores of small congregations from "non-Sunday School" positions, and persuading them to start regular classes for Bible study. Late in the fall of 1934 he was called to Artesia, New Mexico, by the church there for a debate with a "non-Sunday School" brother. He writes:

"Forty and eight years I have been a debater in the church of Christ. Have debated with thirteen denominations, involving three hundred or more debates; and have met both Alva Johnson and J. N. Cowan, leading men with the anti-class faction, representing one of the fourteen factions into which they have split since pulling off from the church of Christ. I thought I was up on their teaching; but in a debate at Artesia, New

Mexico, recently I ran into some new 'arguments' which I'll pass on to Early Arceneaux and give him something to study about. I was called there to meet Musgraves of California. Here are our arguments:

"First argument: I showed that Ezra, in rebuilding Jerusalem had thirteen teachers to help him, as found in the eighth chapter of Nehemiah, as one man could not speak to fifty thousand people at one time. Musgrave argued that as God performed a miracle on Balaam's ass and enabled him to speak with a man's voice, no doubt he performed a similar miracle on Ezra's throat and gave him a miraculous voice so he could speak to fifty thousand at once, and thus avoid the sin of two teaching at the same time.

"Second argument: In Zechariah 13:7-9, the prophet said that the Shepherd would be smitten and the flock would scatter(which Christ applied to himself), and that two parts should be cut off and die, and the third part should be left. Musgraves claimed that the prophecy was literally fulfilled in Artesia, New Mexico. The two parts cut off were the Christian church for using instrumental music and the Church of Christ for using individual communion service, and the part left was his faction because they use one cup. His brethren thought this argument unanswerable.

"Third argument: He argued that Christ gave the disciples the cup and told all to drink of it. Therefore, all must drink out of the same cup, else they violate Christ's command. I replied that in my last meeting at Hope, New Mexico, the country was so dry that a thousand people were hauling water from the same well, thus one thousand were drinking of the one well. Musgrave replied that the cases were not parallel, since the one thousand people had to let down the rope and bucket to get water out of the well. He declared that the only way we could hope to make this parallel would be to set up two tooth-picks, get us a string and a small bucket and draw the wine out of the glass by this contraption. His faction considered this an overwhelming refutation to my parallel.

"Fourth argument: I showed that the Bible taught

one cup, also one baptism; but the 'one baptism' could be obeyed in a thousand different holes of water at the same time and still be the 'one baptism'. Likewise the 'one cup' could be partaken of by a thousand members at once and still.be the same cup. Musgraves replied to this by saying that baptism is one thing and the one cup is another; that a man riding a stick horse had to get astride the horse, but a man riding a train did not get astride the train. Therefore, said he, my parallel was not parallel.

"Fifth argument: He argued that in Luke 22:17, where Jesus took the cup and said 'Divide it among yourselves', that if one disciple separated the wine into separate cups, they did not all 'divide' it, and such was a sin. Each one had to do the 'dividing', just as each one had to do the drinking of the wine.

"Sixth argument: I showed that we had three thousand in the church on the day of Pentecost, and that it would take several hours to go around with one cup and with one plate. He argued that Christ hung on the cross for three hours, and if we were not willing to remain three hours on the Lord's day to carry around the bread and wine, we were not worthy to be his disciples.

"Seventh argument: On women speaking in public, he claimed there were two modes of teaching — one without a tune and another with a tune. God forbade a woman teaching without a tune; but if she would put a tune to her words, she was then permitted to teach.

"Eighth argument: I showed that in the times and places that Jesus taught while he was here, seventy-one times he used the class system, and twenty-one times the entire congregation. He claimed that it was all right for Christ or any other man to take out a class and teach them, provided no one else taught the rest of the assembly while he was gone. If they did, they violated the law of God!

"Brother Musgraves doesn't hesitate to tell that which is incorrect in debate, neither does he have any respect for a man of God who does not stand with his faction. While I am ready to meet him anywhere it is demanded, as I can do no worse than the Son of God did when he met the devil, yet his deportment in debate does not impress one that he is trying to act as a child of God; rather he seems to be determined to win victory, and gain the approval of the ignorant, right or wrong." (Firm Foundation, October 23, 1934.)

III

Late in the fall of 1933 Tant held a debate with D. N. Jackson, Baptist at Texarkana. He wrote:

"This debate, with twenty-three more I am to hold with Jackson, grew out of the Brewer-Jackson debate at Texarkana two years ago. Jackson seems to think Brewer is afraid to meet him again. As I regard Brewer as one of the greatest men we have in the church of Christ, I rather think Jackson is correct. There have always been two animals that Brewer has avoided — the lion on account of his strength and the pole-cat on account of his scent. But Jackson is not in Brewer's class as to ability, and I am sure Brewer does not fear him from the lion standpoint. But as all Baptists look alike to me, I meet any man they endorse.

"I am at home now, working on the farm to help raise my salary for next year. Will be working on the farm for three months in our sunshine while brethren are building fires and freezing up north. During my work on the farm I will hold a tent meeting at Santa Rosa and at Brownsville, thirty and twelve miles from home respectively.

"While working on the farm each day, if not too tired at night to write, I want to write twelve articles on "Fifty Years A Texas Preacher." I hope they may be read with interest by many. After April 1, if I get any calls for my valuable time, I want to spend five months holding meetings if my brethren want me. If not, I'll continue working on the farm and holding mission meetings in reach of home, and try to do all the good possible until called to my eternal home." (Firm Foundation, January 2, 1934.)

He did indeed write his articles (much to the future help

of this writer) and they appeared in the Firm Foundation in various issues through the years 1934 and 1935. The articles created a great deal of interest and led many brethren to have a greater appreciation for the aging warrior. He received hundreds of letters about them from people whom he had baptized in years gone bye, as well as from others who were interested in his work. Even though he was working daily on his farm in the Valley, and writing his articles for the Firm Foundation, he still had time for preaching. He reported:

"A call from the church of Christ at Lockhart asks me to come and hold them a gospel meeting beginning the fifth Lord's Day in May. If the Lord wills, I will be there.

"Fifty-two years ago last October, after being added to the church of Christ, I preached my first sermon in Lockhart at the Christian Church house. We were not divided then, and associated with W. H. D. Carrington, I held my first meeting as a Christian.

"Two years later I was holding a meeting eight miles west of Lockart, and Dr. Blanks, one of the elders at Lockhart, came to the meeting and heard me. He later sent me two dollars, the first fellowship I ever received for preaching. He gave the money to Brother Zachery and told him to 'give it to that boy and tell him if he keeps on he will make a preacher some day'. Other members gave me $2.75 later. I married a couple by riding twenty miles in the rain. They gave me $5.00. Total, $9.75. This was my entire support for my first year as a gospel preacher. . . .

"From Austin to Dripping Springs, San Marcos, and Lockhart, I preached the gospel in most all the school-houses at that time.

"Later on I extended my field of labor and held meetings and put the church on the map and started them to work at Granger, Bartlett, Killeen, and Georgetown. My first meeting at Bartlett was when they had a one-teacher school. At Killeen it was the same. My first meeting at Georgetown was in an old mill at the foot of the bridge across the Gabriel River. Brother Elijah Hansbrough and Brother House were with me. Twenty-two were baptized, and through the efforts of Brother House a church building was erected in North Georgetown. They had seventy-eight members to start with.

"Some time ago I met one of the South Georgetown elders in Houston, and he told me I would be invited in South Georgetown. I hope to get the invitation soon, for my old time friend and brother, J. W. Acuff, lives there. I baptized him forty-one years ago. Many will be singing his songs long after he is gone. I want him to lead songs in one more meeting for me. . . ." (Firm Foundation, March 6, 1934.)

Late in October, 1934, Tant was in a meeting at Broaddus, Texas, staying in the home of Brother Sam C. Beard. He had planned to continue this meeting for two weeks or longer, but closed it a few days early in order to attend the great debate at Fort Worth between J. Frank Norris, Fundamentalist Baptist preacher, and Foy E. Wallace, Jr., of the church of Christ. Tant warned Wallace not to go near Norris' office on any kind of pretext or invitation from the Baptist leader, for, said he, "Norris will shoot you down like a dog, then have one hundred Baptists go to the stand and swear that you pulled a gun on him and he had to kill you in self-defense."

As the fight on premillennialism warmed up among the brethren following the Fort Worth debate, there was much pressure put on Brother J. N. Armstrong of Harding College to "declare himself". It was generally known that most of the premillennial brethren in Louisville, Kentucky, who sent their children to a Christian College preferred Harding College above all the others. Men of known premillennial sympathy had often been welcomed to the Harding Campus, and honored before the student body as great and worthy teachers of the gospel. Many of the Harding students were saying that if Armstrong did not teach pre-millennialism, he certainly did not teach against it. At length Brother Armstrong "took a stand", and wrote a long article explaining his position. Foy E. Wallace, Jr., replied to this by saying that Armstrong had "taken a stand, all right — a stand in opposition to exposing the errors of premillennialism." Tant had had little to say about the premillennial issue, and declared that he had hoped Boll and his followers would soon see the folly of their course, and return to the truth. But when Armstrong and Wallace had their exchange he wrote:

"I was glad some time ago to see Brother J. N. Armstrong come out and declare his college opposed to Bollism.

"I was also glad to see Brother Foy Wallace come out and try to find out which side Armstrong was on. Unfortunately for Brother Armstrong, he can write all day long on a subject and still sometimes you can not tell which side he is on. T. B. Larimore had the same misfortune. When O. P. Speigle tried to force Larimore to take a stand either for or against the organ, Brother Larimore wrote a whole page in the Advocate in favor of, or against the organ. I never could tell which. When Brother Larimore was selected to deliver a week's lectures to the Nashville Bible School, J. A. Harding, one of the greatest men we had, stated that if Larimore came there in favor of the organ, he could lecture; and if he came there opposed to the organ, he could lecture. But if he was on neither side, he was too great and too dangerous to lecture to his boys. After Larimore went on the stand before Harding and Lipscomb, and declared he was on the Lord's side of the organ question, but that he could not tell which side the Lord was on, J. A. Harding side-tracked him right there, and sent for Dr. Brents, a man you never had to guess as to which side he was on.

"For fifty years I am glad I have not had to declare myself, which side I am on, on any Bible subject. If

you hear me one time, and still cannot tell where I
stand, just remember you will not be held responsible
in the judgment day, and you need feel no uneasiness."
(Firm Foundation, March 12, 1935.)

IV

In the summer of 1935 the Tants moved to Brownsville,
Texas, from their farm near San Benito. The church in
Brownsville was very small, and Tant devoted much time
toward trying to encourage them and get them into a permanent meeting place. Nannie writes of his success:

"We were very happy here. The church was small,
and had never owned a house of worship. Through
my husband's advice and encouragement they bought
a building that had been used as a drug store and
dance hall. The store part was remodelled and seated
as an auditorium; the dance hall was divided into a
five room apartment for a preacher to live in. Some
of these rooms 'doubled' as class rooms for the Sunday
School. We were the first occupants of that apartment.

"The small band of disciples in Brownsville was full
of zeal and love and heartily cooperated with us in
every effort to build up the church. I recall this
period we spent there as one of the happiest times
we ever had together. Brother and Sister W. R. Jackson and Brother and Sister Royce Russell were among
the most faithful workers in getting this congregation under way. We stayed there for two years, during which time the work grew constantly. I had a
weekly Bible class for the ladies of the congregation
one day each week, and these ladies, in turn, were
teaching others the way of truth. Our son, Yater,
came for a meeting in the month of May, 1937.

"But my husband's health was failing. He had
never done 'local' work for so long a time with a congregation, and he was restless under the arrangement.
He loved the Brownsville people, and they were almost
fanatically loyal to him; but calls were coming to him
from other places, and he felt that he was more needed

elsewhere than in Brownsville. So many people would write him that they had only one, or two or three members, and would he please, please come and help them get a church started? So when an opportunity came to trade our place in DeQueen, Arkansas, for a little farm near Los Fresnos, having a livable house and fifteen acres of ground, we made the trade. The house was in poor condition, but we fixed it up, and somehow, I felt that we were now located there to the end; I had bought some chickens from Brother Jackson's hatchery, so I started raising chickens again. Husband went off to hold some meetings for some of the places that had pleaded so urgently for him to come. It was July, 1937, when we moved. Husband was now seventy-six years old, and was beginning to feel the weight of years. But he knew nothing of 'slow down' or 'take it easy', but worked to the limit of his strength every day — always in a tremendous hurry." (Reminiscences.)

Tant might be nearing the sunset, all right, but his eagerness to keep on working was never more in evidence. He wrote constantly to both the Gospel Advocate and the Firm Foundation, chiding brethren with their laxity and unconcern about reaching out into new territories, begging the old established churches to send their preachers out into mission fields, pleading with young men to move into virgin territories and make their living by 'making tents' while they got the cause of Christ established.

In the summer of 1936 Tant attended the Digressive State Meeting in Austin, Texas. He wrote:

"I left home May 10 for gospel work. My first stop was at the Digressive State Meeting in Austin. It had been fifty years since I was at the state meeting in Austin when they pulled off to adopt human societies and instrumental music. Chalmers McPherson, Dick Kendrick, and R. D. Smith told me then that within fifty years with their human machinery they would capture Texas. Fifty years have passed. I have lived to see them practice sprinkling for baptism, and use the mourner's bench plan of salvation. So was not surprised to see that some of the young bloods had 'Rev.' before their names on their badges. The day I was there they told me that their ablest man from Indiana would preach. A thousand sermons such as I heard him preach would not save one soul. They all seemed to have forgotten the Bible, and had gone back under the Abrahamic covenant and prayed for the kingdom to come. From the way they talked and acted no one would have ever thought they had once known the word of God.

"I hastened from Austin to Mahomet to meet the noted J. N. Cowan in debate. I found him a much better man than he was fifteen years ago when I met him. He is not so bitter and does not tell one-fourth as many yarns on my brethren. Like N. L. Clark he now claims it is all right to have human literature. He is not so strong in argument. That anti system is now only known in the backwoods and among the ignorant, and I feel like in the next ten years it will be like the Hardshell Baptist doctrine, a thing of the past. I met a number of preachers at the debate, among them John C. Taylor and J. W. Acuff, whom I baptized in the long, long ago.

"From the debate I went to Wichita Falls for a meeting, and after fifty years of preaching I must say I never found such a mess. Brother L. S. White, preacher for the Tenth and Austin Streets church treated me like a Christian gentleman all along the line, came out three nights and was ready to carry me anywhere I wanted to go. But four of his elders wrote me a letter telling me where to head in. I heard they were all common men, each possessing two of the seventeen qualifications the Bible requires an elder to have. I hope they will not try to withdraw fellowship from Brother White for coming to my meeting. If they do, I'll defend him. Polk Street and their located pastor, who seemed to have no mind of his own, boycotted the meeting. But he and his so-called elders seemed to be under the control of the four elders at Tenth Street, and were perhaps not permitted to come.

"We have a splendid church house at Wichita Falls. I held my meeting at Buchanan Street. Brother Ben Taylor, who is known as one of our best song leaders, is working with them; and if they continue to worship the Lord and live right, they will come out ahead in the end.

"I promised to help them for a month next year. They are continually condemned by Tenth Street Church and by the faction at Polk Street. But we trust to see them outlive the opposition and do much good for Christ. It is sad we have so many unconverted members in the church." (Firm Foundation, June 23, 1936.)

G. H. P. Showalter moderated for Tant, and gave an editorial about the debate in the issue of June 2. It had been held in Burnet County. He outlined the arguments used by both men, showing that Cowan rejected the Sunday School because it was "not according to the traditions" — i.e. there was no exact pattern in the Scriptures for the kind of arrangement that characterizes the Sunday School. Tant showed that "teaching" was authorized, and that since this is a GENERIC command, we are left free to use whatever method, way, or arrangement may seem expedient.

A month later N. L. Clark had an article in the Firm Foundation putting his finger on the real point at issue — a separate organization. He contended that the real argument or dispute was not over teaching the Bible, nor yet over teaching it in classes, but over whether or not the Sunday School is a separate organization — either within the church or without the church. He argued that the Sunday Schools among the churches of Christ had "all the earmarks" of denominational Sunday School organizations, and as such were distinct institutions in addition to the church.

The passage of years has shown that this question (like too many other points of argument between sincere brethren) had merit on both sides. There can be little doubt that there was a strong tendency among many congregations to make a separate organization of their Sunday Schools, with Superintendent, Staff, Secretaries, and the entire organization operating relatively independent of the church. They had their own treasuries, determined what works they would do and to whom or where they would send their contributions, selected their own literature, and were clearly headed increasingly toward the denominational arrangement. Perhaps the "no-class" brethren, in their reaction against this, were used by God to save his people from such an extreme. Editor Showalter commented: "If such is the case, Brother Clark has ground that is well taken. I have, myself, many years ago, urged such an objection against the Sunday school. Others have done the same. . . . . ."

V

In 1936 and 1937 Brother G. H. P. Showalter had much to say in the **Firm Foundation** about athletics (particularly foot-ball) in the Christian colleges. He was especially exercised over the "Christian Wildcats" of Abilene Christian College, and carried a dozen or more editorials describing the vicious brutalizing influence of football. Since all the players were noted for their abilities to cripple or maim their opponents, Showalter dubbed them "tom cats — Christian tom cats, that is." He described in horrible detail the sad funeral of some imaginary player who had given his life for grid-iron glory, and suggests:

"There could be a cold marble slab erected at the grave of this boy with an epitaph something like this:

Here Lies A Christian Tom Cat
He fought and scratched as Tom cats do — especially wild cats. He tried to do to the other fellow what they

yelled at him to do — 'kill him', 'break his neck,' 'stomp
on him' — but an opposing player got the drop on him and
in a tackle he was mortally wounded. He lingered a while
and died. Peace To His Soul.".

Tant had lived far too much of the rough life of the
frontier to be much alarmed about the "brutality" of foot-
ball. Staying on the top side of a bucking bronc, wrestling
with wild steers, and trying to wrest a living from Texas
and New Mexico ranches had made the gentle play of the
average football game look like the playful frisking of
lambs gamboling on the green to him. But he did get a
bit of pleasure out of seeing how excited Showalter got
over the question, and enjoyed a quiet chuckle — while
he got in close enough to throw a little gasoline on the
fire now and then. He wrote:

"It has been fifty years since the division took place
at Austin between the church of Christ and the digressives. I was in that meeting and have been fighting
their departures ever since. J. W. McGarvey argued
it is only a 'departure' and they will finally come back.
When he died, those who opposed him, to show their
contempt for him carried his body into the church
house and played the organ over his dead body.

"Brother Lipscomb advised me when I became one
of the editors of the Gospel Advocate in 1895 that
when I went to a place to hold a meeting where there
was internal strife over instrumental music to just
preach the gospel and ignore the trouble — the only
unwise advice he ever gave me. Old Brother Hansborough agreed that the only safe way was to withdraw from all organ agitators before it became popular. If we had done this, we could have saved many
church houses, and many brethren as well. But like
our elders on soft preaching, they did not want to
cause any trouble, and so let them disarm us before
the fight ever began. I can remember during those
years when the battle was raging all along the line,
we had many preachers who would claim, 'We are not
on either side, and when either group sends for us to

hold a meeting, we will go'. Without an exception
every one of those brethren drifted into the Christian
Church and accepted all the innovations. . . .

"So I was more than pleased when Showalter took
his bold stand recently against football in our Christian colleges. In fact, I did not think he had the
courage to make the argument he did." **Firm Foundation, May 4, 1937.)**

J.D. Tant and Nannie Yater Tant on the porch of their home in Los Fresnos, Texas, in the spring of 1941, two or three weeks before Tant's death.

Mrs. J.D. Tant, with her son Yater, while they were working together in writing this book. Memphis, Tennessee,
1957, in thehome of Mozelle (Mrs. Dalton L. Priestley.)

CHAPTER XXVI

"I NEVER DENY ANYTHING THEY TELL ON ME"

J. D. Tant had the rare distinction of becoming legendary even during his lifetime. He was probably the most widely quoted preacher among the churches of Christ during the last decades of his life; and now in the second decade after his death the stories and quotations seem to be growing rather than diminishing. As is always the case with such men, many stories and sayings have been credited to him which never happened, or at least never happened to him. His speech was that of the frontier, and his stories were sometimes such as to shock his listeners; but they were never coarse nor vulgar. He used no profanity, and no by-words at all except his characteristic "before God". This latter was a constant source of embarrassment to Nannie, and more than once she remonstrated with him about it. He always referred her to Paul, declared that Paul used the expression in exactly the same sense he did, and that he had no desire to try to hold himself as being better than one of the Lord's apostles. When he heard of stories and remarks being attributed to him which he knew to be false, he smiled and said nothing.

"I never deny anything they say about me," he once told a visiting preacher with a twinkle in his black Irish eyes. "Let them go ahead and advertise me."

Perhaps one of the most famous of Tant's witticisms was the one he got off at the expense of W. F. Ledlow, and which has been quoted as happening to at least a dozen other preachers and their wives. Tant and Ledlow had been friends for a number of years, but Tant had never met Sister Ledlow. When finally he visited the Ledlow home, Brother Ledlow thought to have a little fun at his wife's expense and introduced the two to each other, remarking, "Brother Tant, this is my wife. I admit she isn't much to look at, but she is a good cook."

Quick to seize the bantering spirit of the occasion, Tant replied, "Will Ledlow, I do believe before God she is the homeliest woman I ever laid eyes on."

"Well, I guess she is at that," said Ledlow, somewhat doubtfully, not knowing exactly whether his wife would be pleased at the raillery. "But after all, Brother Tant, beauty is only skin deep, you know."

"In that case," said Tant without the trace of a smile and in the most earnest and serious tone imaginable, "I'd take her to the barn, where no one could hear her holler, and I'd skin her before morning!"

*   *   *

Tant had a debate with Zeke Sherrill, Baptist, at Benton, Arkansas, in the spring of 1934. While there was a strong Baptist Church in Benton at the time, there were only a few members of the church of Christ. At the close of the first night's session, Sherrill arose and said, "Elder Tant has no strong congregation of his people in Benton like we Baptists have. So, to show that my heart is in the right place, and to let Brother Tant get a taste of Baptist hospitality, I have invited him to stay with me and Mrs. Sherrill during the debate. I want this audience to know about this invitation."

Tant arose and said, "Zeke Sherrill, I received your letter down at my home in the Rio Grande Valley of Texas, where it is always summertime. At first, Wife and I talked it over, and decided I ought to stay in your home, and maybe I could have a good influence on you. But I have thought more about it, and I do not want to be responsible for ruining your happy home. Your wife has had to put up with your ungodly ways for so long that if she had a real Christian gentleman around the house for a few days, and could see the contrast, she would become so dissatisfied she would never live with you again. In view of that condition, I think I'd better stay somewhere else."

*   *   *

In a meeting at Aransas Pass, Texas, in 1936, in which R. T. Towery was leading the singing, somebody put a question in the question-box: "Was Alexander Campbell turned out of the Baptist Church for stealing hogs?"

Tant read the question, looked over his glasses at the audience and said, "Now, I don't know much about that hog-stealing business; but I do know Campbell was not turned out of the Missionary Baptist Church as we know it today. When Campbell lived, the devil hadn't invented that crowd yet."

*   *   *

This happened in the Tant-Cayce debate. In one of his speeches, Tant drew two big circles on the blackboard, then connected them with two parallel lines which he labelled "the straight and narrow way". One of the circles he titled "Earth", the other "Heaven". Then he drew another circle off to one side, and labelled it, "Baptist Church". He made the argument: (a) Baptists all admit it is possible to get from earth to heaven without going through the Baptist Church, but (b) it is not possible to get from earth to heaven without going through the "straight and narrow way;" therefore, (c) to get into the Baptist Church one has to leave the "straight and narrow way," and to get into the "straight and narrow way", he has to leave the Baptist Church. The argument was driven home with considerable force.

Attempting a reply to this, Cayce said, "That blackboard

figure by Tant represents nothing either in scripture or in common sense."

To which Tant responded, "Why, before God, brethren, I did not intend this blackboard figure to represent anything either in scripture or in common sense. This figure represents the Baptist Church and Baptist doctrine! Baptists themselves are the witnesses!"

*   *   *

Not long before his death Tant held a meeting in a little town in the foot-hills of the Arkansas Ozarks. He was met at the depot by a grizzled old tobacco-chewing brother who gave him the sad history of the little congregation as they drove out to the meeting house. Said he, "Brother Tant, I've been in the harness here nigh on to forty years, and this church ain't made no growth at all." After staying for several days in the little town, Tant publicly related one night what the brother had told him, and said, "Brethren, I've been here a week now, and I've had a chance to get a good look at that harness Brother Jones has been in for 'nigh on to forty years'. And the only piece of it that shows any signs of wear at all is the backing strap!"

*   *   *

Tant was scheduled for a meeting in a little country place a few miles out from Trenton, Tennessee. He rode the train into Trenton, expecting someone to meet him there and take him on out to the community where the meeting was to be held. No one met him, but it happened that a sectarian man was at the depot, and as he was driving out toward this community, he offered Tant a lift. It was about a week before Christmas. When the depot agent heard where Tant was going, he called him back into the station and showed him several packages of whiskey, which were addressed to various people in the community where Tant was going. He asked Tant to tell these people that their "merchandise" was at the depot, and would they please come by and pick it up. Tant carefully wrote down the names of all who were receiving the whiskey.

That night, before beginning his sermon, he pulled a sheet of paper from his pocket and announced to the audience, "The depot agent at Trenton wants me to tell the following brethren that their Christmas whiskey has arrived and is now at the depot. He says will you please come in and pick it up." He then read the list of some ten or twelve names which he had taken from the packages at the depot.

* * *

It was one of the hottest and most humid Julys in the memory of anybody in east Texas. Tant was in an outdoor meeting at Appleby in Nacogdoches County. This was before the days of the bug repellant lights, and the big electric bulb directly over the pulpit stand was attracting bugs by the hundreds. They kept hitting the light, having their wings seared, and falling directly on to Tant's bald head. He was obviously annoyed by them, but was deeply immersed in the lesson he was presenting, and made no effort to move out from under the light and away from the blackboard. In fact, he could scarcely have presented that lesson effectively without the use of the charts and diagrams.

Suddenly in the midst of the sermon, without checking for a single instant the rapid flow of his speech, changing the expression on his face, or giving any indication at all that he was doing anything except what was perfectly natural and normal, he walked to the edge of the platform, reached down and picked up a big wide-brimmed sombrero there (it belonged to Mr. Willie Shepherd), clapped it on his head, and went on with the sermon.

*   *   *

In the spring of 1938 Tant attended the Hardeman-Bogard debate in Little Rock, Arkansas. His life was now nearing its close, only three years being left to him. This debate was a time of great pleasure for him, for he met many old time friends, and enjoyed laughing and joking with the preachers who were present. He had become a sort of "institution" among the churches of Christ by this time. From Little Rock he wrote:

"I am now in Arkansas to attend the Hardeman-Bogard debate. Am just back from the far west, where I spent two months in gospel preaching. My first meeting was at Prescott, Arizona. We have only one dozen members there, struggling for an existence. A large Mormon church of five hundred members just across the street have their members under control and will not let them hear the gospel. Also a modern digressive church one block away was going under the name 'Church of Christ'. They have deceived many by wearing such name. I challenged both churches for public debate, but they took to the tall timber. I preached in the digressive house five nights, and told them plainly why the church of Christ does not use instrumental music. I begged them to set it aside, and let us all unite. But they have set up the organ as an idol in their hearts (Ezek. 14:4), and they would rather hear the noise of their idol than to have the fellowship of godly men and women. . . .

"My next stop was at Los Angeles, where I visited that wonderful Pepperdine College. I feel like it is the greatest school we have ever had since the Freed-Hardeman College went into the hands of our brotherhood to become a preacher factory. I learned last year from the writings of two of our college presidents that our Bible colleges do not belong to the church, not to the elders, but to us, and you, and he, and we, and they. As I am not acquainted with those men,

I am still in the dark as to the ownership. But I learned that this college was built and equipped by George Pepperdine as a high class educational institution, and it belongs to none other. So there will not be a drove of gospel preachers running all over the country begging for money to support 'our Bible college' . . . .

"Previous to this trip I had decided to go to Freed-Hardeman College next January and get my degree in penmanship. But when I saw President Baxter, of Pepperdine College, the noted Grover C. Brewer, J. E. Wainwright, and Brother G. W. Riggs, whom I knew in the old Nashville Bible School days, and about twenty-five or thirty young college preachers all coming to my meetings to sit at my feet and learn wisdom from me, I became fearful that if I went to Henderson and got a degree, it would elevate me out of the congenial companionship of those brethren; so I have decided to cut out this degree business for a while.

"My next stop was at Bakersfield. The church there was divided over the preacher. One faction had engaged me since April for a meeting. The other faction, as soon as they heard I was coming, engaged Tice Elkins for the same time to run an opposition meeting. I went to their meeting and begged them to cut it out, and come to our tent, and let Tice and me preach together for two weeks. I assured them Tice and I had been friends for twenty years, and I was sure we could unite the two groups in two weeks. But their located preacher refused to come and the division still exists.

"My last meeting in California was at San Diego. We have two congregations in San Diego. My old time friend and brother, Frank Chambers, was preaching for one of them. Back east where I had known Frank for thirty years he was not a preacher but a school teacher. But he seems to be one among the few school teachers I have ever known who had sense enough to make a preacher. But if reports be true, he is making a wonderful success at preaching." (Firm Foundation, May 31, 1938.)

When Tant lived in Arkansas, in the 1920's he paid a visit one day to Freed-Hardeman College. Brother Hardeman introduced him to the student body at the chapel hour, making some jocular remark about Arkansas, and suggesting perhaps Arkansas and Tant were quite well suited to each other. The students enjoyed this bit of banter immensely.

Tant arose, and told the assembly how glad he was to be there. He admitted he was from Arkansas, but said he was astonished to find out how little most people knew about that state. In fact, the average man could not even locate it on a map! He then told them where it was situated:

"Missouri lies to the north of Arkansas," he said. "Oklahoma lies to the west; Texas lies to the southwest; Louisiana lies to the south; Mississippi and Tennessee lie to the east. In fact, when you come right down to it, ALL the states lie about Arkansas! But it is a wonderful country. We have hardly any hospitals there, because our people are so healthy they rarely ever get sick; we don't have many jails and penitentiaries, because criminals get chased off and go to Texas. We don't have an insane asylum in the state either; if we ever have any idiots there, or anybody becomes a lunatic, we send them to Tennessee, and they are always in great demand in this state as school teachers!"

* * *

Tant's last debate with Ben M. Bogard (his eighth) was held in the Lone Star community about eight miles east of Greenwood, Arkansas, in the fall of 1937. The proposition being discussed was that baptism of a penitent believer is for (or in order to) the remission of past sins. In one of Bogard's speeches of denial he took up his entire thirty minutes trying to prove that there are two figures (pictures) contemplated in I Peter 3:21. Insisting that Noah and his family were saved by faith, and then pictured their salvation in the water of the flood, he declared that we are first saved by faith, and then picture that salvation by baptism. He dwelt at length on the fact that one could not have a picture of a thing or a person without first having the substance of the thing or person. He told of having a picture of his mother, and how highly he prized the picture; but he could not have had the picture unless he had first had the mother! His Baptist brethren seemed elated with this argument, and felt that it was unanswerable.

Tant got to his feet and replied, "My good friends, remember that baptism is just a 'picture'. Ben Bogard says it is, and since Ben seems to be the big 'It' among Baptists, that makes it so. Now, Ben, says baptism is a 'picture'. That does not help Baptist doctrine at all; for it was Jesus Christ himself who said in Mark 16:16, 'He that believeth and gets his picture taken shall be saved'. And when those wicked people on Pentecost asked Peter and the rest of the apostles what they had to do, Peter replied, 'Repent ye, and get your picture taken, every one of you in the name of Jesus Christ for the remission of sins.' And when Ananias came to Saul of Tarsus there in Damascus, he said unto him as recorded in Acts 22:16, 'And now why tarriest thou? Arise and get your picture taken, and wash away your sins, calling on the name of the Lord'. So you can see, Ben, you, too, will have to get your picture taken or you can never be saved!"

There was a roar of laughter from the audience, and Bogard was obviously discomfitted as his bit of sophistry was thus handed back to him.

* * *

It was in September, 1938, while working on an irrigation ditch that Tant suffered a slight stroke, which caused

a temporarily paralysis of his left leg. He refused to let
the dragging leg stop him, however, and kept hobbling
about the place for several weeks, and held three or four
meetings during the fall and winter, sitting down to preach
most of the time. The very week (October 4) in which the
Firm Foundation carried Tant's report of his stroke it carried also the death notice of P. J. Taylor in Oklahoma City.
One month later came the death notice of M. H. Moore, Superintendent of the schools of Fort Worth, and a life-long
friend of Tant's. Concerning Taylor's death Tant wrote:

"P. J. Taylor, an old time gospel preacher and Texas
ranger, has been called home. Of the preachers who
journeyed with me in the long ago, Brother Taylor is
the fifty-eighth to hear the last call. I feel I am almost
standing alone. I am seventy-seven years old. Taylor
was four years my senior. He came to our county,
Hamilton County, Texas, in 1887, and we worked together for four years. At that time, Taylor was considered one of the ablest preachers and debaters in the
state. When he made an argument it was always like
one W. P. Richardson or J. W. Denton would make.
No place to find a flaw. As a debater he stood in the
class of John S. Sweeney, Dr. Brents, or Joe Warlick.
As a speaker, his cousin, Bob Taylor, once governor of
Tennessee, could not beat him.

"In our country he traveled most of the time in a
large hack with his wife and children. When night
came he stopped under a tree, so as not to be a burden
to the brethren. I have been with him in many meetings where he would cook our bread in a frying pan on
the outdoor fire, and stick our meat on a stick and
cook it over the fire. We lived among the common
people and never thought a man had to have the best
hotel in town.

"My last great fight with Taylor by my side was at
Thorp's Spring in March, 1894, at the preachers' insti-
tute, now called 'preachers' meeting'. There we met in
debate J. B. Briney, T. W. Caskey, Chalmers McPherson, J. W. Lowber, W. K. Homan, and a number of the

weaker set. All these brethren had once been loyal
gospel preachers, but went off with the digressives.
We made it so hot for them that as they departed their
chairman, W. K. Homan, lost his head and got up and
said we were a lot of intruders, and that the Digressives were more congenial with the Mormons than
with the church of Christ. Joe Warlick then arose and
apologized for our accepting their invitation to come,
and we went home.

"Brother Taylor's wife, Ollie, was then considered
one of the leading singers of Texas, and she stood behind him in all his work.

"I am glad I spent those years on the firing line with
P. J. Taylor. I regarded him as one of the greatest
men Texas ever had, and am sure many will be in
heaven who would never have known that country if
P. J. Taylor had not lived. I hope in a few more years
to begin eternity with him." (Firm Foundation, November 8, 1938.)

It was P. J. Taylor's son, Glenn Taylor, who as Senator
from Idaho gained some political prominence when he ran
as a vice presidential candidate on the third party ticket
with Henry A. Wallace in the 1940's.

One little incident in that famous meeting at Thorp's
Spring in March, 1894, which Tant did not mention was his
sharp exchange with the venerable J. B. Briney. Tant had
an extended sharp clash with him, in which the irascible
Briney got angrier and angrier as Tant kept throwing at
him the arguments which Briney himself had made as a
younger man against instrumental music. Finally, Briney,
red with anger, arose and said,

"I think it rude beyond description that a stripling like
young Tant here try to question the word and debate the
truth with a man twice his age, and who knows more than
he'll ever learn in a thousand years."

Tant, still on his feet, came back instantly with the re-
tort, "Brother Briney complains that I am too young to de-

bate with him. I remind him that I am thirty-three years
of age. The Son of God was even younger than I when he
debated with the devil. If Jesus Christ at thirty years of
age could debate with the devil, then J. D. Tant at thirty-
three can debate with J. B. Briney. Brother Briney, you
are an old man, but you are not near as old as Satan —
even if you do preach his doctrine!"

*   *   *

The spring of 1939 found Tant back "in the harness"
again, and going strong. He wrote:

"After being out of work for seven months by paralysis, I am glad to state that I am on the firing line
again.

"Just closed my second meeting in Oklahoma, and
am booked for one more meeting in Oklahoma, three in
Tennessee, one in Texas, one meeting and two debates
in California. Then back to the farm. . . .

"After my last meeting in Oklahoma, Wife and I had
a kind invitation from the Highland Church in Abilene,
where Homer Hailey preaches, to attend their meeting, and hear our son, Yater Tant, preach the gospel.
We both went, were treated kindly along all lines, and
shall ever cherish with love and appreciation the members of the church there.

"I was invited while at Abilene to preach one sermon,
which I did to a large congregation. When I saw such
men as Charles Roberson, Jas. F. Cox, President of
Abilene Christian College, Harvey Scott, Homer Hailey,
and fifteen to twenty more up-to-date preachers sit at
my feet and learn wisdom from me, I felt like if I only
had my degree in penmanship, I would be in the ring
as a big preacher. But such is life . . . But withal I
had a fine time and hope to visit the college at Abilene
again." (Firm Foundation, June 6, 1939.)

At the close of the Abilene meeting, Yater Tant took his
father to the railroad depot at Abilene, and watched with
tear-dimmed eyes as the aged soldier of the cross, shoulders

erect and head held high, and with only a trace of a limp, walked down the platform and climbed aboard the train, off to another gospel meeting. He felt fairly certain that he was looking upon his father for the last time. The premonition was not in error. The next time he saw the features of J. D. Tant was two years later when he gazed upon his lifeless body in the Dillon Funeral Home at Cleburne, Texas.

Time was running out for this man. And his companions of many years were dying rapidly all around him. George A. Klingman died on December 10, 1939. Joe S. Warlick had a heart attack in Dallas in January of 1940, and died a year later, January 2, 1941. F. B. Srygley passed away on February 11, 1940. Daniel Sommer died in Indianapolis, Indiana, eight days later, February 19, 1940. J. B. Nelson was killed in a train-car collision in April, 1940. Sister N. B. Hardeman, whom Tant considered one of the noblest women he had ever known, died of a heart attack on May 6, 1940. D. F. Draper died in Texas on June 5, 1941.

The sinking sun had already touch the rim of the hills. But Tant's zest for life was unabated, nor were his quick wit or roguish sense of humor dampened by the approaching night. Nannie reports an incident that happened in the Los Fresnos church:

"Brother James W. Adams conducted a meeting at Los Fresnos in 1940. The church there had almost been wrecked on account of the conduct of one of the leaders (whom I'll call Lacey, since that isn't his name) and Sister Green (which isn't her name either). Both had families, but they seemed to enjoy each other's company more than they did the companions to whom they were married. They spent endless hours together, and conducted themselves in such a fashion as to occasion much talk and much criticism in the Valley. However both Brother Lacey and Sister Green were unusually kind hearted and accommodating, especially

to my husband. Due to Husband's hearing failing
somewhat during the last two or three years of his
life, he did not always get rumors straight, and was
usually inclined to discredit much of what he did hear.
Many stories came to him about the conduct of this
brother and sister, but he refused to believe them guilty of wrong doing. Several of the members, however,
were most unhappy, and were threatening to go elsewhere. Our local preacher Brother Howard Casada, a
fine, godly man, did what he could to preach against
the open misconduct; but his preaching only served to
infuriate Sister Green and she threatened to shoot him.

"During his meeting, Brother Adams preached
much on brotherly love, and each night shamed the
church for calling themselves 'the church of Christ'
when there was so much hatred, non-fellowship, and
even threats of murder right in the congregation. At
each service, Husband was in his chair, up near the
front, as near the speaker as he could get. One night
some fifteen or twenty came forward to confess their
sins.. . . among them Brother Lacey and Sister Green.
Brother Lacey wanted to make his own statement,
and it soon became apparent that he was just wanting
to 'let bygones be bygones', and everybody make a new
start, and he was not confessing to any wrong doing
at all. Husband saw that this was simply some sort
of effort to 'white-wash' things; so he stood up and
made a little speech:

" 'I didn't hear all that was said here tonight', he
began, 'but I am mighty glad to see all these people
come forward, especially Brother Lacey and Sister
Green. There has been an awful amount of talk in the
Valley, as you all know, that they have been running
around together and are guilty of adultery. I want
to give my full approval to what they have done tonight. Because even if they are not guilty of adultery
(and I have never really believed they are), still they
have been chasing around over the countryside together in such a way as to cause everybody to think
them guilty. They have acted foolishly, to say the
least, and I am glad they are going to straighten up
and do better." **(Reminiscences.)**

This speech put the fat in the fire. Sister Green, not green now but livid with anger, jumped to her feet, called Tant a "liar" and an "old devil", and stormed up and down the aisle for several minutes before she could be calmed down and taken out of the building by some of her family. Tant calmly leaned on his cane, chewing on a cough drop, and apparently wasn't the least bit disturbed or excited by the wild outburst. Things finally calmed down a bit, Mrs. Green came back in and did make a specific confession that she had sinned in threatening to shoot the preacher. James Adams dismissed the service, and the meeting ended.

But the trouble was not settled. Some two or three weeks later, some five or six families decided to drive into Brownsville (twelve miles) each Sunday to worship. Tant and Nannie went with them. The Brownsville congregation had a love for him, and he for them, that made these last months of his life some of the happiest he had ever known. Tant was in such condition now that Nannie insisted he should not try to drive. (He fumed at this, and insisted right up to a week before his death that he was plenty capable of driving anything that had wheels!) Some of the neighbors came by every Sunday, however, and took them down to Brownsville to the services and brought them home again. They made the trip twice each day, for both the morning and the evening service. Many Sundays they were invited to spend the afternoon with some Brownsville friends, and did so.

CHAPTER XXVII

INTO THE SUNSET

Tant's last months upon the earth, in spite of failing health, were happy ones. Nannie describes those days in the Valley:

"Much that came to brighten and cheer our old age in those last days was the regular visit each winter of our daughter, Mozelle, (Mrs. Dalton L. Priestley) and her babies. We were in the Valley for some eight or ten years, and Mozelle spent a part of seven winters with us. Her first baby, Nancy, was very frail, and the cold, damp climate at Memphis made it hard for the baby to stay well. But she thrived in the warm sunny days of the Rio Grande Valley.

"Our small citrus grove proved very profitable. In the fall of 1939 we sold twenty-two tons of grapefruit at $4.00 per ton. Oranges were selling at $8.00 per ton. In our grove we had four varieties of grapefruit, three kinds of oranges, besides lemons, papayas, avacadoes, calamundies, limes, and loquots, some eight varieties of citrus. We also had a long arbor of grapes. With all this fruit I was kept quite busy, for I loved to preserve and can, and I had my hands full.

"But my specialty was always chickens. Brother Jackson operated a hatchery at Brownsville. In the spring of 1940 I bought one hundred White Leghorn pullets from him. I was very successful in this venture. I had an electrically heated brooder, and raised the entire batch of one hundred chicks with the loss of only three or four. After culling them, I had left sixty-eight of as fine hens as could be found in the nation. I began trap-nesting them on August 19th. Brother Jackson told me that from all hens which produced as many as 300 eggs in twelve months, he could sell baby chicks for $1.00 each. But I never finished out the year. All my record keeping stopped on June 1, 1941.

"Husband seemed to grow somewhat feebler as the days went by. He was still keeping up a voluminous correspondence, sitting at his table and writing for hours at a time. He had three or four debates 'brewing', as well as several gospel meetings on schedule. But his blood pressure was high, and he seemed to suffer with cramping in the muscles of his legs. Our daughter Zoreta (Mrs. C. R. Keeney) lived at Eldorado, not far from Christoval Wells, which were highly recommended for all muscular pains. We thought maybe the baths there would help him some. So in April of 1941 he went to Zoreta's. She took him to Christoval for the baths. He stayed about two weeks, but we could not see that he was helped very much. He became a bit discouraged, and came back to the Valley. Mozelle was with me during this time. But her baby, Nancy, became ill the last part of May, and Mozelle had to go back to Memphis. Zoreta came down to stay with me after Mozelle left.

"Husband seemed patient now and perfectly resigned to death. He wanted to see his children once again, so I wrote them all and suggested that they come home as soon as they could. His greatest trouble now seemed to be difficulty in breathing. We were so far from a doctor at Los Fresnos that I took him to the hospital in Brownsville, so the doctor could watch him more closely. But that seemed to displease him, so I took him back to our little home at Los Fresnos. The last words our doctor said to him as we were leaving Brownsville were, 'Mr. Tant, you can easily live ten years longer if you will be quiet and try not to work so much.'

" 'Be quiet — not work'! He might as well have told him to stop breathing right then. The very essence of his life was work and activity. Nothing short of death could stop him from that. I believe he loved life more than any person I ever knew. Only a few days before the end he said to me, 'I'd be willing to live a thousand years if it were the Lord's will'. I asked him if he could know that the thousand years would have in them the same hardship, the same incredible toil and labor of the eighty he had just lived, would he still be willing? He said, 'Yes.' I believe he was suffering much, but he gave little outward indication of it. Only once did I hear a sentence fall from his lips that made me think he might be longing for the end to come. One day, sitting quietly in his chair, he said, "There remaineth therefore a rest to the people of God — and I long for that rest!" This was the last bit of scripture I ever heard him quote.

The last two Lord's Days he was not able to attend the services. Brother H. D. Jeffcoat, preacher for the Brownsville church, brought the emblems out to him on May 24. We sang and prayed, and broke the bread together. But on the last day of his life, June 1, he did not partake of the Supper." (Reminiscences.)

All of Tant's children were aware that the end was near. Zoreta was with him in Los Fresnos. All the others were on their way home, or were getting ready to make the trip. Yater had wired from Chicago, Illinois, where he lived, that he would be home on Tuesday, June 3. Tant was cheered at this news, and on Sunday afternoon told some visitors. "Yater will be here Tuesday. I will try to hang on till he gets here, and then I'll die." He seemed completely calm, almost indifferent at the prospect of death. He accepted it as a matter of course, and was neither fearful of it or rebellious against it.

Several visitors came in on Sunday afternoon. One of them was James W. Adams, preacher for the San Benito church, who had visited often in the Tant home these past few months. He noted that Tant was cheerful, but not quite up to his usual joking mood. He was obviously suffering. Adams stayed for about an hour, leaving just 45 minutes before the end came. He had no realization that death was so near his aged friend. It was a typical summer day in the Rio Grande Valley, sunny and pleasant. Brother and Sister W. S. Mullen drove up from Brownsville

in the afternoon, along with their daughter, and her husband, Harold Smith.   Sister Mullen asked Tant how he
was, and he replied that he was all right, but "I'm pretty
sure I'm not long for this world."   They all sat on the front
porch and talked for a little while.   Tant told them that he
had told that doctor in Brownsville that if he did not release
him from the hospital, he was going to get up and walk
the twelve miles home by himself.

Presently the Mullen family got up and prepared to leave.
Tant stood up with them, turned and walked into the front
room, where there was another high backed rocking chair,
similar to the one he had been sitting in on the porch.   He
sat down in this chair, turned his eyes for a last, long
searching look into Nannie's face, and without speaking a
word quietly died.

It was 4:30 o'clock, Sunday afternoon, June 1, 1941.

*   *   *

Two funeral services were held.   The first was conducted
in the building of the Brownsville church on Monday afternoon.   Tant had requested that H. D. Jeffcoat and James
W. Adams be in charge, and had asked that the entire service be conducted like any normal preaching service, with
congregational singing and all.   Brother Jeffcoat read the
scripture and led the prayer.   Adams spoke on II Tim. 4:1-
8, paying tribute to the great fidelity which Tant had all
his lifetime manifested toward the truth in his long and
varied preaching and debating experience.   He emphasized
the sacrificial spirit the deceased had always shown in his
willingness to go into hard and difficult places to preach
the gospel, places where others would not go, and to go
with or without support.

A second funeral service was conducted in the building
of the Central Church of Christ, Cleburne, Texas, on Wednesday morning, June 4.   The principal address here was

made by W. K. Rose, with whom Tant had held a long time agreement that whichever of them survived would speak at the funeral of the other. Scripture was read by G. H. P. Showalter, prayer was offered by Cled E. Wallace, and a short address, preceding Brother Rose's talk, was made by Foy E. Wallace, Jr. The crowd was not large, and was made up mostly of gospel preachers who had come from their fields of labor to pay tribute to the soldier who had fallen. A few old time friends, companions of his youth, were present to shed their tears along with the family. His only surviving brother, James Monroe Tant, was also present. John W. Akin, who had given the suit in which he was to be buried, wept unashamedly as he looked for the last time upon the still and bloodless face of his friend.

The funeral caravan moved slowly and without incident out to old Cleburne Memorial Cemetery, where all that is mortal of "J. D. Tant — Texas Preacher" now sleeps beneath a simple stone bearing the legend:

Jefferson Davis Tant

1861 . 1941

"I have fought a good fight"

Printed in the United States
24467LVS00001B/1-24

9 787770 041150